DEVELOPING READERS AND WRITERS IN THE CONTENT AREAS K–12

Sixth Edition

Developing Readers and Writers in the Content Areas K–12

David W. Moore
Arizona State University

Sharon Arthur Moore
Consultant, Literacy Enrichment and Development

Patricia M. Cunningham
Wake Forest University

James W. Cunningham, Emeritus
University of North Carolina, Chapel Hill

Allyn & Bacon
Boston   Columbus   Indianapolis   New York   San Francisco   Upper Saddle River
Amsterdam   Cape Town   Dubai   London   Madrid   Milan   Munich   Paris   Montreal   Toronto
Delhi   Mexico City   São Paulo   Sydney   Hong Kong   Seoul   Singapore   Taipei   Tokyo

Vice President and Editor-in-Chief: Aurora Martinez
Editorial Assistant: Amy Foley
Executive Marketing Manager: Amy Judd
Marketing Assistant: Robin Holtsberry
Project Manager: Holly Shufeldt
Senior Art Director: Jayne Conte
Manager, Rights and Permissions: Karen Sanatar
Cover Photo: iStockphoto
Cover Designer: Suzanne Behnke
Full-Service Project Management: Chitra Ganesan, PreMediaGlobal
Composition: PreMediaGlobal
Text and Cover Printer/Binder: R. R. Donnelly & Sons
Text Font: Garamond Light

Photo Credits: Pages 4, 25, 64, 67, 95, 98, 127, 131, 132, 161, 169, 173, 176, 205, 215, 220, 239, 242, Shutterstock; p. 23 Getty Images, Inc.- Photodisc; pp. 32, 77, Bob Daemmrich Photography, Inc.; p. 46, Photolibrary/Indexopen; pp. 101, 135, Merrill Education; p. 130, Frank Siteman; p. 175, PhotoEdit Inc; p. 222, Jupiter Images - Image 100.

Library of Congress Cataloging-in-Publication Data

Developing readers and writers in the content areas K-12 / David W. Moore ... [et al.].—6th ed.
    p. cm.
Includes bibliographical references and index.
ISBN-13: 978-0-13-705637-8
ISBN-10: 0-13-705637-0
1. Language arts—Correlation with content subjects. 2. Content area reading. I. Moore, David W.
LB1576.D455 2011
428'.43—dc22

                                    2010015403

10 9 8 7 6 5 4 3 2 1

**Allyn & Bacon
is an imprint of**

PEARSON

www.pearsonhighered.com

ISBN-10:   0-13-705637-0
ISBN-13: 978-0-13-705637-8

CONTENTS

PREFACE

Teaching students how to use reading and writing as tools for learning ranks near the top of the many responsibilities teachers assume. *Developing Readers and Writers in the Content Areas K–12* introduces prospective teachers to this responsibility. Elementary and secondary teachers alike will find this book to be a practical guide. Its engaging prose sheds light on the foundational principles and practices of content literacy.

Even though separate chapters of this text highlight comprehension and writing, each chapter addresses literacy, the combination of reading and writing. Treating written language in its entirety preserves the benefits that reading and writing have for each other and for the exploration of subject matter.

Developing Readers and Writers in the Content Areas K–12 can be used in courses with titles such as *Literacy across the Curriculum, Content Area Reading,* and *Disciplinary Literacies.* Its attention to elementary and secondary teaching makes it appropriate for courses aimed at either audience, as well as for courses with a mixture of upper-grade and lower-grade teachers. It is intended for use in undergraduate or graduate teacher-preparation programs, during staff development activities, and in introductory graduate teacher education courses.

SHARED FEATURES OF EARLIER EDITIONS AND THE SIXTH EDITION

This sixth edition of *Developing Readers and Writers in the Content Areas K–12* retains features of the earlier editions that our students and colleagues found especially noteworthy. These features include the following.

General to Specific Progression

The first three chapters move from general to specific to show how overall instructional planning embeds content area literacy planning. Chapter 1 presents a rationale for content literacy instruction, describes thinking processes that can be promoted across all grades in all activities, and explains the role of academic identities in subject matter reading, writing, and learning. Chapter 2 sets a general stage for content literacy instruction by presenting professional practices, cycles of instruction, and settings that influence literacy and learning. Chapter 3 explains the steps in planning units of instruction that embed reading and writing.

The next seven chapters then concentrate on incorporating the major dimensions of literacy into classroom instruction. The final two chapters address reading proficiency and policy, topics that have become increasingly important as advanced reading becomes more and more politicized.

Disciplinary Literacies

Although the teaching practices described in the comprehension, vocabulary, writing, and studying chapters apply to all disciplines, the applications are not always obvious. For instance, comprehension has many common properties, but comprehending poetry in English/language arts class differs from comprehending explorers' journal entries in history, and both differ from comprehending directions in a technological work environment. Each discipline has distinctive ways of formalizing and communicating knowledge. Consequently, we describe disciplinary literacies at the end of Chapters 5 through 8. The disciplines we address are English/language arts, English language development, mathematics, science, social studies, and activity, a term for hands-on courses.

Standards-Based Teaching and Learning

Educators in the United States teach amid established systems of accountability. Mandated standards and assessments affect teaching and learning in practically every classroom. Chapter 3, "Instructional Units," begins with a clear view of how to design and implement instruction amid accountability systems. Remaining chapters then address this issue, showing how to make standards and assessments work in your students' best interests.

Cultural and Linguistic Diversity

This book addresses the diversity of today's student population. For instance, Chapter 1, "Content Area Reading and Writing," describes the impact socially situated identities exert on youth as they take up academic literacies. Chapter 4, "Reading Materials and Projects," illustrates the great variety of resources and response formats appropriate for students' diverse cultural, linguistic, and cognitive situations. The "Comprehension," "Vocabulary," "Writing," and "Studying" chapters set aside specific sections for students who are learning English. Chapter 10, "Responsive Instruction," focuses entirely on teaching all students fairly.

Thorough Presentations of Key Concepts

Our goal is to enable prospective teachers to implement principled teaching practices readily, and we assume that our audience does not already know these practices. So we present the practices clearly and completely. We use accessible terminology and concrete examples. Additionally, the learning aids in the text are included to enhance understanding and retention. The following aids are found either at the beginning or end of each chapter to promote thinking about the chapter contents:

- *Looking Ahead*, which appears at the beginning of each chapter, presents an overview of that chapter's contents.
- *Key Ideas* are listed in the introduction of each chapter, following the *Looking Ahead* section. They form the main headings for the chapters, indicating the major points within each chapter.
- *Looking Back* summaries occur at the end of each chapter.
- *Add to Your Journal* also appears at the end of each chapter. This learning aid suggests topics to consider and questions to answer when responding to this book in journal form.
- *Additional Readings* suggests books and articles that amplify the material presented in the chapter.
- *Online Resources* recommends instructional resources available through the Web.

Along with the learning aids at the beginning and end of the chapters, we interspersed the following pedagogical features throughout these chapters to promote interaction with the ideas presented:

- *Do It Together* suggests group activities. Small-group collaborative effort can promote learning.
- *Listen, Look, and Learn* contains suggestions for checking out chapter contents with students and practicing teachers. It is a reality check for ideas and an opportunity to develop them.
- *Try It Out* encourages application. Learning occurs best when you do something with the ideas you encounter.

NEW FEATURES IN THE SIXTH EDITION

Educators alter their practices when social and political changes affect school expectations and when scholarship offers new professional knowledge. To keep pace with the changes in content area literacy instruction, we revised the contents of all the chapters. For instance, at least 20 percent of the research cited is new. Especially noteworthy changes in this edition are as follows.

Chapter 11, "Cases of Reading Instruction," Deleted.

Following our reviewers' suggestions, we removed the cases of reading instruction. Students often are prompted to analyze the content literacy instruction they observe during field experiences, then compare their observations with the book's ideas and information.

New Chapter Focus on Responsive Instruction

The U.S. commitment to all students becoming proficient with high levels of literacy means that all learners are expected to accomplish the same standards. Students who start out with different levels of academic preparedness, approaches to learning, and interests deserve instruction that bridges these differences with rigorous, uniform standards of achievement. Chapter 10, "Responsive Instruction," now highlights ways to address literacy with diverse groups of students in particular classrooms. This represents at least a 20-percent change in contents.

New Chapter Focus on Digital Literacies

New dimensions of literacy are entailing new dimensions of literacy instruction. Consequently, in Chapter 9, "Inquiry through Digital Literacies," we continue the focus on inquiry but place it in the context of 21st-century skills. We emphasize the use of digital literacies as students collaborate in problem-solving projects. This chapter highlights the productive uses of practices such as networking academically through blogs and discussion boards, collaboratively composing with wikis, and representing findings through podcasting and multigenre means. These changes represent at least a 20-percent change in contents.

Along this line, each chapter now presents *Online Resources* at the end. This new feature recommends only established and productive instructional resources available through the Web.

New Chapter Focus on High-Stakes Testing

Because specific laws and policies change, Chapter 12, "Reading Policy" no longer focuses on the specifics of the *No Child Left Behind* legislation. It now focuses on a central feature of the policy, high-stakes testing, which appears in various configurations throughout state and federal laws and policies. The opportunities and the challenges of high-stakes testing policies are to ensure that they serve all students well. This represents at least a 20-percent change in contents.

New Focus on Gradual Release of Responsibility

More than ever, this edition highlights and describes the role of teachers in explaining, demonstrating, and gradually releasing responsibility to students. When used appropriately, this model of instruction improves students' control of their cognitive and metacognitive processes while comprehending words and texts, composing, and studying. It is featured now more than ever in Chapters 5 through 8.

Clarifications and Elaborations

We learned which portions of this book communicated better than others while using the fifth edition with our students. Consequently, we clarified the language throughout the chapters and inserted many new key ideas and headings to better signal chapter contents. These edits make up at least a 20-percent modification in wording and style. In particular, we changed the tone of the previous edition. Rather than refer to readers indirectly in the third person ("How do teachers promote literacy when they have so many other responsibilities?"), this sixth edition now addresses readers directly in the second person (e.g., "How do you promote literacy when you have so many other responsibilities?").

This edition also improves certain sections that some readers found confusing or dated. For instance, Chapter 1's previous heading and contents relative to "put the person first" now is the more candid "avoid deficit perspectives." Chapters 2, 5, and 7's previous headings and contents related to "guiding" students now are changed to "providing scaffolds for students."

This edition eliminates redundancies within and across chapters. For instance, we removed the "assess and reflect" portion in Chapter 2's "cycle of instruction" section because it duplicated much of what already was presented in the "practices" section.

This edition deletes minor information. To illustrate, Chapter 4 no longer presents poetry as a central genre during subject matter study, and it no longer distinguishes between seminar and deliberation types of discussions. Our readers found these concepts distracting.

Finally, this edition maintains consistency throughout each chapter. For instance, Chapter 3's treatment of unit planning now provides examples of various unit components that center about one topic, immigration. The term *launch* now is used consistently rather than bringing in new terms like *introduction* or *opening*. Overall, we believe you will find this edition to be very informative and accessible.

ACKNOWLEDGMENTS

The authors would like to thank Gail T. Eichman and Jeanine L. Williams for reviewing this new edition.

CHAPTER 1

Content Area Reading and Writing

LOOKING AHEAD

Elementary-, middle-, and high-school students acquire an incredible amount of knowledge while exploring content areas such as science, mathematics, and history. Because facts and ideas are accessible through print, effective teachers deliberately connect reading, writing, and content area instruction. They teach students how to use print to learn.

At this point, you might be wondering about your role in teaching reading and writing along with content area study. You might think something like, "Shouldn't reading and writing be taught during classes devoted exclusively to reading and writing?" If you are a middle- or secondary-school teacher, you might think literacy skills should be taught only by elementary teachers. These questions and reactions are common when people first consider reading and writing in the content areas.

This book explains productive learning opportunities that occur when reading and writing are linked with subject matter. For instance, it shows how reading and writing about the solar system can improve students' understandings of the sun, planets, and moons. It also shows how literacy skills such as determining the meanings of unfamiliar words and creating effective compositions can be improved while studying something like the solar system.

All K–12 teachers, as never before, are responsible for all students attaining high levels of literacy. Fulfilling this responsibility involves reading and writing across the curriculum.

This opening chapter lays a foundation for understanding how to meet current literacy achievement expectations. It contains three key ideas:

1. Compelling reasons support content area literacy instruction.
2. Thinking underlies reading, writing, and learning.
3. Academic identities drive reading, writing, and learning.

COMPELLING REASONS SUPPORT CONTENT AREA LITERACY INSTRUCTION

Many educators have presented reasons for instruction that links literacy with subject matter (Heller & Greenleaf, 2007; Moje, 2007; Moore, Readence, & Rickelman, 1983). Three compelling reasons for linking students' reading and writing proficiencies with subject matter study are (1) reading and writing are tools for learning; (2) literacy requirements continually increase in school and society; and (3) content area teachers can teach content area reading and writing best.

Reading and Writing Are Tools for Learning

Because content areas consist of language, the study of content entails the study of language. Years ago, Postman (1979) presented the case this way:

> Biology is not plants and animals. It is language about plants and animals. History is not events. It is language describing and interpreting events. Astronomy is not planets and stars. It is a way of talking about planets and stars. (p. 165)

Biologists, historians, and astronomers work with words; they use language to construct and convey meaning. Consequently, thinking and acting like a biologist, historian, or astronomer means being proficient with journal articles, textbooks, Web sites, library books, and other printed materials. It also means being able to write observational notes, character sketches, reactions to experiences, reports, and other forms of expression. This reading and writing associated with academics differs from everyday reading and writing outside of school (Zweirs, 2008). Academic language is the language of school. It is used to formally examine subject matter topics. It follows peculiar language patterns and employs precise terminology. Students benefit from instruction that clearly addresses academic language.

Learning opportunities expand when teachers help students read and write about what they are studying. Individuals who struggle with reading and writing communicate largely through listening, viewing, and speaking, so their opportunities grow tremendously when they gain proficiency with print. Indeed, reputable research syntheses consistently show that literacy learning is connected with subject-matter learning (Alvermann, Fitzgerald, & Simpson, 2006; Biancarosa & Snow, 2004; Kamil et al., 2008; Torgesen et al., 2007; RAND Reading Study Group, 2002). When youth increase their literacy abilities such as organizing ideas found in print, interpreting the meanings of unfamiliar vocabulary, composing reflective responses, recording study notes, and investigating topics independently, they increase their access to ideas and information.

Now that independent lifelong learning is an accepted requirement for staying abreast of our ever-changing worlds in the 2000s, access to print has become especially crucial. What happens when students leave their teachers? What will students do when they have no one to assist them with the print encountered in their personal, political, and occupational lives?

The role of literacy as a tool for learning is neatly encapsulated by the popular aphorism, "Give me a fish, and I eat for a day. Teach me to fish, and I eat for a lifetime." Teaching students to read and write well promotes independent learning in school and lasts a lifetime.

Literacy Requirements Continually Increase

Literacy requirements increase sharply as students become older and as our society and economy continue moving from a manufacturing base to a technical/informational one. Teachers have the responsibility to help students with these increasing literacy demands.

DEVELOPMENTAL CHANGES   Living organisms that develop—including people—progress from relatively simple forms in the beginning to relatively complex forms later on. They elaborate, or expand in detail, from one state to another; they unfold in progressive stages. Through continued development, individuals express all their inherent possibilities. Development applies to reading and writing as much as to physical growth and other areas (Alexander, 2005/2006).

Consider the following well-known quote from Shakespeare's *Hamlet*:

To be, or not to be: that is the question.

Each of the words in this quote appears in books found in any primary-grade classroom, but great maturity and competence are needed to fully come to terms with what these simple words express. Students require instruction to grasp the message and appreciate the beauty of Shakespeare's writing. Novice readers and writers would require support in order to grow into proficient, well-developed readers and writers able to fully understand Shakespeare. The International Reading Association position statement on adolescent literacy referred to development this way:

> Public and educational attention long has been focused on the beginnings of literacy, planting seedlings and making sure they take root. But without careful cultivation and nurturing, seedlings may wither and their growth may become stunted. (Moore et al., 1999, p. 9)

The ever-increasing difficulty of what students read in school unmistakably indicates the need for continual support across the subjects at all grade levels. Students read about neighborhood helpers in the primary grades, world geography in the middle grades, and comparative governments in the upper grades. As students progress through school, they read more and more expository material. Upper-grade students require help learning from their unfamiliar, complex, and abstract passage contents just as lower-grade students do with relatively familiar, simple, and concrete passage contents.

TECHNICAL/INFORMATIONAL CHANGES   Due to the rapid rate of change in our time (Kirsch, Braun, Yamamoto, & Sum, 2007), people require reading and writing abilities that are more sophisticated than those needed decades before. Advanced literacies enhance youths' opportunities to live a meaningful and productive life, earn a decent wage, and compete in today's global economy. All youth, regardless of whether they plan to enter college or the workforce, require advanced literate knowledge and skills (ACT, 2006; College Board, 2006). Lives that call for predictable, simple, stable routines are giving way to ones that require complex procedures, problem solving, and decision making.

In brief, students require reading and writing instruction throughout their school careers and across the curriculum because it is necessary. Literacy instruction provided during only one part of the day for the first few years of school no longer suffices. Extended instruction in reading and writing is needed so that individuals can learn to handle the dramatic changes they will experience in school, in their future workplaces, in society, and in their personal lives.

Content Area Teachers Can Teach Content Area Reading and Writing Best

Primary-grade teachers directing the study of topics such as neighborhoods and animals' habitats can best present ways to read and write about these topics. Senior-high physics teachers presenting a unit on quantum mechanics can best teach strategies for exploring and learning about this topic. Those who regularly guide learners through content areas are in optimum positions to improve students' content area reading and writing competencies.

MULTIPLE LITERACIES   Think how various specialists might perceive a large boulder they encounter during a walk in a meadow: a paleontologist might look for fossils in order to learn about the prehistoric plant and animal life of the area; an anthropologist might look for pictographs to obtain greater insight about ancient cultures; a sculptor might search for the inspiration to compose an original piece; and a metallurgist might analyze the rock to determine what it revealed about the metallic elements in the surrounding area. Because each specialist would approach the boulder differently, each would read and write about it differently. Multiple perspectives require multiple literacies.

Students integrate reading and writing in order to learn content area information.

To further appreciate the different perspectives among content areas, consider the following brief samples of subject matter texts:

Biology: Cells enclose protoplasm, the substance of life. Protoplasm consists of two parts. The nucleus is the more solid central part, and the cytoplasm is the softer, more liquid part. The bulk of protoplasm is made up of carbon, hydrogen, oxygen, and nitrogen.

History: In 1215, a group of barons forced King John of England to sign the Magna Carta. The barons wanted to restore their privileges; however, the Magna Carta grounded constitutional government in political institutions for all English-speaking people.

Mathematics: An angle is the union of two rays that do not lie on the same line. When the sum of the measure of two angles is 90°, the angles are complementary; when the sum of the measure is 180°, the angles are supplementary.

English:
To die, to sleep;
To sleep? Perchance to dream. Ay, there's the rub;
For in that sleep of death what dreams may come
When we have shuffled off this mortal coil,
Must give us pause.

The technical terms in these passages, such as *protoplasm, constitutional government, supplementary*, and *perchance*, refer to somewhat challenging concepts found in various disciplines. Other terms, such as *cell, grounded, angle, ray*, and *rub*, not only can be challenging by themselves, but they also have different meanings in different content areas. Among other things, *cell* can refer to a unit of protoplasm, a holding space in prison, or a receptacle for chemical reactions to generate electricity.

In addition, these passages, like the analyses of the boulder in the meadow described previously, present diverse perspectives on the world. The science passage describes the structure of a substance, the social studies piece explains the outcome of a human event, the math text presents measurements, and the English passage expresses an aspect of the human condition. Each has different ways with words. Indeed, learning in the academic disciplines involves learning the norms for accessing, producing, and communicating knowledge in each discipline. It involves understanding the ways of literate thinking and doing that each discipline authorizes. These disciplinary literacies (Moje, 2008; Shanahan & Shanahan, 2008) involve the reading and writing associated with each particular discipline. Those with deep understandings of a discipline can best explain the reading and writing strategies required by that discipline. People who want help interpreting tax forms typically go to tax preparers rather than reading teachers. Tax preparers are the logical choice because these individuals know the mind-set of the people who produced the material, the special vocabulary of taxation, the structure of the forms, and generally what it takes to make sense of the documents.

TEACHABLE MOMENTS   Along with being the best qualified to explain the demands of different materials, content area teachers also are in the best position to provide support when students are most receptive. Learners typically benefit most from instruction when they wish to accomplish something specific (Lave & Wenger, 1991). Teaching students to take notes about social studies concepts generally is most appropriate when they have the desire to understand and remember these concepts. Teaching students how to solve mathematics word problems is done best in math class when they want to solve such problems. Students who are taught how to take social studies notes or solve math word problems in a reading or an English class frequently lack motivation and have difficulty transferring what they were taught. Literacy learning occurs best when students have the need to know.

DO IT TOGETHER

The preceding section presented three reasons for promoting reading and writing during subject matter study. As a pair or a group, list these reasons and produce personal examples to illustrate each. For instance, how have you used reading and writing as a tool for learning? What experiences have you had with increased literacy requirements? What help with reading and writing have content area teachers provided you in the past?

THINKING UNDERLIES READING, WRITING, AND LEARNING

Thinking is a source of intellectual activity; it is the cognitive basis of reading, writing, and learning. People apply thinking processes in particular ways when they read, write, and accumulate knowledge. Having a firm grasp of the thinking processes that underlie reading, writing, and learning provides a solid base for planning appropriate content area literacy instruction. You can plan your teaching by asking and answering questions like, "What reading practice will best help my students connect what they already know with what they will be reading?" "How could my class best organize this passage?" and "Am I enabling all my learners to form images of what they are reading?"

Since antiquity, philosophers and learning theorists have attempted to identify the thinking processes that underlie reading, writing, and learning. Countless books and articles have been written on this subject, with countless thinking processes suggested. Some classic and contemporary references that we have found to be especially valuable include ones by Bransford, Brown, and Cocking (1999), Dewey (1910), James (1925), Marzano (2004), Pressley & Afflerbach (1995), and Ruddell & Unrau (2004).

The following eight thinking processes account for a large share of the thinking involved in most reading, writing, and learning. These processes help educators plan productive learning experiences. Continually ask yourself how to provide opportunities for students to connect, predict, and so on, in order to enhance their reading, writing, and learning.

Eight Thinking Processes

1. Connect
2. Preview and predict
3. Organize
4. Generalize
5. Image

6. Monitor and fix up

7. Evaluate

8. Apply

Think back to your mid-teens when you were preparing for your driver's license test. You probably obtained a copy of your state's driving manual and set out to learn the driving rules, regulations, and suggested operating techniques. As the eight thinking processes are described in this section, think about the processes you went through to learn from the driving manual.

Connect

Learning involves *connections.* When you encounter a presentation of ideas organized around a topic with which you already have some experience, you connect the new input with what you already know. You call up previous knowledge and experience and either add to the information there or change the information to accommodate the new data. Connecting information is a matter of relating what is being presented to what is already known.

As a teenager studying the driver's manual, you began to call up all those insights and bits and pieces of information about driving that you had absorbed over the years. Without that background knowledge and experience on which to build, learning how to drive would have been nearly impossible to accomplish in the relatively short time you took. Calling up what you already knew about road signs, for example, would have allowed you to skim through that section because the information was so familiar. You probably needed to concentrate on just the few unusual signs that you had not yet learned.

You may never have considered that the road signs you had seen over the years were color-coded. You did know, however, that whenever drivers see a stop sign, they are required to come to a complete stop at the designated location. What you learned when reading your manual was that whenever you saw a red sign, no matter what shape it was or what message it contained, your basic thought should be to stop. DO NOT ENTER, WRONG WAY, and NO LEFT TURN signs are all red. While studying your manual, you might have called up your prior knowledge that a red light signals a stop and related that knowledge to the new fact that any red sign means movement is prohibited. Bridging old information with new information is connecting.

Preview and Predict

When you first obtained your copy of the manual and began to thumb through it, you were *previewing and predicting* what it had to teach you as well as what it contained that you already knew. You engaged in these combined processes automatically, without necessarily being aware of it. For instance, you might have thought there would be sections on starting the car and economizing on gas. In reality, however, you probably found practically no information on those topics. On previewing the manual headings about road signs, on the other hand, you probably expected to find information about their shapes and messages, and your examination of the manual no doubt verified that prediction.

Previewing is a way to get an advance showing of what is to come. The restricted view you receive gives you a head start when you carefully examine passage contents.

Predicting involves thinking about what is to come, giving you a head start on learning. Previewing and predicting also tend to motivate you to get involved with the material. After all, why do movie theaters show previews of coming attractions?

Organize

To have made sense of the driver's manual, you needed to *organize* the information presented there. You analyzed the whole passage, breaking it down into ordered parts. You probably arranged the information according to some type of framework, perhaps according to the headings you found in the manual. Most manuals are divided into chapters with such headings as Parking, Turns, and Licenses. Within each chapter are headings that group the information into related subsets. A chapter on hazardous driving conditions might include topics such as driving at night, driving in adverse weather, and driving under the influence of alcohol and other drugs. Readers and writers who analyze information, grouping it into meaningful categories, go far in making sense of the world.

Generalize

Readers and writers *generalize* when they draw conclusions about information. They form a generalization by noting trends, commonalities, or patterns among specifics; they discover the rule or principle that unites various phenomena. They synthesize information. For instance, when you read the Right of Way section in the driver's manual, you probably found much information about yielding to oncoming vehicles when turning left, yielding to pedestrians whether or not they are in crosswalks, and yielding to emergency vehicles. After reading these laws, you might have concluded this: "The pattern in all this information about yielding right of way is 'Safety first.' Preventing accidents is the thread common to these laws." Coming to this conclusion helped you tie together all the right-of-way laws, which otherwise might have been a meaningless assortment of details to be memorized by rote.

Image

Engaging your senses internally and cognitively as you read and write adds to the learning experience and makes it more memorable. This process often results in an *image*. Visual images are used most frequently, although other sense images certainly come into play. Vicariously seeing, feeling, hearing, smelling, or tasting what is described in print can help you think deeply and richly about the ideas you are reading or writing about.

Imagery may have helped you with your driver's manual. Think about the part of the manual that discussed the appropriate distances to maintain between two vehicles in motion. Safe following distances vary according to how fast you are traveling. For instance, at 50 miles per hour, a safe following distance is 84 yards. You could easily have forgotten these figures if there had been no way to transform them. Thus, you might have imagined a 100-yard football field and then mentally placed a car at one goal line and your car 84 yards down the field. This visual image would have helped you remember the appropriate distance to keep between two vehicles traveling at 50 miles per hour.

Imagery also may have helped you deal with the information about turning at intersections. You probably studied the abstract diagrams and discussions about turning and visualized particular instances of those procedures. In your mind's eye you might have run a little motion picture of pulling up to a multiple-lane intersection and then executing the appropriate turn.

Monitor and Fix Up

Throughout your study of the driver's manual, you needed to *monitor and fix up* how well you were doing with the information. Internally, and probably subconsciously, you asked yourself, "Am I understanding this? Am I getting what I need? Does this make sense?" Part of self-monitoring is checking internally to determine how well your learning or thinking is progressing.

The other part of self-monitoring involves repair work. If you sense a problem with what you are trying to learn, then you need to do something about it. If their understanding breaks down, good thinkers stop, identify the source of the difficulty, and try to get over it. For instance, when you got to the part in your driver's manual about different kinds of licenses, you might have plunged into information about chauffeur's license expirations, the minimum age for driving mopeds, and the cost of instruction permits. Eventually you realized that you were being overwhelmed, so you stopped and thought, "Now, what do I need from this section?" You might have determined that the renewal period and minimum age for a regular operator's license was all that was important, so you selected that particular information for careful study before moving on to the next section. Monitoring your learning by assessing its status and repairing breakdowns is a crucial thinking process.

Evaluate

The difference between monitoring and evaluating concerns processes and contents. Whenever you assess the quality of your reading or writing process while you are actively engaged in it, you are monitoring. Whenever you assess the contents of what you are reading or writing, you are *evaluating*.

One of the hallmarks of proficient readers is deciding whether or not passages are believable, accurate, and appropriate. When you evaluate, you judge the content being presented. The root word of *evaluate* is *value*. Readers and writers who decide the value of information strengthen their grasp of it; those who simply accept information without examining it critically are at a disadvantage. As you read your driver's manual, you might have encountered a section on driving in unsafe conditions that caught your eye. "Does steering in the direction that a car is sliding on ice really help? It sure seems counterintuitive!" you might think. "Are there viable alternatives to what this passage says?"

Insights from critical literacy (see, for example, Fecho, 2004; Lewis, Enciso, & Moje, 2007) have expanded notions of evaluation by concentrating on the links between print and power. Critical literacy educators have readers and writers evaluate the ways print maintains or transforms privilege. They critique media representations of events, looking for bias.

Critical literacy educators might lead students to question state authorities' linking of a driver's license with performance on a pencil-and-paper multiple-choice test. Why must potential drivers succeed in a traditional school-like task? Does this practice support or impede marginalized groups' access to full participation in society? Critical theorists lead investigations into whose interests are served when particular reading materials are selected.

For instance, they call attention to books that predominantly portray scientists as male rather than female. They show how printed messages shape and are shaped by the power structures of society.

Apply

The eighth thinking process is *apply*. The reasons you plowed through the driver's manual were so that you could pass the driver's test, obtain a license, and get behind the wheel of a car. When you finally got behind the wheel, you were required to remember all the rules and regulations: how fast to go on various streets under various conditions, who has the right of way in different situations, and what the road signs mean. Applying goes beyond just telling what you have learned to actually using what you have learned in real or simulated situations.

When you apply knowledge, you select the most appropriate response from all the ones you have acquired. As was noted at the beginning of this chapter, this book is meant to help you teach students to read and write in the content areas. Our goal is to help you plan and actually use (i.e., apply) the thinking processes described here in classroom situations.

TRY IT OUT

Take a passage with which you are quite comfortable, and sit with a classmate. Take turns reading a short section and then explaining how you used—or might use—a few of the thinking processes described previously. Do this until you explain how all eight of the processes were involved in your reading and learning.

Thinking Is Complex

The remaining chapters in this book explain how to generate learning activities that engage students in these thinking processes. When planning instruction, keep in mind several points about the eight thinking processes.

OVERLAP   Our labels and descriptions overlap those presented by many other authors. Fostering thinking is a time-honored common goal among educators, and many types of thinking have been discussed. The professional literature about thinking contains such terms as *hypothesizing, speculating, inferring, extrapolating, elaborating, problem solving, synthesizing, analyzing, creating*, and *categorizing*. *Metacognition* frequently is used to denote a special constellation of thinking processes considered to be above the others.

Our list underlies many of the cognitive behaviors presented in the 2001 revision of Bloom's classic taxonomy of educational objectives (Anderson & Krathwohl, 2001). The essential thinking processes presented in this chapter are listed in the following table alongside the ones presented by Anderson and Krathwohl. Our terms are often synonymous with several others, and ours share most of the characteristics of the others. Our list provides a solid basis for planning content area reading and writing instruction.

Essential Thinking Processes	Taxonomy of Educational Objectives
Connect	Remember
Preview and predict	Understand
Organize	Apply
Generalize	Analyze
Image	Evaluate
Monitor and fix up	Create
Evaluate	
Apply	

FLEXIBILITY A second point about our essential thinking processes is that presenting them separately implies that each is isolated from the others. And listing them from *connect* to *apply* suggests that thinkers do first one, then another, then a third, and so on, in a prescribed sequence. But these thinking processes do not stand alone and are not used in a rigid order. Instead, each thinker orchestrates the processes flexibly according to the demands of each situation. Students might form images and predict upcoming information simultaneously; they might evaluate the first few sentences of what they read or write, organize their thoughts, and continue processing the information. Our point is that students flexibly combine thinking processes and emphasize certain ones at different times in order to conceptualize what they are reading or writing about.

SOPHISTICATION Students at all grade levels can benefit from assistance with these thinking processes. To paraphrase Bruner's famous quotation from *The Process of Education* (1977): We begin with the principle that any thinking process can be taught effectively in some intellectually honest form to any child at any stage of development.

This principle means that organizing, for example, can be presented in the primary as well as the high-school grades. Primary-school children might categorize pictures of animals according to those that fly, those that walk, and those that swim; high-school students might classify one-celled life forms according to their kingdom, phylum, class, order, family, genus, and species. Similarly, very young children can learn to evaluate by thinking about questions like "Did a real boy named Jack climb a beanstalk and meet a giant?" and "Should Jack have climbed the beanstalk?" Older students can ponder how well *Lord of the Flies* portrays basic human nature. In brief, students from kindergarten through twelfth grade connect, preview and predict, organize, generalize, image, monitor and fix up, evaluate, and apply with varying degrees of sophistication.

LISTEN, LOOK, AND LEARN

Visit a class during a subject matter lesson or tape-record a lesson that you present. Pretend that you are a student during this activity and list the chief thinking processes you would use. Which were used most frequently? Which were used least frequently? What could be done to elicit the thinking processes that were not tapped?

ACADEMIC IDENTITIES DRIVE CONTENT AREA LITERACY AND LEARNING

Identity is a source of people's actions individually and in groups; it is the sociocultural basis of literacy and learning (McCarthy, 2002; Lewis & Del Valle, 2009). People enact identities in particular ways when they read, write, and accumulate knowledge. Realizing the importance of students' identities leads educators to approach learners as richly detailed human beings with predispositions, emotions, and motivations—as well as thinking processes—to be addressed during content area literacy instruction.

Identity is linked with individuals' deep-seated understandings and beliefs about themselves. Identity answers "Who am I?" questions. It is found in the answers individuals compose to soul-searching questions about whether or not in school they are leaders, rebels, serious students, readers, and so on. Identities are established when individuals tell themselves and others who they are, act according to these words, and experience strong emotional ties with these words and actions (Holland, Lachicotte, Skinner, & Cain, 1998).

Academic Identities

Educators do well to recognize how youths' academic identities affect their beliefs and actions in school as well as in particular classrooms (McCarthy & Moje, 2002). A positive academic identity means that individuals consider themselves insiders to education; they see themselves as members of scholarly learning communities. Students display positive academic identities when they present themselves as the kinds of people who embrace formal education, who take school seriously. These individuals align themselves with academic cultures, identifying with teachers and conscientious peers. They see themselves connected with academic ways of life. Students with positive academic identities seek to accomplish school-related goals by completing assignments, reading independently, and studying for tests (Jackson, 2003).

On the other hand, students who display negative academic identities in their classes tend to see themselves as lost in school, as educational outsiders, as unsuccessful learners who do not belong in academic settings. Students who demonstrate negative academic identities often act out apathetic, foolish, or defiant behaviors as they resist school and school-related literacies.

Socially Situated Identities

An important distinction exists between individuals' core identities and their socially situated ones (Gee, 2001). Core identities are individuals' stable and continuous manifestations of the self. Core identities are revealed by people's words and actions that generally hold uniformly across situations. When people say, "That's just Pat being Pat," they are referring to Pat acting according to an identity that is relatively fixed, enduring across time and circumstance. Core identities express people's somewhat predictable responses to each and every situation. In contrast, socially situated identities shift across circumstances; they are to be found among particular group environments. Referring to such identities as *socially situated* conveys the idea that individuals act somewhat differently as they move in and out of different social situations (McCarthy & Moje, 2002).

Outside of school, many youth interact with ethnicity, class, gender, community, family, peer group, and popular culture influences whose ways of thinking and communicating differ from mainstream academic ones (DeBlase, 2003; Gándara & Contreras, 2009; Moje, Ciechanowski, Kramer, Ellis, Carrillo, & Collazo, 2004). In order to be successful students, many youth learn to shift their identities across these situations. For instance, a culture that expects girls to regularly interact with the family at home presents different expectations from an academic culture that encourages girls to regularly read silently at home. A culture that regards school success as selling out to an oppressive, dominant establishment differs from an academic one that regards school success with pride. A culture that expects readers to obediently accept the written word holds different expectations from an academic one that expects readers to constantly question what they read. A culture that endorses several individuals participating in story retellings differs from an academic one that expects one individual at a time to retell a story. To cope with social groups' particular cultures that differ from schools' academic cultures, youth adopt flexible identities, shifting what they say about themselves and how they act, according to the social situation.

Not only do many youth learn to alter their outside-of-school identities to fit inside-of-school requirements, they further adjust their identities from class to class. Students learn to cope with different views of learning and ways of thinking and communicating that different teachers present across different content areas (Moje & Dillon, 2006). For instance, students in a math class might be expected to act as problem solvers who calculate unambiguous data precisely and record their findings in meticulous order. These same students in literature class might be expected to act as problem solvers who form several possible interpretations of deliberately ambiguous text and present them in open-ended discussions. To do well, these students need to identify themselves as meticulous problem solvers in the math class and as adventurous problem solvers in the literature class. And in other classes, they may be expected to identify themselves not as problem solvers at all, but as bankers of information who accurately recover what is deposited during class lectures and seat work.

Implications of Socially Situated Identities

Youth shift their identities according to social situations, and they take up particular academic identities to succeed in school in general as well as in your class in particular. Realizing this has implications for your classroom instruction. Acknowledging youths' socially situated identities has implications to (a) Avoid a deficit perspective, (b) adjust classroom instruction to accommodate students' identities, and (c) help students adjust their identities to accommodate classroom instruction.

Avoid a deficit perspective. To discern the value of avoiding a deficit perspective, form an image of different individuals according to the following shortcomings:

1. a distracted learner
2. a reluctant reader

Do you have an image of each? Note that these deficits, or shortcomings, seem to apply to individuals as they participate in each and every situation. The deficits seem to name people's core identities, their fixed traits, to be expected during all school and nonschool activities.

Now form an image of the same individuals according to these descriptors:

1. a learner who acts distracted in Mr. Blanchard's class
2. a reader who participates reluctantly during school time set aside for free reading but who avidly reads about music outside of school

Did the new sentences modify your view of the individuals? Did our putting the person first (e.g., *a learner*) and then characterizing him or her according to a specific social situation (e.g., *who acts distracted in Mr. Blanchard's class*) refine your image of the person, pinpointing your view of him or her?

This demonstration shows how a deficit perspective inappropriately equates people with stable negative traits (e.g., distracted, reluctant). Avoiding deficit perspectives is imperative because classic research is clear that such a view predictably brings down the quality of teaching and learning (Moll & Ruiz, 2002; Oakes, 1985; Rist, 1970). Thinking about students mainly in terms of their perceived shortcomings leads educators to reduce the curriculum to rudimentary skills. Conversations about texts are lowered to answering questions about predetermined facts, and writing is relegated to reproducing barren forms. The quality of teachers' verbal interactions with students declines even when the intention is otherwise.

Deficit perspectives create self-fulfilling prophecies about what a particular student or classroom will be like and what the students can do. Teachers come to treat students as substandard, as broken, so the students, in turn, align their thoughts and actions with the patterns the teachers establish. Students come to identify themselves as deficient, and they act accordingly.

Avoiding a deficit perspective means initially thinking of each student as a human being who is subject to the power of situations rather than as a substandard group member who always acts the same. Knowing that a student acts like a distracted learner in one class does not necessarily mean he or she should be classified as a member of a group of distractible people. This student might be an engaged learner in another class, so you might examine what the engaging class offers. Knowing that a student displays reluctant-reader behaviors inside of school does not mean he or she should be classified as a reluctant reader. This student might be an avid reader outside of school, so you might examine the circumstances of his or her reading outside of school (Alvermann, 2001; Knobel, 2001).

Adjust classroom instruction to accommodate students' identities. Teachers who recognize youths' socially situated identities adjust classroom instruction to accommodate those identities. One way you make such adjustments is by linking your classrooms with what your students bring to them, regularly inviting students to connect experiences and knowledge from their outside-of-school lives with their inside-of-school instruction. During the first day or two of school, have students record their outside-of-school interests and accomplishments on *getting to know you* cards. Then refer to these cards when planning and delivering instruction, explicitly connecting parts of the class to your students' lives. Math teachers might pose geometry problems associated with skateboarding ramps and halfpipes; science teachers might address the physical and chemical processes of cooking; literature teachers might highlight books they think certain students would appreciate; and social studies teachers might show how political and social issues affect people of different ethnicities.

In multicultural settings, honor different patterns of speech and styles of conversation, knowing that cultural groups often differ along these lines. Address examples from students' different ethnic heritages when addressing topics like heroes, historical settlements, and popular literature. Provide culturally relevant materials such as ones presenting African-American, Native-American, and Hispanic groups' experiences with and perceptions of subject-matter topics. Adorn your classroom with positive inclusive images. Do all this so your students can see themselves as members of a classroom community, as insiders to formal education.

Teachers also adjust their classroom instruction to accommodate students' identities by offering instructional voice and choice. Offer a variety of print materials, realizing that your students will find some materials more suitable than others. Present multimedia CDs, pamphlets, brochures, periodicals, alternative textbooks, and online encyclopedias. Finally, provide multiple response options, enabling students to produce PowerPoint presentations, videos, and dramatic presentations, to name a few.

Help students adjust their identities to accommodate classroom instruction. Adjustments and accommodations are two-way streets: You adjust to your students, while your students adjust to you. Instructional support is needed for your students' adjustments to be most effective.

Help your students adjust their identities to accommodate classroom instruction by explicitly presenting the views of learning and ways of thinking and communicating that are needed for success in class. To return to earlier examples, if meticulous problem solving is expected, then inform students of this, explaining and demonstrating the processes and continually supporting your students' identities as meticulous problem solvers. Help youth adopt identities applicable to your class.

The process of flexibly adapting identities to different situations can be considered a form of code switching or border crossing (Mehan, Hubbard & Villanueva, 1994; Zuengler & Miller, 2006). Think of youth regularly crossing community, family, peer group, popular culture, school, and subject-matter borders when they read, write, and learn. Youth might see themselves informally examining multiple texts while pursuing outside-of-school interests in folk dancing, cars, or music while they see themselves focusing on a few core texts inside of school. Code switching and border crossing permit students to maintain their culture and language in nonacademic settings while conforming to different views of culture and language in academic settings. While maintaining stable core identities, youth can cross from one social situation to another, adapting their identities according to the circumstances.

LISTEN, LOOK, AND LEARN

Observe a class for about three sessions. Single out a few students who typically enact positive academic identities in the class and a few who typically enact negative academic identities. Describe the students' actions that led you to your conclusions. Additionally, note the classroom actions that encouraged the students' display of their identities.

LOOKING BACK

Developing students' reading and writing abilities in the content areas is one of the schools' major responsibilities, and content area teachers are the most effective agents in accomplishing this goal. Focusing on thinking processes enables you to plan and deliver learning activities that enhance content area literacy and content acquisition. Students who connect, organize, and apply, among other things, go far in bringing active and effective thought to their schooling. Additionally, youth who identify themselves as members of a community of learners, as insiders to schools and classrooms, have an advantage over those who see themselves as outsiders not fitting in academic settings. This chapter contains three key ideas: (1) Compelling reasons support content area literacy instruction; (2) thinking underlies reading, writing, and learning; and (3) identity drives reading, writing, and learning.

Additional Readings

To examine educational mandates and graduation requirements that each state requires relative to reading and writing, consult the following Web site: Education Commission of the States [www.ecs.org].

The following sources examine how content area reading and writing instruction fits with teachers' backgrounds, beliefs, and practices. They provide a good overview of typical content reading practices.

Barry, A. L. (2002). Reading strategies teachers say they use. *Journal of Adolescent and Adult Literacy, 46,* 132–141.

Spor, M. W., & Schneider, B. K. (2001). A quantitative description of the content reading practices of beginning teachers. *Reading Horizons, 41,* 257–268.

Sturtevant, E. G., & Linek, W. M. (2003). The instructional beliefs and decisions of middle and high school teachers who successfully blend literacy and content. *Reading Research and Instruction, 43*(1), 74–90.

The following six syntheses of research provide a solid base for the instructional recommendations presented in this first chapter and in succeeding ones.

Alvermann, D. E., Fitzgerald, J., & Simpson, M. (2006). Teaching and learning in reading. In P. Alexander & P. Winne (Eds.), *Handbook of Educational Psychology I* (2nd ed., pp. 427–45). New York, NY: Simon & Schuster/Macmillan.

Biancarosa, F., & Snow, C. E. (2004). *Reading next—A vision for action and research in middle and high school literacy: A report to Carnegie Corporation of New York.* Washington, DC: Alliance for Excellent Education. Retrieved May 3, 2006, from www.all4ed.org/publications/ReadingNext/index.html

Kamil, M. L., Borman, G. D., Dole, J., Kral, C. C., Salinger, T., & Torgesen, J. (2008). *Improving adolescent literacy: Effective classroom and intervention practices: A practice guide* (NCEE #2008-4027). Washington, DC: Institute of Education Sciences, U.S. Department of Education. Retrieved September 4, 2008, from http://ies.ed.gov/ncee/wwc

National Reading Panel. (2000). *Teaching children to read: An evidence-based assessment of the scientific research literature on reading and its implications for reading instruction: Reports of the subgroups.* Bethesda, MD: National Institute of Child Health and Human Development, National Institutes of Health.

RAND Reading Study Group. (2002). *Reading for understanding: Toward an R&D program in reading comprehension.* Santa Monica, CA: Science and Technology Policy Institute, RAND Education.

Torgesen, J. K., Houston, D. D., Rissman, L. M., Decker, S. M., Roberts, G., Vaughn, S., Wexler, J., Francis, D. J., Rivera, M. O., & Lesaux, N. (2007). *Academic literacy instruction for adolescents: A guidance document from the Center on Instruction.* Portsmouth, NH: RMC Research Corporation, Center on Instruction. Retrieved May 3, 2007, from the Center on Instruction site: www.centeroninstruction.org

Content area reading and writing is based on the assumption that advantages occur when literacy and subject matter are integrated. The following reference presents subject-specific insights from mathematics, the arts, history, and science about such integration.

Alvermann, D. E., & Reinking, D. (Eds.). (2004). New direction in research: Cross-disciplinary collaborations [Special section]. *Reading Research Quarterly, 39*(3).

The following call for attention to the literacies that are peculiar to each discipline. They refer to content area literacy as *disciplinary literacy* to highlight the idea that each discipline calls for distinctive reading and writing.

Conley, M. W. (2008). Improving adolescent comprehension: Developing learning strategies in content areas. In S. E. Israel & G. G. Duffy (Eds.), *Handbook of research on reading comprehension.* New York, NY: Routledge.

Moje, E. B. (2008). Foregrounding the disciplines in secondary literacy teaching and learning: A call for change. *Journal of Adolescent and Adult Literacy, 52*(2), 96–107.

Shanahan, T., & Sanahan, C. (2008). Teaching disciplinary literacy to adolescents: Rethinking content-area literacy. *Harvard Education Review, 78*(1), 40–59.

This is a scholarly treatment of the ways learners' cultures and identities interact with their literacy learning.

Lewis, C., Enciso, P. E., & Moje, E. B. (Eds.). (2007). *Reframing sociocultural research on literacy: Identity, agency, and power*. Mahwah, NJ: Erlbaum.

An indictment of the deficit perspective is contained in the following:

Valencia, R. R. (2009). A response to Ruby Payne's claim that the deficit thinking model has no scholarly utility. *Teachers College Record*. Retrieved July 24, 2009, from www.tcrecord.org/Content.asp?ContentID=15691

Valencia, R. R. (Ed.). (1997). *The evolution of deficit thinking: Educational thought and practice*. Washington, DC: Falmer Press.

Online Resources

The following sites, which are listed by content area, represent instructional resources available through the web that link content with literacy.

English-Language Arts

East of the Web
http://www.eastoftheweb.com

International Reading Association
http://www.reading.org/

Literacy Connections
www.literacyconnections.com

Literature Lesson Plans
http://litplans.com

National Council of Teachers of English
http://www.ncte.org/

Studyguide.org
http://www.studyguide.org/index.htm

Teaching Literature
http://www.teachingliterature.org/teachingliterature/ index.htm

Web English Teacher
www.webenglishteacher.com

English Language Learning

Colorín Colorado
http://www.colorincolorado.org/educators/content

National Association for Bilingual Education
http://www.nabe.org/

National Clearinghouse for English Language Acquisition and Language Instruction Educational Programs
http://www.ncela.gwu.edu

Teachers of English to Speakers of Other Languages
http://www.tesol.org

TEFL.net–Because You Teach English
http://www.tefl.net/

Mathematics

How to Read Mathematics (a single source)
http://www.stonehill.edu/compsci/History_Math/math-read.htm

MathStories.com
http://www.mathstories.com/strategies.htm

National Council of Teachers of Mathematics
www.nctm.org

Science

Action Bioscience
http://actionbioscience.org/

How Stuff Works
http://www.howstuffworks.com/

National Science Teachers Association
http://www.nsta.org/

Try Science
http://www.tryscience.org/home.html

United States Geological Survey and Science Education
http://education.usgs.gov/

Social Studies

American History Teachers' Collaborative
http://www.americanhistoryteachers.org/

National Council for the Social Studies
http://www.socialstudies.org/

Reading Quest
www.readingquest.org

SCORE History/Social Science
http://score.rims.k12.ca.us/

C-SPAN Classroom
www.c-spanclassroom.org

These sites present resources for K–12 content area literacy programs.

Just Read Now
http://www.justreadnow.com/index.htm

The Knowledge Loom
http://knowledgeloom.org/index.jsp

Learning Point Associates
http://www.learningpt.org/expertise/literacy/

This site presents resources for elementary literacy programs.

Reading Rockets
http://www.readingrockets.org/

These sites present resources for middle-and high-school literacy programs.

Adlit.org
http://www.adlit.org/

Adolescent Literacy Toolkit
http://www.ccsso.org/projects/
Secondary_School_Redesign/
Adolescent_Literacy_Toolkit/

Literacy Matters
www.literacymatters.org/

References

ACT. (2006). *Ready for college and ready for work: Same or different?* Iowa City, IA: Author. Retrieved November 13, 2008, from the ACT site: www.act.org

Alexander, P. A. (2005/2006). A path to competence: A lifespan developmental perspective on reading. *Journal of Literacy Research, 37,* 413–436.

Alvermann, D. E. (2001). Reading adolescents' reading identities: Looking back to see ahead. *Journal of Adolescent and Adult Literacy, 44,* 676–690.

Alvermann, D. E., Fitzgerald, J., & Simpson, M. (2006). Teaching and learning in reading. In P. Alexander & P. Winne (Eds.), *Handbook of educational psychology* (2nd ed., pp. 427–455). Mahwah, NJ: Erlbaum.

Anderson, L. W., & Krathwohl, D. (Eds.). (2001). *A taxonomy for learning, teaching, and assessing: A revision of Bloom's taxonomy of educational objectives.* New York, NY: Longman.

Biancarosa, F., & Snow, C. E. (2004). *Reading next—A vision for action and research in middle and high school literacy: A report to Carnegie Corporation of New York.* Washington, DC: Alliance for Excellent Education. Retrieved May 3, 2006, from www.all4ed./publications/ReadingNext/index.html

Bransford, J. D., Brown, A. L., & Cocking, R. R. (Eds.). (1999). *How people learn: Brain, mind, experience, and school.* Washington, DC: National Academy Press.

Bruner, J. (1977). *The process of education.* Cambridge, MA: Harvard University Press.

College Board. (2006). *College Board standards for college success: English language arts.* Princeton, NJ: Author. Retrieved September 15, 2006, from the College Board site: www/collegeboard.com

Deblase, G. L. (2003). Missing stories, missing lives: Urban girls (re)constructing race and gender in the literacy classroom. *Urban Education, 38,* 279–329.

Dewey, J. (1910). *How we think.* Boston, MA: D. C. Heath.

Fecho, B. (2004). *"Is this English?" Race, language, and culture in the classroom.* New York, NY: Teachers College Press.

Gándara, P., & Contreras, F. (2009). *The Latino education crisis: The consequences of failed social policies.* Cambridge, MA: Harvard University Press.

Gee, J. P. (2001). Identity as an analytic lens for research in education. In W. G. Secada (Ed.), *Review of research in education* (v. 25) (pp. 99–125). Washington, DC: American Educational Research Association.

Heller, R., & Greenleaf, C. L. (2007). *Literacy instruction in the content areas: Getting to the core of middle and high school improvement.* Washington, DC: Alliance for Excellent Education. Retrieved August 25, 2007, from the Alliance for Excellent Education site: www.all4ed.org/adolescent_literacy/index.html

Holland, D., Lachicotte, W., JR., Skinner, D., & Cain, C. (1998). *Identity and agency in cultural worlds.* Cambridge, MA: Harvard University Press.

Jackson, D. B. (2003). Education reform as if student agency mattered: Academic microcultures and student identity. *Phi Delta Kappan, 84,* 579–585.

James, W. (1925). *Talks to teachers on psychology, and to students on some of life's ideals.* London, England: Longman.

Kamil, M. L., Borman, G. D., Dole, J., Kral, C. C., Salinger, T., & Torgesen, J. (2008). *Improving adolescent literacy: Effective classroom and intervention practices: A practice guide* (NCEE #2008-4027). Washington, DC: Institute of Education Sciences, U.S. Department of Education. Retrieved September 4, 2008, from http://ies.ed.gov/ncee/wwc

Kirsch, I., Braun, H., Yamamoto, K., & Sum, A. (2007). *America's perfect storm: Three forces changing our nation's future.* Princeton, NJ: Educational Testing Service. Retrieved February 10, 2007, from the ETS site: www.ets.org/research/pic

Knobel, M. (2001). "I'm not a pencil man": How one student challenges our notions of literacy "failure" in school. *Journal of Adolescent and Adult Literacy, 44,* 404–414.

Lewis, C., & Del Valle, A. (2009). Literacy and identity: Implications for research and practice. In L. Christenbury, R. Bomer, & P. Smagorinsky (Eds.), *Handbook of adolescent literacy research* (pp. 307–322). New York, NY: Guilford.

Lewis, C., Enciso, P., & Moje, E. (2007). *Reframing sociocultural research on literacy: Identity, agency, and power.* Majwah, NJ: Erlbaum.

Marzano, R. J. (2004). *Building background knowledge for academic achievement: Research on what works in schools.* Alexandria, VA: Association for Supervision and Curriculum Development.

McCarthey, S. J., & Moje, E. B. (2002). Identity matters. *Reading Research Quarterly, 37,* 228–238.

Mehan, H., Hubbard, L., & Villanueva, I. (1994). Forming academic identities: Accommodation without assimilation among involuntary minorities. *Anthropology and Education Quarterly, 25,* 91–117.

Moje, E. B. (2008). Foregrounding the disciplines in secondary literacy teaching and learning: A call for change. *Journal of Adolescent and Adult Literacy, 52,* 96–107.

Moje, E. B., & Dillon, D. R. (2006). Adolescent identities as mediated by science classroom discourse communities. In D. E. Alvermann, K. A. Hinchman, D. W. Moore, S. F. Phelps, & D. R. Waff (Eds.), *Reconceptualizing the literacies in adolescents' lives* (2nd ed.; pp. 85–106) Mahwah, NJ: Erlbaum.

Moje, E. B., Ciechanowski, K. M., Kramer, K., Ellis, L., Carrillo, R., & Collazo, T. (2004). Working toward third space in content area literacy: An examination of everyday funds of knowledge and discourse. *Reading Research Quarterly, 39,* 38–70.

Moll, L., & Ruiz, R. (2002). The schooling of Latino students. In M. Suarez-Orozco & M. Paez (Eds.), *Contexts for learning: Sociocultural dynamics in children's development* (pp. 19–42). New York, NY: Oxford.

Moore, D. W., Bean, T. W., Birdyshaw, D., & Rycik, J. A., for the Commission on Adolescent Literacy of the International Reading Association. (1999). *Adolescent literacy: A position statement.* Newark, DE: International Reading Association.

Moore, D. W., Readence, J. E., & Rickelman, R. (1983). An historical exploration of content area reading instruction. *Reading Research Quarterly, 18,* 419–438.

Oakes, J. (1985). *Keeping track: How schools structure inequality.* New Haven, CT: Yale University Press.

Postman, N. (1979). *Teaching as a conserving activity.* New York, NY: Delacorte.

Pressley, M., & Afflerbach, P. (1995). *Verbal protocols of reading: The nature of constructively responsive reading.* Hillsdale, NJ: Erlbaum.

RAND Reading Study Group. (2002). *Reading for understanding: Toward an R&D program in reading comprehension.* Santa Monica, CA: Science and Technology Policy Institute, RAND Education.

Rist, R. (1970). Student social class and teacher expectations: The self-fulfilling prophecy in ghetto education. *Harvard Educational Review, 70,* 257–301.

Ruddell, R. B., & Unrau, N. J. (Eds.). (2004). *Theoretical models and processes of reading* (5th ed.). Newark, DE: International Reading Association.

Shanahan, T., & Shanahan, C. (2008). Teaching disciplinary literacy to adolescents: Rethinking content-area literacy. *Harvard Education Review, 78*(1), 40–59.

Torgesen, J. K., Houston, D. D., Rissman, L. M., Decker, S. M., Roberts, G., Vaughan, S., Wexler, J., Francis, D. J., Rivera, M. O., & Lesaux, N. (2007). *Academic literacy instruction for adolescents: A guidance document from the Center on Instruction.* Portsmouth, NH: RMC Research Corporation, Center on Instruction. Retrieved May 3, 2007, from the Center on Instruction site: www.centeroninstruction.org

Zuengler, J., & Miller, E. R. (2006). Cognitive and sociocultural perspectives: Two parallel SLA worlds? *TESOL Quarterly, 40*(1), 35–58.

Zwiers, J. (2008). *Building academic language: Essential practices for content classrooms, grades 5–12.* San Francisco, CA: Jossey Bass.

CHAPTER 2

Setting the Stage

LOOKING AHEAD

Teachers who promote students' essential thinking processes and academic identities while reading and writing across the curriculum go far in promoting students' literacy. But how do you promote literacy when you have so many other responsibilities? How do you organize instruction that promotes reading and writing along with subject matter learning? How do you set the instructional stage for developing readers and writers in the content areas? This chapter addresses these questions. It presents three key ideas:

1. Practices are a basic ingredient of literacy instruction.
2. Literacy instruction occurs in cycles.
3. Settings influence literacy teaching and learning.

PRACTICES ARE A BASIC INGREDIENT OF LITERACY INSTRUCTION

Practices are a basic ingredient of any profession or craft. Practices consist of recurring actions, or routines, that enable practitioners to accomplish their goals. To illustrate, medical professionals follow certain practices in the course of their day. When a patient comes in for a physical exam or an ailment, doctors and nurses measure, record, and interpret body temperature, blood pressure, and so on according to established procedures. Those in the legal profession base their actions on established practice, too. When representing clients, they exercise due diligence toward professional notices and documents.

Like other professionals, educators have access to established practices (Morrow, Gambrell, & Pressley, 2007; Stone, 2002; Zemelman, Daniels, & Hyde, 2005). This section introduces five practices commonly used for developing literacy in content area classrooms. Only a brief overview of each is offered here; the remaining chapters of this book specify how you might implement them to fit specific circumstances. Five general practices applicable to content area literacy are as follows:

1. Provide access to reading and writing that students can and want to accomplish
2. Provide scaffolds for challenging passages
3. Provide explicit instruction in reading and writing strategies
4. Facilitate collaborative literacy efforts
5. Assess literacy to inform teaching and learning

Provide Access to Reading and Writing That Students Can and Want to Accomplish

Students who read and write much tend to improve their reading and writing (Cunningham, 2005; Krashen, 2004). Time spent reading and writing connected text is associated with increased levels of word knowledge, fluency, and comprehension. Knowledge of the world and attitude toward literacy also tend to improve with opportunities to read and write each day. Content area teachers who provide students with access to literacy materials, time, and support go far in promoting literacy.

When students participate in units of instruction, they can locate and read appropriate materials by themselves. They can select topic-related books for sustained reading and response. Teachers often provide class time for students to read self-selected materials (Pilgreen, 2000; Lenski & Lainer, 2008). One way to accomplish this in an era of crowded curriculums is to have students read on their own when they finish assigned tasks. However, many teachers provide reading opportunities by setting aside a certain time on certain days for reading.

Maintaining journals about what has been read is a powerful way for individuals to interact with materials. The reading materials could be selected for the whole class, small group, or the individual, but the journal entries would be produced only by individuals.

Listening to well-crafted English read well orally provides class members access to the magic of the spoken word (Santoro, Chard, Howard, & Baker, 2008). Listening also presents subject matter that might remain inaccessible to students who struggle with reading. For instance, as someone skillfully reads *The Witch of Blackbird Pond*, students can vicariously experience Hannah's and Kit's adventures and learn about the Puritans' disdain for outsiders.

Most of the reading students do should be silent because it is most efficient; however, student oral reading has a place during content area instruction. Students might read aloud short sections to each other and then examine what they encountered. Oral interpretation is another good practice that allows students to prepare and present selections to a group.

In order to entice students to select and read materials, you can display posters, book jackets, and other attractions in the classroom. These displays change along with the units of study. You might invite members of the community to speak about their reading and writing preferences and habits.

Teachers who demonstrate a deep-seated commitment to literacy offer classrooms with multiple reading materials and regular attention to literacy. Classroom interactions often center around print; classroom success depends on reading and writing. These teachers believe that formal education should result in highly literate graduates. They see the role of schools, the purpose of the subjects they teach, and the way students should be treated as naturally leading to a concentration on literacy.

Younger students enjoy time to read a good book.

Provide Scaffolds for Challenging Passages

Students deserve assistance and support with difficult passages. If your students are expected to learn from a demanding passage, then you are obliged to help them meet the expectations. For instance, you might prepare readers for a challenging text by connecting it with ideas encountered earlier, explaining the new ideas students will read about and presenting unfamiliar vocabulary. You might have students take notes or record questions while they are reading. And you might schedule after-reading activities in which students share what they understand and receive feedback. Scaffolds like these help readers grasps the unfamiliar, complex, and abstract ideas their academic texts commonly present.

Provide Explicit Instruction in Reading and Writing Strategies

If your instructional plans call for students to obtain information from the Internet, then you would show how to accomplish this, such as how to go online and record pertinent information, before having students do so on their own. You would provide students explicit instruction in how to accomplish what they are expected to accomplish now and in the future.

Students require well-developed repertoires of independent reading and writing strategies. Some of the more common ones teachers address during content area study include the following:

- Reading with fluency and expression
- Synthesizing information from various sources
- Identifying, understanding, and remembering key vocabulary
- Recognizing how a text is organized and using that organization as a tool for learning
- Taking notes
- Searching resources such as the library and the Internet for information
- Keeping a learning log
- Generating questions to guide inquiry

These strategies enable individuals to understand difficult passages on their own, when no teacher or any other form of assistance is available. These strategies are what enable people to become independent, life-long learners.

Facilitate Collaborative Literacy Efforts

The photo on page 25 shows students studying in a group, having formed a community of readers. One youth begins a conversation about a passage and others join in. Those who have read something else question the reader and react to what they hear in order to learn what is new. Interaction is prized; students collectively think through the task at hand. Collaborative literacy efforts bring students together to talk about and support each other's undertakings. Students hear what others have to say about possible interpretations and meaning-making strategies. Through dialogue, they generate new ideas and new ways with words. Collaborative efforts in which students talk about what they are reading go by names such as *Socratic circles, book clubs* and *literature circles*.

Collaborative literacy efforts might concentrate on reading strategies. For instance, students might participate in Reciprocal Teaching (Palincsar, 2002) by talking about their summaries of passage contents. Sometimes, individuals form pairs, or "study buddies," and take turns orally reading and summarizing passages.

Individuals often collaborate in groups to accomplish projects. Along with the activities just described, they work together dramatizing what they read, gathering timeline information for a particular era, or completing inquiry projects. They brainstorm what individuals might say in a writing activity, and then they react to the person's rough draft. They work as a team to plan compositions, although they produce each composition individually.

Another form of collaboration involves teacher–student conferences. During conferences, teachers assume the role of facilitator more than examiner. Teachers often schedule individual conferences with students to talk about what they are reading or writing.

Assess Literacy to Inform Teaching and Learning

Assessment is a regular part of instruction. Assessments measure what students have attained in order to monitor current actions and inform decisions for the future.

Literacy assessments promote learning in large part by maintaining focus. Setting aside time during initial teaching to show how reading and writing will be assessed clarifies expectations and signals what is important.

Youth in a book study group.

Literacy assessments also promote learning through self-reflection. Teachers and students determine how they are doing. Teachers find out what they need to reteach, and learners determine what they still need to learn.

Perhaps the most promising literacy assessments come from individuals' ongoing reading and writing amid daily practices (Shepard, Hammerness, Darling-Hammond, & Rust, 2005; Stiggins, 2007). Many opportunities exist during the school day to observe and document individual students' literacy strategies and subject learning. For instance, samples of individuals' writing plans, rough drafts, and polished work are compared. Students reflect on their own literacy performance after assessing it with a rubric. The amount of reading accomplished in a certain time period is recorded. Completed study guides are examined for patterns of performance. Teachers and students continually reflect on their daily work to make informed decisions about on-the-spot actions as well as the future (Andrade & Valtcha, 2009; McCann, Johannessen, Kahn, Smagorinsky, & Smith, 2005).

LISTEN, LOOK, AND LEARN

Visit a class and observe approximately three content area lessons. Describe the literacy practices that occurred and the organization of the class during each practice. Which literacy practices were most frequent? Which were least frequent?

LITERACY INSTRUCTION OCCURS IN CYCLES

In classrooms that effectively promote reading and writing along with subject matter, students sense that they are improving as readers and writers, that they are getting somewhere. Progress is apparent. However, such movement is not in a straight line. Teachers and students build on the reading and writing that came before; they revisit prior experiences to add new layers of learning (Good & McCaslin, 1992). This pattern of movement is a cycle.

Cycles consist of regularly recurring events. As Figure 2.1 shows, four events, or phases, make up cycles of instruction. Teachers repeatedly plan, introduce, guide, and culminate during content area reading and writing instruction.

Planning

In the planning phase, you determine what you wish to accomplish and how you will approach it. Planning can be for different blocks of time (e.g., hour, day, week, grading period, semester, year) and for different blocks of content. If you are studying the solar system for three weeks, you decide what standards to take up relative to descriptions and distances of the planets, sun, moon, comets, asteroids, and so on. You consider issues about linking subject matter with learning processes such as image and apply. You gather print and nonprint resources for your class. You decide on reading and writing options.

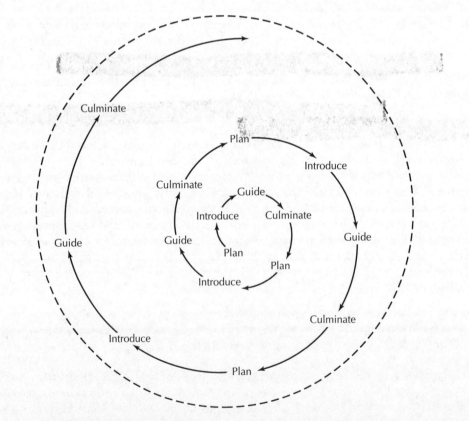

FIGURE 2.1 Cycles of Instruction.

Introducing

As with planning, introducing applies to different blocks of time and subject matter. You might devise introductions that apply to general procedures for the entire year (e.g., how to gain the floor during class discussions, how to take notes) or to specific content being explored during the next hour (e.g., the distances between planets).

While the bulk of planning is done away from learners, introducing occurs in their presence. During this stage of instruction, you prepare learners by sharing your plans, arousing curiosity and interest, and acquainting everyone with your expectations and available resources. You orient learners to the topics being addressed, the reasons for exploring them, and the procedures for accomplishing the learning activities. Then you show students—through modeling and explaining—how to do what they are expected to do.

Guiding

After planning and introducing learning activities, you continue your interactions with learners by offering guidance. You oversee their work. Learners get in on the act during this phase, exploring ideas on their own or practicing and applying what has been modeled. This phase of the instructional cycle typically consumes the most time.

Guiding learners takes innumerable forms. If class members are discussing what they have read, you might facilitate the discussion. If everyone is writing, you might consult with individuals. If small groups are brainstorming generalizations about a passage, you might move from group to group, asking probing questions. If students are solving problems, you might contribute to their efforts. During this phase, you monitor learners' progress, offering feedback, encouragement, and praise where appropriate.

Culminating

Culminating activities bring events to a close. Effective culminations help learners reflect on their experiences, clarify what they have learned, review what is unclear, and celebrate accomplishments.

Culminating activities can last only a few minutes, such as when you review and summarize an hour's lesson, or they can last a week or more, such as when students exhibit science projects to different audiences. Culminations can take a class period when you administer a formal a quiz, test, or exam. No matter what type of culminating activity you use, follow up the results and reteach what is needed either as part of the culmination or in the next cycle of instruction.

Cycles of Literacy Instruction Are Complex

It is important to realize that effective literacy instruction moves through phases of a cycle. But there is more to it than just moving through phases. Cycles of instruction involve scaffolding and fading as well as spiral curriculums.

SCAFFOLDING AND FADING   You might teach students how to take notes from passages in your content area. To teach note taking through the cycle of instruction just presented, first select a passage that seems within the grasp of your students. Then introduce how to take notes from the passage by actually producing notes and explaining how you decided to write what you did. Next, guide students as they practice note taking. Direct them to a portion of the passage, telling them to write notes about it like you just did. Compare your notes with some of the students' notes and have students compare their notes with one another's. Provide feedback about how they are doing. Eventually, in order to culminate your instruction, direct students to record their notes in a notebook and check them occasionally.

The note taking instruction just described moves from planning to introducing to guiding to culminating. The terms *scaffolding* and *fading* capture the essence of this instructional progression. Teachers use scaffolds to introduce students to subject-related literacy activities and then gradually fade back so the students can perform independently. Scaffolds are in place when they are needed, but then are gradually removed—or faded—when the learning can stand alone.

Scaffolds consist of the assistance, or support, teachers provide so that students can accomplish academic work. A common instructional scaffold is dialogue among teachers and students as well as among students themselves when they are engaged in a learning activity. Another instructional scaffold consists of the relatively simple reading passages that teachers often provide when introducing complex strategies like critiquing an author's writing style. Other scaffolds include visuals that represent vocabulary terms, classroom charts that serve as instructional reminders, and cooperative learning. Scaffolding is based on the idea that students require substantial support at the beginning of learning, then less and less support as they gain independence (Duke & Pearson, 2002). It involves a gradual release of responsibility, a practice where teachers initially assume responsibility for students' learning, then fade out as students fade in and assume responsibility for their learning.

SPIRAL CURRICULUM As Figure 2.1 shows, instructional cycles move in a continuous spiral. One series of events merges into and builds on another. Although the culminating phase of the instructional cycle involves closure, it simultaneously is a beginning for the next round of instruction. Every exit is an entrance. What students learned yesterday about Jupiter leads into today's consideration of Saturn.

Dewey's (1938) time-honored notion of a spiral curriculum emphasizes how ideas and insights obtained in one setting become the ground for ideas and insights in another. Procedures for solving two-step math word problems become the basis for solving three-, four-, and five-step problems. Understanding characterization in a Brothers Grimm story leads to understanding Shakespeare's characters. Expert teachers routinely help students connect what they already know with what they are learning. Especially when planning instruction, think of a spiral and look for ways that students can build on earlier learning experiences.

DO IT TOGETHER

Do you recall a class that explicitly layered ideas and information onto what had gone before? Gather in pairs and relate past teaching and learning that occurred in a spiral.

SETTINGS INFLUENCE LITERACY TEACHING AND LEARNING

Two classes with the identical title might be taught at the same time of day, have the same course outline and standards, employ the same materials for teaching and testing, and have the same teaching practices. Despite these identical circumstances, the students' reading and writing in the two classrooms probably would be affected differently (Moore, 1996). The differences would be due to classroom settings.

In this section, we present five dimensions of classroom settings to consider when planning reading, writing, and subject matter teaching. The five are vision, authenticity, active participation, academic challenge and support, and social support.

Vision

Effective classroom settings are characterized by a clear vision, or purpose. Teachers and students know where they are going.

A statement of vision expresses where you see yourself and others in the future. It is a sign pointing in a certain direction. It articulates reasons for pursuing academics in your class.

Course visions are stated numerous ways. For instance, in one high-school literature classroom in which students read lengthy classics such as *Beowulf* and *Canterbury Tales,* the motto is, "If anything is odd, inappropriate, confusing, or boring, it's probably important" (Rex, 2001, p. 294). This somewhat sophisticated motto prompts students to invest energy in the tricky parts of texts they often overlook. It guides their close reading of novels throughout the year.

Another class devoted to general reading competencies centers about the statement, "It's cool to be confused" (Braunger, Donahue, Evans, & Galguera, 2005). This affirmation prompts students to regularly and confidently make public how they figure out text difficulties.

When you express your course vision, state it in such a way that it never can be mastered fully. For instance, statements like "Learning leads to power, self-sufficiency, and opportunity" express goals that people never reach completely; power, self-sufficiency, and opportunity are ever expanding. They resemble balloons that continually touch new space as they expand. Being committed to such goals keeps everyone pressing forward. Bringing such lofty, far-reaching, and enduring ideals to life can capture students' imaginations and sustain their academic actions.

Authenticity

Authentic classroom settings are relevant to students' lives, engaging them at personal levels (Newmann & associates, 1996). Students learn information and strategies because they are seen as being useful. Students address important timely goals, such as making sense of a chaotic world, preparing for an occupation, and expressing a sense of self.

Linking learning activities to the world beyond the classroom promotes authenticity. When students' personal, societal, and occupational worlds are connected to the academic world, schooling can be seen as an authentic bona fide enterprise. For instance, personal health is an issue that students face daily, so it has an intrinsic appeal that more academic topics, such as propaganda techniques and government controls, lack. Deciding on a healthy lifestyle is a personal value-based decision that individuals make.

Consequently, when instructional standards call for the study of propaganda techniques or governmental powers, have your students examine how these forces affect their decisions about their personal health. When studying golden ages of civilizations, ask students to describe golden ages in their own lives. When examining the ATP cycle in biology, have students analyze the foods they're eating and digesting and figure out the caloric content.

Authentic instruction involves students in the range of thinking processes presented in the previous chapter. Learners in authentic situations transform information and make it their own. They use their minds fully to solve problems and construct significant ideas. Rather than participate in rote recitations about the contents of a driver's manual, students in authentic classroom settings explain situations that exemplify driver's manual guidelines, participate in decision-making simulations, and demonstrate their knowledge while actually driving a car. Authentic writing occurs when students expect a response from real audiences, such as classmates online, subject matter authorities, and celebrities. It moves students from relying on lifeless end-of-chapter textbook questions.

Active Participation

Active participation is another aspect of classroom contexts associated with effective literacy learning. Learners who are active participants do more than just passively receive information through lectures, assigned readings, and audiovisuals. They manipulate ideas, paraphrasing them, reorganizing them in visual displays, identifying the most important points, asking questions about them, talking with others about them, and applying them to novel situations. They are animated in class, taking part in lively activities.

Classrooms with active participation exhibit flexible grouping practices. Students sometimes meet as a whole class for teachers to introduce something new, build common experiences, and review what has been presented. But students then might meet in small groups to collaborate on projects and share ideas. Next, they might work on their own to pursue individual goals, apply strategies, and assess their learning. If your class were producing possible solutions to a community problem, your initial explanation and demonstration might occur before the whole class, your students might meet in small groups to brainstorm potential problems and solutions, and individuals might draft their own letters to community leaders.

Another way to enhance active participation is to provide students with choices. When you provide activities for students, offer them choices regarding which ones to perform and the order in which to complete them. Given two possible writing assignments, your students could pick the one they are more interested in completing. Given certain vocabulary words, your students could select their own ways of presenting the words' meanings. Given a set of short stories, your students could decide the sequence in which to read them.

Along with choice, give your students a voice in deciding their academic work. Students have the right to be heard, to get in on the act, relative to learning. If they are to retell a passage, have them suggest ways to do so. Will they use props? If so, which ones? Will they orally interpret selected portions? If so, which ones? Will they dramatize the retelling? If so, how?

Ensuring that every pupil responds to your oral questions is another way to elicit active participation. Imagine that you want to review the major aspects of communicable diseases. You could ask, "Who remembers something we learned about communicable diseases?" You probably would elicit some comments, but you might notice that they regularly come from the same few individuals. Do those who remain silent not know or simply not care to participate? A review activity that gets everyone involved would be to have everyone take out a sheet of paper and quickly write three things they remember about communicable diseases. Then you might randomly nominate students to share their thoughts.

Academic Challenge and Support

One of us (David Moore) played racquetball regularly. David marks his greatest gain in racquetball enjoyment and skill during a two-year time span when he had a weekly game with Dean, a one-time state-level doubles champion in Iowa. Dean loved the game; he would play anyone just so he could be on the court. The first time they played, David scored only a few points, but Dean commented on his potential and suggested ways he could improve his backhand stroke. David remembers walking away from that game believing he could do better.

Sometimes Dean would give David an advantage by hitting only straight drives to his backhand or serving only at half speed, and Dean continued demonstrating stroke and court positioning techniques. Over time, David's racquetball technique improved so much that Dean actually worked up a sweat when they played—and David even won a few of their matches just before moving from the state.

As with racquetball, literacy improves in situations with appropriate challenges, ones that stretch students' abilities. Appropriate challenges call for special effort from learners, but they are not defeating. They strengthen students' wills to succeed. They are at the cutting edge of students' abilities—neither too easy nor too demanding. Appropriate challenges are tasks that students are unable to accomplish at first but are able to accomplish with the help of others or with reasonable individual effort. Such levels of challenge allow students the pleasure of exerting themselves and experiencing success. Dean's racquetball challenge was such that David always believed he was within sight of a higher level of play.

For challenging learning environments to be most effective, students require support. David's racquetball would have improved little if Dean had left him in a sink-or-swim situation. Fortunately, they entered into something like a master–apprentice relationship. Before, during, and after the games, Dean supported David's development by offering encouragement—along with an occasional criticism—and demonstrating and explaining pertinent techniques to get to the next level. Using terminology from the previous section of this chapter, Dean scaffolded then faded his instruction. Dean bridged the gap between David's existing racquetball abilities and more sophisticated abilities, then Dean removed his supports as David's performance improved.

Social Support

Social support calls attention to interpersonal relations and to identity formation. It focuses on the emotional and attitudinal climate of a class. Social supports are as necessary as the preceding academic supports in promoting learning. Teachers provide social support and promote positive academic identities by shaping their classrooms so students see themselves belonging there.

Perhaps the key social support is respect. Among other things, respect is apparent when teachers and students treat each other like long-time members of a club. Each member is an insider; there is a sense of community. Social markers such as achievement level, ethnicity, gender, and peer affiliation do not affect concerns for individuals' well-being. Rapport is evident during face-to-face interactions; efforts are made to enfranchise those who feel alienated.

Students can actively participate in collaborative learning groups.

Positive expectations are an important type of social support that indicates respect. Teachers' expectations for students are especially important because they often result in self-fulfilling prophecies: teachers who believe students will (or will not!) succeed with challenging activities communicate this to students, and students follow suit. Positive expectations assume that all students can and will learn. Positive expectations counteract deficit perspectives that are based on stereotypes of the academic performance expected of members of certain groups. Learners do best when they and their teachers expect their efforts to result in high-quality accomplishments. To return to the racquetball account, Dean seemed convinced that David's racquetball game would improve to an A level, and David came to believe it, too.

Projecting enthusiasm is another way to support learners. You project enthusiasm when you convey an intense eagerness to explore class contents. Being theatrical or being low-key is not crucial as long as you are passionate and sincere about the value of the topics under consideration. As with respect and expectations, enthusiasm is contagious.

LISTEN, LOOK, AND LEARN

Talk with a student about the classroom settings he or she prefers, asking this person to describe the best teacher he or she had. What did the teacher do that he or she liked? What was so good about that teacher's class? Compare your findings with the dimensions of effective settings presented in this section.

LOOKING BACK

Instructional practices, cycles, and settings set the stage for developing readers and writers in the content areas. These staging devices provide good general structure for your instructional plans. Three key ideas were presented in this chapter: (1) Practices are a basic ingredient of literacy instruction; (2) literacy instruction occurs in cycles; and (3) settings influence literacy instruction.

ADD TO YOUR JOURNAL

Think about the three key ideas of this chapter, and use the eight thinking processes from Chapter 1 to compose a response. You might organize the chapter by summarizing or outlining it. You might connect the chapter's information with past experiences. You might evaluate the chapter. What is your opinion of the ideas so far? Why do you think this way? Finally, you could begin to apply what you have read. What applications do you foresee between what has been presented in this chapter and your future teaching?

Additional Readings

These books describe exemplary literacy teaching and learning that occur in actual classrooms.

Allington, R. L., & Johnston, P. H. (Eds.). (2002). *Reading to learn: Lessons from exemplary fourth-grade classrooms*. New York, NY: Guilford.

Block, C. C., & Mangieri, J. (2009). *Exemplary literacy teachers: What schools can do to promote success for all students* (2nd ed.). New York, NY: Guilford.

Langer, J. A. (2002). *Effective literacy instruction: Building successful reading and writing programs*. Urbana, IL: National Council of Teachers of English.

Pressley, M., Morrow, L. M., Block, C. C., Wharton-Macdonald, R., & Allington, R. L. (Eds.). (2001). *Learning to read: Lessons from exemplary first-grade classrooms*. New York, NY: Guilford.

Sturtevant, E. G., Boyd, F. B., Brozo, W. G., Hinchman, K. A., Moore, D. W., & Alvermann, D. E. (Eds.). (2006). *Principled practices for adolescent literacy.*

A framework for instruction and policy. Mahwah, NJ: Lawrence Erlbaum Associates.

These books are popular descriptions of basic, general instructional settings and practices.

Daniels, H., & Bizar, M. (2005). *Teaching the best practice way: Methods that matter, K-12*. Portland, ME: Stenhouse.

Jones, F. H. (2000). *Tools for teaching*. Santa Cruz, CA: Fredric H. Jones & Associates.

Marzano, R. J., Pickering, D. J., & Pollock, J. E. (2001). *Classroom instruction that works: Research-based strategies for increasing student achievement.* Alexandria, VA: Association for Supervision and Curriculum Development.

Wong, H. K., & Wong, R. T. (2004). *The first days of school: How to be an effective teacher*. Mountain View, CA: Harry K. Wong Publications.

Online Resources

These sites contain lesson plans and instructional resources that connect literacy and subject matter.

> ### Read-Write-Think
> http://www.readwritethink.org/
>
> ### Technology Assisting Literacy Knowledge
> http://teach.fcps.net/talk

Videos of teachers modeling teaching practices that help upper-grade students improve their reading are available here.

> ### Literacy and Learning: Reading in the Content Areas
> http://www.lpb.org/education/classroom/itv/litlearn/
>
> ### More Reading Strategies in Action
> http://www.marion.k12.ky.us/Strategies/Math/readingspecialist/activate.htm
>
> ### Reading Strategies in Action
> http://www.jackson.k12.ky.us/readingstrategies/module1.htm
>
> ### Strategic Literacy Initiative: Reading Apprenticeship Videos
> http://www.wested.org/cs/sli/print/docs/922

A profusion of lesson plans and instructional resources, including many that explicitly connect literacy and subject matter, are represented by the following.

> ### 4Teachers
> http://www.4teachers.org/
>
> ### Discovery Education
> http://school.discoveryeducation.com/index.html
>
> ### The Educator's Reference Desk
> http://www.eduref.org
>
> ### Edutopia
> http://www.edutopia.org/
>
> ### Greece, New York Academics
> http://web001.greece.k12.ny.us/academics.cfm
>
> ### The Literacy Web at the University of Connecticut
> http://www.literacy.uconn.edu/index.htm
>
> ### National Education Association
> http://www.nea.org/home/ToolsAndIdeas.html
>
> ### Ohio Resource Center
> http://www.ohiorc.org
>
> ### Scholastic Publishing
> http://www2.scholastic.com/browse/home.jsp
>
> ### Teaching that Makes Sense
> http://www.ttms.org

References

Andrade, H., & Valtcha, A. (2009). Promoting learning and achievement through self-assessment. *Theory into Practice, 48*(1), 12–19.

Braunger, J., Donahue, D. M., Evans, K., & Galguera, T. (2005). *Rethinking preparation for content area teaching: The reading apprentice approach.* San Francisco, CA: Jossey Bass.

Cunningham, A. E. (2005). Vocabulary growth through independent reading and reading aloud to children. In E. H. Hiebert & M. L. Kamil (Eds.), *Teaching and learning vocabulary: Bringing research to practice* (pp. 45–68). New York, NY: Routledge.

Dewey, J. (1938). *Experience and education.* New York, NY: Macmillan.

Duke, N. K., & Pearson, P. D. (2002). Effective practices for developing reading comprehension. In A.E. Farstrup & S. J. Samuels (Eds.), *What research has to say about reading instruction* (pp. 205–242). Newark, DE: International Reading Association.

Gambrell, L. B., Morrow, L. M., & Pressley, M. (Eds.). (2007). *Best practices in literacy instruction* (3rd ed.). New York, NY: Guilford.

Good, T. L., & Mccaslin, M. M. (1992). Teaching effectiveness. In M. C. Alkin (Ed.), *Encyclopedia of educational research* (6th ed., pp. 1373–1388). New York, NY: Macmillan.

Krashen, S. (2004). *The power of reading* (2nd ed.). Englewood, CO: Libraries Unlimited.

Lenski, S., & Lanier, E. (2008). Making time for independent reading. In S. Lenski & J. Lewis (Eds.), *Reading success for struggling adolescent learners* (pp. 133–152). New York, NY: Guilford.

Mccann, T., Johannessen, L. R., Kahn, E., Smagorinsky, P., & Smith, M. W. (2005). *Reflective teaching, reflective learning: How to develop critically engaged readers, writers, and speakers*. Portsmouth, NH: Heinemann.

Moore, D. W. (1996). Contexts for literacy in secondary schools. In D. J. Leu, C. K. Kinzer, & K. A. Hinchman (Eds.), *Literacies for the 21st century: Research and practice*. Forty-fifth Yearbook of the National Reading Conference (pp. 15–46). Chicago, IL: National Reading Conference.

Newmann, F. M., & Associates. (1996). *Authentic achievement: Restructuring schools for intellectual quality*. San Francisco, CA: Jossey-Bass.

Palincsar, A. S. (2002). Reciprocal teaching. In B. J. Guzzetti (Ed.), *Literacy in America: An encyclopedia of history, theory, and practice* (vol. 2; pp. 535–538). Santa Barbara, CA: ABC-CLIO.

Pilgreen, J. L. (2000). *The SSR handbook: How to organize and manage a sustained silent reading program*. Portsmouth, NH: Boynton/Cook.

Rex, L. A. (2001). The remaking of a high school reader. *Reading Research Quarterly, 36,* 288–314.

Santoro, L., Chard, D. J., Howard, L., & Baker, S. K. (2008). Making the very most of classroom read-alouds to promote comprehension and vocabulary. *The Reading Teacher, 61*(5), 396–408.

Shepard, L., Hammerness, K., Darling-hammond, L., & Rust, F. (2005). Assessment. In L. Darling-Hammond & J. Bransford (Eds.), *Preparing teachers for a changing world: What teachers should learn and be able to do*. San Francisco, CA: Jossey-Bass.

Stiggins, R. J. (2007). *Student-involved assessment for learning* (5th ed.). Upper Saddle River, NJ: Pearson/Merrill-Prentice Hall.

Stone, R. (2002). *Best practices for high school classrooms: What award winning secondary school teachers do*. Thousand Oaks, CA: Corwin.

Zemelman, S., Daniels, H., & Hyde, A. (2005). *Best practice: Today's standards for teaching and learning in America's schools* (3rd ed.). Portsmouth, NH: Heinemann.

The following describes specific reading and writing practices that are consistent with the general ones this chapter describes.

Buehl, D. (2009). *Classroom strategies for interactive learning* (3rd ed.). Newark, DE: International Reading Association.

Burke, J. (2000). *Reading reminders: Tools, tips, and techniques*. Portsmouth, NH: Boynton/Cook.

Tierney, R. J., & Readence, J. E. (2004). *Reading strategies and practices* (6th ed.). Boston, MA: Allyn & Bacon.

CHAPTER 3

Instructional Units

LOOKING AHEAD

The first two chapters of this text provide general background on the teaching of reading and writing in content areas. This chapter more specifically explains how to plan your teaching so that you promote students' literacy along with subject matter learning.

By moving from general to specific—by first planning the year, then units, then lessons—you produce a series of connected experiences. Yearly plans are at the long-term end of instructional decision making. Yearly planning is the time to think about grand outcomes. It calls for you to decide on the major goals you want students to accomplish. At this level of planning, you think about all the content to be covered (or uncovered!) and about helping students become critical thinkers, autonomous learners, productive individuals, and so on. Establishing year-long outcomes before meeting students the first day of class is crucial because, as the old saying goes, "When you're up to your neck in alligators, it's hard to remember that you came to drain the swamp!" Having a vision for your class helps maintain your aim at what is important while managing immediate everyday details.

Lessons are at the short-term end of instructional planning. Lessons specify day-to-day learning activities; they detail, sometimes down to the minute, the actions you and your students will perform. Beginning teachers often write lesson plans that are specific enough for a knowledgeable outsider—such as a substitute teacher—to step into a classroom, read the lesson plans, and lead a class.

Units, which are at the middle level of teachers' planning, offer a productive means for bringing together and teaching information, ideas, and literacy (Erickson, 2007; Wiggins & McTighe, 2006). Units indicate how the year's curriculum will be divided among blocks of time, lasting from a few days to a few weeks. They relate coursework about a manageable central focus that foregrounds particular knowledge and skills. Space, pushes and pulls, and plants name science units commonly addressed in the early grades. Science teachers in middle school often divide their courses among units devoted to astronomy, meteorology, geology, and so on. Senior-high biology teachers might address population genetics, bacteriology, and metabolism.

What follows are some major decisions to be made when planning units. This chapter presents three key ideas:

1. Selecting a topic begins unit planning.
2. Framing a topic structures unit planning.
3. Working within a frame focuses unit planning.

SELECTING A TOPIC BEGINS UNIT PLANNING

Topics express in one or two words what units are about. They can be considered the titles, or organizing centers, of units. If you ask teachers or students what a class is studying, they generally will respond with something like "Fractions," "We're doing cell differentiation," or "We're reading *Ender's Game*."

When looking over what needs to be taught during the school year, begin with what your school district, school, academic department, grade-level committee, or textbook has listed. Dinosaurs, neighborhoods, and the weather are unit topics in countless primary-grade classrooms. Pioneers, land formations, and adventure often appear in the middle grades. Radiation, constitutional government, and identity are found in the upper grades. These subject matter topics readily divide into even more parts. For instance, land formations readily divide into mountains, plains, valleys, and plateaus, to name a few. These subtopics often are presented as individual lessons.

You might choose topics that are deliberately open ended and invite exploration. These are called *themes* rather than *topics* because they underlie so much. For instance, patterns, flight, and bridges open the door to much creative thinking and exploring. Bridges, for instance, physically connect land and socially connect people. Themes such as justice and relativity have proven effective because they offer rich possibilities for inquiry. The following table lists common secondary-school topics and themes that form the basis of units:

Content Areas

Language Arts	Mathematics	Science	Social Studies
The Giver	Congruent triangles	Atomic theory	Civil rights
Heart of Darkness	Logic	Bonding	Legislative branch
Drama	Nonpolynomial equations	Digestive system	Macroeconomics
Shakespeare	Quadratic equations	Genetics	Mexico
Angelou	Statistics and probability	Plate tectonics	Westward expansion
Identity		Water cycle	World War II
Flight			
Conducting research			
Writing essays			

As the table shows, English/language arts teachers often employ distinctive topics. They might select ones that consist of

- a novel (*The Giver, Heart of Darkness*)
- a genre (drama, short story)
- an author (William Shakespeare, Maya Angelou)
- a theme (identity, flight)
- a skill (conducting research, writing essays)

Novels frequently serve as unit topics during English/language arts instruction and occasionally during social studies instruction. A middle-grade English/language arts teacher might select *A Wind in the Door*. In this story, Charles Wallace is seriously ill and others must miniaturize themselves and enter his body in order to combat his disorder. Students could examine plot along with human anatomy, cell structure, and medical innovations. As students read *Roll of Thunder, Hear My Cry* during middle-grade social studies instruction, they could explore issues such as injustice, rural life, and post–Civil War social patterns.

Once you determine the topics for your units, you are ready to begin more detailed planning. Establishing frames for the topics is an important next step in this process.

LISTEN, LOOK, AND LEARN

Visit a high-school department head, middle-school team leader, or elementary-school grade-level leader and ask for a list of units taught during the year. Then ask how these particular unit topics were chosen. How were they sequenced in their particular order of presentation? Compare your findings with those of others in your class.

FRAMING A TOPIC STRUCTURES UNIT PLANNING

Frames provide structure. They enclose items and mark borders. A picture frame, for instance, holds a picture while setting it off from others. When producing units, teachers frame their unit topics by planning student-friendly objectives, central questions, and culminating activities.

Student-friendly Objectives

Student-friendly objectives state what students are responsible for learning as a result of a particular unit. They designate what students are expected to know and be able to do, and they provide clear direction when planning units (Conley, 2005; March & Peters, 2008). Student-friendly objectives establish what educators and students are responsible for accomplishing. Practically every department of education in every state in the United States now is explicit about what they expect of students following each unit of instruction.

The terminology related to student-friendly objectives is confusing. Some educators use terms such as *objectives, standards* and *outcomes* interchangeably, and some differentiate these terms. Some use other terms, such as *goals* or *benchmarks,* and some distinguish such things as *content standards* from *performance standards.*

We use the term *student-friendly objectives* because it is relatively brief, descriptive, and common—but not universal. The *student-friendly* wording in this term is important. It emphasizes the idea that the language of the objective is appropriate for the age group of the students. You take the official language of your state- or district-mandated standards and, when necessary, convert it to wording that your students will find clear and comprehensible.

PRODUCING STUDENT-FRIENDLY OBJECTIVES   If you are in a situation in which student-friendly objectives are not established explicitly for each unit you teach, begin with the unit's topic—immigration, for instance. Working by yourself or with a team, consult applicable state or local standards-based outcomes—including those that address reading and writing—for ones that fit the unit topic.

Considering the mandated standards and your students' learning needs at the particular time of the school year when the unit will be presented, you might decide that students will require understandings of noteworthy immigrations, personal experiences of immigrating, conditions that generate immigrations, and the consequences of immigrations. These decisions can be articulated into student-friendly objectives such as the following:

1. Students will be able to describe noteworthy immigrations.
2. Students will be able to portray personal experiences of immigrating.
3. Students will be able to explain conditions that produce immigrations.
4. Students will be able to evaluate the consequences of immigrations.

FEATURES OF STUDENT-FRIENDLY OBJECTIVES   A crucial feature of how these objectives are stated is their plan for observable actions. Each outcome calls for students to do something that can be seen or heard. The terms *describe, portray, explain*, and *evaluate* emphasize overt, external responses. They are not entirely covert, internal processes such as *understand, appreciate*, and *learn*. To be sure, understanding, appreciating, and learning are critical, but they are not appropriate terminology for planning units of instruction because they can remain invisible too easily. Ask yourself, "What might learners do that demonstrates, or provides evidence of, understanding, appreciating, or learning?" "What might learners do that allows me to observe their competence with the objective?"

Another crucial feature of these outcomes is their overall plan for essential thinking processes. The majority of the outcomes call for students to go beyond the information given, to transform what they encounter. Expecting students to *describe, portray, explain,* and *evaluate* what they learn about immigration goes beyond recalling or reproducing ideas already stated. *Describing, portraying, explaining*, and *evaluating* engage students in thinking that generates ideas. These actions point to enduring understandings that can last a lifetime; they do not address trivial ideas and information to be regurgitated on a test and then promptly forgotten.

Some verbs useful for producing student-friendly unit objectives are as follows:

analyze	express
characterize	identify
classify	interpret
compare	invent

compose	judge
construct	justify
convince	map
create	paraphrase
critique	persuade
debate	portray
decide	produce
defend	rate
describe	recommend
design	recount
develop	sequence
distinguish	show
dramatize	solve
explain	summarize

A third important feature of the objectives just presented is their focus on the end points of learning rather than on the means to the ends. These objectives call attention to destinations rather than to the vehicles for the destinations. For instance, an objective like "Students will break into small groups and discuss noteworthy immigrations" is inappropriate because it does not go far enough. It does not reveal why students are to break into small groups and discuss; it does not specify the end point, the take away. You might have students break into small groups and discuss noteworthy immigrations in order for them to be able to describe noteworthy immigrations.

Finally, for the reasons Chapter 1 presented, include a minimum of at least one reading or writing outcome with each unit topic. Many schools now have curriculum guides, or maps, that order reading and writing outcomes across content area curriculums. You might enter a teaching situation that expects you in September to present summarizing along with your subject, self-questioning in October, visualizing in November, and so on. If you do not inherit such guidance, then decide on literacy objectives on your own.

To decide on a literacy objective, determine how reading and writing connect with each of your objectives, then determine which connection would require preliminary teaching in order for your students to accomplish it. To illustrate, with the immigration unit, you might realize that you expect students to explain in writing the conditions that produce immigration. You also might realize that your students will require extensive teaching to write this proficiently. Then you would consult your state's literacy standards, identify what best expresses your expectation, and produce another student-friendly objective that focuses only on literacy like this:

Students will be able to write an explanatory, multiparagraph essay.

Central Questions

Central questions are individual queries that provide students with an overarching purpose for examining unit topics and accomplishing unit objectives. Each is a single question that drives your unit's teaching and learning. With regard to immigration, a productive central question could be, "Why do people immigrate?" If 1950 to 2000 were the topic of a middle-grade history unit, you might pose a central question such as, "In which decade of the late 1900s were people better off?"

Central questions position students as problem solvers in authentic situations. They serve as a stimulus, provoking and sustaining students' thinking and learning during day-to-day unit activities. They serve as a connector, too, gluing together what students encounter across several days of instruction. They allow all students to form an appropriate answer, although the sophistication of the answers might vary.

When addressing a unit's central question, you help students grasp the numerous facts associated with the topic by treating these facts as the building blocks of thinking. With central questions in mind, students treat potentially inert ideas and facts as ideas-in-action and facts-in-action. Students use facts and ideas to construct personal insights into the topic. Examples of central questions include the following:

History/Social Studies

- Is the United States today more like Athens or Sparta?
- What are appropriate limits to freedom of speech?
- Was the U.S. civil rights movement successful?

Literature

- What in a short story keeps you reading?
- What does it take to be a hero?
- What is the heart of darkness?

Mathematics

- How economical is it to buy food from a convenience store compared to a full-service grocery store?
- How can a statements such as "The lake has an average depth of 3 feet" mislead people?
- Is a straight line always the shortest possible distance?

Science

- What would happen if the Earth's gravity doubled?
- What factors most influence plant development?
- Why is the weather difficult to predict?

Interdisciplinary

- What new city in our state would be ideal?
- How can we stop violence?
- How can our community be better prepared for natural disasters that probably will occur?

Producing central questions is difficult. They need to be general enough to provoke thinking yet specific enough to guide it. They need to allow multiple responses and have no single, simple answer, yet they need to elicit answers that are supportable. They need to encompass substantial amounts of content, yet be limited to what can be explored deeply during the unit. They need to provoke students' thinking and hold their interest, yet cover content mandated by state standards and tests.

To produce central questions, begin by using "wh" words (*who, what, when, where, why*) and *how* to combine the unit's outcomes into a question. Search for commonalities underlying the outcomes. For instance, answers to "Why do people immigrate?" touch on economic, political, social, and environmental issues.

To maintain attention to central questions, post them on a bulletin board and on unit handouts for continual reference. At the end of each class, for instance, direct students to the central question with inquiries such as, "How does what you learned today help you answer the central question?" Students use their minds fully to solve the problem, bringing together information and constructing significant ideas.

Culminating Activities

Culminating activities end units of instruction. They provide closure, ending units on a high note, a big finish. They provide opportunities for learners to consolidate their new understandings and celebrate their successes. Like central questions, they focus and connect what is being taught and learned. Culminating activities specify how students are to express their final responses to units of instruction.

Culminating activities can consist of students' written, spoken, or artistic exhibits produced during the unit. To illustrate, students might respond to "Why do people immigrate?" in one of the following ways:

Performance: a panel discussion, role play, persuasive speech, poster talk, or debate
Product: editorial, essay, magazine article, art display, multigenre report, multimedia production, videotape, PowerPoint presentation, pamphlet, or children's book.

As these possibilities suggest, exhibits can be somewhat open ended (e.g., a debate) as well as closed (e.g., a newspaper report). Exhibits can capitalize on creative outlets such as dramatic productions and visual displays. Students can be offered choice and they can have a voice in designing their own.

Exhibits involve some public display of what students accomplish. Students share what they learned with their classmates, with younger or older students, and with adults such as parents, teachers, school administrators, political leaders, and community members. The public nature of such displays offers a chance to refine students' presentation abilities and recognize what they accomplished. The next chapter, "Reading Materials and Exhibiting Responses," details several additional types of exhibits appropriate for a culminating activity.

Another type of culminating activity consists of a unit exam. Unit exams have served as culminating activities in many upper grades over many years. These assessments can be especially productive when students know they will encounter a specific constructed-response, essay-type test item that involves about 15 minutes of writing. For instance, at the beginning of a unit on immigration, you might inform your class that they will respond to the essential question, "Why do people immigrate?" during the end-of-unit exam. A culminating activity like this helps learners maintain focus and connect ongoing course work.

Finally, culminating activities can be enrichments, activities that celebrate and augment students' accomplishments without involving grades or additional work. Having your students share their exhibits with an external audience is a prominent example of a culminating enrichment activity. You also might have your students interact with guests who are experts in the unit's topic, conduct a gallery walk of peers' posters, watch and respond to a relevant video clip, or participate in a game-like simulation or a game like Jeopardy. Students might tour a museum, a historical site, a business or manufacturing center, an arboretum, or a zoo. Such activities end the unit on a high note.

Framing Units Coherently

Student-friendly objectives, central questions, and culminating activities work best when they fit together as a coherent frame, when they correspond with each other. In effective units, one part of a frame leads to another; each is consistent with the other. For instance, an objective calling for critical thinking corresponds with a central question asking about reasons for immigration. And this objective and central question fit a culminating activity calling for a persuasive pamphlet. The parts are coherent; they fully match one another.

DO IT TOGETHER

Discuss characteristics of student-friendly objectives, central questions, and culminating activities. Practice generating possibilities. First, select a topic you anticipate teaching. Then construct possible objectives, central questions, and culminating activities for the topic. In class, share these possibilities for framing instructional units and decide on the most effective sets.

WORKING WITHIN A FRAME FOCUSES UNIT PLANNING

After establishing a unit's topic and frame, you are ready to plan the details. Working within a clear, coherent frame enables you to focus instruction effectively. You are better able to plan assessments, launches, resources, general instruction, and a schedule.

Assessment

As noted in Chapter 2, assessment involves gathering information to monitor actions and inform decisions. Regularly gathering information helps you determine how you are doing in the present and decide what you will do in the future. Assessing student performance contributes to teaching and learning several ways. Assessment clarifies outcomes and signals what is important in the unit. Assessment also alerts you to what needs to be retaught, and it alerts your students to what needs additional attention. What follows are two assessment concerns that are especially pertinent when planning instructional units: scoring guides and student self-assessment.

SCORING GUIDES   Scoring guides, or rubrics, describe what is needed to achieve certain levels of performance. If a culminating activity is a panel discussion, the scoring guide would specify how the discussion is to be scored. If a culminating activity is a pamphlet, the scoring guide would specify how the pamphlet is to be scored. The following scoring guide has been used to assess Grand Canyon presentations that middle-school students produced:

Grand Canyon

Origin of Grand Canyon's strata					
Complete description of the origin of the Grand Canyon's strata	12	10	8	6	Partial description of the origin of the Grand Canyon's strata

Formation of Grand Canyon					
Complete description of how weathering and erosion formed the Grand Canyon	12	10	8	6	Partial description of how weathering and erosion formed the Grand Canyon

Writing Organization					
Strong introduction that does much to engage readers	5	4	3	2	Weak introduction that does little to engage readers
Clear categories in the body of the report	6	5	4	3	Unclear categories in the body of the report
Complete wrap up in the conclusion	5	4	3	2	Partial wrap up in the conclusion

Scoring guides like this one consist of three components: criteria, scales, and performance indicators.

Criteria are what assessors look for when scoring. They are the specific features, or traits, to be scored. The preceding Grand Canyon scoring guide contains three criteria: *origin of Grand Canyon's strata, formation of Grand Canyon,* and *writing organization.* Other criteria certainly contribute to Grand Canyon presentations, but the three listed here are the ones to be emphasized and directly taught this time. Other writing criteria that might have been scored earlier or later in the school year are *ideas* and *content, voice, vivid language,* and so on. A *conventions* criterion might have been divided among *spelling, grammar,* and *legibility.*

Scales are the series of points possible for each criterion. Most scoring guides consist of 2-, 4-, or 6-point scales. Having an even number of points requires scorers to stay off the middle, choosing either the high or the low side of the scale.

The points possible for each criterion depend on the emphasis placed on each. For instance, in the scoring guide shown here, *origin of Grand Canyon's strata* and *formation of Grand Canyon* are of equal maximum value (12), and the total of these two subject matter criteria (24) is worth more than the total of the *writing organization* criterion (16). The highest points possible for *origin* and *formation* are the same because the teachers decided these were of equal importance; the *writing* criterion was considered to be worth fewer points.

Performance indicators describe what each scale point represents. A 12 for *origin of Grand Canyon's strata* means the description is complete; a 6 means the description is partial. This scoring guide does not contain performance indicators for every scale point (i.e., 10 or 8 on this scale), although many guides do. Writing performance indicators for every scale point—not just the points at the extremes—is especially important for tests with high stakes, such as whether students graduate or enter special education.

STUDENT SELF-ASSESSMENTS   Student self-assessments are a valuable practice that involves learners in estimating their own proficiencies. Bringing your students into the assessment process promotes independence, removing them from reliance on others. It helps your students internalize outcomes. Having your students assess their own academic work promotes self-reflection, self-awareness, and self-direction. It engages your learners with subject matter specifics, clarifying the standards you use. It increases personal responsibility.

There are numerous ways to promote your students' self-assessments:

1. Enlist your students in completing scoring guides for their own work. After a scoring guide such as the one provided here is distributed, have your students act as the scorer for their own and others' work before you do so.
2. Enlist your students in producing guides for their own work. Present an activity, then have your students design their own criteria, scales, and performance indicators. Ask something like, "How should your pamphlets be assessed?"
3. Display student-friendly unit objectives, refer to them throughout the unit, and reflect on progress toward them. You might display a unit objective such as "You will be able to write an explanatory, multiparagraph essay," then regularly ask your students about their proficiencies doing this.
4. Have your learners gauge their ongoing reading and writing development by completing questionnaires and supporting their ratings. This might occur during small-group discussions, during individual conferences, or as journal entries. Your students might answer open-ended questions—without a scoring guide—such as "I rate my summaries . . . because . . ." or "This paper deserves a . . . because . . . ."
5. In writing and during conferences and discussions, have your learners explain how they accomplished strategies such as learning key vocabulary or following the author's organization. Your learners also might estimate how well they performed the strategies.
6. During units' culminating activities, have your students reflect orally or in writing on their growth as learners. For instance, they might answer questions such as, "What advice would you give someone who is doing this project next year?" and "What did you find out about your reading and writing while completing this activity?"

Features of effective self-assessments (Stiggins, 2007) are evident in the ways to promote student self-assessments just listed. Note that the six ways all emphasize clear targets; they generate understandable goals and objectives. All six also provide opportunities for students to define quality work. Each of the ways to promote student self-assessments also permits feedback, allowing students to obtain reactions to their work. Finally, there are opportunities for-self correcting. Students can consider the feedback and decide on improvements.

TRY IT OUT

Construct a scoring guide for a unit's culminating activity. Decide what criteria, scales, and performance indicators are appropriate for the activity. Obtain feedback from your classmates about your guide. Additionally, describe at least one way you would promote students' self assessment during your unit.

Teachers continually address students' literacy during instructional units.

Launch

Once you have framed a unit topic and determined your assessments, you know where you and your students are headed. You then can plan how to launch, or kick off, the journey. You can plan how to set learning in motion. Unit launches prime students for upcoming reading, writing, and subject matter (Readence, Moore, & Rickelman, 2000).

To launch a unit on immigration, for example, you might display and talk about maps and census data depicting mass movements of people; visuals of poverty, warfare, and other conditions that trigger immigrations; and terms such as *melting pot, cultural pluralism*, and *brain drain* that address immigrations' effects. Such an introduction goes far in setting the stage for instruction that centers around why people immigrate.

Five practices that are especially appropriate as launches are real-world observing/participating, reading aloud, previewing passages, brainstorming, and writing. These practices are flexible; they fit countless units and combine with each other in countless arrangements.

REAL-WORLD OBSERVING/PARTICIPATING Engaging your students with real-world objects, media, and guest speakers puts students in touch with abstract ideas (Guthrie, Wigfield, & Perencevich, 2004). For instance, the following content areas and unit topics might begin with the following real-world observation and participation:

Language Arts	Mathematics

Shabanu, Daughter of the Wind
   Photos, slides, and videos of rural
   Middle Eastern life
   Guest speakers with firsthand
   experiences and mementos
 Incense and Middle Eastern music
	Measures of central tendency
	   Survey of food or entertainment
	   preference
	   USA Today portrayal of data

Science	*Social Studies*
Oceans and marine life	Middle Ages
Photos, slides, and videos of oceans and marine life	Photos, slides, and videos of Middle Ages
Sea shells, seaweed, driftwood	Action figures/dolls representing people at different positions in society
Maps and globes	Cardboard cutout of castle

READING ALOUD   Reading aloud passages that introduce a topic and engage students with it is a good unit launch (Albright & Ariail, 2005; Lesesne, 2006). Hearing vivid presentations of personal experiences and exciting or unusual events arouses interest. When hearing someone read aloud well, students can come into contact with ideas they might miss due to a passage's difficulty. Picture books—those in which pictures and print independently convey a message—launch units well for lower- as well as upper-grade students (Carr, Buchanan, Wentz, Weiss, & Brant, 2001). Picture books typically can be read aloud in one class sitting, so students experience the entire telling of something, and the books' artistic representations engage students in ways that words do not.

PREVIEWING PASSAGES   Previewing passages is like touring reading materials before studying them (Readence, Moore, & Rickelman, 2000). When students have been led through a number of passage previews by their teacher, they can do so with any material they choose.

- Display library and classroom materials related to unit contents. Teachers often set aside a table or display case to hold these materials and allow student access during the unit.
- Show the cover of several reading materials related to the unit. Have your students describe what they see in the cover and predict upcoming unit contents.
- Have your students examine interior pages with an open discussion of what they encounter. Direct attention to pictorial displays such as illustrations, photographs, maps, diagrams, tables, and graphs as well as the text notes about these displays. Also examine the materials' titles, section headings, and boldface print. Insert target vocabulary into your comments about the material. Elicit from your students the materials' commonalities.

BRAINSTORMING   Having students brainstorm what they know about a topic is a flexible and popular way to introduce units. Brainstorming occurs best in a freewheeling atmosphere with just enough structure to maintain focus. First, stimulate your students' brainstorms with real-world observations and participations, reading aloud, or previewing passages as previously suggested. Then use a device such as KWL or a web to record what students call up.

KWL is an abbreviation for the three steps of a well-known procedure: What we *know*, what we *want* to learn, and what we *learned* (Blachowicz & Ogle, 2008). The following chart adds *focus questions* to KWL to promote deep examination of subject matter in a manageable way (Huffman, 2000). When launching a unit, students complete the first

KWL Chart for Washington, D.C.

	Where is it located?	Why is it district and not a state?	What are its major landmarks
What We Know			
What We Want to Learn			
What We Learned			

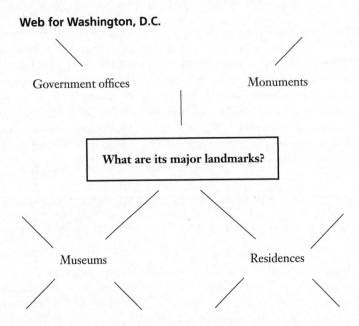

Web for Washington, D.C.

Government offices   Monuments

What are its major landmarks?

Museums   Residences

two rows of the chart. During the unit, they return to the chart and revise the second row, "What we want to learn," and complete the third row, "What we learned." Consider including other rows, such as, "How we will find out," "What we still need to learn," and "What we think about what we're learning."

Webs such as the one displayed for *Washington, D.C.*, also can be used to graphically depict relationships among the ideas and information students brainstorm. You might provide headings like the ones in the figure to direct students' thinking toward certain topics. Or you might simply list whatever students produce, then revisit the list and organize the items in web form.

WRITING   Writing as a unit launch is especially appropriate because it helps clarify thinking. It goes far in focusing attention on a topic. Two writing practices useful as launches are quick writes and extended personal writes.

Quick Write
- You now have had a brief introduction to desert habitats. Take sixty seconds and write down all that you think of when you think of a desert. The clock starts now!

- Starting with pennies, list all the different currencies we have in the United States. Then jot down any patterns you see.

These writing prompts are quick writes, the least formal kind of writing and, in some ways, the easiest one to fit into a crowded curriculum. When using quick writes to launch units, emphasize the pace of this practice. Students have a very brief time to blast down what they are thinking in "sloppy-copy," first-draft, rough fashion. Occasionally have students tell what they have written down as you list this on the board and point out that this is the starting point, the "What we know" phase of a KWL-type event. Occasionally collect the quick writes, using these to help guide the planning of later activities. And occasionally use small index cards for recording the quick writes and have students hand them to you as their "tickets" for exiting class.

Extended Personal Write

- Pretend you are your current age in 1845, heading for the Oregon territory. Based on what you know of the westward movement, write a letter home to your best friend, describing your experiences and feelings.
- You are a saltwater fish who is able to keep a journal. Based on what you know of these animals, describe a day in your life.

Extended personal writes such as these take longer than quick writes, but they are intended to produce deeper, longer-lasting knowledge. Extended personal writes encourage students to synthesize ideas and connect with subject matter at a somewhat emotional level. When using extended personal writes to launch units, have students maintain the writing in a journal. Redirect students to the compositions for revision as the unit progresses, and have students read their compositions in groups or to the class.

DO IT TOGETHER

Get together in groups and examine the unit frames each individual produced. Then plan launches that would start the units effectively.

Collecting Resources

At this point, you should be clear about where the unit is going and how you intend to launch it. You have in mind the unit's ending and its beginning—the culminating days and the introductory day. You have a plan for assessing student performance. Now you are ready to begin devoting attention to the unit's middle—what happens throughout the unit that actually takes up most of the time.

The resources available to you go into your decision making as you plan your unit. Instructional resources define what you have to work with. Be sure to determine what instructional resources you have for the unit.

Effective, experienced teachers learn to collect resources over time. When a classroom magazine contains a good article about a topic, teachers save that issue. They might maintain picture files for what they teach. They locate and request library books and audiovisual materials each year when the appropriate unit of study comes up because they have kept a list with their unit materials, and they update that list to include new resources and eliminate ones that are less useful. They bookmark good Web sites for teacher and student use.

There are many ways to obtain print resources for your students without spending money. You can check materials out of the school or the public library to use in your classroom. Many public libraries will compile a "Book Box" for teachers, with fifty to one hundred books on a topic. Although searching is time consuming, the number of books and magazines available makes it worthwhile.

Planning General Instruction

To structure general instructional planning for your unit, list your objectives and culminating activities, then begin deciding how you could best enable students to accomplish them. Ask yourself what support students require to meet these challenges. To illustrate, the immigration objectives noted earlier are challenging:

1. Students will be able to describe noteworthy immigrations.
2. Students will be able to portray personal experiences of immigrating.
3. Students will be able to explain conditions that produce immigrations.
4. Students will be able to evaluate the consequences of immigrations.
5. Students will be able to write an explanatory, multiparagraph essay.

How would you enable students to accomplish these outcomes? How would you provide access to subject matter as well as to reading and writing strategies? During this planning stage, seek help from department heads, team leaders, media specialists, and experienced teachers. Personally contact potential helpers. Notify your colleagues about units you are planning; you may be amazed at the amount of assistance you receive.

The remaining chapters in this book describe how to help students accomplish the reading and writing of your units. They suggest how to support students as they engage in comprehension, vocabulary, writing, study, and inquiry. They detail practices that guide students toward course content through literacy.

Scheduling Unit Events

The final step in unit planning is to design a timetable of events. You decide the sequence, the order, in which instruction will occur.

Figure 3.1 shows a three-week calendar for a unit on immigration. Seeing what is to be done each day helps you determine the feasibility of your plans. If your unit turns out to need three months, then you will need to reduce it. Schedules also help determine how to overlap activities. For instance, you can plan to have students work in groups on one aspect of the unit while you confer with individuals about another aspect. As Figure 3.1 shows, the schedule concentrates on when to launch the unit, introduce and culminate instruction devoted to each objective, then culminate the unit.

A schedule of unit events also helps organize your efforts and monitor the pace of your instruction. To be sure, your schedule might change once you begin a unit: a school assembly, fire drill, or power outage might disrupt a day's planned activities; particular resources such as a video or a guest speaker might not arrive as scheduled; and students might accomplish tasks more quickly or slowly than expected. While you can expect minor disruptions when following a unit's schedule, you can look forward to a complete breakdown if you don't even have a schedule.

TRY IT OUT

Figures 3.2 through 3.6 present plans and schedules for units on space for the primary grades, Native Americans of the Southwest for the intermediate grades, and smoking for the upper grades. These figures show how unit plans can be portrayed as webs; they show finished products rather than what is produced at each step of the planning process. Evaluate the unit plan appropriate for the grade level you intend to teach. Determine what you would keep and what you would change for your classroom instruction.

	Monday	Tuesday	Wednesday	Thursday	Friday
Week 1	Launch unit. Brainstorm understandings, beliefs, and questions.	Continue launch. Introduce objectives.	Present DVD program on noteworthy immigrations and have students take notes. Present readings on immigration.	Engage students in cooperative groups with the task of describing noteworthy immigrations.	Have groups complete their descriptions, then report to the class what they learned.
Week 2	Have guest speaker share personal immigration experience.	Engage students with the task of portraying personal experience of immigrating through poetry.	Conduct a brainstorming discussion of the human conditions that produce immigrations. Display resources on human conditions.	Demonstrate how to produce the explanatory, multiparagraph essay on human conditions that produce immigrations. Have students examine the resources.	Have students produce their essays; circulate through the class to support the writing.
Week 3	Present the consequences of immigrations through a lecture and video clips.	Have students evaluate the consequences of immigrations.	Finalize essay on conditions triggering immigrations.	Culminate unit.	Culminate unit. Display exhibits.

FIGURE 3.1   A Three-Week Calendar for a Unit on Immigration.

Unit
Launch

Practices

(wg) Announce topic and
read aloud book excerpts.

(wg) Start bulletin board
of solar system.

(i or sg) Place books, DVDs, and
activity cards in center.

(wg) Chant poems and sing songs.

(sg) Select space body
to learn and report on.

(sg) Begin planning for planetary
bazaar and museum.

Resources

Commander Toad series—J. Yolen
Space Case series—E. Marshall
The Magic School Bus: Lost in the Solar System—J. Cole
If You Were an Astronaut—D. L. Moche
Gravity and the Astronauts—M. Freeman
A Day in Space—S. Lord & J. Epstein
Our Solar System and Beyond—Q. L. Pearce
Amazing Space Facts—D. L. Moche
Songs and poems on space
Space Songs—M. C. Livingston
DVDs, space songs from media center

Students will be able to describe space exploration equipment.

Practices

(wg) Guided viewing and discussion of films
on space exploration

(i) Nighttime viewing of stars with telescopes

(wg) Presentation by head of astronomy club

Assessment

(sg) Each group selects a kind of tool,
instrument, or machine used for
exploration and examination of space
bodies. Produce a picture and a
description of what it does and what it
has found.

Resources

The First Space Pioneers and *Lunar Landings*
DVDs from district office
Rockets and Satellites—F. M. Branley
How to Draw Spacecraft—E. Fischel & A. Ganeri
Telescopes borrowed from astronomy club
Guest speaker—Dr. Artis, president of local
astronomy club
Online pictures of space exploration equipment

Key:	i = individual
	sg = small group
	wg = whole group

FIGURE 3.2   Primary-Grade Unit on Space.

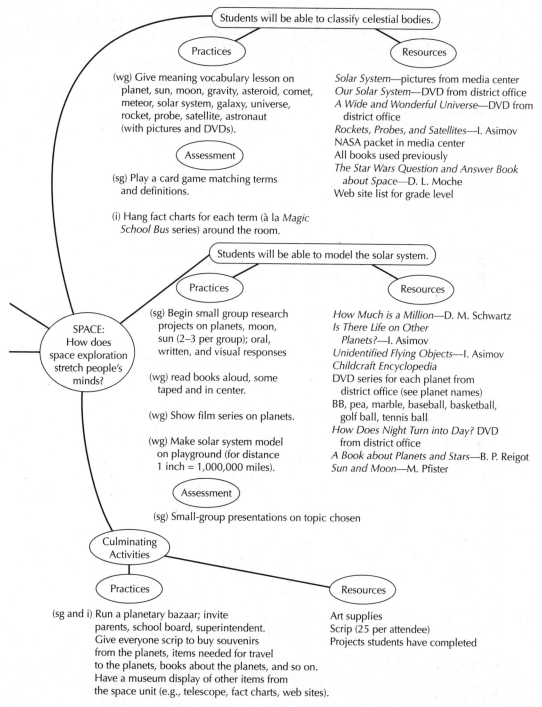

Students will be able to classify celestial bodies.

Practices

(wg) Give meaning vocabulary lesson on
planet, sun, moon, gravity, asteroid, comet,
meteor, solar system, galaxy, universe,
rocket, probe, satellite, astronaut
(with pictures and DVDs).

Assessment

(sg) Play a card game matching terms
and definitions.

(i) Hang fact charts for each term (à la *Magic
School Bus* series) around the room.

Resources

Solar System—pictures from media center
Our Solar System—DVD from district office
A Wide and Wonderful Universe—DVD from
district office
Rockets, Probes, and Satellites—I. Asimov
NASA packet in media center
All books used previously
*The Star Wars Question and Answer Book
about Space*—D. L. Moche
Web site list for grade level

Students will be able to model the solar system.

Practices

(sg) Begin small group research
projects on planets, moon,
sun (2–3 per group); oral,
written, and visual responses

(wg) read books aloud, some
taped and in center.

(wg) Show film series on planets.

(wg) Make solar system model
on playground (for distance
1 inch = 1,000,000 miles).

Assessment

(sg) Small-group presentations on topic chosen

Resources

How Much is a Million—D. M. Schwartz
*Is There Life on Other
Planets?*—I. Asimov
Unidentified Flying Objects—I. Asimov
Childcraft Encyclopedia
DVD series for each planet from
district office (see planet names)
BB, pea, marble, baseball, basketball,
golf ball, tennis ball
How Does Night Turn into Day? DVD
from district office
A Book about Planets and Stars—B. P. Reigot
Sun and Moon—M. Pfister

SPACE:
How does
space exploration
stretch people's
minds?

**Culminating
Activities**

Practices

(sg and i) Run a planetary bazaar; invite
parents, school board, superintendent.
Give everyone scrip to buy souvenirs
from the planets, items needed for travel
to the planets, books about the planets, and so on.
Have a museum display of other items from
the space unit (e.g., telescope, fact charts, web sites).

Resources

Art supplies
Scrip (25 per attendee)
Projects students have completed

FIGURE 3.2 *Continued*

Unit Launch

Practices

(wg) Elicit what students already know and establish categories of study.

(wg) Read books daily—fiction, folklore, and informational.

(sg) Show materials in the social studies learning center.

Students will be able to distinguish Southwest Native American groups.

Resources

Post large sheet of paper with "Native Americans of the Southwest" at the top.
Coyote the Trickster—G. Robinson & D. Hill
Raven the Trickster: Legends of the North American Indians—G. Robinson
Teacher information packets from the Heard Museum (Phoenix)
Corn is Maize—Aliki
Word Book Encyclopedia
Childcraft Encyclopedia

Practices

(wg) Present meaning vocabulary: Cochimi, Navajo, Apache, Pueblos (Hopi, Zuni, Zia, San Ildefonso, Laguna, Acoma, Taos), Yaqui, Yuma, Pima, Papago, Waiguri.

(wg) Discuss similarities and differences in beliefs and lifestyles.

(i) Create models of homes. Write how it is uniquely adapted for its population.

(i) Choose a tribe for final report about selected tribe.

(wg) Make traditional Native American foods from recipes.

Resources

Annie and the Old One—M. Miles
The Hopi—A. Tomchek
Indians of the Southwest, Facts on File—K. Liptak
Southwestern Indian Arts and Crafts—R. Manley
Tapestries in Sand—D. Villasenor
Wildlife of the Southwest Desert—L. Scott
Kachina Dolls—L. Spizzirri (Ed.)
Indian Festivals—P. Showers
The Taos Indians and Their Sacred Blue Lake—M. Keegan
Alice Yazzie's Year—R. Maher
Web sites for grade level

NATIVE AMERICANS OF THE SOUTHWEST
How does my family's heritage compare with a Native American family's heritage?

Assessment (i) Use score guide to evaluate final report done as book. Check home models for accuracy.

Students will be able to compare traditional and contemporary Southwest Native American cultures.

Practices

(wg) Present meaning vocabulary: loom, silver, turquoise, treaty, reservation, tribal council, sheep, gaming, poverty, BIA.

(wg) Guided viewing and discussion of DVDs on Native Americans.

(i) Participate in weaving class rug on a loom; discuss math principles.

(wg) Compare different styles of jewelry making among tribes.

Resources

After Columbus: Native Americans Today film
The Navajo—A. Osinski
Hawk, I'm Your Brother—B. Baylor
Life on the Reservation DVD from district office
Sky City: The Life of the Acoma Pueblo Peoples DVD from district office
Looms and yarn
Display of turquoise and silver jewelry
Morning Arrow—N. C. Dodge
Web sites for grade level

Assessment (i) Use score guide to evaluate notes made by individuals during discussions about Native Americans.

FIGURE 3.3 Intermediate-Grade Unit on Native Americans of the Southwest.

Students will be able to reconstruct pre-contact Southwest Native American cultures.

Practices

(wg) Meaning vocabulary; kachina, pottery, adobe, hogan, wickiup, tepee, pueblo, kiva, agave, cactus, yucca.

(i) Make clay pots and decorate with traditional designs.

(sg) Wash with yucca root soap.

(i) Paint with yucca brushes.

(wg) Examine music and learn dances.

(sg) Compare folktales among tribes.

Resources

Ancient Indians—R. Gallant
Indians of the Southwest— K. Liptak
North American Indian Ceremonies—K. Liptak
The Smithsonian Book of North American Indians before the Coming of the Europeans—P. Kopper
Sweet Salt—R. F. Locke
Meditations with the Navajo— G. Hausman
Yucca plants, clay, kiln, and paints
Kids Discover magazine, "America 1492"
Boy Scout with Indian lore merit badge

At the Center of the World— B. Baker
North American Legends— V. Hamilton
Arrow to the Sun—G. McDermott
And It Is Still that Way: Legends Told by Arizona Indian Children—B. Baylor
God on Every Mountain— B. Baylor
A Cry from the Earth: Music of the North American Indians— J. Bierhorst
The Desert Is Theirs—B. Baylor
Moonsong—B. Baylor
The Indians Knew—T. S. Pine and J. Levine
Web sites for grade level

Assessment

(i) Use score guide to assess projects for accuracy of designs and information.

Students will be able to evaluate reasons why certain Southwest Native American groups have disappeared.

Practices

(wg) View and discuss DVD.

(wg) Present meaning vocabulary: Mogollon, Hohokam, Mimbres, anthropologist, dig, petroglyph, pictograph, cliff dwelling, artifact, archaeologist.

(sg) Write letters to archaeologist at local university or Heard Museum.

Resources

The Old Ones: The Story of the Anasazi DVD from district office
The Old Ones: A Children's Book about the Anasazi Indians—B. & J. Freeman
Picture packets on archaeology, Southwest Indians from media center
When Clay Sings—B. Baylor
Before You Came This Way— B. Baylor

Assessment

(sg) Use score guide to assess accuracy information in letters to archaeologist.

Culminating Activities

Practices

(wg) Visit Heard Museum for day.
Finish books on tribes.
Write thank-you letters to guide.

Resources

Tour guide for the Heard (focus on Southwest Indians).
Notebooks to record information.

Key:
i = individual
sg = small group
wg = whole group

FIGURE 3.3 *Continued*

	Monday	Tuesday	Wednesday	Thursday	Friday
Week 1	Launch Space unit. Read books throughout day. Sing songs. Read poems. Introduce science center. Explain planetary bazaar.	Launch Space unit. Read throughout day. Sing songs. Read poems. Start bulletin board (add to as possible).	Launch Space unit. Read throughout day. Sing songs. Read poems. Choose space body for report. Explore web sites	Meaning vocabulary lesson. Present *Solar System* pictures. Present *Our Solar System* DVD. Continue reading.	Meaning vocabulary lesson. Present *Solar System* pictures. Present *Wide/ Wonderful Universe* DVD. Continue reading. Play card game to practice terms.
Week 2	Meaning vocabulary lesson. Present *Solar System* pictures. Use pictures and information in NASA space packet. Continue reading. Construct and hang fact charts.	Present *Sun* DVD. Read books and parts of encyclopedias. Visual display by small group.	Continue to read. Oral report by small group. Explore web sites	Continue to read. Written report by small group.	Present *Earth* DVD. Visual display by small group. Make solar system model on playground with balls to show distances and proportional sizes.
Week 3	Present *Moon* DVD. Oral report by small group. Present *How Does Night Turn into Day?* film.	Written report by small group. Plan for bazaar and museum. Explore web sites	Visual display by small group. Prepare materials for planetary bazaar and museum. Explore web sites	Oral report by small group. Prepare materials for planetary bazaar and museum.	Present *Jupiter* DVD. Written report by small group. Prepare materials for planetary bazaar and museum.
Week 4	Visual display by small group. Prepare materials for bazaar and museum.	Oral report by small group. Prepare materials for bazaar and museum.	Present *1st Space Pioneers* film. Evening: View stars with telescopes.	Present *Lunar Landings* DVD. Select tool for research. Make pictures and one-paragraph report of tool.	Culminate unit. Hold planetary bazaar and museum. Guest speaker. Display pictures and report.

FIGURE 3.4 Schedule for Unit on Space.

	Monday	Tuesday	Wednesday	Thursday	Friday
Week 1	Launch unit. Present pictures. Present map. Read passage from informational packet.	Launch unit. Brainstorm knowledge. Browse and free read. Explore web sites	Launch unit. Brainstorm knowledge. Share learning objectives. Browse and free read. Explore web sites	Meaning vocabulary: Southwest tribes. Emphasize similarities and differences among groups as shown in DVD.	Choose a tribe/ group to study and report in book form. Begin collecting information from classroom resources.
Week 2	Meaning vocabulary: Precontact cultures and artifacts. Illustrate and plan construction of models of homes and cultural artifacts.	Read folktales aloud. Construct models of homes and cultural artifacts. Explore web sites	Monitor tribe/ group reports. Perform traditional dances.	Read folktales aloud. Construct models of homes and cultural artifacts.	Display models of homes. Cook traditional recipes.
Week 3	Meaning vocabulary: Extinct groups. Read folktales aloud.	Compare folktales. Construct cultural artifacts. Explore web sites	Meaning vocabulary: modern and ancient lives. Monitor tribe-group reports.	Watch DVD and orally compare differences in modern and ancient lives. Plan letter to archaeologist.	Display artifacts (pots, rugs). Cook traditional foods from recipes.
Week 4	Submit letter to archaeologist.	Plan questions and observations for museum visit.	Monitor tribe-group reports.	Culminate unit. Visit museum.	Culminate unit. Write thank-you letters to museum guide. Share books on tribes.

FIGURE 3.5   Schedule for Unit on Native Americans of the Southwest.

Unit Launch

Practices

(wg) Present smoking artifacts.

(wg) Present background on extent of smoking and its effects.

(sg) Browse through materials.

(i) Brainstorm plans for culminating activity.

Resources

Cigarette packs, loose tobacco, pictures of people smoking.

Thank you for smoking DVD clips

Assorted literature; from National Clearinghouse for Smoking and Health

Grade level web sites

Students will be able to portray the health risks and performance effects of smoking.

Practices

(wg) Present composition of smoke.

(sg) Examine smoking-related diseases.

(wg) Portray effects of smoking on life-size diagram of human body.

Resources

DVD of lung surgery
The Scientific Case against Smoking—R. Winter
The Stop Smoking Book for Teens—C. Casewit
Grade level web sites

Assessment

Quiz on effects of smoking

Students will be able to analyze governmental supports and challenges to smoking.

Smoking: What is my response to smoking?

Students will be able to express a personal commitment relative to smoking.

Practices

(wg) Present health warnings plus price supports for tobacco.

(i) Compose a letter to a young child explaining why U.S. government simultaneously supports and challenges tobacco industry.

Resources

Tobacco product packages

Newspaper editorials

Magazine articles

Web sites

Culminating Activity

Share commitments about smoking

Practices

(wg) Present need for commitment.

(sg) Debate reasons for and against smoking.

(i) Compose message using any media expressing commitment.

Resources

Previous study

Family, friends and community interviews

Smoking: Fact and Fiction— B. Szumski

Assessment

Use score guide to assess letter to young child.

Assessment

Use score guide to assess media message

Key: i = individual
       sg = small group
       wg = whole group

FIGURE 3.6 Upper-Grade Unit on Smoking.

	Monday	Tuesday	Wednesday	Thursday	Friday
Week 1	Present clips from DVD, *Thank You for Smoking* Display smoking artifacts Discuss central question.	Present effects of smoking and health warnings Explore resources	Present smoking-related diseases Explore resources Plan interviews	Portray effects of smoking on life-size diagram of human body	Compare interview findings Plan responses to central question
Week 2	Present composition of smoke Explore web sites	Present medical effects of smoking	Plan and begin drafting letter	Draft letter Review effects of smoking	Quiz on effects of smoking
Week 3	Share letters Review resources	Plan and begin draft of media message	Plan for debate Draft media message	Debate responses to smoking	Share media messages about smoking

FIGURE 3.7 Schedule for Unit on Smoking.

LOOKING BACK

In this chapter, we emphasized unit-level planning. This chapter is meant to get you started with plans for meaningfully engaging students with reading and writing. It contains three key ideas: (1) Selecting a topic begins unit planning; (2) framing a topic structures unit planning; and (3) working within a frame focuses unit planning.

ADD TO YOUR JOURNAL

Record in your class journal your reactions to unit planning. What units have you experienced? What were their strengths and limitations? What were their similarities and differences? How do you plan on implementing units in your teaching and why?

Additional Readings

This is an enormously popular and influential source for planning instructional units.

Wiggins, G., & Mctighe, J. (2006). *Understanding by design* (expanded 2nd ed.). Upper Saddle River, NJ: Pearson/Merrill-Prentice Hall.

Descriptions of unit planning that include reading and writing are found in the following:

Donoghue, M. R. (2009). *Language arts: Integrating skills for classroom teaching*. Thousand Oaks, CA: Sage.

Erickson, H. L. (2007). *Concept-based curriculum and instruction for the thinking classroom*. Thousand Oaks, CA: Corwin Press.

March, J. K., & Peters, K. H. (2008). *Designing instruction: Making best practices work in standards-based classrooms*. Thousand Oaks, CA: Corwin Press.

Wood, K. E. (2005). *Interdisciplinary instruction: A practical guide for elementary and middle school teachers* (3rd ed.). Upper Saddle River, NJ: Pearson/Prentice Hall.

Concept-oriented reading instruction (CORI) is a promising research-based framework for integrating language arts and subject matter instruction that emphasizes academic engagement. These sources detail the theory, practice, and results of implementing CORI in elementary classrooms:

Guthrie, J. T., Wigfield, A., & Perencevich, K. C. (Eds.). (2004). *Motivating reading comprehension: Concept-oriented reading instruction*. Mahwah, NJ: Lawrence Erlbaum Associates.

Swan, E. A. (2003). *Concept-oriented reading instruction: Engaging classrooms, lifelong learners*. New York, NY: Guilford Press.

Online Resources

These sites present abundant unit-based lessons and instructional resources.

Awesome Library
http://www.awesomelibrary.org/

Beacon Learning Center
http://www.beaconlearningcenter.com

Blue Web'N
http://www.kn.pacbell.com/wired/bluewebn/

EduHound
http://www.eduhound.com/

eThemes
http://www.emints.org/ethemes/index.shtml

Thinkfinity
www.thinkfinity.org

Virtual Middle School Library
http://www.sldirectory.com/virtual.html

Concept-oriented reading instruction (CORI) incorporates reading strategy instruction and inquiry science to increase students' reading comprehension and motivation as well as science knowledge.

CORI
www.cori.umd.edu

References

Albright, L. K., & Ariail, M. (2005). Tapping the potential of teacher read-alouds in middle schools. *Journal of Adolescent & Adult Literacy, 48*(7), 582–591.

Blachowicz, C., & Ogle, D. (2008). *Reading comprehension: Strategies for independent learners* (2nd ed.). New York, NY: Guilford.

Carr, K. S., Buchanan, D. L., Wentz, J. B., Weiss, M. L., & Brant, K. J. (2001). Not just for the primary grades: A bibliography of picture books for secondary content teachers. *Journal of Adolescent and Adult Literacy, 45*, 146–153.

Conley, M. W. (2005). *Connecting standards and assessment through literacy*. Boston, MA: Allyn & Bacon.

Erickson, H. L. (2007). *Concept-based curriculum and instruction for the thinking classroom*. Thousand Oaks, CA: Corwin Press.

Guthrie, J. T., Wigfield, A., & Perencevich, K. C. (Eds.). (2004). *Motivating reading comprehension: Concept-Oriented Reading Instruction*. Mahwah, NJ: Erlbaum.

Huffman, L. E. (2000). Spotlighting specifics by combining focus questions with K-W-L. In D. W. Moore, D. E. Alvermann, & K. A. Hinchman (Eds.), *Struggling adolescent readers: A collection of teaching strategies* (pp. 220–222). Newark, DE: International Reading Association.

Lesesne, T. S. (2006). Reading aloud: A worthwhile investment? *Voices from the Middle, 13*, 50–54.

March, J. K., & Peters, K. H. (2008). *Designing instruction: Making best practices work in standards-based classrooms*. Thousand Oaks, CA: Corwin Press.

Readence, J. E., Moore, D. W., & Rickelman, R. J. (2000). *Prereading activities for content area reading and learning* (3rd ed.). Newark, DE: International Reading Association.

Stiggins, R. J. (2007). *Student-involved assessment for learning* (5th ed.). Upper Saddle River, NJ: Pearson/Merrill-Prentice Hall.

Trelease, J. (2006). *The read-aloud handbook* (6th ed.). New York, NY: Penguin Books.

Wiggins, G., & Mctighe, J. (2006). *Understanding by design* (expanded 2nd ed.). Upper Saddle River, NJ: Pearson/Merrill-Prentice Hall.

CHAPTER 4

Reading Materials and Exhibiting Responses

LOOKING AHEAD

Think of traveling via different types of roads. Freeways hurry you through the landscape quickly and efficiently. Although freeways speed your journey to a certain point, you probably would use them for only part of your trip if you want to take in the surroundings or get to a special area of interest such as a small town, a lake, a state park, or an historical site.

Traditional content area textbooks are like freeways. They move you through a lot of territory, but they do it so quickly that you are unable to obtain close, personal insights into the area. In order to genuinely know the area, you need to exit the freeway and travel the connecting roads. The connecting roads of subject matter study are materials such as library books, magazines, newspapers, Web sites, and computer software. These materials provide multiple avenues to thinking and learning. This chapter, which introduces content area reading materials and ways readers might respond to them, contains three key ideas:

1. Students deserve diverse reading materials during instructional units.
2. Diverse reading materials are available for instructional units.
3. Exhibits take many forms.

STUDENTS DESERVE DIVERSE READING MATERIALS DURING INSTRUCTIONAL UNITS

Students benefit from exiting the subject matter freeways of textbooks and traveling the connecting roads of diverse materials because such reading enriches the mind (Cunningham 2005; Krashen, 2004). Students deserve a variety of content area reading materials for at least four reasons: (1) depth of information, (2) distinctive points of view, (3) materials that fit reading competencies, and (4) opportunities for a range of thinking.

Depth of Information

A major reason for providing students access to diverse reading materials during subject matter study is to deepen understanding. Reliance on a single source of information can lead to superficial knowledge. Think of how a typical middle-school social studies textbook presents the ancient Greeks. The textbook probably devotes ten to twenty pages to such topics as Greek mythology, government, social order, culture, art, architecture, warfare, and overall influence on modern life. This is quite a lot of ground to cover in only ten pages, but the Roman Empire comes next, and it, too, has several noteworthy features that must be covered.

But now think of library books and magazine articles on ancient Greece. For instance, *Gods, Men, and Monsters from the Greek Myths* takes 156 pages to describe only one aspect of ancient Greek life: mythology. This book contains a full account of the exploits of the mythical characters, memorable graphics depicting scenes from the various myths, a chart depicting the relationships and roles of the gods, and an index. Prometheus, Apollo, Jason, Helios, and others come alive in this book. Such a carefully detailed, well-crafted treatment of a topic is not possible in a textbook because textbooks must cover too many topics.

To further appreciate the differences between the depth available in traditional textbooks and well-written library books, think back to what you learned in this text about the "organize" and "connect" thinking processes. Remember that good readers arrange information into categories and form associations between what they already know and what a passage contains. Likewise, good writers enable readers to readily apprehend the organization of a passage and make connections. Proficient authors are well aware of the pitfalls of typical textbook writing, so they make organizing and connecting seem effortless. They do not produce baskets of facts.

Distinctive Points of View

Students also deserve a variety of content area reading materials because such resources can present distinctive points of view on a topic, whereas textbooks tend to present no specific viewpoint or only a traditional perspective (Ravitch, 2003). For instance, *The Way Things Never Were: The Truth about the "Good Old Days"* (Finkelstein, 1999) presents an alternative history of the United States during the 1950s and 1960s that includes sections on health care, eating habits, family life, environmental issues, and the condition of the elderly. It demonstrates that looking at the past only through rose-colored glasses misrepresents actual conditions. *Lies My Teacher Told Me* (Loewen, 2007) takes this stance even further by revealing ways that American history textbooks slant and even distort the past. Content area materials also present alternative, interesting points of view on issues such as the environment, genetic engineering, UFOs, war and conflict, and those with mental or physical disabilities. Diverse materials go beyond singular accounts of topics and events, revealing multiple paths to them and alternative conceptions of them.

Materials That Fit Reading Competencies

If you took your students out on a football field and had them run 100 yards, individuals would finish at different times, and some would enjoy the exercise more than others, no matter how they placed. In fact, the differences between students' running times and feelings about running probably would increase as they got older. The same holds true for literacy. When you give your class a reading and writing assignment, you can count on students finishing at different times, with different amounts of understanding and degrees of interest. Thus, diverse materials are needed to match your diverse students.

Incorporating diverse reading materials into the study of subject matter allows students to work with what they can handle. Students learn best when reading and writing tasks are within their limits. Understandably, students tend to avoid frustrating assignments and search for something else to do. Making available a variety of reading materials allows more students to succeed.

Opportunities for a Range of Thinking

A final reason why students deserve diverse content area materials involves opportunities to employ the various thinking processes. Teaching practices centered about a textbook tend to emphasize only recall. This situation seems due partly to the authoritative tone of textbooks. Textbook language has an all-knowing stance, dispensing information in domineering fashion. Multiple materials help demystify print by showing that some authors present a topic more clearly and completely than others.

Multiple materials also are conducive to problem solving and decision making. For instance, teachers who use a variety of materials can have students compare different versions of the same Greek myth or compare Greek myths with those from other cultures. In brief, multiple materials give students a chance at getting something meaningful from their reading; they meet students halfway. Some of the time you might spend guiding your students through their textbooks would be better spent getting other materials into their hands.

Students enjoy opportunities to browse through a variety of reading materials.

LISTEN, LOOK, AND LEARN

Informally interview a teacher who uses diverse reading materials during subject matter study. Ask why he or she uses multiple materials rather than a single text. Compare the reasons you obtain from the interview with the ones listed in this section.

DIVERSE READING MATERIALS ARE AVAILABLE FOR INSTRUCTIONAL UNITS

This section presents general types of materials for students to access. It describes six major categories of content area reading materials: reference materials, periodicals, digital resources, trade books, multicultural literature, and textbooks. We offer these six categories as a sample of what is available. You can engage your students with countless types of reading materials during instructional units throughout the year.

Reference Materials

Students consult reference materials for facts or general background information. These materials typically display information in a straightforward, concise manner. Two types of reference materials are common: compendiums and special-interest publications.

COMPENDIUMS Compendiums are handy collections of information. They include encyclopedias, dictionaries, atlases, almanacs, and yearbooks. Students frequently are intimidated by compendiums because the information in them is presented differently than the information in other books. Compendiums usually have extremely dense text summarizing a great deal of information in very little space. Nonetheless, some materials are better than others. Some publications contain striking visuals, accurate information, and accessible writing. In one book's presentation of the layers of the atmosphere, an illustration shows the sea, the world's tallest building, an eagle flying, Mount Everest, and an airborne jumbo jet in order to provide concrete examples of height.

Computer-based compendiums have features that are lacking in traditional print. Multimedia sound and film clips enhance available information. Seeing and hearing portions of President Kennedy's inaugural address through multimedia differs from reading about it. Computerized encyclopedias also allow searches using combinations of terms (e.g., mammals + North American), and they offer immediate links from one topic to another. Finally, computer-based encyclopedias allow students to copy information from the reference and paste it into a word-processing application. Although this might raise concerns about plagiarism, it offers opportunities to explain how reports are to be constructed in the Information Age.

Technological innovations continue affecting the world of encyclopedias. CDs overwhelmed print-based materials, and the Web seems to be overwhelming CDs. To illustrate, the Encyclopaedia Britannica (www.britannica.com) affords searches through its more than 76,000 entries and provides fresh information daily, along with links to other Web sites.

SPECIAL-INTEREST REFERENCES   Brochures and pamphlets exemplify special-interest references. When studying cities or states, students often obtain colorful promotional literature from chambers of commerce. When investigating occupations, students examine brief publications produced by trade unions, professional organizations, and government agencies. Classrooms stocked with special-interest references have filing cabinets and shelves full of such real-life reading materials as maps, application forms, menus, food labels, legal documents, and telephone books. More and more they have Web bookmarks, such as the following that lead to travel information, in place of print versions.

- www.travel.state.gov
- www.travelinformation.com
- www.lonelyplanet.com

When searching for reference materials, keep student reading abilities in mind and examine the composition of the materials. Are they well organized? Are examples provided? If the material is too sparse, students will not be informed and may even go away from the material confused because information was missing.

Periodicals

A wide range of published material is available by subscription. Periodicals are excellent content area materials because they are timely and include short, lively, well-illustrated articles on interesting topics. Periodicals can provide students with an introduction to a new subject, pique student interest in a subject not considered interesting, and summarize information after students have done other research. Periodicals from *Ranger Rick's Nature Magazine* to *Popular Mechanics* to the community newspaper are available for class or individual subscriptions. Practically every subject area has at least one periodical appropriate for upper-grade students, and general periodicals that report the weekly news and special features exist for all grades. The Thomson Gale Web site (www.gale.cengage.com/title_lists) maintains the *InfoTrac Kids, InfoTrac Junior Edition*, and *InfoTrac Student Edition* databases that provide extensive lists of magazines for young people.

Digital Resources

Fundamental shifts in education occurred when print replaced the oral tradition and again when printing presses resulted in affordable books. Learners depended less on others and more on themselves to become educated; learners also could access quantities of information and ideas that previously had been inaccessible. Computer technology is affecting education every bit as much as these past innovations. Educators now talk about *digital literacies* and *new literacies*, the reading and writing of digital, multimodal, multigenre representations displayed on screens, as opposed to traditional *print literacy* (Coiro, Knobel, Lankshear, & Leu, 2008; Lankshear & Knobel, 2008). As the International Reading Association put it, "To become fully literate in today's world, students must become proficient in the new literacies of the Internet and communication technology" (International Reading Association, 2001).

Your students now can click and enter vast storehouses of information. They can experience multimedia presentations that include print but go far beyond the capacity of books. They can participate in real-time video conferencing and long-distance collaborations. They can observe and produce vivid presentations with streaming technology.

Separating the hype from the reality about what technology actually offers classrooms can be difficult, but educational possibilities and occupational realities make digital resources an important part of content area materials. The most suitable digital resources include online sites, simulations, gamelike simulations, and multimedia.

ONLINE SITES   Separating the wheat from the chaff is essential for effective use of online sites. The incredible richness of contents ranging from primary sources such as slave narratives, weather data from around the world, and views from space, as well as secondary sources such as that provided by online multimedia encyclopedias, make the search worthwhile.

edheads. org

A good way to locate useful information is to rely on selection guides. Selection guides list only recommended sites, sometimes annotating Web site contents and offering links that bypass introductory menus and go directly to the heart of the information. These guides provide access to instructional tips, lesson plans, event updates, and subject matter information. Three examples of reliable selection guides that provide links to useful online sites are the following:

- *Blue Web'n*
  http://www.kn.pacbell.com/wired/bluewebn/
- *Ohio Resource Center*
  http://www.ohiorc.org
- *Thinkfinity*
  http://thinkfinity.org/

SIMULATIONS   Students who cannot participate in scientific or historical events firsthand can take part in them vicariously through computer simulations. Simulations allow students to investigate phenomena through virtual reality.

Students access literacy through computer technology.

For instance, the *Teachers' Domain* Web site (http://www.teachersdomain.org) presents *Ice Shelf and Ice Sheet Simulation* under the *Climate* heading in their *Water Cycle, Weather and Climate* section. This scientific simulation allows students to quickly see the difference between water levels when floating ice and shelf ice melt. Another simulation, *Harness the Power of Wind,* is found in the *National Geographic* site under Global Warming (http://environment.nationalgeographic.com). This simulation allows students to create their own turbine, then manipulate variables such as wind speed and altitude to determine the amount of energy that would be produced and how many homes would be supplied electricity. In *Operation Frog Deluxe* (www.tomsnyder.com), students explore multiple biological aspects of this amphibian through virtual reality.

GAMELIKE SIMULATIONS   Many simulations have gamelike features, with points scored for desirable decisions, that only hint at actual firsthand experiences. For instance, the classic *Oregon Trail,* 5th edition (www.broderbund.com) has students reenact part of the westward expansion saga. Players decide what provisions they should set out with; what food rations and travel pace they should follow; and how they should acquire food, cross rivers, and handle adversity. Successful players reach Oregon's Willamette Valley; unsuccessful ones are said to die on the trail. On the *Europe Inspirer* 4.0 (www.tomsnyder.com), teams of students compete against each other as they participate in a scavenger hunt for resources across Europe. They interpret maps, recognize geographic patterns, and collaborate to be successful. The *O2 Speculator* game (http://www.altruisticworld.com/Environment_Play.aspx) is an interactive financial game based on stock market trading, although students trade oxygen in this future world where oxygen is in short supply. They try to turn their $10,000 game money into a fortune in one day, learning about short selling, commodity prices, and the volatility of the market.

MULTIMEDIA   Like the electronic encyclopedias noted previously, multimedia contains incredible amounts of information in the form of print, still images, graphics, sound, animation, and video. Students can view multimedia individually on a monitor or as a group by having the visuals projected onto a screen. The presentation of multimedia can be controlled by moving from one link to another in a desired order. For instance, science teachers might talk through the human heart's system of blood circulation by presenting pictures one at a time, then showing a video of an actual heart beating, then displaying a diagram of the human body's arteries and veins. Deciding whether to show blood passing through the lungs can be made relative to how the class is responding.

The PBS award-winning documentary *Eyes on the Prize II*, which is available on DVD (www.pbs.org), presents America's Civil Rights movement from the mid-1950s to 1980s. It contains videotaped speeches by equal rights activists, texts from pertinent documents, anthems and theme songs, maps, and profiles of key people and organizations. In this case, students have access to the sights, sounds, and printed words of a social movement. National Geographic (www.nationalgeographic.com) offers multimedia kits with titles such as *Geokit: Cells & Microorganisms, Age of Exploration,* and *Immigration.* These collections include stunning pictures and drawings, narration accompanied by music and sound effects, and interactive picture buttons that invite exploration.

Multimedia projects are possible as students gather, organize, and report on information contained in multimedia courseware. For instance, in *Decisions, Decisions 5.0: Town Government* (www.tomsnyder.com), students learn about local government as they figure out how to manage rapid population growth, decide on new city services and how to pay for them, grapple with lifestyle changes resulting from increased population, and deal with crime. Students engage in a range of interactions in whole-group and team settings. They are able to track their reasoning, decision making, and consequences on-screen. *Prime Time Math* (www.tomsnyder.com) engages intermediate-grade students in real-world dramatic stories about professional people using math in compelling situations, such as wilderness search and rescues, medical emergencies, crimes, and fires. The situations portray how math applies to the world in which students live.

In a comparison of students' uses of digital resources inside and outside of school (Project Tomorrow, 2008), students reported needing to power down when they entered school. When prompted to name digital features and functions they would like in their textbooks, the youth in this survey said they would like to be able do the following:

- personalize their books with electronic highlights and notes (63 percent);
- take quizzes and tests on their own to assess their own content proficiency (62 percent) or use self-paced tutorials (46 percent);
- access links to real-time data such as NASA and Google Earth (52 percent);
- tap into the expertise of an online tutor whenever necessary (53 percent);
- link to PowerPoints of class lectures that support the textbook content (55 percent);
- explore concepts through games (57percent) or animations and simulations (55 percent);
- access content outside of school through links to videoconferences (30 percent) or podcasts from subject experts (34 percent); and
- watch video clips about topics they are studying (51 percent) and create podcasts or videos to support their own learning (48 percent).

TRY IT OUT

The Web site www.teachersdomain.org is a cornucopia of simulations for the arts, English language arts, mathematics, science, and social studies. You may use the site several times without registering; registration is free. Explore some of this site's lessons in your content area, then decide how you could use a few lessons in your classroom.

Trade Books

Trade books are intended for sale in general bookstores; they make up a bookseller's trade. Some educators use the terms *trade book* and *library book* as synonyms.

Content area trade books come in a wide range for preschool children through adults. Trade books are available for all content areas, even those that typically limit wide reading. For instance, Atkinson, Matusevich, and Huber (2009) recommend science trade books and an approach for selecting them that is appropriate for elementary classroom use. Marlette and Gordon (2004) present various texts physical education teachers can incorporate into their classes when addressing issues like body image, wellness, and teamwork. Hunsader (2004) presents trade books appropriate for mathematics topics. Along with books that focus on one mathematical topic like exponential growth or fractals, others deal with fundamental personal issues connected with mathematics. For instance, *The Curious Incident of the Dog in the Night-time* sensitively discloses an autistic boy's logical mathematical predisposition toward experiencing and coping with life.

The following are good examples of reliable, online selection guides for children and youths' trade books:

Adolescent Literacy: Booklists for Adolescent Readers
www.literacy.uconn.edu/adolit.htm

American Library Association
www.ala.org/ala/aboutala/offices/library/libraryfactsheet/alalibraryfactsheet23.cfm

Carol Hurst's Children's Literature Site
http://www.carolhurst.com/

International Reading Association: Choices Booklists
http://www.reading.org/Resources/Booklists.aspx

Kathy Schrock's Guide for Educators
http://school.discovery.com/schrockguide/index.html

Literacy Matters
www.literacymatters.org/adlit/selecting/literature.htm

Vandergrift's Young Adult Literature Page
www.scils.rutgers.edu/~kvander/YoungAdult/index.html

Here we present only a few major genres appropriate for subject study in order to exemplify the possibilities. The following are some major genres likely to be found in elementary-, middle-, and secondary-school libraries: picture books, fiction, nonfiction narrative, nonfiction exposition, and biography.

PICTURE BOOKS   Picture books, which are appropriate for all ages, refer to texts whose artwork is crucial for their understanding and experience. For young children, these books introduce such concepts as size, shape, color, spatial relations, the alphabet, numeral recognition, and number sets. For instance, *Exactly the Opposite* depicts various opposites. This wordless book of photographs allows preschoolers and early readers to identify more than one correct response. In *Animalia*, each page contains dozens of lavish pictures of items that begin with that page's letter of the alphabet. *First the Egg* art fully presents stages of natural development.

For older readers, *One Grain of Rice* vividly portrays the mathematical principle of exponential growth. Language arts teachers might introduce literary elements and writing traits through picture books and then transfer the lesson to more challenging material (Culham 2004; Zile & Napoli, 2009). They could present alliteration with *Some Smug Slug*, imagery with *Owl Moon*, and parody with *Dusty Locks and the Three Bears*. Social studies teachers could portray young people's lives in Kabul, Afghanistan, with *Afghan Dreams*.

FICTION   A great deal of your knowledge about the climate, language, flora, fauna, and ethnic groups in certain parts of the world probably came from reading fiction set in those locations. For instance, *Downriver* is an exciting story about troubled teens escaping their Colorado River guide, then battling themselves and the river. Readers access much information about the terrain and conditions of the U.S. southwest's Colorado Plateau while following this adventure. Another book that follows a story line while presenting extremely valuable and valid information is *Voices of the Wild*.

Two types of fiction especially suitable for content area classrooms include realistic fiction and historical fiction. *Realistic fiction* portrays events and people that seem to be involved in the recognizable trials and uncertainties of life. Books such as *I'll Get There, It Better Be Worth the Trip*, and *A Day No Pigs Would Die* are classic statements of young adults' changes from dependent children to independent adults. Many books are now available that deal with such issues as divorce, developing sexuality, mental and physical disabilities, and death and dying. Homelessness becomes more than a word to young children when they read engaging literature like *Fly Away Home* and *Monkey Island*.

Historical fiction attempts to re-create a believable past. Authors of such works often create fictional characters who interact with people who actually shaped events in history. Readers step into the past when they vicariously experience events through imagined and real characters. After reading *Across Five Aprils, Bull Run*, or *Behind the Lines*, students begin to understand much better why the Civil War was so devastating on a personal as well as a national scale. Historical fiction portrays countless eras and events, from prehistoric Ice Ages to the present.

NONFICTION NARRATIVE   A content area trade book genre that deserves attention is accounts of actual happenings, called *nonfiction narratives*. This genre presents events and dialogue as they are remembered or recorded by the participants. Authors typically maintain a journal of the events if they were participants, or they interview those who actually participated and present a story that documents the events. Classic examples of nonfiction narratives appropriate for secondary students include *Black Like Me, The Double Helix, Into Thin Air, Never Cry Wolf*, and *The Right Stuff*.

You could accommodate readers' ranges of ability by offering a range of nonfiction narrative that addresses the same topic. When examining the end of World War II and the first use of an atomic bomb, you might offer *Hiroshima*, which is somewhat challenging, along with *Sadako*, which is quite accessible.

NONFICTION EXPOSITION   Much nonfiction examines a single topic in expository fashion, with no story line for conveying ideas. This genre contains some exceptionally vivid writing and visual display. Nonfiction exposition is written for very young children through adults. *Wolfsnail, Frogs,* and *When the Wolves Returned* are examples of nonfiction exposition books about animals written for young readers. Books within this genre that address particular social groups and are appropriate for upper-grade readers include *Lest We Forget: The Passage from Africa to Slavery and Emancipation* and *World of Our Fathers: A History of Jewish Life from Eastern Europe to America*. A vivid depiction of the human body is found in *The Way We Work*.

BIOGRAPHY   Books about people who have made contributions to the content areas are numerous. Biographies are available about people prominent in reform movements, politics, sports, medicine, war, and entertainment, to name only a few fields. Abraham

Lincoln, Jim Thorpe, Marie Curie, James Audubon, Anne Frank, Elizabeth Blackwell, and Bill Cosby are only a small sampling of those whose life histories have been written. Young readers often appreciate biographies as they search for heroes and heroines to emulate. Unfortunately, some biographers let their own infatuation with the subject interfere with the honest depiction of a multifaceted human being. Students need to be on the alert for folklore that passes for truth from one book to another. For instance, the story about George Washington and the cherry tree is not substantiated. Some myths are easily spotted; others pass into the general culture as truths. Though more biographies exist for people in the content areas of the arts, humanities, and social sciences, biographies have been written about important figures associated with all major curricular areas.

Multicultural Literature

Multicultural literature is a genre that differs from the others in this section because it refers to the content of materials rather than to their form. Multicultural literature is printed matter that recognizes human features such as ethnicity, language, race, religion, age, gender, socioeconomic class, and exceptionality. It acknowledges our cultural diversity, embracing literacy as a civil right and an essential element of social justice (Greene, 2008). It can affirm individuals' cultural identities. Multicultural literature is part of educators' responses to a pluralist vision of society (Au, 2006; Boyd & Brock, 2004).

Your students should have access to reading materials whose contents, illustrations, and language accurately and fairly represent them. This approach goes beyond merely displaying posters, having a one-day multicultural fair with ethnic foods for lunch, and adding a list of diverse heroes and holidays to be memorized. When studying the age of discovery, provide *The First Voyage of Christopher Columbus*, which maps out the voyage in exceptional detail, along with *The Encounter*, an account of the arrival of Columbus as seen through the eyes of the Tianos people who met him.

Myriad books with multicultural perspectives fit the myriad topics covered in school. Young children studying shelter will gain perspective on the children who live in different types of houses built throughout the United States in *The House I Live In: At Home in America*. *Rosa Parks: Mother to a Movement* offers older children a personal account of the events that led this courageous woman in 1955 to refuse to give her bus seat to a white man in Alabama, turning the civil rights movement into a national issue. *The Storyteller's Candle/La Velita de los Cuentos* is a bilingual volume that tells the story of Pura Belpré, the first Puerto Rican librarian hired by the New York Public Library.

The emphases you place on passage contents go far in determining what students make of diversity. For instance, *Shabanu, Daughter of the Wind*, a novel about a Pakistani girl commonly found in middle schools, can be approached different ways. You might help students enter the novel through multiple entry points, such as enacting key scenes from the book and bringing in Middle Eastern artifacts (Benedicty, 1995). Or you might approach the novel with a critical eye, using it as a resource for discussing and cultivating positive views toward women (Ruggieri, 2001). You might directly address two issues the book portrays—violence toward women and girls' attitudes toward their physical appearance—along with other more subtle issues, such as gender roles in the household and gendered customs relative to universal actions like weddings and childbearing. Or you might approach it from a multicultural stance (Boyd, 2003). Journal responses, PowerPoint presentations, and body biographies could all be pointed toward comparing Shabanu's traditions and customs with others.

Textbooks

Textbooks play a needed role in education: They systematically introduce readers to a body of knowledge; they save you time by outlining learning sequences for students; and they specify content beforehand so you know how to plan. Textbooks provide the glue that holds together a wide assortment of facts and generalizations.

Effective teachers use textbooks selectively. They guide students through parts of the book that present content appropriately, point out textbook portions that reinforce what was introduced in class, and consult the text as a reference source. They selectively use accompanying textbook resources.

Assessing the match among textbooks, students, and the curriculum is an important aspect of teaching. Deciding if one book—or one section of a book—is more effective than another comes into play when you adopt materials for course use and decide what specifics to use when teaching. One way to make such an assessment involves textbook rating scales.

TEXTBOOK RATING SCALES Rating scales call for you to examine material and assign a subjective, but informed, rating. Rating scales pinpoint aspects of a text, and you judge their quality.

Figure 4.1 contains a textbook rating scale that we have found to be useful. As you rate each aspect of text this scale identifies, continually ask yourself how much support your students would require.

As you study this scale, ask yourself what you might add, modify, or delete. For instance, you might add to item 15, which addresses bias. One way to check on bias is to examine materials for stereotyping, omissions, distortions, and language bias:

- Stereotyping occurs when all individuals in a particular group are depicted as having the same attribute: Are Native Americans characterized as warlike? Are women presented as dependent?
- Omissions occur when the contributions of particular groups are underrepresented: Are women's roles in westward expansion described? Are scientific discoveries by physically disabled individuals noted?
- Distortions systematically misrepresent certain groups. For instance, referring to Asian Americans rather than to Japanese or Chinese Americans gives a false impression of uniformity between these two groups. And depicting Native Americans in only historical or ceremonial settings ignores their contemporary status.
- Language bias happens when subtle, frequently subconscious choices about words affect the message about certain groups. Are revolutionaries working to overthrow an established government called terrorists or freedom fighters? Did Americans in the 1860s fight a Civil War or a War Between the States? Were African Americans given the right to vote, or did they win it?

The most effective textbook rating scales seem to be ones that school and school district staff produce on their own. Such scales can be based on the one shown in Figure 4.1 yet modified to fit local standards and particular student populations. Among other things, one group of social studies educators might consider primary sources to be essential in a textbook; a group of math teachers might emphasize vivid and feasible application activities; and a group of English instructors might be quite interested in authors from a particular region.

Title _____

Author(s) _____

Publisher _____ Copyright date _____

School district's intended audience _____

Directions: Rate the text according to each item below using a four-point scale, with 4 being high and 1 being low. Compare the text to an ideal instead of known materials.

After rating each item, decide how much you would need to guide students through the material in order to compensate for its shortcomings. Finally, form a holistic rating of the overall value of the text.

Very Desirable—"I would love to teach with this text!"

Desirable—"With a little support on my part, this text could be quite useful."

Undesirable—"I would have to spend a great deal of time and energy making up for the shortcomings of this text."

Very Undesirable—"I would not even hand out this text to my students!"

Adjunct Aids

____1. The text contains a detailed table of contents, index, and glossary.

____2. Objectives, introductions, graphic overviews, and summaries occur at appropriate intervals and indicate major ideas.

____3. Headings, subheadings, and italic and boldfaced words occur at appropriate intervals and indicate major ideas.

____4. Graphic aids such as illustrations, maps, and tables occur on the same page as the discussion or at least the facing page. These graphics clarify major ideas presented in the text; they do not introduce new ideas or simply decorate the page.

____5. Review, extension, and application activities such as questions, suggested readings, and projects occur at appropriate intervals. They relate directly to the major ideas and elicit a wide range of thinking.

Conceptual Development

____6. The chapters emphasize fundamental concepts or principles; they are more than encyclopedic collections of related information. Facts are presented to develop the explicitly stated concepts or principles.

____7. Explanations of new ideas include memorable analogies, clear references to previously presented information, and concrete examples. The explanations consist of more than dull dictionary-type wording.

____8. The amount of technical vocabulary on each page is appropriate for the intended audience.

Motivation Arousal

____9. The text includes introductory comments, questions, and scenarios to arouse curiosity about the upcoming contents.

____10. The text explains how learners might use the information in real-life situations.

____11. The text cover, print size, graphics, and layout are appealing to the intended audience.

Organization

____12. The chapters could be outlined easily. The paragraphs and sections move forward in a logical manner.

____13. The text explicitly signals how information is arranged. Topic paragraphs and sentences include such statements as, "There are three reasons for this outcome" and "The following presents the key events."

Special Concerns

____14. The text fits the course objectives.

____15. Groups of people are presented authentically. There is no bias.

____16. A teacher's manual provides helpful suggestions for presenting the textual information.

FIGURE 4.1 Textbook Rating Scale.

DO IT TOGETHER

Form small groups of three or four students each according to academic specialization (e.g., social studies, mathematics, English). If you teach all subjects, select a particular one for this activity. Go on a scavenger hunt to locate and bring to class on a certain date published materials that fit your specialization in each of the following categories. On the day that everything is brought in, share the materials you found. Indicate what is special about their contents, writing styles, and potential classroom uses.

Reading Materials Scavenger Hunt List

Reference materials
Periodicals
Digital resources
Trade books
Multicultural literature
Textbooks

EXHIBITS TAKE MANY FORMS

The term *exhibit* refers to what students construct after they engage with instruction. Exhibits typically are somewhat open ended and flexible. As noted in the preceding chapter, students often produce exhibits in response to units of instruction. Exhibits also can be in response to any single reading material or set of materials and be assigned by you or designed by your students. Effective exhibits include combinations of visual displays, concrete displays, dramatizations, writing, and discussing.

Visual Displays

If a culminating activity is to "Describe why people immigrate" or "Explain why the Grand Canyon is so grand," visual displays might be a key part of the exhibit. Visuals can stretch minds in ways that words cannot (Zoss, 2009). Visuals such as the following might be computer generated, produced freehand, or gathered from available resources.

ILLUSTRATIONS   Students often draw pictures, use computer graphics, collect photographs, take their own photographs, and make posters or bulletin boards in order to depict ideas and information. Realistic or impressionistic sketches also are appropriate. Such visuals graphically depict what words can only suggest. For example, the Grand Canyon, cell division, parts of the body, and geometric figures are natural candidates for illustrated projects.

TIME LINES AND MURALS   The key events of a phenomenon are frequently displayed on a time line. Any number of illustrations, or none at all, may be on the time line. The essential feature is that events are labeled and represented in sequence on a linear chart. Murals can be similar to time lines in that they represent a sequence of events; the difference, of course, is that murals consist solely of pictures.

STORYBOARDS   The film industry originated storyboarding to represent scenes to be filmed, but educators now use the term to refer to any set of illustrations that depict a sequence of events. Your students can storyboard the key scenes from a narrative they have read or plan to write. They can storyboard scientific processes such as photosynthesis and the water cycle as well as social events such as the 1920s or the labor movement.

MAPS   Representing an area visually requires careful reading, reviewing, and composing. Students need to decide what locations to represent and then produce that representation. Illustrations can be added to maps for greater detail. Maps can depict locations on many scales. For instance, locations within a building, a neighborhood, a community, a state, a nation, the world, or the universe can be mapped.

COLLAGES   Collages are groups of pictures and various other materials glued to a surface. These artistic compositions generally symbolize a topic. Making a collage of an area of study such as ethnic and racial groups, geographic locations, inventions, or animal groups can benefit students of all ages.

TABLES, GRAPHS, AND CHARTS   Displays of numerical data represented through tables, graphs, and charts and accompanied by written explanations are effective visuals. Your students might present findings from their polls, experiments, and surveys.

Concrete Displays

Your students can buy, borrow, or make concrete displays as part of their exhibits. Such displays could be the centerpiece of what students then talk or write about. Science fairs and open-house displays, which are traditional parts of many schools' curricula, are excellent examples of projects centering around concrete displays.

REPRESENTATIONS   Concrete displays frequently represent, or model, real-world phenomena. Students who study the formation of islands could fashion clay-and-water representations of their geological actions. Large entities such as buildings and land formations, as well as invisible processes such as evaporation and covalent bonding, can be modeled through concrete representations.

REALIA   Actual phenomena being studied, called *realia*, might be collected and displayed as part of an exhibit. Displaying pieces of sandstone, limestone, and shale concretely depicts types of sedimentary rock when exhibiting land formations. Young students constructing a exhibit on frontier living might collect objects that represent life on the western frontier in the 1800s. They can bring into class farm tools, kitchen implements, clothing, and assorted household items.

Dramatizations

Performing before others is a powerful device for promoting reading, writing, thinking, and learning (Pogrow, 2009; Zingher, 2006). Dramatically reading selected portions of a passage to classmates or to older or younger students is one form of dramatization.

Students can form pairs to review what they have read, with one student emphasizing the positive features and the other stressing the negative. Finally, students engaged in oral interpretation, dramatically reading selected portions of a text to their classmates or younger students, is another form of dramatization.

Dramatizations are ways for students to express ideas and understandings in a highly visible and active format. Four popular formats are described here.

SKITS   Many students like to stage short skits in reaction to what they have read and studied, simulating certain phenomena through action and dialogue. For example, older students might take Studs Terkel's *Working* and present selected scenes wherein people talk about the emotional side of their jobs and how their jobs affect their whole lives.

Reader's Theater

PANTOMIMES   With pantomime, students use creative physical movement to nonverbally represent a procedure, event, or concept. One person, often the teacher, might begin pantomime in the class by orally reading a passage while student-actors use gesture and movement to represent what is being said. As class members become adept with this technique, they can pantomime subject matter with no accompanying reading. After the performance, discuss the actors' accomplishments and the audience's thoughts. Some content area topics conducive to pantomime are as follows:

- *Mitosis* can be enacted with same-sex pairs of students wearing identically colored jerseys to represent chromosomes and students without jerseys encircling the pairs by joining hands in a large ring to represent a cell membrane. The group then depicts how it would produce another cell like itself (Wyn & Stegink, 2000).

Orally interpreting a passage is an effective book project.

- *Viral infections* can be presented with students acting as viruses entering, multiplying, and exiting cells.
- *The French Revolution* can be depicted with students acting as Louis XVI, members of the second estate, Robespierre, national assembly members, and Napoleon Bonaparte.
- *Paul Revere's ride and the battles of Lexington and Concord* can be portrayed with students acting as Paul Revere, colonists and the minutemen, and the British military.

ROLE-PLAY INTERVIEWS In role-play interviews, investigative reporters put questions to important figures from science, social studies, literature, or mathematics. The questioning can occur during a fictional news conference, talk show, or on-the-scene report.

Demonstrate role-play interviews before your students perform one. Generate questions that prompt long responses; follow up short yes/no responses with "Why?"; include various types of questions. Have your students dress and talk (as much as possible) in the manner of the participants. After the interview, discuss the actors' accomplishments and the audience's thoughts.

- When studying the ancient world, famous individuals can be interviewed, such as

Alexander the Great	Confucius	Siddharta Gautama
Iceman of the Alps	Liu Bang	Menes
Paul	Socrates	Thutmose III

- Interviews can be conducted with unnamed individuals representing groups such as

archaeologists	artisans	barbarians
caravan riders	disciples	martyrs
patricians	plebeians	regents

As students become adept with role-play interviews, they can include multiple reporters and/or figures during one interview session (e.g., bring together and interview Confucius, Siddharta Gautama, and Paul). Another option is for students to break into pairs or small groups and simulate an interview with the author of or a character from a text. Television talk shows provide a model for this interviewing format.

READERS' THEATER Readers' theater is a productive way for students to dramatize what they have read (Campbell & Cleland, 2003; Flynn, 2007). It is a method of oral interpretation that provides a relevant purpose for reading orally. You do not need to prepare special scripts for readers' theater; have students read directly from the passage. Most children who have basic reading proficiencies enjoy reading plays; readers' theater allows playlike reading with regular prose.

When you first introduce readers' theater, have a small group demonstrate the process. Show how each speaking part is indicated in the text with quotation marks and how the speaker is revealed by the flow of the conversation. The narrator's role of reading all the material outside the quotation marks should be made clear. When first presenting this activity, the narrator might read all the "he said" and "she said" phrases, but this practice should be stopped when the students become adept. Explain that only the key parts of a book and the parts that contain extensive dialogue should be selected for readers' theater.

When readers' theater groups are formed, have the students first react to the entire passage so they have a good understanding of what they are staging. Then have them identify and practice their parts before reading. Some groups tape-record themselves and submit the recording as their exhibit, and others perform for the class. Simple props and sound effects frequently are included. Readers' theater is quite popular among students, so you might consider setting aside a certain time of the week for these presentations.

TRY IT OUT

Produce a visual display, a concrete display, or a dramatization in response to this chapter. Share your exhibit with your class or a small group of classmates.

Writing

Writing is part of most exhibits. You might have students regularly write very brief compositions, such as notes or reactions during a unit, and then collect all the writing as a culminating exhibit. Or you might have students work toward one large composition to submit at the end of a unit. Chapter 7, "Writing," and Chapter 9, "Inquiry through Digital Literacies," add to what we present here relative to writing.

To stimulate and structure students' exhibits, provide writing prompts. Prompts urge and inspire action; they cue people to move forward. Prompts can be questions ("What was the most important word in what you just studied?") or directives ("Describe the most important word in what you just studied.").

Generic prompts fit any material. They contain language that is appropriate for anything students read. Generic prompts apply to more than one piece of text. For instance, students can learn to ask, "What have I learned?" after each reading. To do so is a powerful strategy. In addition, teachers can regularly demonstrate how they answer a question such as, "What have I learned?" thereby providing a pattern for students to follow. Figure 4.2 contains numerous generic prompts. Two common writing projects that utilize prompts are response journals and reaction guides.

RESPONSE JOURNALS   Response journals allow students to explore ideas, ask questions, and express feelings about what they are learning. Teachers often introduce journals by presenting an entry or two and showing how they respond to particular prompts.

Numerous response journal prompts can be added to the questions presented in Figure 4.2. When reading a narrative, readers might respond in the form of a character journal, a written log readers keep as they assume the identity of a main character. Another option is to provide writing stems that address various aspects of a passage. After first exemplifying appropriate responses, you might have students complete stems such as the following:

- The most important word in the chapter is . . .
- The most important thing about . . . is . . .
- The most incredible thing about . . . is . . .
- The worst thing about . . .
- An unbelievable thing about . . .
- The simple facts about . . .
- The truth about . . .

Universal Reading-Response Prompts

What will I/you remember about this material?

What ideas did I/you gain from my/your reading?

How did this material help me/you better understand the world?

What is the most important word, sentence, or section?

What materials have I/you read that are similar?

What does this material remind me/you of?

What was the author trying to share?

What is the most important message of this material?

How will I/you think differently after reading this material?

What questions did the material leave unanswered?

Information for a Best Friend

How could I convince my best friend to read this material?

What would my/your best friend like to know about this material?

Should I/you tell a friend to read this? Why?

Image

What pictures, sounds, and other sensory feelings did I/you experience while reading this material?

Evaluation

What did I/you like best about this material?

What was my/your favorite part of this material?

Should the material receive a literary award? Why?

Is anything missing that should be included? What?

If I/you rewrote this, what would I/you change?

Is the material unique? Why?

What part of the material was realistic or unrealistic?

Literary Structure

What event begins the story?

What situation in the story reminded me/you of a situation from my/your own life?

What did I/you think was going to happen when _____?

How would I/you have reacted to the situations in the story?

If I/you were _____, what would I/you have done when _____?

If I/you could become a part of the story, at what point would I/you like to enter? What would I/you do?

Characterization

Why did the main character behave as he or she did?

Which characters, if any, did I/you especially like or dislike? Why?

Did any characters change? If so, how?

What did the characters learn?

What advice would I/you give the characters?

FIGURE 4.2 Generic Prompts for Written and Oral Compositions.

Emotions

How did _____ feel when _____ happened?

What parts made me/you feel the strongest?

Did any part of the material surprise me/you? Why?

Author's Craft

How did the author hold my/your attention?

How did the author signal important information?

How did the author reveal the meanings of difficult or unfamiliar terms?

How did the author organize the material?

How did the author balance illustrations and print?

How did the author develop his or her ideas?

FIGURE 4.2 *Continued*

Students typically write in their journals several times a week. Replying to the students as an aunt or uncle instead of as teacher-as-examiner goes far in allowing you to express interest in students' insights and strategies. A special feature is that these journals allow you to stay in touch with each individual in class, not just the vocal ones; you can maintain a dialogue with the shyest student through journals.

REACTION GUIDES Teachers frequently distribute reaction guides to promote students' thinking. Reaction guides typically offer more structure than journals. Reaction guides for literary writing during English language arts instruction might contain items grouped according to traditional literary elements such as character, plot, setting, and theme. For instance, Figure 4.3 displays a sample guide for older readers that contains two items under

Directions: Complete one task that is listed under each literary element.

Character

1. Write to a friend, a member of your family, or an actor or actress a letter that describes how he or she is like a character in your book.
2. Pretend that you are one of the characters in your book. Write a letter to Ann Landers to get her advice on coping with the main problem you faced. Write her response.

Plot

1. Produce a calendar of events that reflects the story line. (The calendar can be divided among hours, days, weeks, months, or years.)
2. Produce a diary that one of the characters might have kept in order to chronicle the events of his or her life.

Setting

1. Pretend that the book is being turned into a one-hour special or a miniseries for television. Describe at least five locations where five different scenes should be filmed.
2. You are responsible for obtaining the props for a stage production of your book. List five props that are essential for the production and justify their use.

Theme

1. Describe at least one insight that the main character gained by the end of the book.
2. Describe how another book that you know makes the same point as the one you read.

FIGURE 4.3 Sample Literary Response Guide for Older Readers.

1. Tell how far you read before you knew for sure that you wanted to finish the book.
2. Describe your favorite part of a chapter or of the entire book.
3. Think of a book that is like the one you just read and explain how the two are alike.
4. Identify the main problem and its solution in the book.
5. Explain why you would or would not choose someone in the book for a friend.

FIGURE 4.4 Sample Literary Response Guide for Younger Readers.

each literary element; others certainly might be included. Figure 4.4 shows a sample literary response guide for young readers.

Reaction guides for expository writing differ from guides for literary materials because expository guides do not refer to story characters or the main problem and solution of the plot. Figure 4.5 shows an expository guide that fits younger as well as older readers.

Guides also can be produced that contain items fitting only the one book under consideration. For instance, if an adolescent chooses *Shipwreck at the Bottom of the World*, an award-winning account of the ill-fated 1914 Shackleton expedition to Antarctica, then the teacher or peers might help him or her decide which questions to address: Should the student portray and explain what caused Shackleton's ship, the *Endurance*, to be destroyed? Should he or she generate the most important reasons for no one dying during this ordeal? Should connections be made among this saga and contemporary ones? Should the quality and accuracy of Armstrong's presentation be evaluated?

You might produce reaction guides that fit certain types of materials. For instance, the following prompts fit only their respective genres:

- *Biography*: Describe how the individual was influenced by others as well as how he or she exerted an influence on others.
- *Movie tie-in*: Describe at least three differences between the book and the movie.
- *Mystery*: List the clues that led to the solution.

You might have students choose the items they wish to complete or create ones for themselves. You might require one or two activities, provide options (e.g., "Select two of the following four choices"), and encourage students to create their own way to react. Figure 4.6 displays a reaction guide that calls for choices.

Discussion

Discussions are verbal explorations of ideas among teachers and students and among students themselves. Individuals purposefully exchange their views.

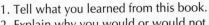

1. Tell what you learned from this book.
2. Explain why you would or would not choose to read other books by this author.
3. Describe what information in this book you would like to know more about.
4. Describe what made this book interesting.
5. Explain how you might use what you learned from this book.

FIGURE 4.5 Sample Expository Response Guide.

Directions: Complete items 1 and 2 listed below.
1. Describe what became clear to you while reading this material.
2. Describe one question you had after reading.

Directions: Mark one item from the list below and complete it.
_____ Poster advertising the book
_____ Display of at least five items representing the book
_____ Skit depicting an event from the book
_____ Conference on selected parts of the book

Directions: Create one additional way to react to your book. Describe below what you will do.

_____

_____

FIGURE 4.6 Sample Reaction Guide Offering Choices.

Discussions provide opportunities for participants to think of things they otherwise might not have considered. They obtain new insights and perspectives (Applebee, Langer, Nystrand, & Gamoran, 2003; Nystrand, 2006). "I hadn't thought of that!" is a common response during effective discussions.

Discussants engage in a dialogue—not in a recitation in which an answer or a solution has been determined beforehand. Ideal patterns of group talk move from student to student rather than only from teacher to student in ping-pong fashion. The talk lasts at least several minutes, with you and your students taking up others' ideas, expanding them, or asking follow-up questions.

When using discussion as a unit's culminating activity, be sure to plan for it. Present a unit's essential question and highlight on the class calendar when your class will be able to publicly and thoroughly discuss responses to it. Prepare students for the culminating discussion by helping them gather and organize ideas for this event. You might have your class move their seating arrangement into a large circle in order to face one another during the discussion; sometimes you might have your classes move into several small circles.

To begin a discussion, you might use an open-ended item such as one of those listed in Figure 4.2. An important rule is to ask only those questions that you consider to have more than one possibly acceptable answer. If you are committed to a single correct answer, then the students' task becomes one of determining what is in your mind rather than of thinking on their own terms. Discussions are give-and-take dialogues in which teachers are not committed to single correct answers.

To keep talk going after a student has finished speaking, consider these classic four moves: statements, student questions, signals, and silence:

1. *Statements* are someone's selected thoughts related to what has just been said. You might state your understanding ("As I understand it, you're saying . . ."), describe what you would like to have expanded ("I'm interested in hearing more about . . ."), indicate your state of mind ("I'm confused about . . ."), or relate what has just been said with what has been previously stated ("So you're saying . . . , while _____ is saying . . .").

2. *Student questions* often seem to invigorate discussions more than teachers' questions. Your role, then, is to encourage and facilitate such questions. You might state, "This seems to be a good time to know what else we should be asking about," then wait for someone to initiate a new direction in the exchange. Many teachers post questions for students to ask to keep a discussion moving. Questions such as the following move a discussion forward while addressing rigor and accountability: "Can you support that?" "Where did you find that information?" "Can you give us some examples?" "Why do you think that?" and "Can you explain that more fully?"

3. *Signals* are somewhat neutral gestures that indicate you heard what a student said and are ready for someone else to talk. Signals might consist of a comment such as, "All right," "Well said," or "Okay." You can nod your head in agreement or lift your hands and eyebrows in wonder.

4. *Silence* can go far in encouraging students to speak. Keeping silent for at least five seconds after a prompt by you or after a comment by a student might not seem like much, but it is a clear indication that someone should speak. This wait time can be powerful.

Maintaining appropriate social support during discussions is especially important. Free-flowing talk about compelling issues risks inflaming passions and diminishing civility. It potentially enables powerful, outspoken individuals to marginalize others. Consequently, a classroom climate that promotes respect is essential. Respectful discussions are accomplished in part by articulating and demonstrating what respect looks like, sounds like, and feels like. Clarify expectations along these lines, have students enact them in small-group demonstrations, and hold individuals accountable for them. You might display expectations such as the following:

Respectful Discussions

Look Like	Sound Like	Feel Like
• People face each other.	• One person at a time talks.	• My ideas are being taken seriously.
• People concentrate on what each other is saying.	• Remain on task.	• I'm confident that I will learn from others and they will learn from me.
• Friendly faces	• Give-and-take of ideas	

Finally, discussions conducted online are promising sites for exchanging ideas about literacy and learning (Grisham & Wolsley, 2006). An online discussion group consists of individuals who make use of a particular Web site to post their ideas and opinions about a topic and comment on others' postings. Individuals over time receive comments about their postings along with new postings for them to comment on. This is done asynchronously, not at the same time, with the postings accumulating in the central site. Asynchronous dialogue retains the interactive nature of traditional discussions and adds deliberative, self-paced time to reflect and write.

As with any teaching plan, online discussion groups require structure. Online discussants benefit from models of online discussions so they realize expectations for theirs. They benefit from scoring guides that help identify and ensure fair assessments of the frequency and content of their postings. And they profit from ongoing monitoring and reminders of netiquette, academic focus, and Web site access. Such structure goes far in enhancing learners' voices in what and how they are learning.

LOOKING BACK

When you use diverse reading materials in your classroom, you and your students can benefit greatly. Your teaching and your students' learning are energized. Reading materials vary from computer technology to trade books to periodicals. Students can respond to these materials in many ways, too. In this chapter, you encountered three key ideas: (1) Students deserve diverse content area reading materials during instructional units; (2) diverse content area reading materials are available for instructional units; and (3) exhibits take many forms.

ADD TO YOUR JOURNAL

Think about the role of diverse reading materials in the classes that you will be teaching. How far beyond the text do you intend to go? What types of materials will you use? How do you intend to have students respond to what they read? What exhibits will you use as culmination activities?

Additional Readings

These four references provide valuable ideas and information about reading engagement and motivation.

Gambrel, L. (1996). Creating classroom cultures that foster reading motivation. *The Reading Teacher, 50*(1), 14–25.

Guthrie, J. T., & Wigfield, A. (2000). Engagement and motivation in reading. In M. J. Kamil, P. B. Mosenthal, P. D. Pearson, & R. Barr (Eds.), *Handbook of reading research* (vol. 3, pp. 406–424). Mahwah, NJ: Lawrence Erlbaum Associates.

Marinak, B. A., & Gambrell, L. B. (2007). Rewarding reading? Perhaps authenticity is the answer. *Teachers College Record.* Retrieved June 2, 2009, from www.tcrecord.org/PrintContent.asp?ContentID=15608

Margolis, H., & Mccabe, P. P. (2006). Improving self-efficacy and motivation: What to do, what to say. *Intervention in School and Clinic, 41,* 218–227.

This book is a comprehensive yet accessible guide to children's and young adult literature:

Gillespie, J.T. (2005). *The children's and young adults literature handbook: A research and reference guide.* Santa Barbara, CA: Libraries Unlimited.

The following present literature across the curriculum for children:

Culinan, B. E., & Person, D. G. (Eds.). (2005). *The Continuum encyclopedia of children's literature.* New York, NY: Continuum.

Lima, C. W., & Thomas, R. L. (2008). *A to zoo:* Santa Barbara, CA: Libraries Unlimited.

Olness, R. (2007). *Using literature to enhance content area instruction.* Newark, DE: International Reading Association.

Zarian, B. B. (2004). *Around the world with historical fiction and folktales: Highly recommended and award-winning books, grades K–8.* Lanham, MD: Scarecrow Press.

These references present literature across the curriculum for young adults:

Barr, C., & Gillespie, J. T. (2009). *Best books for high school readers: Grades 9–12* (2nd ed.) Westport, CT: Libraries Unlimited.

Koelling, H. (2009). *Best books for young adults* (3rd ed.). Chicago, IL: American Library Association.

Nilsen, A. P., & Donelson, K. L. (2008). *Literature for today's young adults* (8th ed.). Boston, MA: Allyn & Bacon.

Wise uses of digital resources for subject matter study are suggested in the following:

Grabe, M., & Grabe, C. (2006). *Integrating technology for meaningful learning* (5th ed.). New York, NY: Wadsworth Publishing.

Kuiper, E., Volman, M., & Terwel, J. (2005). The web as an information resource in K–12 education: Strategies for supporting students in searching and processing information. *Review of Educational Research, 75,* 285–328.

Reading materials that expose students to new, possibly controversial ideas risk offending parents and community members. Prepare for this possibility by examining the following.

Reichman, H. (2001). *Censorship and selection: Issues and answers for schools* (3rd ed.). Chicago, IL: American Library Association.

Simmons, J. S., & Dresang, E. T. (2001). *School censorship in the 21st century.* Newark, DE: International Reading Association.

Leading discussions of what students have read is complex. The following books suggest ways to conduct productive discussions.

Copeland, M. (2005). *Socratic circles: Fostering critical and creative thinking in middle and high school.* Portland, ME: Stenhouse.

Holden, J., & Schmit, J. S. (Eds.). (2002). *Inquiry and the literary text: Constructing discussions in the English classroom.* Urbana, IL: National Council of Teachers of English.

The following multicultural book selection guide suggests appropriate children's and young adults' titles:

Cai, M. (2006). *Multicultural literature for children and young adults.* Charlotte, NC: Information Age.

The following summarize what researchers have learned about readers' interactions with literature.

Galda, L., Ash, G. A., & Cullinan, B. E. (2000). Children's literature. In M. J. Kamil, P. B. Mosenthal, P. D. Pearson, & R. Barr (Eds.), *Handbook of reading research* (vol. 3, pp. 361–379). Mahwah, NJ: Lawrence Erlbaum Associates.

Marshall, J. (2000). Research on response to literature. In M. J. Kamil, P. B. Mosenthal, P. D. Pearson, & R. Barr (Eds.), *Handbook of reading research* (vol. 3, pp. 381–402). Mahwah, NJ: Lawrence Erlbaum Associates.

Martinez, M., & Roser, N. L. (2003). Children's responses to literature. In J. Flood, D. Lapp, J. R. Squire, & J. M. Jensen (Eds.), *Handbook of research on teaching the English language arts* (2nd ed., pp. 799–813). Mahwah, NJ: Lawrence Erlbaum Associates.

Morrow, L. M., & Gambrell, L. B. (2000). Literature-based reading instruction. In M. J. Kamil, P. B. Mosenthal, P. D. Pearson, & R. Barr (Eds.), *Handbook of reading research* (vol. 3, pp. 563–586). Mahwah, NJ: Lawrence Erlbaum Associates.

Online Resources

You can access rich collections of digital media for your units in these sites.

Annenberg Media
http://www.learner.org/index.html

Federal Resources for Educational Excellence
http://www.free.ed.gov/index.cfm

The Library of Congress Teacher Resources
www.loc.gov/teachers/

The National Archives
http://www.archives.gov/education/

National Geographic Society
http://www.nationalgeographic.com/education/

PBS
http://www.pbs.org/teachers/

Smithsonian Education
http://www.smithsonianeducation.org/educators/

Teachers' Domain
http://www.teachersdomain.org

These sites are central sources for classroom media and technology.

Center for Media Literacy
http://www.medialit.org/best_practices.html

Technology in Education Resource Center
http://www.rtec.org/index.cfm

This site allows you to identify award-winning literature according to options such setting, historical period, and ethnicity/nationality of the protagonist or tale.

Database of Award-Winning Children's Literature
www.dawcl.com

Children's and Young Adults' Trade Books Noted in Chapter 4

Armstrong, J. (1999). *Shipwreck at the bottom of the world*. New York, NY: Crown.

Armstrong, W. H. (1969). *Sounder*. New York, NY: Harper & Row.

Base, G. (1987). *Animalia*. New York, NY: Abrams.

Bishop, N. (2008). *Frogs*. New York, NY: Scholastic.

Bunting, E. (1991). *Fly away home*. New York, NY: Clarion.

Campbell, S. C. (2008). *Wolfsnail: A backyard predator*. Honesdale, PA: Boyds Mills Press.

Coerr, E. (1993). *Sadako*. New York, NY: Putnam.

Demi. (1997). *One grain of rice: A mathematical folktale*. New York, NY: Scholastic.

Donovan, J. (1969). *I'll get there, it better be worth the trip*. New York, NY: Harper & Row.

Edwards, P. D. (1996). *Some smug slug*. New York, NY: HarperCollins.

Fleischman, P. (1993). *Bull run*. New York, NY: HarperCollins.

Fox, P. (1991). *Monkey island*. New York, NY: Orchard.

Gibson, M. (1982). *Gods, men, and monsters from the Greek myths*. New York, NY: Schocken.

González, L. (2008). *The storyteller's candle/La velita de los cuentos*. San Francisco, CA: Children's Book Press.

Griffin, J. H. (1977). *Black like me*. Boston, MA: Houghton Mifflin.

Haddon, M. (2003). *The curious incident of the dog in the night-time*. New York, NY: Vintage.

Hersey, J. (1946). *Hiroshima*. New York, NY: Knopf.

Hoban, T. (1990). *Exactly the opposite*. Westport, CT: Greenwillow.

Hobbs, W. (1996). *Downriver*. New York, NY: Dell.

Holland, I. (1994). *Behind the lines*. New York, NY: Scholastic.

Hunt, I. (1964). *Across five Aprils*. Chicago, IL: Follett.

Krakauer, J. (1997). *Into thin air*. New York, NY: Villard.

London, J. (1993). *Voices of the wild*. New York, NY: Crown.

Lowell, S. (2004). *Dusty Locks and the three bears*. New York, NY: Owlet.

Macaulay, D. (2008). *The way we work: Getting to know the amazing human body*. New York, NY: Houghton Mifflin

Meltzer, M. (1996). *World of our fathers: A history of Jewish life from Eastern Europe to America*. Northvale, NJ: J. Aronson.

Mowat, F. (1963). *Never cry wolf*. Boston, MA: Little, Brown.

O'brien, T., & Sullivan, M. P. (2008). *Afghan dreams: Young voices of Afghanistan*. New York, NY: Bloomsbury.

Parks, R. (1992). *Rosa Parks: Mother to a movement*. New York, NY: Dial.

Patent, D. H. (2008). *When the wolves returned: Restoring nature's balance in Yellowstone*. New York, NY: WalkerBooks.

Peck, R. N. (1972). *A day no pigs would die*. New York, NY: Dell.

Pilling, A. (1993). *Realms of gold: Myths and legends from around the world*. New York, NY: Kingfisher.

Seeger, L. V. (2007) *First the egg*. New York, NY: Roaring Brook Press.

Seltzer, I. (1992). *The house I live in: At home in America*. New York, NY: Macmillan.

Smith, B. (1992). *The first voyage of Columbus*. New York, NY: Viking.

Staples, S. F. (1989). *Shabanu, daughter of the wind*. New York, NY: Knopf.

Terkel, S. (1981). *Working*. New York, NY: Simon & Schuster.

Thomas, V. M. (1997). *Lest we forget: The passage from Africa to slavery and emancipation*. New York, NY: Crown.

Watson, J. D. (2001). *The double helix*. New York, NY: Touchstone.

Wolfe, T. (1979). *The right stuff*. New York, NY: Farrar, Straus & Giroux.

Yolen, J. (1992). *The encounter*. San Diego, CA: Harcourt Brace Jovanovich.

Yolen, J. (2007). *Owl moon*. New York, NY: Philomel Books.

References

Applebee, A. N., Langer, J., Nystrand, M., & Gamoran, A. (2003). Discussion-based approaches to developing understanding: Classroom instruction and student performance in middle and high school English. *American Educational Research Journal, 40*, 685–730.

Atkinson, T. S., Matusevich, M. N., & Huber, L. (2009). Making science trade book choices for elementary classrooms. *The Reading Teacher, 62*(6), 484–497.

Au, K. H. (2006). *Multicultural issues and literacy achievement*. Mahwah, NJ: Erlbaum.

Benedicty, A. (1995). Reading *Shabanu,* creating multiple entry points for diverse readers. *Voices from the Middle, 2*(1), 12–17.

Boyd, F. (2003). Experiencing things not seen: Educative events centered on a study of *Shabanu. Journal of Adolescent and Adult Literacy, 46*, 460–470.

Boyd, F. B., & Brock, C. H. (Eds.). (2004). *Multicultural and multilingual literacy and language: Contexts and practices*. New York, NY: Guilford.

Campbell, M., & Cleland, J. V. (2003). *Readers theatre in the classroom: A manual for teachers of children and adults*. Lincoln, NE: Iuniverse.

Coiro, J., Knobel, M., Lankshear, C., & Leu, D. J. (Eds.). (2008). *Handbook of research on new literacies*. Mahwah, NJ: Erlbaum.

Culham, R. (2004). *Using picture books to teach writing with the traits*. New York, NY: Scholastic.

Cunningham, A. E. (2005). Vocabulary growth through independent reading and reading aloud to children. In E. H. Hiebert & M. L. Kamil (Eds.), *Teaching and learning vocabulary: Bringing research to practice* (pp. 45–68). New York, NY: Routledge.

Finkelstein, N. H. (1999). *The way things never were: The truth about the "good old days."* New York, NY: Atheneum.

Flynn, R. M. (2007). *Dramatizing the content with curriculum-based readers theatre, grades 6–12*. Newark, DE: International Reading Association.

Greene, S. (Ed.). (2008). *Literacy as a civil right: Reclaiming social justice in literacy teaching and learning*. New York, NY: Peter Lang.

Grisham, D. L, & Wolsey, T. D. (2006). Recentering the middle school classroom as a vibrant learning community: Students, literacy, and technology intersect. *Journal of Adolescent and Adult Literacy, 49*, 648–660.

Hunsader, P. D. (2004). Mathematics trade books: Establishing their value and assessing their quality. *The Reading Teacher, 57*, 618–629.

International Reading Association. (2001). *Integrating literacy and technology in the curriculum: A position statement*. Retrieved August 25, 2005 from the International Reading Association Web site: www.reading.org/resources/issues/positions_technology.html.

Krashen, S. (2004). *The power of reading* (2nd ed.). Englewood, CO: Libraries Unlimited.

Lankshear, C., & Knobel, M. (Eds.). (2008). *Digital literacies: Concepts, policies and practices*. New York, NY: Peter Lang.

Loewen, J. W. (2007). *Lies my teacher told me: Everything your American history textbook got wrong* (2nd ed.). New York, NY: Touchstone.

Marlette, P. B., & Gordon, C. J. (2004). The use of alternative texts in physical education. *Journal of Adolescent and Adult Literacy, 48*, 226–237.

Nystrand, M. (2006). Research on the role of discussion as it affects reading comprehension. *Research in the Teaching of English, 40*(4), 392–412.

Pogrow, S. (2009). *Teaching content outrageously: How to captivate all students and accelerate learning, grades 4&12*. San Francisco, CA: Jossey-Bass.

Ravitch, D. (2003). *The language police: How pressure groups restrict what students learn*. New York, NY: Knopf.

Ruggieri, C. A. (2001). What about our girls? Considering gender roles in *Shabanu*. *The English Journal, 90*(3), 48–53.

Wyn, M. A., & Stegink, S. J. (2000). Role-playing mitosis. *The American Biology Teacher, 62*, 378–381.

Zile, S. V., & Napoli, M. (2009). *Teaching literary elements with picture books: Engaging, standards-based lessons and strategies*. New York, NY: Scholastic.

Zingher, G. (2006). *Theme play: Exciting young imaginations*. Westport, CT: Libraries Unlimited.

Zoss, M. (2009). Visual arts and literacy. In L. Christenbury, R. Bomer, & P. Smagorinsky (Eds.), *Handbook of adolescent literacy research* (pp. 183–196). New York, NY: Guilford.

CHAPTER 5

Comprehension

LOOKING AHEAD

Most of the time, readers take comprehension for granted. They decode words and automatically understand the message. But comprehension does not always occur automatically. Excellent decoding skills sometimes are not enough. The following passage from a classic statistics book (Kirk, 1972) shows that comprehension is more than a matter of merely pronouncing each word correctly:

> Fractional factorial designs have much in common with confounded factorial designs. The latter designs, through the technique of confounding, achieve a reduction in the number of treatment combinations that must be included within a block. A fractional factorial design uses confounding to reduce the number of treatment combinations in the experiment. As is always the case when confounding is used, the reduction is obtained at a price. There is considerable ambiguity in interpreting the outcome of a fractional factorial experiment, since treatments are confounded with interactions. For example, a significant mean square might be attributed to the effects of treatment A or to a BCDE interaction. (p. 256)

Did you understand this passage? Could you retell it to someone in your own words without looking back at the text?

Comprehension is automatic when reading about topics for which you have adequate background, know most of the appropriate vocabulary, and understand enough to sort out important from trivial information. People who are knowledgeable about statistics fully comprehend the sample paragraph; typically, it makes little sense to nonstatisticians. Students often are in this position when reading in the content areas, so they require support. This chapter on supporting comprehension contains three keys:

1. Plan levels of comprehension support.
2. Provide scaffolds for challenging passages.
3. Teach reading comprehension strategies.

PLAN LEVELS OF COMPREHENSION SUPPORT

Not all content reading is—or should be—like what you probably just experienced with the fractional factorial design passage. As Chapter 4 showed, countless well-written, richly presented books, pamphlets, online sites, and so on, are available. Extensive reading of high-quality informational literature increases students' subject matter knowledge and reading competence. Engaging your class with accessible materials as Chapter 4 described goes far in promoting comprehension. However, students often require support with even the best reading materials.

Planning appropriate levels of support is a good way to begin planning how to give students what they need to comprehend satisfactorily. Sometimes substantial support is needed because students are far from ready for the challenge certain materials present. Sometimes, practically nothing is needed. In order to begin planning comprehension supports appropriately, consider reader–text matches.

Reader–Text Matches

Assessing the match between readers and the texts they have to read informs your instructional decisions. It involves determining how challenging particular passages are relative to particular readers. Educators traditionally have discerned three levels of reader–text match: frustration, instructional, and independent.

FRUSTRATION   When passages are as challenging as the one on fractional factorial designs presented earlier, frustration readily sets in and students often skip it, have others explain it, or—if there is a test—try to memorize its contents. When your students read material at their frustration levels, they will retell only about half of the key ideas and information. Their oral reading will by choppy and halting, and they will miscall more than 10 percent of the words. They frequently will show signs of frustration such as fidgeting, scowling, and sighing. They will tend to avoid the task, although such avoidance might be due to limited motivation, engagement, and literate academic identity more than technical reading competence. Students might eventually gain partial knowledge of the passage, but it would take too much time to be productive.

The fractional factorial designs passage presents nonstatisticians an academic challenge that requires undue amounts of help and individual effort to be a worthwhile classroom teaching tool. For ease of reference, reading educators refer to this reader–text match simply as *frustration*.

INSTRUCTIONAL   Reader–text matches conducive to effective instruction are called *instructional*. A good word for matches at this level is *teachable*. Like the racquetball situation between David and Dean described in Chapter 2, instructional level is at the cutting edge of learners' abilities—neither too difficult nor too easy. After receiving some support, learners can accomplish a task independently, and they can learn to accomplish similar future tasks independently.

Your students who are reading material at their instructional levels will retell about three-quarters of the key ideas and information. Their oral reading will flow rather smoothly, and they will miscall no more than 10 percent of the words. If the work is engaging, they will tend to remain on task and successfully work through the few difficulties they encounter.

Instructional, teachable text is one that students will best understand and remember if someone supports their efforts. It also is the level at which students develop their strategies best. Teachable text is just challenging enough that a teacher is needed to help the majority of students understand and remember it. It is not so easy that most students can read and learn from it on their own. In brief, instructional-level, teachable texts are those in which your support is appropriate.

INDEPENDENT   When you read about something that is so familiar and well known to you that comprehension seems effortless and automatic, you probably are reading text with a challenge educators describe as *independent*. The write-up in the sports page of last night's basketball game, which your favorite team won, is probably independent for you. Even if you did not see the game, you know all the players, their positions, and the likely moves they would make. You could independently use the essential thinking processes described in Chapter 1, seeing scenes from the game in your mind's eye, connecting new information with what you already knew, organizing the ideas, and so on.

When your students are reading independent-level materials, they will retell about 95 percent of the key ideas and information. Their oral reading will flow smoothly, and they will miscall no more than 5 percent of the words. Assuming engaging work, they will tend to complete tasks with little or no trouble.

To be sure, readers match up with texts according to more than three isolated levels. Frustration, instructional, and independent reader–text matches are best seen as points on a support continuum, such as the following:

Frustration	Instructional	Independent
Maximum Support		Minimum Support

When readers are fully independent with materials, they require minimum support. When readers are on the frustration end of the continuum, they benefit from maximum support. Most of the time, however, readers are somewhere between these points.

Another way of considering reader-text matches and appropriate levels of support involves Vygotsky's (1978) zone of proximal development (ZPD). This zone designates what learners can accomplish only with assistance. For instance, many young students could comprehend Eve Bunting's *Fly Away Home* as long as someone assisted them by orienting them to the contents and explaining some key words. These same students could not comprehend Watson's *The Double Helix* no matter how much assistance they received because the concepts and words simply would be too complex for them. *Fly Away Home* would be in the students' ZPD, and working there would afford students maximum learning opportunities. As you present units to your students, be sure to provide a range of reading materials so that some are within your students' instructional reading levels—their zones of proximal development—where the most effective instruction occurs.

DO IT TOGETHER

Bring to mind the textbooks and other reading materials you read in previous courses. Think about the ones that approached your (a) frustration, (b) instructional, and (c) independent levels. Then think about what you learned from these different materials and how you responded to them. Share your experiences with a few classmates to personalize and apply your knowledge of reader–text matches.

Study Guides

When readers encounter instructional-level passages, they require more support than what is needed with independent-level passages. They do best with guidance. A common support along these lines is a study guide (Wood, Lapp, Flood, & Taylor, 2008). Study guides consist of questions and statements that direct students' reading. Study guides can help you clarify materials. Think of them as substitutes for the support you would provide your students if you, personally, could sit next to each of them and steer them through a passage.

Two useful and appealing study guides are point-of-view and interactive reading guides. Point-of-view reading guides (Figure 5.1) engage readers by making their reactions the central focus of the questions. The guide invites students to become one of the participants in what is being described and asks for their thoughts about and reactions to the events. Notice the use of the words *you* and *your*.

The distinctive feature of the interactive reading guide (Figure 5.2) is the interaction it ensures among students. Activities are to be done by individuals, pairs, small groups, and the whole class. As you look through the guide, notice that students have clear purposes for reading and that the actual reading is often done alone or with partners. The whole class gets together at certain points to brainstorm and discuss what is being learned.

Roman Empire

1. You are Julius Caesar preparing to march your troops across the Rubicon. Record your thoughts and feelings about this bold action.
2. As a plebeian, explain to a group of patricians why you wish to form the Concilium Plebis and elect tribunes.
3. As a farmer who lived before and during the beginning of the Pax Romana, tell how it affected your life.
4. As a gladiator talking with your peers, tell why you are appearing in the Colosseum.
5. As Marcus Aurelius, portray your concerns about the decline of the Roman Empire to your son, Commodus.

FIGURE 5.1 Point-of-View Guide.

Types of Rocks

Task: Acting as a geologist, produce a brief picture book appropriate for primary-grade children that explains the three main kinds of rocks.

1. As a class, brainstorm what we know about the three main kinds of rocks:

    Igneous   Sedimentary   Metamorphic

2. Read the section in your text on igneous rocks (pages 204–205), then work with your partner to revise what was brainstormed about this topic.
3. Read the section in your text on sedimentary rocks (pages 205–207), then work again with your partner to revise what was brainstormed about this topic.
4. Read the section in your text on metamorphic rocks (pages 207–208), working one last time with your partner to revise what was brainstormed.
5. As a class, generate what we now know about the three main kinds of rocks:

    Igneous   Sedimentary   Metamorphic

6. In groups of three, each person selects one of the three types of rock to explain. Each person then talks through what he or she plans to produce for the section of the picture book.
7. Each person produces a section of a picture book explaining one kind of rock.
8. Combine the three explanations into one finished product appropriate for donating to a primary-grade class.

FIGURE 5.2 Interactive Reading Guide.

LISTEN, LOOK, AND LEARN

Interview two teachers and two students who have used study guides. If possible, look at sample study guides and compare them with the two samples here. How do the teachers feel about the study guides? Is this different from how the students feel? Summarize what you learned, including the benefits and pitfalls of using study guides with instructional-level reading materials.

PROVIDE SCAFFOLDS FOR CHALLENGING PASSAGES

Imagine now that it is the first week of school. You have a list of state reading standards. You have met your students and have a general idea of their varied abilities. You also have one or more books and other resources that provide you with some teachable text for most of your students. You have a unit plan, but you now are thinking about specific lessons. You are looking through the available reading, listening, and viewing materials and have several critical decisions to make about providing scaffolds for challenging passages.

Planning Comprehension Scaffolds

CHOOSING WHAT MATERIAL TO USE   Using your time well is one of the keys to successful teaching. Books, curriculum guides, and other resources are filled with information. You know that you cannot teach it all and that, if you try, many students will retain very little.

As you look through your available resources, rate the various sections, chapters, parts, and so forth, on a three-star scale. One-star selections are parts or resources that may not be used at all or may be used by individual students as they pursue their own interests. Two-star selections are interesting, important, but not critical. You may have students work with these selections individually or in small groups, possibly with a study guide, as time and student needs permit. Three-star selections contain critical content in instructional, teachable text. Use whatever class time you can to guide readers through these three-star selections.

DETERMINING WHAT EVERYONE IS TO LEARN   Once you have determined which part of your books and other resources get the three-star rating and deserve full attention, decide what critical concepts you expect students to learn. Read the selection first, then list the most important ideas and information that are aligned with your unit's objectives, essential questions, and culminating activities. Listing what is critical does not limit students to learning or thinking about only these critical ideas, but it does mean that your students' attention will be focused on what is important, thus greatly increasing the chances that most students will learn. You now have the beginnings of objectives for your lesson.

DECIDING HOW TO ENGAGE STUDENTS WITH READING   Once you know what critical concepts you want students to take away from their reading, you must think about why they might want to learn them. Two factors substantially affect engagement (Guthrie &

Comprehension lesson planning involves many decisions.

Wigfield, 2000). One, expectations for success lead students to dedicate themselves to the task at hand. When your students feel they can successfully do what is being asked of them, they will be more determined to try. Many students have experienced failure with reading to learn, so they identify themselves as nonreaders. When reading is assigned with little support, students do not know what they are supposed to get out of it, so many just read and hope they will know whatever it is the teacher asks. Many give up because their past experience tells them they won't know it. Guidance in which you provide maximum support will convince students that they can successfully read in your subject and, over time, change their expectations of failure.

Interest is another factor to consider. How do you engage students' interest? A partial answer to this question comes from the unit launch practices described in Chapter 3 because engaging learners with lessons is much the same as engaging them with units. Realworld observing/participating, reading aloud, previewing passages, brainstorming, and writing can effectively grab students' attention and promote desire to learn during a lesson. Creating analogies and arousing curiosity are two other ways to accomplish this.

- Create analogies. A social studies teacher might create an analogy between parliamentary and congressional forms of government when the class is studying England, Canada, or Israel. A science teacher might create an analogy between airplane and bird wings when the class is studying birds. An algebra teacher might compare solving an equation with two or more unknowns to how Sherlock Holmes solves mysteries.
- Arouse curiosity. A health teacher might arouse readers' curiosity by explaining that the "no cholesterol" printed on packages of cookies or potato chips will not protect them from increasing their cholesterol level as a result of eating those foods. A French teacher might arouse readers' curiosity by stating that they will be reading a conversation in French between an advocate and an opponent of nuclear power plants.

BUILDING BACKGROUND KNOWLEDGE Students vary in the background knowledge they are able to call up about a particular topic. Students who live in Florida or California may know about oceans and oranges; midwestern students may be more familiar with wheat and blizzards. The author of your textbook may have assumed that your students can call up certain information that you know they lack. For instance, a passage on volcanoes may assume that students are aware of the bubbling action of heated liquids. Thus, the passage may deal primarily with volcanoes' effects on the earth's crust while failing to explain what pushes magma up through it. If students are confused about the initial thrust of the magma, they may not be able to follow the rest of the description of volcanic action. Thus, if certain information seems prerequisite to your students learning with a text, then you should plan to present it before having them read or listen to the text.

DESIGNING A GROUP TASK Once you know what students are to learn, how you will engage them with reading, and what background knowledge to build, you decide on a group task that students will complete during and after reading. This task must meet two criteria: completing the task must result in the students learning what is important, and the task must be clear to the students before they read.

Imagine, for example, that your objective is for students to be able to compare the composition and examples of the three main types of rocks. You might first present and have students feel actual rocks that exemplify the different types, put on view land formations composed of the different types, and invite students to share what they already know about the rocks. After engaging students' interest and activating their background

Type of Rock	Composition	Examples
Sedimentary		
Igneous		
Metamorphic		

FIGURE 5.3 Comparison Chart: Rocks.

knowledge, you might display a comparison chart like the one in Figure 5.3 as the joint task everyone is to complete en route to learning the texts' critical concepts.

This chart is one example of a group task that makes the objective clear and focuses on the important information. Depending on what you want students to learn, there is an endless variety of group tasks that will clearly communicate a purpose for reading. You might have students respond to an open-ended question ("How are the major types of rocks alike and different?"), rewrite the ideas and information in a picture book for children, or produce a display with actual rocks and a poster. You will see more examples of group tasks in the *Disciplinary Literacies* section at the end of this chapter.

Implementing Comprehension Scaffolds

As the section just presented shows, planning scaffolds to support your students' reading comprehension involves decisions about (a) instructional-level materials, (b) the critical concepts to emphasize, (c) engagement with the material, (d) background knowledge, and (e) a group task. Now you decide how you will implement the scaffolds.

Comprehension lessons have discernible beginnings, middles, and endings. While it is impossible to set firm guidelines about how much time to spend in each phase, many teachers find that dividing the time roughly into thirds is reasonable. With this distribution of time, the before-, during-, and after-reading phases are seen as more or less equally important in determining what students will learn from their scaffolded reading.

BEFORE READING Perhaps the most important part of the before phase of a scaffolded comprehension lesson is clarifying the students' group task. What is clear to you as the teacher is often a mystery to your students. Has an English teacher ever told you to read so that you can discuss how the setting of a story or novel affects the plot development? In order to accomplish this purpose, you must understand clearly what setting and plot entail, then clearly perceive the setting, follow the plot, and finally get to the task of thinking about how setting and plot interact. This complex task is further complicated by the jargon— *setting* and *plot*. Many students are confused by such terminology as *setting, plot, main idea*, and *summary*. When alerting students to the purposes for which you would like them to read, try to avoid unnecessary jargon or make the jargon clear by including examples.

In a situation in which the interaction between setting and plot was important, students would be more apt to understand what you wanted them to read for if you drew on the board a diagram such as Figure 5.4. Note the similarities between this plot/setting diagram and the comparison chart presented in Figure 5.3; both are meant to convey publicly and clearly what students are to take away from the text.

After displaying the diagram, you could explain to students that the setting changes three times during the story and that certain things happen in the different settings. Students should read so they can fill in the three settings and the major events that happened in each

Teachers scaffold student's comprehension.

	Setting (Time and Place)	Plot (What Happened)
Beginning of story		
Middle of story		
End of story		

How did the setting at different points in the story affect what happened?

FIGURE 5.4 Plot/Setting Diagram.

setting. They should also think about how the different times and places affected what did and did not happen.

In this example, you have clarified the task by explaining what is meant by the jargon *setting* and *plot*. You have also written the chart and the question on the board so that as students read, they can look up and think about what they can contribute to the group task of filling in the chart and responding to the question. When students have the necessary background knowledge, engagement and know their purpose for reading, they are ready to move into the next phase.

DURING READING   Now as your students read to complete the group task, provide other scaffolds. Often students read silently, but the reading can take other forms. Students can be paired and read the passage together, with each one taking a page or a paragraph. They might highlight important ideas by recording notes or posting sticky notes at appropriate spots in a passage. As they read, you may notice their eyes going up to the board as they come upon some piece of information they want to include. You may need to interrupt the reading after a few minutes and point to the task on the board to remind students of it.

AFTER READING   If you have set a clear task, clarifying the objective, and provided your students scaffolds during their reading, what happens afterwards is done readily: students complete the task, then review it.

Talk about what your students accomplished and how they did it. For the setting–plot task discussed above, you might have students share their responses about how the setting affected what happened at different points in the story. Offer feedback to the responses. You might then be ready to take this learning to a new level by teaching your students how to write their own stories where the setting clearly affects the plot.

Closing Words about Comprehension Scaffolds

Scaffolding readers through challenging—but not defeating—texts as presented here goes far in developing comprehension of future passages as well as the particular one at hand. This practice promotes knowledge of the world, which is crucial background for making sense of print (Hirsch, 2003). As students develop their understandings of concepts such as the types of rocks and plot-setting relationships, they bring this new knowledge to future readings. They learn about the world incrementally, across multiple exposures, constantly connecting new ideas and information with what they already know. Providing scaffolds before, during, and after reading is a time-honored practice. It is a sensible way to support learners' efforts, and it mirrors what good readers do independently. The following lists additional scaffolds appropriate to offer your students before, during, and after they read.

Before Reading

- asking and answering questions
- brainstorming
- examining pictures and graphic aids
- graphically organizing related information
- listening to selected portions being read aloud
- observing media presentations
- predicting

- previewing key vocabulary
- previewing the passage
- receiving directions and recommendations
- writing

During Reading

- answering interspersed questions
- completing a study guide
- posting sticky notes on the passage
- reading along with a passage recording or another individual reading
- writing notes while reading
- silently reading individually
- taking turns reading and talking about the passage with a partner, group, or class

After Reading

- applying contents to a related situation
- asking and answering questions
- completing assessments
- discussing with a partner, small group, or class
- following directions
- graphically organizing information
- paraphrasing or summarizing the passage
- producing concrete displays
- producing dramatic responses
- producing visual, artistic responses
- writing

DO IT TOGETHER

Bring to class a section of a textbook or other reading material you foresee using with your students. As a group, decide before, during, and after reading scaffolds that would be appropriate. Share your plans with other groups to personalize and apply your knowledge of planning comprehension scaffolds.

TEACH READING COMPREHENSION STRATEGIES

Reading comprehension strategies are procedures that active readers use to enhance their understandings of text (Dole, Nokes, & Drits, 2008). Active readers do more than internally listen to themselves pronounce words; they direct their attention to various aspects of print and build meaning for themselves. In one of the first scientific investigations of reading comprehension, Thorndike (1917) put it this way:

> Reading is a very elaborate procedure, involving the weighing of many elements in a sentence, their organization in the proper relations one to another, the selection of certain of their connotations and the rejection of others, and the cooperation of many forces to determine final response. (p. 323)

Teaching students comprehension strategies fosters their independence, and it promotes lifelong learning. Some reading comprehension strategies that have been shown to reliably enhance understandings of text include graphically organizing ideas and information, predicting what comes next in a passage, summarizing passages, forming images, generating and answering questions, and monitoring comprehension (National Reading Panel, 2000). The following explains these strategies.

Graphic Organizing

Both the rock comparison chart and the setting/plot chart in the preceding section are graphic organizers. *Graphic organizers* are visual diagrams that depict the relationships among concepts. There are many kinds, and you can create your own variations. Figures A.1 to A.6 contained in this chapter's Appendix, *Graphic Organizers*, show popular graphic organizers in various stages of completion by students.

On the semantic feature matrix (Figure A.1), students indicate with a plus or minus which qualities are possessed by various Americans depicted in poetry. On the Venn diagram (Figure A.2), students compare and contrast how animals and humans communicate. These graphic organizers are helpful in comparing and contrasting members of a particular group.

The time line (Figure A.3) is an excellent device to use when sequence is important. Here, students fill in the important event that occurred on each date. A variation is to give students a time line of events and have them fill in the dates. If you want more details, draw two lines under each event line and have students fill in two details about each event.

Both the whale web (Figure A.4) and the Yukon outline (Figure A.5) help students organize information when they are to learn a variety of detailed information

Students construct time lines in order to display information they have gathered.

about one topic. Most students find it easier to web ideas than to outline them because when they outline they often get lost in the trivia of upper- and lowercase letters and indentation. The partially completed outline allows students to concentrate on the information and the relationships because the skeleton and a few pieces of information are included.

Notice in the cause-and-effect chain (Figure A.6) that some causes have multiple effects, some effects have multiple causes, and an effect often becomes a cause of another effect. These diagrams help students sort through the complex relationships that comprise much of the information they need to understand in the real world.

When you determine that students need to learn compare–contrast relationships, time/order relationships, topic/subtopic relationships, or causal relationships, a graphic organizer is often your most efficient strategy. It is obvious that graphic organizers involve organizing. What may not be so obvious is that thinking processes like generalizing evaluating, imaging, and applying can often be included productively. Consider the following:

- After completing the Venn diagram on human and animal communication in Figure A.2, you may lead the students to conclude that "there are many similarities between humans and animals," a generalization based on the data students have put into the graphic organizer.
- After students complete the World War II time line (Figure A.3), you may lead them to talk about the events and imagine what it would have been like fighting those battles on either side. This discussion would involve the students in forming images of the events they had just organized.
- Students who learned about whales and organized the information into a web (Figure A.4) might take a stand on whether whales should be hunted. This discussion would involve evaluating.
- Applying can also occur. After learning about the Yukon or Washington, D.C., you could ask students if they would like to live there.

TRY IT OUT

Select a five- to ten-page section of text. Consider the important facts and relationships. Construct a graphic organizer that portrays the relationships among the facts.

Predicting

You are predicting whether a particular book will interest you when you peruse the title, author name(s), and cover illustration. You are predicting when you thumb through a magazine, looking at the pictures before you start to read. You are predicting when you read a heading such as "Are We Once Again Headed into Disaster?" and assume that the author will give you reasons to believe you are or are not. Two practices with some unique practical features for teaching prediction include an anticipation guide and DRTA.

ANTICIPATION GUIDE   An *anticipation guide* is a list of statements or key words, some of which are true and some of which are false. The students are presented with the statements or key words, and they predict which are true and which are false. Doing this prompts students to anticipate what they soon will learn. They then read to check their predictions. Below is an anticipation guide used before students read about the life of Babe Ruth. What are your predictions?

Babe Ruth

1. Orphan
2. Good kid
3. Only child
4. Irish
5. German
6. Over six feet tall
7. Right-handed
8. Pitcher
9. Catcher
10. New York Yankee

Students who have made some predictions want to read to see if they were right. Students who predict before reading are usually engaged and clear about their purposes for reading.

DRTA   A Directed Reading Thinking Activity—DRTA—is a way of teaching students to predict what they will learn. In a DRTA, the teacher usually leads the students to make predictions, read portions of the text, stop and make more predictions, read some more, and so on until the text is finished. Predictions are written on the board, checked when confirmed, and erased when not confirmed. How many times the students stop and make predictions depends on the length of what they are reading and their maturity. Here is an imaginary script for a modified DRTA centered on an elementary school science text about sound:

TEACHER: Today we are going to begin learning about sound. Look at the front and back. What do you think we will learn?

The teacher waits for students to respond, then writes these responses on the board:

What sound is.
How you hear.
What different kinds of sounds there are.
Where sounds come from.

TEACHER: Let's open our books now and see if we can predict anything else we might learn just by looking at the visuals.

The teacher directs students' attention to several pictures, a chart, and a diagram. Students add predictions, which the teacher writes on the board:

Sound travels in waves.
You make sounds with guitars.
Your ears let you hear sounds.
Sounds are measured in decibels.
Bats can hear sounds.

The teacher reads all the predictions aloud and asks students to read the first three pages to see which predictions are supported by the text. Students do so. They read a section of the text to confirm each prediction, then the teacher puts a checkmark next to that prediction. The teacher asks if there are more predictions students would like to add before finishing the sections. After students make suggestions, the teacher writes this:

> Soft sounds have decibels.
> Loud sounds have really big decibels.
> Pitch is how high or low the sound is.

Students finish reading the section on sound, then tell which predictions should be checked because they are supported and which should be erased because they either are not supported or not mentioned.

Anticipation guides and DRTAs differ in how much input the teacher and students have into the predictions. Both, however, motivate students to think about what they know and might find out and then to read with clear purposes. Both lead students to think about what they expect to learn then determine whether or not they learned what they expected.

Summarizing

Summarizing is producing a condensed version of what one reads or hears. Readers form generalizations about the text message, integrating information and stating its main ideas in a few words. *GIST* is one productive practice that promotes students' summarizing.

In *GIST*, the group task is to write a summary in twenty words or less. The teacher explains that sometimes we do not need to remember all the details but read just to get the general idea of the material. The teacher displays twenty word-size blanks and explains to the students that, after reading, they will write a sentence or two of no more than twenty words that captures the gist of what they have read.

The students read a short section—no more than three paragraphs—then work with the teacher to record the gist of what they have read. Students take turns telling the teacher part of what to write. In no case will the teacher write a twenty-first word. Students must revise what they want the teacher to write so that it will fit into the twenty blanks. The discussion challenges students to distill what is really important. This is an example of a GIST statement a class might produce:

Tropical	rain	forests	are	lush
forests	near	the	equator	that
are	hot	and	get	a
lot	of	rain.		

Next, the teacher tells them to read the following section and says that they must now incorporate the information from both the first section and the second in just twenty words. Students groan but usually rise to the challenge of trying to compact twice the amount of information into the same limited set of words. This is an example of the revised GIST statement, including information from both sections:

Tropical	rain	forests	are	hot,
rainy,	and	important	because	of
the	many	species	of	plants
and	animals	that	live	there.

It is possible that the teacher might then have the students read a third short section and attempt to incorporate its information into the GIST statement. (No more than three sections should be used with this challenging task.) This is an example:

Leafy	full	tropical	rain	forests
lower	the	carbon	dioxide	
in	the	air	and	
provide	new	medicines	and	products.

During this process, students learn how to get to the core of what they are reading. Most students will be able to make a contribution at some point during the GIST process.

Imaging

Imaging is using the senses to learn. It involves imagining something, seeing it, and putting yourself there. When you want students to image, you must move away from a two-dimensional world. You might first read a brief section of text, then describe whatever visual, aural, tactile, olfactory, and taste images you experienced most vividly. Here are some other suitable tasks:

- Draw, paint, or sculpt a pioneer.
- Create a diorama of a scene from pioneer days.
- Pick or create a piece of music that evokes Switzerland.
- Create a skit or play in which you act out a confrontation between the president and Congress.

Asking and Answering Questions

Learners who ask and answer their own questions about what they are reading have a powerful comprehension strategy. Learners best acquire and develop this strategy when they begin with question signal words and stems such as the following (Kiewra, 2002).

Question Signal Words

- Who _____?
- What _____?
- When _____?
- Where _____?
- How _____?
- Why _____?

Question Stems

- What have I learned about _____? What should I remember about _____?
- What does _____ mean?
- What are the components of _____?
- How are _____ and _____ alike? How are _____ and _____ different?
- What are the strengths of _____? What are the limitations of _____?
- What caused _____ to happen?
- How does _____ affect _____?
- How does _____ relate to what I already know? How does _____ relate to _____ in the passage?

- What does _____ look (and sound) like?
- What is the significance of _____?

MONITORING UNDERSTANDING   Monitoring understanding means that readers determine how their comprehension is progressing. They assess the status of their reading, and they repair breakdowns as needed. Providing students with prompts such as the following that question the author (Beck & McKeown, 2006) and point to areas needing clarification (Palincsar, 2002) are especially productive:

- How did the author put the ideas in order? How can I duplicate this arrangement of ideas on my own?
- What did the author do to help me understand the passage? How can I use this help?
- What are the key vocabulary words? How can I understand and remember them?
- What did the author not explain clearly? What concepts, words, or phrases are unclear? What can I do to improve my understanding?

Comprehension Strategy Instruction

Teaching reading comprehension strategies involves first selecting the strategies you plan to teach, then deciding when to introduce them. In this current era of standards-based education, such decisions frequently will be made for you, so mark your plan book accordingly. If no district- or school-level decisions have been made, you might begin with one or two comprehension strategies at the beginning of the year that you intend students to use all year long, then you might introduce others during the units that naturally call for them. When teaching reading comprehension strategies, make use of direct, explicit as well as discussion-based instruction.

DIRECT, EXPLICIT INSTRUCTION   Once you decide when to introduce comprehension strategies, expect positive effects by presenting them directly and explicitly (Alvermann, Fitzgerald, & Simpson, 2006). A highly regarded model of instruction for directly and explicitly teaching reading comprehension strategies is based on a gradual release of responsibility (Duke & Pearson, 2002; Lapp, Fisher, & Grant, 2008). In this model, teachers initially assume responsibility for using a particular strategy, then they fade out as students fade in and assume responsibility. This model of instruction, informally known as "I Do, We Do, You Do," contains the following five steps:

Describe the Strategy (I Do)
Explain what the strategy is and when and how to use it. If you are introducing forming images, tell students about them and their value when reading text that benefits from such nonverbal representations.

Model the Strategy (I Do)
Show students how to use the strategy by thinking aloud as you read. You might read aloud a brief portion of text accessible to everyone, then stop and think-aloud the images you are forming and the mental moves you are making to form them. You might explain the internal movie, the series of still scenes, or the senses of touch and smell you are constructing. You could record on a chart prompts such as, "First I imagine . . . ," "Then I imagine . . ." to publicize your mental processing. Such thinking aloud and recording reveals proficient readers' mental processes that otherwise remain concealed.

Collaboratively Use the Strategy (We Do)

Work with students to jointly apply the strategy. To begin fading your instruction, read aloud or have students read silently another section of text, then get them in on the act. Have students share with the class the images they formed, then provide feedback on their efforts. You might share your own images along with the images your students describe.

Guide Application of Multiple Strategies (You Do)

Gradually release responsibility to students to use the strategy along with other strategies they have learned. At this point you might have students share their images with a partner or small group. Sharing images might be only part of what the students talk about after reading sections of a text.

Support Independent Application of Multiple Strategies (You Do)

Continue releasing responsibility to students to use strategies they have learned when they are reading independently. When students demonstrate control of the strategy, remind them to apply it along with other strategies to passages that come up in the future. Have students tell how the strategy affects their reading comprehension. Fading, gradually releasing responsibility, is not difficult to do, but it is sometimes difficult to remember to do. Just when your lessons are going well and your students are succeeding with your support, you must remember that someday they will have to apply these strategies on their own.

A good supplement to the gradual release of responsibility model involves self-assessment. And a good form of self-assessment involves scoring guides as described in Chapter 3. Students rate their performance while completing literacy tasks, and afterward they set aside time to monitor what they have accomplished and what they might do to improve. Learners develop self-assessment as both a habit and an ability when regularly completing and talking about scoring guides for their strategies.

DISCUSSION-BASED INSTRUCTION Discussion-based instruction brings people together to improve their understandings of texts. Chapter 4 of this text focuses on promoting free yet rigorous exchanges among students so they explore passages from multiple perspectives and generate rich understandings of them. Here, we focus on discussions as a tool for developing comprehension strategies.

Discussion is essential during the fading process (Keene & Zimmerman, 2007). Talking with others about reading-related graphic organizers, predictions, images, and so on, goes far in developing independence (Vaughn, Klingner, & Bryant, 2001). Discussion exposes learners to diverse options. It provides opportunities to reflect on and refine the effectiveness of strategies.

As you release responsibility for reading and learning to your students, structure opportunities for them to talk about their strategies. Such talk should be in the form of a dialogue, with speakers responding to what each other said. It should make public what readers and learners do internally (Lloyd, 2004).

Learners benefit from common shared approaches to academic work (Palincsar & Herrenkohl, 2002). To develop commonalities, record and post the mental processes involved in comprehension strategies. Displaying such processes publicizes what to

Collaboration Rubric

Productivity

We stayed on task and accomplished much. Comments:	4	3	2	1	Often got off task, accomplishing little.

Participation

Everyone acted like an insider, contributing ideas. Comments:	4	3	2	1	Some acted like outsiders, contributing little.

Communication

We listened attentively and responded to ideas in a give-and-take conversation. Comments:	4	3	2	1	We often ignored others' ideas and had a one-sided conversation.

Climate

We disagreed agreeably; the atmosphere was friendly and relaxed. Comments:	4	3	2	1	We often disagreed disagreeably; the atmosphere was tense and quarrelsome.

Roles

Each member played preferred (or assigned) roles to help the group move along. Comments:	4	3	2	1	Only a few played preferred (or assigned) roles to help the group move along.

FIGURE 5.5   Discussion Rubric.

do and serves as a reminder to do so. Learners also require opportunities to lead the discussions about reading strategies. Keeping track of group roles and distributing them evenly accomplishes this. Further, group members share approaches best after teachers have modeled the expectations several times and had groups demonstrate them before the class. Finally, learners do well to construct a common culture of support, a community of learners, where they are willing to expose their confusions and misunderstandings about comprehension strategies. Adhering to a rubric such as the one in Figure 5.5 goes far in specifying what discussion requires and in designating areas for improvement.

LISTEN, LOOK, AND LEARN

Interview a teacher about enabling students to apply reading comprehension strategies. Determine what strategies are taught and the most productive ways to teach them. Ask about the teacher's perspective on direct, explicit instruction as well as discussion-based instruction. Summarize what you learned about comprehension strategy instruction.

DISCIPLINARY LITERACIES

Comprehension in English/Language Arts Classrooms

Attention to reading comprehension in English and language arts generally centers about novels, short stories, plays, and poetry. English teachers have countless options for promoting students' understanding of these literary forms. Given this situation, the following focuses on one specific piece of literature. What you gain from examining this example in depth can be used to guide decisions about other materials and other situations.

Shabanu, Daughter of the Wind is a novel about a 12-year-old nomadic Islamic girl in Pakistan. This 240-page narrative tends to hold the interest of middle-school students. There are numerous ways to scaffold understanding of it.

BEFORE READING   A good way to begin supporting students would be to enrich their understandings of the book's setting, desert life in Pakistan. You could accomplish this by displaying scenes of rural Middle Eastern life and showing videos. You might elicit students' images and the information they have about this topic. If you are fortunate, you might have someone from your class or community share firsthand experiences they had in this region of the world. List housing, transportation, and clothing features mentioned in the book, and portray them as vividly as possible.

While helping students experience the setting of a novel or short story before reading serves to develop background knowledge, it often arouses curiosity, too. After viewing scenes from a Middle Eastern desert, students might begin to wonder what life there would be like. You might pique their interest by asking what differences they would expect if they moved to rural living in Pakistan. By focusing on one feature—transportation, for instance—you could have students imagine all the ways life with camels would differ from life with cars.

Supporting readers' comprehension also can be accomplished by focusing attention on a central question. There are many possibilities for *Shabanu*; your choices depend on how this novel fits the unit you are presenting and the school curriculum guide you are following. One productive central question might be "What is the same and what is different about my life and Shabanu's?" This question is promising because the novel touches on universal coming-of-age themes such as clashing with parental expectations and meeting a first love. It portrays events common to all cultures, such as wedding rituals and religious worship, yet it offers insights into distinctive customs such as arranged marriages and informal schooling. Other questions might be "How does Shabanu change during the course of the novel?" "What is different about the qualities and concerns of the men and women in this novel?" and "How do the characters' attitudes toward obedience affect their actions in this novel?" Of course, students might produce their own central question(s) once they get into the novel, or they might choose from several offerings.

Reading aloud the first few chapters is a good way to support students' initial efforts with the novel. If you intend to read orally to the class, practice your presentation so you can effectively convey the information and tone of the story while enjoying it with your class. Demonstrate your interest in *Shabanu* by commenting on what you find fascinating and what you hope to learn in the future. To help students with self-monitoring, focus their attention on a central question: "So far, what similarities and differences have you found between your lives and Shabanu's?"

DURING READING Once students are under way with *Shabanu*, provide enough scaffolds to support their comprehension while you fade in and out of center stage. Many teachers use response journals for this purpose. Having students maintain a folder, perhaps a spiral-bound notebook or a stapled collection of papers, helps in recording thoughts about what they are reading. Be sure to produce a schedule so everyone knows when certain chapters—and the whole book—are to be completed. Also include a set of prompts to accompany the central question(s) and elicit thinking about what has been read. The prompts can be generic (e.g., "What will I remember about this section?") or content specific (e.g., "Should Shabanu marry her cousin?"). They can address essential thinking processes such as organizing (e.g., "Summarize the events of this chapter"), previewing and predicting (e.g., "What do you think will happen in the next chapter?"), and monitoring and fixing up (e.g., "What have you learned about Muslim life?").

Along with prompts that focus attention on the contents of the novel, you can list prompts that encourage student responsibility, reflection, and self-assessment. Students might respond to questions such as "What part of this chapter was the most difficult to understand?" and "What did I do when I encountered the difficult parts of this chapter?" Questions such as these enhance students' thinking about and control of their reading.

Arranging a weekly schedule for moving through *Shabanu* allows you to structure your plans. You might establish outside-of-class expectations for students to read silently and record responses in their journals, realizing that time for these activities can be offered during class, too. Designate inside-of-class time for whole-class or small-group discussions and for conferring with individuals.

Setting aside time during the week for addressing key incidents in the novel is a good way to provide needed scaffolds. For instance, powerful events occur when Shabanu's father sells their prize camel and when her grandfather dies in a storm. Sharing these passages orally through a teacher or student read-aloud session or through readers' theater could be time well spent. When talking about these episodes, you can refer to the central question(s), and you can explain how you employed essential thinking processes such as image, connect, and evaluate while making sense of these parts of the novel.

AFTER READING Culminating students' experiences with *Shabanu* can be accomplished many ways. If a central question is followed throughout the novel, then students' answers to it are shared. Using ideas recorded in their journals, students express differences between their lives and Shabanu's through visuals such as illustrated and captioned time lines, collections of concrete objects, skits, or essays. These forms of expression can be combined. Writing about Shabanu as a multiday project or as a one-day in-class exam are options. Displaying individuals' reactions to *Shabanu* through a class book, bulletin board, or presentations to an audience also build on the activities conducted while reading the novel.

Comprehension in English Language Development Classrooms

Comprehension processes are quite similar when students read in their primary and new languages because in both instances readers tap essential thinking processes, such as call up, connect, image, and organize. The main difference between comprehending passages written in one's primary and one's new language centers on the support that is required. English language learners require comprehensible input, exposure to language that they can and are motivated to make sense of.

READING MATERIALS   To ensure that reading materials provide comprehensible input—that they are challenging but not defeating—effective teachers provide a range of commercial and student-produced materials for students to read. They offer abridged, simplified versions of core reading materials so all students can access basic story lines or expository structures. They provide access to print written at various levels of difficulty so students can learn from and experience materials within their range of competence.

Effective teachers also provide high-quality culturally relevant literature for students to read. They incorporate novels into their instructional units that center on settings and events their students recognize and characters with which their students identify. For instance, authors such as Rodolfo Anaya, Nicholasa Mohr, Gary Soto, and Gloria Velasquez have produced many young-adult novels with Hispanic characters. Providing access to such literature honors the cultural backgrounds of many Hispanic students while linking home and school endeavors. It goes far in helping Spanish-speaking adolescents gain proficiency and comfort in English.

READ-ALOUD SESSIONS   Reading aloud to students who are somewhat proficient in their second language provides many opportunities to develop comprehension strategies. When reading aloud, take special care to select passages that are within students' capabilities. In fact, you might read vivid and interesting passages more than once so students are able to grasp them at different levels. As students listen, they should concentrate on understanding the passage's ideas and experiencing the characters' worlds. Teachers and students then might share what images they formed while listening, what connections they made between the passage and their lives, how they organized the information, and so on.

RESPONSE SKETCHES   English learners often benefit from responding to literature verbally and through sketches rather than through writing. After reading, have students sketch an illustration that represents their understanding of the passage. They might react to prompts such as "What did the passage mean to you?" "What is the author's message?" or "What do you see after reading the passage?" You might display some sketches you or your students drew for previously read texts to demonstrate the possibilities. (In our case, we rely on minimal stick figures and geometry as art forms!) After displaying a sketch to the class or small group, the illustrator remains silent and the audience interprets its message about the passage. The sketcher then explains what he or she meant the drawing to express. Following these sharings, you might talk about the variety of alternative interpretations the sketches represent.

FLUENCY   Teachers also support English learners' comprehension by enhancing their fluency, their ability to decode a passage's words automatically, so they can attend to the passage's ideas. To promote fluency, teachers often have students first read silently and then orally. They occasionally have students prepare to read orally just as they would for an oral interpretation event. They encourage groups of students to read selected portions of passages chorally.

Having students read a passage repeatedly until fluency is achieved is a powerful teaching practice. Students might tape-record themselves, repeating a passage several times until they are satisfied with their performance. Teachers often provide audiotaped recordings of passages with which students repeatedly follow along while looking at the text. Students also carry books home so they can have daily access to repeated reading in their home environment. These fluency practices always are conducted with meaningful passages connected to units of study, and students always respond to the meanings of what they have read fluently.

SOCIAL SUPPORT   Another way effective teachers support English learners' comprehension involves social support during classroom interactions. Effective teachers recognize cultural sources of students' behaviors and adjust their instruction accordingly. For instance, students' culturally patterned ways of taking turns and gaining the conversational floor during text-based discussions might differ from their teacher's. If students are used to interrupting others and the teacher is not, then the situation should be addressed. Get the issue out in the open and talk about it. The case could be that students view interruption as a way for group members to express community and solidarity and jointly produce a message, whereas teachers view an interruption as a takeover attempt by an outspoken individual. If this is the case, teachers might promote discussions that follow students' expectations, or they might promote students' self-monitoring so they can behave differently in different situations.

Effective teachers also accommodate the uncertainties and pressures English learners typically experience. Realizing how vulnerable language users can feel when practicing another language, teachers promote risk-free, nonthreatening learning climates. They make it clear to students that linguistic miscues are expected and are considered learning opportunities rather than mistakes. They allow English learners ample time to reply to questions, and they repeat and rephrase questions that appear unclear. They encourage students to initiate questions about what has been read. They elicit comments from all students in whole-class and small-group settings so that more than just a few vocal individuals participate.

Comprehension in Mathematics Classrooms

Because math teachers generally received no comprehension scaffolding when they were K–12 math students and did not observe other math teachers providing it when they were in teacher education, they often feel that it has no place in the mathematics classroom. Yet math word problems are difficult for most students. Math is among the most homework-intensive subjects; students need to be able to understand the explanations and directions in their math textbooks when they have trouble figuring out their homework problems. As in the example from a statistics book presented early in this chapter, you must not assume that students can comprehend math word problems or text explanations and directions simply because they can read them aloud, pronouncing most of the words correctly. Fortunately, the current standards for teaching mathematics recognize the failure of traditional mathematics instruction to address the literacy demands of mathematics. Here are some specific ways math teachers use the ideas in this chapter to help students learn how to comprehend the written language of mathematics.

COMPREHENDING WORD PROBLEMS Students for whom word problems are highly challenging benefit from being taught short comprehension lessons with a single word problem as the text. Before they read the problem, they are given the task they will complete after reading the problem. For example, when students have difficulty interpreting word problems, you can follow the five-step, gradual release of responsibility instructional model to teach them strategies for solving the problems. Begin by determining how you go about solving such problems, then share this problem-solving process with your students. Describe it, model it, then begin handing it over to your students by collaboratively performing and applying it with multiple problems. Discussion is essential. Fading from whole-class to small-group to individual participation gradually helps students learn how to interpret word problems.

As another example, when students fail to read word problems systematically before trying to solve them, you can use GIST. In GIST, when the text is a word problem, the group task is to write a summary of the problem in twelve words or less. Draw twelve word-size blanks on the chalkboard or on a transparency and explain to the students that they will write a sentence of no more than twelve words that captures the gist of the word problem. The students read the first sentence in the problem and then work with you to record the gist of that sentence. In no case do you write a thirteenth word. Students must revise what they want you to write so that it will fit into the twelve blanks. Next, have them read the following sentence and say that they must now incorporate the information from both the first sentence and the second in just twelve words. Continue in the same way through all the sentences of the problem. During this process, students learn how to distill the essence of the word problem. At the end, the resulting GIST statement is solved and then compared with the solution to the full problem to see if the GIST statement is correct and complete.

Finally, students who have some difficulty with word problems benefit from marking through every word in a problem that will not actually be part of the computation they do to solve it. This is particularly helpful to students who are confused by extraneous numbers in a problem.

COMPREHENSION OF TEXT EXPLANATIONS AND DIRECTIONS On occasion, students should be taught how to read explanations in the math textbook of how to solve problems. A problem of the type being introduced that day, and different from any in the book, is presented, then you again follow the five-step, gradual release of responsibility instructional model for interpreting such explanations. This instruction mirrors the instruction typically used when computing solutions for problems; now you are teaching how to read the problems, completely blending the teaching of literacy with mathematics.

Comprehension in Science Classrooms

Science is a subject that presents a great deal of new information. Students (and teachers!) are often overwhelmed by the sheer volume of what needs to be taught and learned. When there is so much, helping children develop comprehension strategies is particularly critical. Here are some specific ways science teachers use the ideas in this chapter to help students understand critical science concepts.

GRAPHIC ORGANIZERS   Earlier in this chapter, you learned that graphic organizers help students see the relationships between various facts and pieces of information. Learning to create graphic organizers also helps students become aware of text structure. Text structure is the way ideas are tied together in written language. Two common science structures are description and compare and contrast. Students can learn to construct webs when the information they are reading describes one main topic, Venn diagrams when the information is organized to compare and contrast two or three topics, and data charts when the information includes many different members of the same category.

Most teachers begin with the web because it is the easiest graphic organizer to teach and the most valuable for helping students organize and remember descriptive information presented hierarchically use the gradual release of responsibility mode. Working together, you and the students write the main topic in the center of the web and then put the other information going out from the center, using subtopics as needed. After describing and modeling, you and the class work together to create the first several webs, and then students work together in small groups to create several more; finally, ask students to create individual webs. (Figure A.4 shows the beginning of a science web on whales.)

Once students have become proficient at making their own webs, you can teach a second graphic organizer format. Direct students' attention to a part of the text that describes two things, telling characteristics they share and differences between the two. Using the same gradual release of responsibility, students can learn to create a Venn diagram like that shown in Figure A.2. Some teachers call this Venn diagram a "double bubble."

When students are good at creating webs, double bubbles, and triple bubbles, direct their attention to a text passage in which many different members of a category are described/compared and contrasted. Interlocking circles would get impossible to construct when there are more than three things being contrasted, so students can learn to make data charts such as that shown in Figure 5.3.

Once students have learned to create these separate graphic organizers, help them see that, depending on the structure of the text they are reading, one or the other of these would help them better organize the material. If the students already know how to create these graphic organizers or if the text you want them to read and understand has many passages in which sequence or cause–effect is the dominant structure, use the same procedures to teach them to create time lines (Figure A.3) or cause–effect chains (Figure A.6). Deciding which graphic organizer to use is the final step, which allows students to use this valuable comprehension strategy independently when reading on their own.

ANTICIPATION GUIDES   In science class, prior knowledge, which is generally helpful in comprehension, can sometimes actually impede comprehension. Based on observation and prior experience, some students have misconceptions about the way things work. Students may have seen objects falling and assumed that objects always fall in a straight line. Some students may have been told that warts are caused by frogs or that getting one's feet wet would cause a cold. To help students monitor their misconceptions, some teachers create anticipation guides in which some of the statements directly confront the possible misconceptions. Students indicate whether they agree or disagree with the statements before reading and then read to see which of the statements are actually true. Research on misconceptions has shown that students must have their misconception directly refuted either by the text, the teacher, or peers. Otherwise they may learn the new information but fail to discard the old misconception. Many students who learn that colds are caused by viruses still believe that they are also caused by getting your feet wet!

An anticipation guide, which directs students to think about and predict what they will learn, can directly confront common misconceptions. Going back to the statements after reading (or listening or viewing), students discuss what their misconceptions were and how they now understand the phenomenon under consideration.

OPEN-ENDED TASKS Students develop their science content and literacy learning best when their overall purpose is to learn science. This means using literacy to develop conceptual knowledge, to seek out relationships among scientific phenomena. It means learning to view scientific facts and ideas found in print as facts-in-action and ideas-in-action. It means learning to use print as a tool for investigating and learning about the natural world.

To emphasize literacy as a tool for learning science, pose open-ended, essential questions. To illustrate, primary-grade teachers can pose questions like "How do plants and animals depend on each other?" "What can you see in the sky?" and "How do liquids and solids change?" before students read. These open-ended questions promote conceptual knowledge because they have no single simple answers and they encourage resourcefulness. These questions urge students to share and compare their emerging understandings, to work out with others the meanings they are making of their texts and inquiries.

Comprehension in Social Studies Classrooms

GRAPHIC ORGANIZERS Earlier in this chapter, you learned that graphic organizers help students see the relationships between various facts and pieces of information. Learning to create graphic organizers can also help students become aware of text structure. Text structure is the way ideas are tied together in written language. Some common text structures include sequence, compare and contrast, cause and effect, problem–solution, and description/listing of important characteristics. While all of these idea structures appear in social studies texts, sequence, cause, and problem–solution structures are omnipresent. Students can learn to construct time lines when sequence or dates are important, cause–effect chains when causal relationships are what matters and problem–solution maps when that is the dominant theme.

Time lines are fairly easy to construct and are often the first graphic organizer taught in history classes. Use the gradual release of responsibility model. Working together, you and the students draw the line and put in a starting date and an ending date. Next, go through the text and add other dates and important events. In the space under the event, add one or two key facts to each event. After describing and modeling, you and the class work together to create the first several time lines, and then students work together in small groups to create several more; finally, students are asked to create individual time lines.

Once students become proficient at making their own time lines, you can teach a second graphic organizer format. Direct students' attention to a part of the text in which a certain "chain of events" unfolds, with each event resulting in another event. Using the same gradual release of responsibility model, students learn to create a cause–effect chain like that shown in Figure A.6.

Another common text structure seen in social studies texts is one in which there is a problem and various attempts at a solution. Sometimes, the solution creates an unforeseen new problem, which then needs some kind of solution. Students can learn to create a problem–solution map.

Once students have learned to create these separate graphic organizers, you can help them see that depending on the structure of the text they are reading, one or the other of these would help them better organize the material. Deciding which one to use is the final step, which allows students to use this valuable comprehension strategy independently when reading on their own.

KWLS Social studies tends to be a subject in which the pooled prior knowledge and interest of the whole class about any topic is substantial. When most students already know a little and a few students know a lot, a KWL is an effective way to activate everyone's prior knowledge and interest. You place a large sheet of roll paper across the board, label a column *K* for *what we know* and say, "We're going to be learning about the civil rights struggle in this country, but I know that you already know a lot about this so I want to list here everything that we jointly know." Student interest is piqued. As you list everything they brainstorm (even if it is not correct and will need to be edited or deleted later in the unit), students enlarge their prior knowledge stores by listening to their most important experts—their peers. Perhaps you spend most of one period creating a gigantic list. For homework, you assign them to discuss this issue with someone they know who lived through or participated in the struggle and see if they can come to class the following day with something to add. After adding what they learned from their "informed sources," you begin the second column, the *W—what we want to know*! Again, list all questions, even if you know some of the answers can probably not be found or agreed on. As you begin your class study of this unit, return each day to the scroll and add to the *L* column—*what we have learned*. You may want to also let them add to the *W* column because as students learn more, they generate more questions.

Prediction is the major thinking process used to launch and sustain the KWL activity. Prediction happens when a little voice inside our minds whispers, "I wonder if . . ." "I think that . . ." or "I wish I knew . . . ." Prediction helps keep our brains, and sometimes our hearts, actively engaged in learning.

OPEN-ENDED TASKS Students develop their social studies content and literacy learning best when their overall purpose is to learn social studies. This means using literacy to develop conceptual knowledge, to seek out relationships among phenomena. It means learning to view facts and ideas found in print as facts-in-action and ideas-in-action. It means learning to use print as a tool for investigating and learning about the social world.

To emphasize literacy as a tool for learning social studies, pose open-ended, essential questions. To illustrate, upper-grade history teachers can pose questions that address the big issues of history like cause and effect ("What happened and why?"), change and continuity ("What changed and what remained the same?"), turning points ("How did events of the past affect the future?"), through their eyes ("How did people in the past view their lives and world?"), and using the past ("How does studying the past help us understand our lives and world?"). Such open-ended questions promote conceptual knowledge because they have no single simple answers and they encourage resourcefulness. These questions urge students to share and compare their emerging understandings, to work out with others the meanings they are making of their texts and inquiries.

Comprehension in Activity Classrooms

Have you been to a large newsstand lately? Isn't it amazing how many different kinds of magazines there are? Think about classifying all those magazines into the different content areas in school. There are a few titles that would fit best under English, a few more that would fit best under social studies, and several more that would fit best under science. There are almost none that would fit best under foreign language or mathematics. A very large number, however, would fit best under our "activity" category. In other words, they are magazines for people who engage in a particular pursuit, say gardening, golf, or gun collecting. And many of the articles in these magazines actually outline procedures for doing some aspect of the pursuit to which the magazine is devoted. Likewise, time spent in a major bookstore reveals that this is an era of "self-help" books and manuals for doing, using, or repairing almost anything. In your course, you are attempting to teach your students to do a number of varied procedures, so it is helpful for them to learn how to *read to do* in your subject.

You may well have a textbook for your course. If not, you may have access to brochures, manuals, or even trade books and magazines that exist to help people perform better in your field. That is the material, diagrams and all, that you can teach your students how to comprehend as a part of your course. If so, your students will be more able to take advantage of the books, magazines, and other reading materials available to them after they no longer have you for their teacher.

Most students are totally dependent on their teachers in activity courses because they are unable to use reading. Reading should never become a major part of any activity course, but reading what to do is one aspect of what it means today to be educated in any field, from playing the guitar to playing the stock market, and from painting with watercolors to losing weight.

LOOKING BACK

Most of what we choose to read is on topics for which we have a great deal of background knowledge; thus, motivation is usually quite high. When we read this easy (for us) material, comprehension seems to occur effortlessly and automatically as we process the words. In content area classrooms, however, students often read materials for which they have little prior knowledge and motivation. It is when students are reading teachable text that comprehension scaffolds are needed. In this chapter, you learned the why and how of supporting students' comprehension and some strategies for weaning them off this support. These are the three keys:

1. Plan levels of comprehension support.
2. Provide scaffolds for challenging passages.
3. Teach reading comprehension strategies.

ADD TO YOUR JOURNAL

Reflect on this chapter's key ideas: Do you see why students need support as they read unfamiliar text? Can you imagine yourself providing scaffolds for students through the before, during, and after phases of reading? Finally, what do you think of the gradual release of responsibility and discussion models as ways to help students become more independent learners? What do you believe will be most useful to you?

Additional Readings

The following present specific hands-on teaching practices that focus on particular aspects of reading comprehension:

Buehl, D. (2008). *Classroom strategies for interactive learning* (3rd ed.). Newark, DE: International Reading Association.

Burke, J. (2002). *Tools for thought: Graphic organizers for your classroom.* Portsmouth, NH: Heinemann.

Harvey, S., & Goudvis, A. (2007). *Strategies that work: Teaching comprehension to enhance understanding* (2nd ed.). Portland, ME: Stenhouse.

Wormeli, R. (2004). *Summarization in any subject.* Alexandria, VA: Association for Supervision and Curriculum Development.

Zwiers, J. (2004). *Building reading comprehension habits in grades 6–12: A toolkit of classroom activities.* Newark, DE: International Reading Association.

These texts provide research-based insights into reading comprehension instruction:

Block, C. C., & S. Parris, S. (Eds.). (2008). *Comprehension instruction: Research-based best practices* (2nd ed.). New York, NY: Guilford Press.

Keene, E. O. (2008). *To understand: New horizons in reading comprehension.* Portsmouth, NH: Heinemann.

Keene, E. O., & Zimmerman, S. (2007). *Mosaic of thought: The power of comprehension strategy instruction* (2nd ed.). Portsmouth, NH: Heinemann.

The following summarize research on reading comprehension:

Alvermann, D. E., Fitzgerald, J., & Simpson, M. (2006). Teaching and learning in reading. In P. Alexander & P. Winne (Eds.), *Handbook of educational psychology* (2nd ed., pp. 427–455). New York, NY: Simon & Schuster/Macmillan.

Edmonds, M. S., Vaughn, S., Wexler, J., Reutebuch, C., Cable, A., Tackett, K. K., et al. (2009). A synthesis of reading interventions and effects on reading comprehension outcomes for older struggling readers. *Review of Educational Research, 79,* 262–300.

Israel, S. E., & Duffy, G. (Eds.). (2008). *Handbook of research on reading comprehension.* New York, NY: Routledge.

McNamara, D. S. (Ed.). (2007). *Reading comprehension strategies: Theories, interventions, and technologies.* Mahwah, NJ: Erlbaum.

National Reading Panel. (2000). *Teaching children to read: An evidence-based assessment of the scientific research literature on reading and its implications for reading instruction: Reports of the subgroups.* Bethesda, MD: National Institute of Child Health and Human Development, National Institutes of Health.

Nystrand, M. (2006). Research on the role of discussion as it affects reading comprehension. *Research in the Teaching of English, 40*(4), 392–412.

Rand Reading Study Group. (2002). *Reading for understanding: Toward an R&D program in reading comprehension.* Santa Monica, CA: Science and Technology Policy Institute, RAND Education.

Torgesen, J. K., Houston, D. D., Rissman, L. M., Decker, S. M., Roberts, G., Vaughn, S., Wexler, J., Francis, D. J., Rivera, M. O., & Lesaux, N. (2007). *Academic literacy instruction for adolescents: A guidance document from the Center on Instruction.* Portsmouth, NH: RMC Research Corporation, Center on Instruction. Retrieved May 3, 2007 from the Center on Instruction site: www.centeroninstruction.org

Online Resources

These sites contain templates for numerous graphic organizers; many provide guidelines for using these tools.

The Graphic Organizer
www.graphic.org/index.html

Houghton Mifflin Education Place
www.eduplace.com/graphicorganizer/

A Periodic Table of Visualization Methods
http://www.visual-literacy.org/periodic_table/periodic_table.html

References

Alvermann, D. E., Fitzgerald, J., & Simpson, M. (2006). Teaching and learning in reading. In P. Alexander & P. Winne (Eds.), *Handbook of educational psychology* (2nd ed., pp. 427–455). New York, NY: Simon & Schuster/Macmillan.

Beck, I. L., & Mckeown, M. G. (2006). *Improving comprehension with Questioning the Author: A fresh and expanded view of a powerful approach*. New York, NY: Scholastic.

Block, C. C., & Parris, S. R. (Eds.). (2008). *Comprehension instruction: Research-based best practice* (2nd ed.). New York, NY: Guilford.

Dole, J. A., Nokes, J., & Drits, D. (2008). Cognitive strategy instruction: Past and future. In S. E. Israel & G. Duffy (Eds.), *Handbook of research on reading comprehension* (pp. 347-372). New York, NY: Routledge.

Duke, N. K., & Pearson, P. D. (2002). Effective practices for developing reading comprehension. In A. E. Farstrup & S. J. Samuels (Eds.), *What research has to say about reading instruction* (pp. 205–242). Newark, DE: International Reading Association.

Guthrie, J. T., & Wigfield, A. (2000). Engagement and motivation in reading. In M. J. Kamil, P. B. Mosenthal, P. D. Pearson, & R. Barr (Eds.), *Handbook of reading research* (vol. 3, pp. 406–422). Mahwah, NJ: Lawrence Erlbaum Associates.

Hirsch, E. D., Jr. (2003). *Reading comprehension requires knowledge—of words and the world*. Retrieved August 28, 2005, from the American Educator Web site, www.aft.org/pubs-reports/american_educator/spring2003/index.html

Keene, E. O. (2008). To *understand: New horizons in reading comprehension*. Portsmouth, NH: Heinemann.

Keene, E. O., & Zimmerman, S. (2007). *Mosaic of thought: The power of comprehension strategy instruction* (2nd ed.). Portsmouth, NH: Heinemann.

Kiewra, K. A. (2002). How classroom teachers can help students learn and teach them how to learn. *Theory into Practice, 41,* 71–80.

Kirk, R. E. (1972). Classification of ANOVA designs. In R. E. Kirk (Ed.), *Statistical issues: A reader for the behavioral sciences* (pp. 241–260). Belmont, CA: Wadsworth.

Lapp, D., Fisher, D., & Grant, M. (2008). "You can read this—I'll show you how": Interactive comprehension instruction. *Journal of Adolescent and Adult Literacy, 51,* 372–383.

Lloyd, S. L. (2004). Using comprehension strategies as a springboard for student talk. *Journal of Adolescent and Adult Literacy, 48,* 114–124.

McNamara, D. S. (Ed.). (2007). *Reading comprehension strategies: Theories, interventions, and technologies*. Mahwah, NJ: Erlbaum.

Nystrand, M. (2006). Research on the role of discussion as it affects reading comprehension. *Research in the Teaching of English, 40*(4), 392–412.

Palincsar, A. S. (2002). Reciprocal teaching. In B. J. Guzzetti (Ed.), *Literacy in America: An encyclopedia of history, theory, and practice* (vol. 2, pp. 535–538). Santa Barbara, CA: ABC-CLIO.

Palincsar, A. S., & Herrenkohl, L. R. (2002). Designing collaborative learning contexts. *Theory into Practice, 41,* 26–32.

Thorndike, E. L. (1917). Reading as reasoning: A study of mistakes in paragraph reading. *Journal of Educational Psychology, 8,* 276–282.

Vaughn, S., Klingner, J. K., & Bryant, D. P. (2001). Collaborative strategic reading as a means to enhance peer-mediated instruction for reading comprehension and content-area learning. *Remedial and Special Education, 22*(2), 66–74.

Vygotsky, L. (1978). *Mind in society: The development of higher psychological processes.* Cambridge, MA: Harvard University Press.

Wood, K. D., Lapp, D., Flood, J., & Taylor, D.B. (2008). *Guiding readers through text: Strategy guides for new times* (2nd ed.). Newark, DE: International Reading Association.

APPENDIX: GRAPHIC ORGANIZERS

Famous Americans in Four Poems

Qualities (+ / –)	Abraham Lincoln	Georgia O'Keeffe	Martin Luther King, Jr.	Betsy Ross
proud				
controversial				
artistic				
political				
———				
———				
———				
———				

FIGURE A.1 A Semantic Feature Matrix is especially appropriate for comparing and contrasting as well as choosing among alternatives (e.g., Which famous American is least controversial?).

Human and Animal Communication

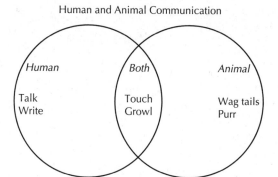

FIGURE A.2 A Venn Diagram is especially appropriate for comparing and contrasting as well as describing (e.g., How does human communication differ from animal communication?).

World War II

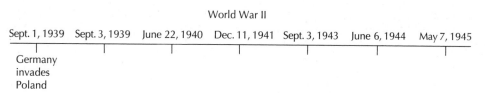

FIGURE A.3 A Time Line is especially appropriate for describing sequences (e.g., Describe the major turning points of World War II.).

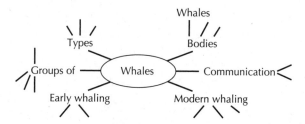

FIGURE A.4 A web is especially appropriate for grouping items into categories and portraying relationships among the categories. Often used to begin and monitor the gathering of ideas and information during units and unit projects (e.g., What can we learn about whales?).

THE YUKON
A. Geography
   1.
   2.
   3.
   4.
B. Economy
   1. Fishing
     a.
     b.
   2. _____
     a. lynx
     b.
     c.
   3. Manufacturing
     a.
     b.
     c.

4. _____
   a. gold
   b.
   c.
   d.
   e.
C. Government
   1. Canadian
     a.
     b.
     c.
   2. Territorial
     a.
     b.

FIGURE A.5 An outline is especially appropriate for grouping items into categories. Often used to introduce expository writing (e.g., List main points about the Yukon in the order that they are to be presented.).

The Election of Abraham Lincoln

Lincoln-Douglas Illinois Senate race
  c
    e
Lincoln-Douglas debates
    c
     e
National fame
for Lincoln
    c
    e

Democratic   c
Party splits

Lincoln nominated
for president by   c
Republican Party
    e

Third party   c

Lincoln elected
president
   c
    e
Seven Southern
states secede

FIGURE A.6 A Cause-and-Effect Chain is especially appropriate for explaining how events affect one another (e.g., How did events associated with Abraham Lincoln contribute to secession?).

Meaning Vocabulary

VOCABULARY DEVELOPMENT IS COMPLEX

Given the importance of vocabulary development to academic success, there are many aspects to consider. When planning vocabulary instruction, think about addressing concepts and labels for concepts, depth of word knowledge, related words, and symbols (Blachowicz, Fisher, Ogle, & Watts-Taffe, 2006; Graves, 2006).

Concepts and Labels for Concepts

Examine the following two sentences:

> The avuncular man scratched his philtrum.

> She painted all but her lunules.

These are simple sentences. You probably gained a general idea that a "certain" man scratched "something" that belonged to him, and that the woman painted all but some specific "things" that belonged to her. Because you probably lack meanings for some key words, however, your comprehension of these sentences is impaired. If you located definitions of these key words, starting with *avuncular*, you found that it meant "acting like an uncle." Depending on your experiences with uncles, you then conjured up a meaning for the previously unfamiliar word, *avuncular*. You also discovered that you have both a philtrum (groove in the middle of the upper lip, below the nose) and lunules (moon-shaped white areas at the base of the fingernails that at one time were fashionable for women to leave white while painting the rest of their nails). Now you know exactly what the sentences are telling.

Notice that you did not lack meanings for the three words in the preceding example. You just were unable to connect the meanings with the words. You had the concepts—how uncles behave, the groove in the middle of your upper lip, the moon-shaped white areas at the base of your fingernails. What you didn't have were these particular labels, or words, for the concepts. Having concepts and labels for concepts are two aspects of vocabulary knowledge.

Consider another example:

> The pharmacist needed lupulin and lupulone.

Again, you know that the pharmacist needed two "things." But which two things? When you look up *lupulin*, you discover that it is the "glandular hairs of the hop." Lupulone is "a white or yellow crystalline solid." These meanings are not very informative because you probably do not know what the meanings mean. In this example, you probably lack the labels as well as the concepts.

Dictionaries are very helpful when we have a concept but not the particular label by which it is being called. Dictionaries have limited usefulness when we lack both the labels and the concepts. Indeed, Beck, McKeown, and Kucan (2002) provide data-based support for their assertion that "the reality is that definitions are not an effective vehicle for learning word meanings" (p. 33).

As you consider how to teach word meanings, keep in mind the aspects of labels and concepts. If the word to be taught is one for which students already have the appropriate concept and lack only the label, the teaching task is relatively simple. If, as is more common during subject matter study, students lack both the concept and the label, the task is more difficult.

Depth of Word Knowledge

Knowing a word is like knowing a person. Asking, "How many words do you know?" is like asking, "How many people do you know?" If we ask the latter question, you will probably not respond, thinking that we could not be serious. If we persist, however, you might answer with a question of your own: "What do you mean by *know?*" There are many aspects to knowing word meanings.

There are many people whom you know only by name. There are also many words you know only by name, for which you have the label, but whose concept remains vague. *Truffles* is a word known to many people, but perhaps the whole extent of your meaning for *truffles* consists of "I think you eat them." Your meanings for the word *potatoes*, on the other hand, probably could fill pages. You might think of all the French fries you have eaten at fast-food restaurants, of the baked potatoes your mother served, and of the potato-head toy you had as a young child. You might call up your knowledge that potatoes are "vegetables," "underground tubers of a plant," "sometimes covered with eyes," "grown in great quantities in Idaho," "eaten in many forms: baked, mashed, french fried," "the crop that failed during the Irish famine of the 1840s," and so on. Your knowledge of *truffles* probably is shallow, while your knowledge of *potatoes* most likely is deep. You probably are able to connect many nuanced ideas with *potato*, and you most likely are able to pronounce and spell it as well as make use of it adeptly while reading, writing, speaking, and listening. Of course, our example of knowing *potato* so well best applies if you've lived in a culture that makes the most of them. If you live in a culture that makes more use of cassavas or rice, then you might not have much knowledge of potatoes.

Related Words

Just as most names stand for many different people, some of whom are related and some of whom are not, most words stand for many different meanings, some related, some not. Look up *root*, for example, and you will find many meanings. Plant roots, tooth roots, root words, and square roots all share a common concept, the idea of a basic part, often hidden, from which other parts, usually visible, emerge and grow. The related meanings of a word may be compared to related people who share the same name. Such people often share a family resemblance: physical (red hair, big bones) or behavioral (mannerisms, gestures, idiosyncrasies of speech). In some families, these resemblances are striking. In others, only the most astute observer would be able to detect family resemblances. So it is with words. The relationship among the many meanings for some words is apparent to everyone; other words reveal their kinship only to philologists. For instance, did you know that the words *sedimentary* and *presidential* are related? Their *sed/sid* bases both refer to *settle*. Sedimentary material is the sediment that settles at the bottom; presidents wield their presidential power when they preside over groups, settling them down. Thus, most students need a teacher's help to perceive the family aspect of words.

People also mean different things to others when they are in different situations. For instance, you can be a parent or offspring, spouse or sibling, friend or enemy depending on your relationship with others. So it goes with words; they can mean different things according to how they are used. Consider the word *spring* as found in *offspring*. It can mean different things as a verb (to leap), a noun (the season following winter), or an adjective (able to cushion, like a spring mattress). Multiple-meaning words like *base, power, prime, principal, radical, set, square,* and *table* that have specific meanings across the disciplines present many challenges to learners, especially English learners.

Symbols

You also ought to be concerned with some terms not usually considered *words*. A few examples should illustrate this point:

> The FBI and CIA directors met last week.
>
> AB = CD.
>
> N.Z. is ESE of Australia.
>
> The president of ASCAP was a member of CORE.

Phrases, symbols, abbreviations, initials, and acronyms all occur in the material students read in content areas. While these terms are not technically "words," they are entities for which meaning must be built, and teachers should remember to teach meanings for any symbols that students will need to understand in order to read and write effectively in a particular content area.

TRY IT OUT

Obtain a textbook or other reading material in a subject you will be teaching. Pick a section you might have students read and identify about five words that are key to understanding the section. Then assess the challenges and possibilities each word presents learners according to the features presented here, concepts and labels for concepts, depth of knowledge, and related words. Share your assessment of the words with a few classmates to personalize and apply your knowledge of the features of words presented here.

PROMOTE RICH AND MEANINGFUL EXPERIENCES WITH LANGUAGE

About 88,700 word forms (e.g., *history, historian, historical*) occur in print from the first through the twelfth grade (Nagy & Anderson, 1984). If students are to learn enough of these word forms to become literate adults, they need to know about 45,000 by the end of high school. Perhaps the best way to enable students to develop such a vocabulary is to promote rich and meaningful experiences with language. Content area study is a premier site for such experiences.

In rich and meaningful experiences, students use the natural language that is provided by books, guest speakers, role plays, informative media, and classmates as they explore ideas. Experiences are rich and meaningful when they relate to students' worlds, when they tap individuals' interests and concerns. Students in these experiences want to acquire new words for genuine reasons; they intend to apply what they learn. They develop vocabulary while engaging their minds fully in worthwhile ideas.

Rich and meaningful experiences are developed in units of study as described in Chapter 3, "Instructional Units." Units present the big picture before focusing on details, so students have something to help organize all the new words they encounter.

Secondary students find a range of reading materials engaging.

This whole-to-part approach enhances vocabulary development. Such settings are the opposite of antiseptic ones filled with worksheet lists of unrelated words to define, synonyms to match, and rote drills to perform.

Rich and meaningful unit-based experiences are especially appropriate for the complexities of teaching and learning vocabulary. In fact, the words that naturally emerge during units are the ones many teachers use as the core of their vocabulary instruction.

Wide reading is a crucial ingredient in rich and meaningful language experiences (Krashen, 2004). Reading self-selected materials provides a plentiful source of new words. Research is clear that students engaged with interesting and important books, periodicals, online sites, and so on grasp the meanings of unfamiliar words, and they review and refine the meanings of familiar ones. When reading on their own, students tend to independently understand and remember the meanings of about fifteen of every one hundred unknown words they encounter. Reading only ten minutes per day can result in students learning about one thousand new words each year (Cunningham & Stanovich, 1998). In brief, if you want to increase your students' vocabularies, you should do everything possible to increase the amount of your students' wide reading.

15 out of 100 words!

Fictional and nonfictional printed accounts add to your students' funds of knowledge about the world and about words. Reading about the Donner party, the Shackelton expedition, the way animals adapt, and how *Star Wars* was produced—to name a few topics—can be compelling experiences in their own right as well as valuable contributions to one's knowledge base. Chapter 4 of this text, "Reading Materials and Projects," describes materials appropriate for wide reading and explains how to set up and manage opportunities for reading, responding, and learning vocabulary.

TEACH SETS OF WORDS DIRECTLY

Making new words available and accessible through rich and meaningful experiences with language is essential for vocabulary development, but more needs to be done. Learners also benefit from studying particular sets of words that correspond to units of instruction. Teaching sets of unit-based words presents your students conceptually related items that are linked in meaningful networks. It shows students how to go about learning words well.

Selecting Sets of Words

Selecting sets of words that correspond to your units of instruction involves several considerations:

1. *Consider the unit you are presenting and list all the key words.* As Chapter 3 indicated, much instructional decision making occurs when planning units of instruction. When planning units, be selective about the vocabulary you intend to teach. Begin by identifying key words. Key words are words that unlock the meaning of a topic. Be sure to include multimeaning words, such as *root*, for which the students might know a meaning that is not appropriate.

2. *Pare down this initial list by setting priorities.* Determining how many words to teach is a difficult task, but research indicates that ten new words per week per class is what we can expect students to learn (Beck, McKeown, & Kucan, 2002). Ten words per week may not sound like much, but consider that it means 360 new words per year! Furthermore, if a student is studying five subjects and each subject includes ten new words each week, that would add up to 1,800 new words per year—a considerable increase in vocabulary.

   To pare your list, first select the words that are important not only to the unit of study but also to understanding the content area (Hyland & Tse, 2007). The word *cell* in a science unit on plants should be kept because it is crucial not only to understanding plants, but also to the whole study of biology. Likewise, the word *angle* is crucial to the whole study of geometry. In addition to words crucial to the whole discipline, keep on your list words that occur repeatedly in the unit of study and that are crucial to understanding it. A word appearing only once is probably less important than a word that occurs frequently throughout the unit.

3. *Include words that will be of particular interest to your students.* Sometimes, there is a word or two that are not critical to your discipline but that are interesting words. Including these words will increase the engagement of your students and help convince them that words are wonderful!

4. *Display the words for intensive study.* Many teachers set aside a word wall or reserve one of the bulletin boards in the room to display the important words associated with a unit. Sometimes these words are part of a graphic organizer such as a web or a chart. Other times, the words are displayed with pictures that help to clarify their meanings. Still other times, they are simply written on index cards and attached to the board. Some teachers put all the important unit words up at the beginning of the unit and refer to these words throughout the unit, periodically asking students what else they have learned about these important words. Other teachers prefer to add words gradually as the words occur and do some culminating activities at the end of the unit to help students tie all the words together.

TRY IT OUT

Select a unit of study you might teach to a group of students. Consider what you want them to learn. As you think, preview, and read, list all the key words. Be on the lookout for multi-meaning words. These are hard to spot because when we know the appropriate meaning, we often forget that students may only know the more common meanings.

Once you have listed your key words, cut the list to a reasonable number (no more than ten per week) following the guidelines given. Assume your unit will last three weeks, and cut your list of words to teach down to thirty.

Representing Word Meanings Productively

As you move through units of study, you can use numerous productive strategies for presenting the key words you have selected. How to teach something should parallel how something is learned. Because people remember best the things that they do, direct experience with the concept represented by the word is the most powerful and lasting way to teach. Providing this real experience, however, is not always possible, so you might look to the next best thing, media representations. You also can teach new words by helping students see the relationships between new words and already known words. The best instruction involves practices that reveal words' meanings in multiple ways. This instruction focuses on deep and thorough understandings of the words, so learners will have them for a lifetime.

Introduce your units' words as each one comes up during the normal course of instruction. If you are presenting a middle-grades unit on rocks, then introduce words like *sedimentary, limestone, sandstone,* and *shale* as they come up in your lessons. For example, when you are initially focusing on the types of rocks and the word *sedimentary* first appears, show its written form and pronounce it clearly and slowly, emphasizing its syllables. Next, explain its meaning with student-friendly definitions (e.g., rocks formed from materials deposited by water, wind, or glaciers), media representations, actual examples, and verbal connections (e.g., unlike igneous rocks that emerge bottom-up from the earth, sedimentary rocks materialize from the top down). Finally, encourage elaboration by having students respond to your prompts (e.g., Are sedimentary rocks more like layer cakes or ice cream?).

To ensure deep knowledge of your unit's key words, do more than introduce them when they first come up in your lessons. Consider the following practices to represent the words' meanings productively and involve your students actively and meaningfully in learning them.

REAL-WORLD INTERACTIONS   Real-world interactions are exactly what they sound like. You want students to develop a meaning for a word, so you put them in direct contact with the thing that the word represents. Field trips are often good ways to show students the real thing. If you have ever taken a field trip to a state capitol to watch the legislative process, your teacher was providing you with real experience for a number of words: *capitol, legislature, gavel, quorum, debate, adjourn.* Field trips are some of the best ways of providing students with direct experience on which to base meaning for new words, but they are expensive and time consuming, and often the things you need to show students are not available at a reasonable distance from the school.

When you cannot take your students to the real, thing, the next best option is to bring something to the students. Learners at all levels learn something best when they have actually seen it, touched it, smelled it, listened to it, or even tasted it.

Sometimes the actual subject of study could never be available for students to interact with, but a model could. Models of the human heart, a pyramid, or a DNA molecule, while differing in size and other features from the real thing, are still three-dimensional representations that can be explored by the senses.

You can provide students real experience with verbs like *cringe, catapult,* and *pontificate* by demonstrating these actions, then letting students act them out. You provide students with experience with such concepts as *assembly line* and *electoral process* by simulations in which each student takes part as the class manufactures something assembly-line style or participates in a mock election. Because of time and other constraints, not all meanings can be developed through this method. But the time and effort involved in providing the real thing must be weighed against the depth and the permanence of the learning and excitement that this method generates.

SCAVENGER HUNTS Have you had firsthand experience with a scavenger hunt? Have you actually gone to gather assorted items, competing to be the team that found the most in a limited time? If you have not, perhaps you have had visual experience of watching others go on one. Scavenger hunts are fun because they develop both competition and a sense of team spirit. For a scavenger hunt that helps your students build word meanings by collecting real things and pictures, follow these steps:

1. *Make a list of the items for which you want students to scavenge.* Include anything for which students might be able to find a real object, model, or picture. Be sure to

Students link concrete objects with vocabulary learning during instructional units.

Media help develop meanings for words.

add some well-known, easy-to-collect items so that some of the finds will be easy and immediately satisfying. Here is a list used for a scavenger hunt employed during a unit on the desert:

sand	woodpecker	cactus	vulture
skunk	dune	fox	kangaroo rat
mesquite	dates	oasis	
roadrunner	coyote	yucca	

2. *Divide your class into teams of three or four.* Explain how scavenger hunts work. Be sure students understand that they must bring in objects and pictures by a certain date.

3. *Allow the teams to meet briefly once or twice more.* Teams should check things off their lists and see what is still needed. If students protest that "No one could find a . . . ," assure them that "No one could possibly get objects or pictures for everything. The goal is to collect as much as you can."

4. *On the appointed day, have teams bring their finds.* Cards on which each word is printed might be attached to bulletin boards and all the pictures representing that object can be arranged in collage fashion around the word. Objects that are not alive, dangerous, or valuable can be labeled and placed on tables near the bulletin boards.

MEDIA AND TECHNOLOGY Media provides us with the next best thing to being there. All of us have numerous concepts that we have not experienced directly but have developed through movies, television, still photographs, paintings, diagrams, or maps. Computer software and Web sites now offer simulations that allow students to observe

Active participation engages learners with terminology.

science phenomena like the body systems and mathematical phenomena like tessella-tions that were difficult to portray before. Imagine trying to explain the Grand Canyon to someone who has never seen it, or trying to describe with words the color teal, what fencing looks like, or life at the bottom of the ocean. Your words are meaningful mainly to those who have seen what the words represent.

Fortunately, we are surrounded by visual stimuli. Television programs offer great possibilities for content teachers. Most school system media centers contain DVDs, CDs, and other media. As you consider how to build meaning for words, ask yourself, "Where could I find an image of this?" Often, the answer is as close as your textbook or computer.

When you have your list of words for which you must build meaning, look at the textbooks and other books you have available. Note page numbers where various concepts are portrayed visually. You can introduce these concepts by writing the word on the board, pronouncing it and having students pronounce it with you, and directing their attention to the appropriate text visual.

In the case of visuals, if one is good, two are twice as good. Remember that developing a concept is not a matter of "one time—now you've got it." Your meaning for *ancient Greece* is not based on having seen just one image. If your students see several visuals, the depth of their meaning for the word will be much greater than if they see only one. In addition to broadening their concepts, each visual provides review of the meaning represented by the word.

ORGANIZING WORDS   Organization is a powerful avenue to understanding and remembering words and their meanings. If you provide category names before students organize words, correct answers would be expected. If students are allowed to invent their own category names, correctness is based on the students' explanations of their organizational schemes. Students typically like recording each word on a separate slip of paper in order to physically manipulate and group them. For instance, if young children were reading about food, they might organize the following items into categories:

apple	fried chicken	ice cream
hamburger	cake	peach
orange	hot dog	pie

You might produce one or more category topics, then have students supply subordinate terms in a format such as the following:

Fruit	Dessert	Meat Dish

Older students exploring land formations caused by glaciers might depict the relationships of the following words:

drumlin	rocking stone	moraine
erratic boulder	valley	continental
esker	kame	

You and your class might display the categories in a graphic organizer such as a semantic feature matrix, Venn diagram, or a web according to the words' relationships with each other (see pages 120 and 121 of this text). Displaying terms in topic–subtopic or sequential arrangements promotes deep understandings of the connections among vocabulary. It is like producing a map of a group of words.

CREATING ANALOGIES   To create an analogy, think of something your students are apt to know that is like the thing they do not know. It is very important that students be familiar with the concept being used to teach the unknown concept. Telling you that cricket is a lot like rounders is not helpful if you do not know rounders either. Once you have decided which analogy to make, consider the similarities and differences between the familiar and unfamiliar concepts.

Imagine that you want to teach the students about taxation without representation and its relationship to the Revolutionary War. You decide to compare this concept with the idea of belonging to a club to which you have to pay dues. You do not mind paying the dues, even though the club founders meet each year and decide how the dues are to be spent. After a while, it occurs to some club members who are not founders that because the dues are partly theirs, they should have some say in how the dues are spent. The founding members will have no part of this and insist that the power to spend the dues is theirs, as is written in the club's bylaws. Then explain that taxation is like dues and that representation, in this case, means the power to decide how something is spent. A difference that should be pointed out is that you as a club member always have the right to quit the club and stop paying dues. When the colonists quit and stopped paying taxes, a war ensued.

PROMOTE WORD CONSCIOUSNESS

Word consciousness is an awareness of and interest in words as units of language (Graves & Watts-Taffe, 2008; Scott & Nagy, 2004). Youth who are conscious of words willingly note their presence in different settings, analyze their distinctive spellings and meanings, judge whether certain ones are more appropriate than others in particular situations, and generally appreciate the power and wonder of language. Developing youths' word consciousness goes far to produce life-long readers and writers who value print. The following describes practices used to promote word consciousness.

Model Word Wonder

what is a logophile?

If you are fascinated by words, you need to realize that you probably developed that sense of wonder by interacting with someone—a parent, teacher, friend—who communicated his or her love of words. That gift is now one that you can pass on to your students, regardless of what subject you teach. If you have not yet developed an appreciation for words, it is never too late! Read a few books such as ones by Isaac Asimov, Willard Espy, Charles Funk, Richard Lederer, or William Safire that describe words' histories, or etymologies. These and other sources will help you overcome any lingering logophobia and help you and your future students become logophiles!

Predict Word Relationships

Have students predict the relationships among words in a passage before reading the passage. You can do this with Passage Impressions and Word Splash.

PASSAGE IMPRESSIONS In Passage Impressions, students compose a brief passage by fitting together words in a given order, reading a passage that contains the words, then refitting their original impressions. Here are the four steps of Passage Impressions:

1. Students write paragraphs using displayed words in order. Show students a list of key vocabulary, then say: *Here are some words contained in what we are going to be reading. First, write your own paragraph using all these words in the order they are presented.*

Grand Canyon Geology
Colorado Plateau
uplift
erosion
strata
sedimentary
limestone
sandstone
shale

2. After writing, have a few students read their paragraphs aloud to the class.
3. Then have students read the target story or passage and see how their ideas compare with the author's.
4. After reading, have students compare the similarities and differences between the contents of their paragraphs and the author's actual composition. This comparison can be done through discussion, writing, or both.
5. Have students rewrite their paragraphs as needed to align them with the text.

WORD SPLASH While Passage Impressions has students order words from first to last in entire paragraphs, Word Splash has students relate words in any order through graphic organizers and sentences.

A student organizes words by looking for words with similar meanings.

To begin Word Splash, identify key terms from the reading passage that are adequately defined by their context. Display the words, like the Grand Canyon ones above, on cards so they can be manipulated. Then follow six steps:

1. Explore word relationships. Students might come to the front of the class and graphically organize the words to portray how they fit with each other.
2. Have students write sentences that each contain at least two of the key words, underlining them in each sentence. Words may be used in more than one sentence, but every word must be used at least once.
3. After writing, have a few students read their sentences aloud to the class.
4. Students then read the text to see how it supports their sentences.
5. Revise the sentences. Using the passage as a reference, students evaluate the information in each of their original sentences to determine which ones are supported and which ones need revision. Unsupported sentences should be made accurate.
6. Share the revised sentences. Ask for new sentences from the word list that conform with the passage information.

Have Students Select the Words to Be Learned

Ruddell and Shearer (2002) suggest a vocabulary self-collection strategy in which students list words they consider important and relatively unknown. The list of words that students suggest can be supplemented to fit the criteria for choosing which words to teach offered earlier in this chapter. Students involved in the vocabulary self-selection practice tend to consistently select challenging words that contribute to their subject matter knowledge. They also devote substantial effort to learning the meanings of the words they collect, tending to engage in extended and multilayered discussions of the words. Engaging learners in selecting words gives them considerable voice and choice in their vocabulary development, contributing to their word consciousness and learning.

Help Students Develop Self-Assessment Strategies

Helping students self-assess is one of the major ways of helping them develop word consciousness. Help students self-assess by presenting them with a knowledge-rating scale and have them assess their knowledge of the unit's key words using that scale at the beginning and end of the unit. Students could then add up the number of points they have moved for tangible proof of their vocabulary growth in your subject.

Vocabulary Self-Assessment Scale

0 = I never heard of that word in my whole life.

1 = I have heard it, but I have no idea what it means.

2 = I couldn't tell you what it means, but I might be able to pick the right meaning from four choices.

3 = I can tell you a little about that word.

4 = I could put that word in a good sentence that would show its meaning.

5 = I could use that word correctly in discussion and writing.

Another way to support students' vocabulary self-assessment is to post questions such as the following that invite thinking about what to do upon encountering unfamiliar words:

1. What unfamiliar word should I figure out in order to understand the selection?
2. Have I seen this word before? What do I know about it already?
   Do I understand the word well enough to continue?
3. Does this part of the selection help me understand the word? Do other parts of the selection help me understand the word?
   Do I understand the word well enough to continue?
4. Do any parts of the word help me understand it?
   Do I understand the word well enough now to continue?
5. Who or what can help me understand the word right away?
   If I still don't understand the word, mark it and come back to it later.

Maintain Word Books

Many teachers have students maintain word books—vocabulary notebooks in which students record the words they are learning. Students may use a notebook or sheets of paper stapled together and decorated with an interesting cover. Words are then usually entered according to their first letter, but in the sequence in which they are introduced, alphabetical by first letter only. Depending on the age of the students and the type of word being studied, different information can be included with each word. Many teachers like students to write a personal example for each word ("*Frigid* is a February day when the thermometer hits 20°F.") as well as a definitional sentence

("*Frigid* means very, very cold."). Although students may consult the dictionary for help, it is best not to let them copy dictionary definitions because this requires little thought or understanding. In addition to an example and definitional sentence, other information may be included. The following table lists productive dimensions of words to use in word books.

Dimensions of Words

Dimension	Example
1. Original Sentence (Copy the sentence containing the word.)	Pat was not used to the frigid weather conditions he now faced.
2. Dictionary Definition (What does the dictionary say the word means?)	extremely cold
3. New Sentence (Use the word in a sentence that shows what it means.)	A winter day at the north pole would be frigid.
4. Closest Experience (When have you seen it?)	My aunt has a big freezer, and the inside of it is frigid.
5. Explanation of Meaning (In your own words, what does it mean?)	Frigid means very, very cold.
6. Main Idea (What is it?)	a way to describe temperature
7. Details (What are some parts of it?)	you can see your breath, ice and snow
8. Synonym/Comparison (What words have nearly the same meaning?)	cold, freezing, polar
9. Antonym/Contrast (What words have nearly the opposite meaning?)	warm, hot, burning
10. Word Family Members (What words share the same root, or base?)	Frigidaire, refrigerator, fridge
11. Origin (What does the word come from?)	*Frigid* comes from the Latin word *frigus*, which means frosty or cold.
12. Translation (What is the Spanish [or other home language] word for it?)	Frígida
13. Visual (Illustrate the meaning of the word.)	
14. Learning Key (How will you remember this word?)	The *fr* beginning makes me think of the first two letters in frosty, freezing and frozen, and the *rigid* part reminds me of something frozen solid. So frigid is something that is so cold that things barely move.

Play with Words

As Blachowicz and Fisher (2004) put it, word play puts the *fun* back into *fundamental*. Word play is a motivating way to position youth as active manipulators of words, as being conscious of words. It focuses on different dimensions of word structures and meanings. The following word plays join time-honored activities such as classroom baseball, charades, Password, and Pictionary for promoting word consciousness.

STUMP THE EXPERT   Students play either individually, in pairs, or in small groups.

1. Designate the expert.
2. A stumper then offers an academic challenge in an attempt to confound the expert. With vocabulary, stumpers typically present a definitional statement (e.g., "This word is used a lot in the winter to describe extremely cold weather.") and the expert has a set time (e.g., ten seconds) to produce the term (e.g., *frigid*).
3. If the expert responds accurately, the next stumper offers a challenge. This continues until the expert is stumped—or until the expert answers a certain number of challenges (e.g., seven) and earns recognition (e.g., applause), a prize (e.g., food treat), or both.
4. Whoever successfully stumps the expert becomes the new expert, and the procedure begins anew.

AROUND THE WORLD   A student designated as the traveler moves from his or her seat and stands by a student in the next seat. Orally, present the traveler and the challenger a definitional statement; whoever says the matching word first is the traveler and stands by the student in the next seat. A traveler who continues responding first and returns to his or her seat has successfully gone Around the World.

CONCENTRATION   Patterned after the popular card game, vocabulary concentration relies on card pairs containing a term on one and a definitional statement on another.

1. Tape the cards containing the terms to one section of the board; randomly tape the cards containing the definitional statements on another section.
2. Students playing either individually, in pairs, or in small groups then direct the teacher or an assistant to uncover one card from each section. If a matching pair is uncovered, the students keep it and try to match another pair. If they do not make a match, the next set of students tries.
3. When all the pairs are matched, students determine who uncovered the most pairs.

TWENTY QUESTIONS   One student silently holds in mind a word from the unit's vocabulary list. Other students then take turns asking yes–no questions—no more than twenty—to determine the word that was selected. One particular questioner might continue until he or she receives a "no," or questioners might be allowed to ask only one question at a time to allow greater participation. Questions should progress from general to specific.

JEOPARDY   Patterned after the popular television show, Jeopardy contains columns with about five terms in each column, arranged from simple to difficult. The columns might be headed by unit categories (e.g., sedimentary rocks, metamorphic rocks, methods of erosion) or simply by letters.

A	B	C	D
5	5	5	5
10	10	10	10
15	15	15	15
20	20	20	20
25	25	25	25

Students then select a cell (e.g., "C for 15"), listen to the definitional statement, and attempt to produce the appropriate term.

WHATTA YA KNOW   Put two words together in a way that students can answer only with "yes" or "no." You or your students can be the ones to make up the sentences. The responses can be written or stated orally, and hands can be raised for yes and then for no. For instance, the following questions might be asked about words associated with *volcanoes*:

1. Do *igneous* rocks come from *magma*?
2. Are *volcanoes* made from *lava*?
3. Would you find *igneous* rocks around *volcanoes*?
4. *Lava* is what *magma* is called when it's under the ground.

Be sure to talk about students' reasons for their answers. Points can be kept for appropriate responses if desired.

DO IT TOGETHER

In a small group or pair preparing to teach the same subject, discuss the meaning vocabulary teaching practices described in the last section. Choose the strategies that your group or pair would be most likely to use with students and write a one-sentence rationale for choosing each. Compare your list and rationales with other groups or pairs to personalize and apply your knowledge of the practices.

TEACH WORD LEARNING STRATEGIES

Students who learn new words on their own are active, independent learners (Edwards, Font, Baumann, & Boland, 2004; Harmon, Wood, & Medina, 2009). They note important unfamiliar words, then use strategies to learn them. Independent word learning strategies involve making use of context, morphemes, and external resources.

google for top 5

Context

Do you know what a jingo is? Imagine that you are reading and come across the unknown word *jingo* in this context:

> All he ever talked about was war. His country was the best country, and anyone who disagreed should be ready to fight in battle. He was really quite a jingo!

You could now infer that a jingo must be a militaristic person ready to defend his or her country (or have someone else defend it) at the drop of a hat. The word *jingo* may have been unfamiliar, but if you have had experience with nationalistic, militaristic people, the concept was not. The context helped you associate your old meaning with a new label. Context is a valuable tool for associating meaning with words, because once you learn how to use context, you can do so independently without a teacher's help. Many students, however, do not make proficient use of context. They do not know how surrounding words give clues to unfamiliar words.

There are a variety of context clues, and you ought to present all the common ones so that students become familiar with them. Common types of context clues include explanatory sentences, as in the jingo example; synonyms ("mean, cruel, and truculent"); antonyms ("Some things are easy, others are arduous"); similes and metaphors ("as fervid as a stove"); and appositives ("the pandowdy, a pudding made with apples").

Teach your students how to use context clues early in the year, then apply uses of the clues throughout the year. The subject matter texts you and your students will encounter will provide plenty of opportunities to develop proficiencies with context clues. The direct explicit model for teaching reading comprehension strategies (Duke & Pearson, 2002) presented in Chapter 5 is appropriate for teaching word learning strategies, too. The model, based on a gradual release of responsibility and known informally as "I Do, We Do, You Do," fits the use of context clues as follows:

I do
we do
you do

Describe the Strategy (I Do)

Explain what the strategy is and when and how to use it. Present a sentence like the following that is grade appropriate, call attention to the unfamiliar (underlined) word, then describe how context can be used to figure it out.

They used <u>indigo</u> to dye the shirt and get the blue color they wanted.

Model the Strategy (I Do)

Show students how to use the strategy by thinking aloud as you read. Read the sentence again, but stop and think-aloud the mental moves you are making to figure out the unfamiliar word. Call attention to the explanatory words *used*, *dye*, and *blue* that suggest the meaning of *indigo*. Emphasize that context gives only clues to words, and sometimes these clues can lead readers astray. Ideas about what a word means when seen in context should be considered tentative. Context-based guesses, however, are more likely to be right than guesses made without context.

Collaboratively Use the Strategy (We Do)

Work with students to jointly apply the strategy. To begin fading your instruction, read aloud or have students read silently another sentence like the one below, then get your students in on the act. Have them share with the class the context clues they used to figure out the meaning of *volubility*, then provide feedback on their efforts. You might share your own thinking, making sure to highlight the way *in sharp contrast to* signals an antonym to *quietness*.

John's quietness was in sharp contrast to Glen's <u>volubility</u>.

As you and your students figure out word meanings from context and explain your reasoning, have volunteers look up the words in a dictionary and read the appropriate definitions to the class. This reinforces the notion that context typically gives only clues, not certain answers, and it models for students how to use the dictionary authentically for checking hunches and gaining more precise information.

Guide Application of Multiple Strategies (You Do)

Gradually release responsibility to students to use the strategy along with other strategies they have learned. At this point you might have students read a section of text, then share their uses of context clues with a partner, small group, or the class. Sharing uses of context might be only part of what the students talk about after reading sections of a text. For instance, they might note their uses of dictionaries to confirm word meanings. If they encounter *volubility* again, they might note that the base word *volume* underlies it.

Support Independent Application of Multiple Strategies (You Do)

Continue releasing responsibility to students to use strategies they have learned when they are reading independently. When students demonstrate control of context clues, remind them to apply all their strategies for figuring out unfamiliar words that come up. Have students tell how the use of context affects their reading.

In addition to these planned lessons, you have the opportunity on a daily basis to explore with students how context helps in figuring out meanings for words (Harmon, 2002). When you and your class encounter a word whose meaning even you—the teacher—are not sure of, that is a perfect opportunity to model authentically how you use context as your first line of attack on a new word. In the next section of this chapter, we discuss the role that morphemes play in figuring out meaning for big words. Context and morphemic sophistication are a powerful combination for learning new word meanings.

Morphemes

Here is the first sentence from a *USA Today* article in which all the words of three or more syllables have been replaced with X's.

> French XXXXXXXXX are XXXXXXXXX ways to XXXXXXXXX should the United States enforce laws XXXXXXXXXXX XXXXXXXXXXXX trade.

You can easily see that without some ability to pronounce and access meanings for these words, comprehension would be impossible. Now, read the sentence again and put these words where the X's are: *officials, exploring, retaliate, restricting, international.*

Imagine that you are teaching a unit in economics on international trade, and you want your students to write a letter to the editor expressing their opinions related to this topic. Writing a sensible letter would be impossible unless they could use some of these big, specific words in their writing. Even if you allow them to spell the words as best they can on a first draft and then fix them on a final draft, they must be able to remember the words and make some attempt at spelling them, or their writing will not reflect the kind of thinking you want them to do.

The simple truth is that learning about any content area topic requires students to learn to speak, understand, read, and write a new vocabulary. Throughout this chapter, we have emphasized strategies you can use to teach new vocabulary, but your students are going to meet many more words than you can possibly teach, and if they have a "skip it" or "quit reading" reaction to text with lots of big, not-immediately-familiar words, they are not going to be able to read much independently. This sets off a vicious downward cycle because vocabulary is developed primarily through wide reading, and students who avoid reading are cut off from this most important source of vocabulary development.

Let's look again at those five words your students might not have immediately recognized:

officials, exploring, retaliate, restricting, international

Two of these words, *exploring* and *restricting*, are what linguists call "morphologically transparent," that is, they are related to smaller words and would be almost instantly identified by a reader who knew the words *explore* and *restrict*. Two other words, *officials* and *international*, also have related words, but it requires a level of "morphological sophistication" to recognize the similarities. The word *officials* is related to the words *office* and *officers* and also to words such as *nationals* and *professionals*. *International* is related to the word *nation* and also to *interstate* and *intersection*. The only word for which many readers would not have some related words to help them figure out its pronunciation and meaning is *retaliate*.

Morphemes →

The English language contains innumerable word families based on common morphemes (Venezky, 1999). (*Morphemes* are meaning-bearing parts of words, including prefixes, roots, and suffixes.) Linguists estimate that for every word you learn, you can transfer some part of its pronunciation, spelling, and meaning to seven other words! That is the good news. The bad news is that in order to do this transferring, you have to notice the letters, sounds, and meanings that words share! Even many high-school students do not notice common meaningful word parts!

Of the ten thousand new words students from fifth grade and up encounter in school each year, only one thousand are probably truly new words, not related to other more familiar words. If we can help our students become more morphologically sophisticated, they will be able to take advantage of these morphological relationships when reading and writing on their own (Nagy, Berninger, & Abbott, 2006; Templeton, 2004). Word Bench is a practice designed to help students notice these relationships.

WORD BENCH   To help students become aware of the helpful links words share, there are two questions you should get them in the habit of asking themselves:

1. "Do I know any other words that look like this word?"
2. "Are any of these look-alike words related to each other?"

These two simple questions can be used by every teacher in every subject area. Imagine that students in a mathematics class encounter this new term:

improper fraction

Assuming you selected *improper fraction* as a key term for your unit and displayed it for intensive study, you would introduce it naturally as it came up in your lessons. You would show its written form and pronounce it clearly and slowly, emphasizing its syllables. You would explain its meaning with student-friendly definitions, media representations, verbal connections, and several examples. You would encourage elaboration by having students work with improper fractions, converting them to mixed numbers, and comparing them with proper fractions. Then, to focus on the morphemes in the term, you would set aside no more than ten minutes to examine *improper fraction* on a wordbench.

Display the word, saying that this is on the *wordbench*, something like a *workbench* where carpenters and mechanics assemble and reassemble objects. In this case, the objects are words. Ask your students to pronounce and look at both words and see if they know any other words that look like these words: For *improper*, students might think of

impossible, important, impatient
property, properly, proper

For *fraction*, they might think of
fracture, motion, vacation, multiplication

List the words, underlining the parts that are the same. Then explain that words, like people, sometimes look alike but are not related. If this is the first time this analogy is used, you will want to spend some time talking with the students about people with red hair, green eyes, and so on, who have some parts that look alike but are not related and others who are.

"Not all people who look alike are related, but some are. This is how words work, too. Words are related if there is something about their meaning that is the same. After we find look-alike words, we try to think of any ways these words might be in the same meaning family."

With your help, your students will discover that *impossible* is the opposite of *possible, impatient* is the opposite of *patient*, and *improper* is the opposite of *proper. Proper* and *improper* are clearly relatives! Depending on their word sophistication, someone might be able to point out that a *fracture* is a break into two or more parts and that *fraction* also involves parts.

Imagine that your students who were introduced to the morphemes in *improper fractions* on Monday using Word Bench had a science teacher on Tuesday who is beginning a unit on weather and does some experiments with the students using *thermometers* and *barometers*. At the close of the lesson, the teacher uses Word Bench with these words and helps them notice that the *meter* morphemes are related to one another and refer to measurement.

Now imagine that your lucky class of students has a social studies teacher on Wednesday who uses Word Bench to point out the morphemes in the new word *international*, an art teacher on Thursday who has them do the same with *sculpture*, and an English teacher on Friday with whom they encounter the new word *personify*. Such instruction benefits all students, and it is especially appropriate for Spanish-speaking English Language Learners when they capitalize on Spanish–English cognates (e.g., violencia/violence, farmacia/pharmacy) (Carlo et al., 2004). Examining possible morphemes in the key vocabulary introduced in any content area adds to the instruction and pays students back manyfold (Kieffer & Lesaux, 2007).

External Resources

As you began this chapter on vocabulary, did you expect to find a chapter full of dictionary activities? This is a common yet unproductive practice. It is like expecting that you could get to know new people by looking them up in *Who's Who* and writing down their distinguishing characteristics. Such a practice is helpful only if you already know something about the people and want to find out more. In the same way, dictionaries are wonderful resources for adding to or clarifying a word's meaning.

Students need to see how people use the dictionary authentically. People do not look up lists of words and write definitions that they memorize for a test. People consult a dictionary when they cannot figure out the meaning of a word they encounter in their reading. They look up a word they know a little about when they meet it in a new context and need some clarification or elaboration on its meaning. Sometimes a dictionary is used to check the spelling of a word needed in writing.

The heading for this section is *external resources* to acknowledge the funds of word information available in places other than standard print dictionaries. When examining word meanings, you can consult a glossary, thesaurus, online resources like Onelook or Google, resources that come with your word processing software, and knowledgeable people. When students meet a new word and ask what it means, you may respond with a little information and then say, "I don't really know exactly what that means. Let's look it up and find out." As described in the context section, you can have students use the dictionary to check or flesh out a meaning derived from context. When you are at the board recording a brainstormed list or some other student-generated responses, you can model how to check the spelling of a word of which you are unsure. Showing your students that you see external resources as the natural tools to discover and clarify meanings and check spellings will go a long way toward their independent vocabulary learning.

LISTEN, LOOK, AND LEARN

Interview three of your friends about their vocabulary remembrances: Are they logophiles or do they suffer from logophobia? Do they remember looking words up and writing the definitions? How did this affect how they felt about the dictionary? Do they use a dictionary now, and how do they use it?

DISCIPLINARY LITERACIES

Vocabulary in English/Language Arts Classrooms

Two primary goals of reading novels, short stories, plays, and poetry are to gain insights into the human condition and to participate vicariously in the text worlds authors create. To accomplish these goals, readers must understand the words they encounter. Understanding vocabulary, then, is the means to the end of literary insights and experiences. Understanding vocabulary is not the end.

vocab. is means to an end

Effective English teachers perform a balancing act when addressing vocabulary: They work at developing word understandings while keeping those understandings subservient to the larger purposes for which students read. They achieve balance before students read by teaching the specific word meanings needed to grasp overall passage meanings. Effective English teachers achieve balance after reading by focusing attention on the key words that elicited the messages and experiences students gained. This balancing act fits situations involving single passages as well as multiple passages.

SINGLE PASSAGES   To consider effective ways to promote vocabulary when students are reading a single passage, think of *Shabanu, Daughter of the Wind*, the novel addressed in Chapter 5 (pages 109–110). Vocabulary learning readily can be folded into the study of this piece of literature.

Before students read *Shabanu*, introducing unfamiliar words that are crucial to understanding a section but are not fully explained is a good way to balance vocabulary and passage understandings. To illustrate, desert *oases* play a large role in *Shabanu*. Readers who lack clear and extensive understandings of this term risk substantial difficulties with the novel because it assumes readers already know about oases. Presenting the word in depth to students before they read the book is appropriate. As part of the introduction to the novel, you display *oasis* before the class and call attention to its pronunciation, then develop in-depth knowledge of its meaning. You ask students to call up what they already know about oases, present pictures and videos of them, and create analogies. You connect this individual term to the overall novel by explaining how it is a central part of the setting.

Folding vocabulary instruction into the study of *Shabanu* also can be done in the during- and after-reading phases. Asking students, "What is the most important word in this section?" and discussing their choices goes far in promoting active comprehension and in-depth vocabulary learning. A student who selects *storm* for the scene in which Shabanu's grandfather dies might focus on the denotations and connotations of this word. What exactly is a storm? Does *storm* refer to a physical weather disturbance or to characters' turmoil? How can personal relationships or the course of one's life be stormy?

If students are maintaining response journals for *Shabanu*, some of the writing prompts can highlight vocabulary. Offering a menu of prompts allows readers to select a vocabulary response format they find most productive. For instance, students illustrate the meanings of three words from a chapter (e.g., show people wearing *chadors* and *turbans* or having their bodies painted with *henna*). They present word families (pilgrim, pilgrimage; nomad, nomadic). They maintain a list of "words I should learn more about" for weekly follow-ups, or they complete vocabulary self-assessment scales of words that peers select. Students maintain a "language gems" section in their journals for recording vivid comparisons, strong verbs, and other phrases they find compelling.

MULTIPLE PASSAGES A standard recommended practice for increasing vocabularies is for students to read widely in materials that are within their capabilities. This recommendation is based in part on the inefficiency of teaching isolated terms in a word-by-word fashion. A large volume of reading provides students opportunities to encounter the thousands of new terms they need to develop their vocabularies.

English teachers who stimulate their students to read widely for pleasure and academics assist vocabulary development, but additional actions are needed to enhance this practice. Because it is impossible to introduce unfamiliar words that are crucial to understanding a section when each student selects his or her own materials, focusing on vocabulary in the during and after phases of self-selected reading is appropriate.

A good way to incorporate word study while students are reading on their own is to have them maintain journals with a section devoted to vocabulary. Students select their own materials for silent reading, and they enter into their journals sections of text that contain words or phrases they find appealing, that they want to remember, and that they believe deserve sharing with classmates. They might cite author, title, and page number for each section they record. About once a week, students share what they have recorded, and they engage their peers in a discussion of the passage context and meaningful word parts (if any) that determine the word's meaning. Students might first meet in groups to nominate a few words they consider most important for class consideration. When group representatives present their words to the class, they explain why they believe others should know them by articulating their contribution to the unit of study being conducted. You then post these words on a bulletin board or word wall and revisit them occasionally through word games and other review practices.

Vocabulary in English Language Development

Understanding the words of another language is only part of understanding the language, but it is a crucial part. Here are some ways to build on the suggestions presented in this chapter when teaching word meanings to English learners.

SCAVENGER HUNTS Realia and visual aids are used in many English Language Development classrooms to teach vocabulary meaningfully. One way to add to these concrete teaching tools is by enlisting students' help through scavenger hunts. Present a list of terms for each instructional unit, and have students individually or in groups bring in concrete objects, models, pictures, and illustrations that represent the terms. Afterwards, you have an almost instant bulletin board or display table for introducing and applying vocabulary.

Looking beyond obvious sources and representations is a good way to extend what you gather during scavenger hunts. For instance, children's action figures, dolls, and other toy people often come with physical settings such as dollhouses, forts, and farms. Leading your class of youngsters to describe the locations and actions of scenes ("The man is hiding behind the large house hoping to surprise the enemy.") can result in active participation and meaningful applications of terms. You also might provide Web sites and well-illustrated magazines for students to scavenge during class time.

CAPSULE VOCABULARY   The capsule vocabulary teaching strategy provides students good practice using English vocabulary. In this strategy, you first present the pronunciations and meanings of topically related words (e.g., fruits), then students use these words (e.g., apples, oranges, bananas) while conversing with each other. This strategy is most productive when the terms refer to known concepts because the emphasis here is on students practicing and applying new terms in a supportive setting. Capsule Vocabulary stresses attaching labels to concepts already understood more than developing conceptual knowledge.

Several options are available for practicing the Capsule Vocabularies that are introduced. Using the words in oral conversations certainly is appropriate. In written conversations, or buddy journals, students take turns composing notes to each other in a manner similar to the surreptitious note passing that sometimes occurs during class. Written conversations are like pen pal situations; however, the pals are in the same classroom and they are using certain terms associated with units of study.

Another Capsule Vocabulary practice option is for students to write one term each on a card and categorize the cards in whatever groupings come to mind. Additionally, students might write sentences with each one containing two or three target terms. The class could play Twenty Questions in English, a game in which one word is selected and players try to determine what it is by asking yes–no questions ("Is it an animal?" "Is it four-legged?" "Is it domestic?"). Charades and Password are two other games appropriate for practicing Capsule Vocabulary Terms.

USING COGNATES   English learners often apply their knowledge of word cognates when they encounter unfamiliar vocabulary. Cognates are words derived from a common earlier form. Spanish and English have especially large numbers of cognates due to their historical bases in Latin. Here are some Spanish–English cognates:

naturalmente	naturally	novelas	novels
clima	climate	decidir	decide
curioso	curious	farmacia	pharmacy

Using cognates to help understand and remember unfamiliar words involves several mental operations. Learners identify unfamiliar words that justify the time and energy to be figured out, they examine target words' spellings and pronunciations to determine if they might be cognates of known words, and they test possible meanings for the unfamiliar words in the contexts of the passages to decide upon specific meanings.

Teaching students to transfer their knowledge of word meanings in one language to help in another can be done according to the recommendations in this chapter for teaching morphological sophistication. Indeed, a shared morpheme is what makes up a cognate pair. In essence, students act as detectives when figuring out word meanings, and cognate relationships are powerful clues to solving the mystery of what many words mean. When attention is directed to long unfamiliar words, remind students to ask themselves,

"Do I know any other words that look like this word?"

"Are any of these look-alike words related to each other?"

And when meanings are suggested through possible cognates, have students ask themselves,

"Does my understanding of this word make sense in this passage?"

Consider the following description by a Mexican American woman of one of the healing plants in her garden:

> Estas hojas tienas se hiervan para hacer un te. Este te es para los diabeticos. Ellos lo toman para su enfermedad. (These tender leaves are boiled to make a tea. This tea is for diabetics. They drink it for their illness.) (Brozo, Valerio, & Salazar, 1996, p. 164)

Te–tea and *diabeticos–diabetics* are two word pairs with obvious cognate relationships. Students could be expected to capitalize on these relationships when assigning meaning to what they read. Somewhat more obscure relationships are apparent in *un–a* and *enfermedad–illness*. Explaining that the *un* in *unit, unite,* and *union* refers to *one* or *single* and that *infirmity* is a synonym for *illness* would offer students powerful clues for understanding and remembering the meanings of *un* and *enfermedad*.

Vocabulary in Mathematics Classrooms

When most people think of mathematics, they think of numbers, but math is a subject with its own very particular vocabulary, and if you don't know precisely what its words and symbols mean, you just can't do mathematics! Here are some practices teachers use to help students master the vocabulary of math.

A SYMBOL BOARD   Cover a bulletin board or attach a banner to your wall and add symbols to it as they are introduced. Put up the symbol and a class-created, user-friendly definition. Add pictures and opposites as appropriate. Use different colored markers and make it as appealing as possible.

MATH MORPHEMES   The Word Bench activity in which you ask your students if they know any other words that look and sound like a new mathematics term and determine if any of these words are related will help your students become more morphologically sophisticated. In addition, you have the unique opportunity to teach your students the meaning for some morphemes that occur most commonly in mathematics words. Seize this opportunity when teaching one of these words, because your students might not meet these morphemes in any of their other classes:

Morpheme	*Math Usage*	*General Usage*
bi (two)	bisect, binomial, bimodal	bicycle, bifocals, bilingual
cent (hundred)	centimeter, percent	century, centipede
circu (around)	circle, circumference	circumvent, circuit
co, con (with)	cosine, collinear	cocaptains, coordinate, concurrent
dec (ten)	decimal, decagon	decade, decibel
dia (through)	diagonal, diameter	dialogue, diagram
equi (equal)	equilateral, equiangular	equator, equinox, equitable
inter (between)	intersect, interdependent	interdisciplinary, international
kilo (thousand)	kilometer, kilogram	kilowatt
milli (thousand)	millimeter, milligram	millennium, million

peri (around)	perimeter	periphery, periscope, periodontal
poly (many)	polygon, polynomial	polygamy, polyunsaturated
quadr (four)	quadrant, quadruple	quadrangle, quadruped
tri (three)	triangle, triple	tricycle, tripod, trilogy
uni (one)	unilateral,	unicycle, unify unidimensional

MATH WORD BOOKS   Math word books are powerful devices for analyzing, recording, and reviewing math vocabulary. Some teachers have students maintain separate books for vocabulary. Other teachers have students set aside a special section of their math notebooks for vocabulary entries to go along with their class notes, problem sets they have worked, journal entries, and questions. Still others have students maintain separate math word cards, usually devoting the front and back of one card for each term.

Following the guidelines for word books presented earlier in this chapter, you might have students respond to three prompts when examining math vocabulary:

a. List a key math term
b. What does the term mean?
c. How will you remember the term?

You might encourage students to respond visually and with examples to the third prompt, "How will you remember the term?" They might respond to *improper fraction* by displaying 16/5, 27/9, 42/14; they might represent *multiples* with 18, 36, 54, 72, 90.

Maintaining math word books is especially important for clarifying the mathematical denotations of multiple-meaning words. The meanings of *base, face, gross, line, mean, power, prime, principal, product, radical, set, square, table,* and *times*—to name a few— depend on the way the words are used. Students require great sensitivity to the differences in their meanings, and creating and reviewing math word books as glossaries for these words go far in clarifying them.

Vocabulary in Science Classrooms

MULTIPLE-ENTRY-POINT DISPLAY   Each content area has unique vocabulary, but the technical vocabulary load in science is probably greater than in any other subject. Look at the key vocabulary listed for each chapter in a typical textbook and you will often find thirty to fifty words. Another problem is that much of the vocabulary used in science falls into the lupulin/lupulone category—students know neither the word nor the concept—rather than the lunules/philtrum/avuncular category in which students have the concept but simply lack the label.

One advantage that science teachers have is that much of their class time is spent with hands-on activities and experiments that are intended to provide the direct experience essential for building meanings for completely new concepts. Generally, the hands-on experience should occur first and then students should be led to attach the associated vocabulary with the phenomena experienced.

Science teachers must be ruthless about limiting the number of words, following the guidelines listed earlier. Textbook and curriculum guide writers often list all words not apt to be known by students without considering the fact that some listed words only occur once and are not essential for understanding the unit, much less the whole discipline.

Once you have identified the key vocabulary, let students know exactly which words are critical to master. One way to do that is to post critical vocabulary on a board along with a plain-English translation, picture, or diagram whenever possible. Show the phonetic pronunciation next to each word because many students have difficulty pronouncing these strange, big words. Students who understand what they are reading and what you are telling and demonstrating for them may lack the auditory route to retrieve that information if they cannot pronounce the critical words.

SCIENCE MORPHEMES   The Word Bench activity, in which you ask your students if they know any other words that look and sound like a new science term and determine if these words are related, will help your students become more morphologically sophisticated. In addition, you have the unique opportunity to teach your students the meaning for some morphemes that occur most commonly in science words. Seize this opportunity when teaching these words.

Morpheme	*Science Usage*	*General Usage*
aud (hear)	audible, audiometer	auditorium, audience
astro (star)	astronomy, astronaut	astronomical, asterisk
bio (life)	biology, biome, biosphere	biography, antibiotic
cardio (heart)	cardiovascular, cardiac	cordial, concord
chlor (greenish)	chlorophyll, chloroplast	chlorine, chlorosis
corp (body)	corpuscle, corpse	corporation, corps
dent (teeth)	dental, dentifrice	indent, trident
eco (habitat)	ecology, ecosystem	economy, eco-friendly
hydro (water)	hydrogen, hydroelectric	hydrant, hydroplane
hypo (under)	hypothermia, hypodermis	hypodermic, hypothesis
hyper (too much)	hyperglycemia, hyperphonia	hyperactive, hypertension
logy (science)	biology, geology, physiology	chronology, psychology
meta (change)	metamorphosis, metabolism	metaphor, metaphysical
micro (small)	microscope, microorganism	microphone, microfilm
ped (feet)	biped, quadruped	pedestrian, pedicure
photo (light)	photosynthesis, phosphorescent	photograph, photocopy
psych (mind)	psychosis, psychogenic	psychology psychiatrist
sym, syn (together)	symbiosis, symmetry	symphony, synchronize
therm (heat)	thermometer, thermal	thermos, thermostat
vor (eat)	omnivore, herbivore, carnivore	devour, voracious

Vocabulary in Social Studies Classrooms

FIGHTING WORDS   In social studies more than in any other subject area, students have to become attuned to the connotations as well as the denotations of words. In describing various events, the point of view of the writer colors the reporting and interpretation of these events, and this point of view is evidenced by the words used. To help students become sensitive to word choice and to review important vocabulary, give students lists of words/terms and have them indicate with a plus, check, or minus sign whether they think the word generally has positive, neutral, or negative connotations, respectively. After students complete this activity separately, have them get together with peers and discuss their decisions. This is an activity in which you want them to use the evaluate thinking process. Don't expect everyone to agree, because their point of view will affect their decisions. But considering the different connotations of common social studies terms will help them be more critical readers and better understand and retain the word meanings. Here are some starter words/terms. Pick similar words from your units.

liberal	conservative	corporation
pro-choice	pro-life	revolutionary
capitalist	reactionary	feminist
media	minority candidate	third world

SOCIAL STUDIES MORPHEMES   The Word Bench activity in which you ask your students if they know any other words that look and sound like a new social studies term and determine the words that are related will help your students become more morphologically sophisticated. In addition, you have the unique opportunity to teach your students the meaning of morphemes that occur most commonly in social studies words. Seize this opportunity when teaching these words because your students might not notice these morphemes in their other classes:

Morpheme	*Social Studies Usage*	*General Usage*
anti (against)	antitrust, antislavery	antibody, antisocial
com, con (with, together)	community, congress, conspiracy	compile, committee, company,conform
counter, contra (against)	counterintelligence, counteroffensive	counterfeit, contradict
ex (out)	exports, explorers	expedition, exit
form (shape)	conform, reformers	deformity, formula
geo (earth)	geography, geopolitical	geometry, geology
im, in (in)	imports, immigration, invasion, inauguration	implant, impoverish, indent, intruder
im, in (opposite)	immoral, independence	impatient, inefficient
inter (between)	international, intervention	interrupt, interfere
ism (state of)	communism, capitalism	patriotism, alcoholism
ist (person)	communist, nationalist	pianist, scientist
mono (one, same)	monarchy, monopoly	monorail, monolingual
non (opposite)	nonviolence, nonpartisan,	nonprofit, nonstop nonproliferation
sub (under)	subcontinent, subculture	subway, substitute
trans (across)	transAtlantic, transcontinental	transport, transfer
uni (one, same)	unilateral, unified, universal	uniform, united

ACRONYM AND ABBREVIATION BOARD   Cover a bulletin board or attach a banner to your wall and add acronyms and abbreviations to it as they occur in your study. List the items and the name for which they stand. Have your artistically talented students draw something to symbolize each one. Here are some examples of common social studies acronyms and abbreviations:

AID—Agency for International Development

CNN—Cable News Network

CORE—Congress of Racial Equality

HUD—Housing and Urban Development

MIA—Missing In Action

NATO—North Atlantic Treaty Organization

SADD—Students Against Destructive Decisions

WHO—World Health Organization

Vocabulary in Activity Classrooms

In many subjects, the emphasis is on doing rather than on reading and writing. In order to do anything successfully, however, you have to develop the vocabulary of that area. Whether you teach physical education, music, art, a vocational subject, or some other activity-oriented course, your students will learn more and like it more if you expend a small amount of time and effort identifying the key vocabulary in your area and making sure your students attach the appropriate meanings to the words and symbols. Here are some specific activities teachers in nontextbook courses have used to develop meanings for critical words.

WORD BOOKS Word books are powerful devices for analyzing, recording, and reviewing the new vocabulary encountered in activity classes. Some teachers have students maintain separate books for vocabulary. Other teachers have students set aside a special section of their class notebooks for vocabulary entries to go along with their class notes, illustrations, journal entries, and questions. Still others have students maintain separate word cards, usually devoting the front and back of one card for each term.

Following the guidelines for word books presented earlier in this chapter, you might have students respond to three prompts when examining vocabulary in your class:

a. List a key term
b. What does the term mean?
c. How will you remember the term?

You might encourage students to respond visually and with examples to the third prompt, "How will you remember the term?" They might respond to *vibrato* by linking it with *vibration*, they might link *nocturne* with *nocturnal*, and they might connect *libretto* with *library*.

Maintaining word books is especially important for clarifying the denotations of multiple-meaning words encountered in your specialization. In auto mechanics the meanings of *charge, clutch, counter, crank, file, hex, tap and die,* and *thread*—to name a few—depend on the way the words are used; music presents terminology with multiple meanings like *bar, beat, flat, key, note, pitch, scale, score,* and *sharp*. Students require sensitivity to the differences in these words' meanings, and creating and reviewing word books as glossaries for these words go far in clarifying them.

WORD/SYMBOL/PICTURE BOARD   Fortunately, many of the new meanings that students must learn in activity courses are words that represent concrete, real things. Learning the names of the parts of the lathe becomes a much simpler task when a picture or diagram is displayed with these parts labeled. Coaches have long made use of diagrams for various plays and positions. A music board might display the symbols for *sharp, flat, note, repeat*, and so forth, along with the words for which they stand. A display of art labeled for its style and media catches the eye while simultaneously giving reality to confusing terms such as *impressionist, neoclassical*, and *acrylic*.

MORPHEMES   Just as in all areas, many of the new words your students will encounter are big words for which your students have other words that will help them figure out and remember pronunciations, spellings, and meanings. Students in an art class who are dealing with the concepts of *foreground* and *background* and whose attention is drawn to words such as *forehand, forehead, backhand*, and *backpack* should have no trouble understanding and using the new art terms. The strange new words *micrometer, variometer*, and *magnetometer* are not so strange when connected with *speedometer, thermometer, microscope, variations*, and *magnetic*. With a little help, students can even be led to see the "strong" relationship in such words as *fortress, fortitude, fortify*, and *fortissimo*.

When you are on the lookout for these morphemic relationships between words and point them out to your students, your students benefit in two ways. The obvious benefit is that they can more easily learn your new vocabulary and retain it fairly effortlessly. Less obvious—but actually more important in the scheme of things—you help your students become independent word learners who, whenever they encounter a new word, are apt to look for clues in already-known words and thus grow in vocabulary knowledge from all the reading they do. Not a bad return on a small investment of time and energy!

LOOKING BACK

Having a thorough knowledge of the key words is essential to learning in any content area. The vocabulary of each content area is specific to that area and not apt to occur in normal conversation, recreational reading, or television viewing. All content area teachers must teach the vocabulary essential to communicating their subjects. These are the keys you explored in this chapter: (1) Vocabulary development is complex; (2) promote rich and meaningful experiences with language, (3) teach sets of words directly, (4) promote word consciousness, and (5) teach word learning strategies.

ADD TO YOUR JOURNAL

Reflect upon the five key ideas in this chapter. Which teachers best taught you the meanings of specific words? Which teachers helped you learn to use context or become morphologically sophisticated? Think about the teaching strategies described. Which ones could you most profitably use in your teaching? Emphasize independence. Students will not always have you there to ferret out the critical words and devise ways to learn them. What will you do to help your students become independent word learners?

Additional Readings

Some notable books devoted specifically to vocabulary instruction are as follows:

Baumann, J., & Kame'Enui, E. J. (Eds.). (2004). *Vocabulary instruction: Research to practice*. New York, NY: The Guilford Press.

Beck, I. L., Mckeown, M. G., & Kucan, L. (2002). *Bringing words to life: Robust vocabulary instruction*. New York, NY: The Guilford Press.

Beck, I. L., Mckeown, M. G., & Kucan, L. (2008). *Robust vocabulary: Frequently asked questions and extended examples*. New York, NY: Guilford.

Blachowicz, C., & Fisher, P. (2009). *Teaching vocabulary in all classrooms* (4th ed.). Upper Saddle River, NJ: Merrill Prentice Hall.

Graves, M. F. (2006). *The vocabulary book: Learning and instruction*. New York, NY: Teachers College Press.

Lubliner, S. I., & Scott, J. A. (2008). *Nourishing vocabulary: Balancing words and learning*. Thousand Oaks, CA: Corwin Press.

Stahl, S. A., Nagy, W. E. (2006). *Teaching word meanings*. Mahwah, NJ: L. Erlbaum Associates.

This survey reports the vocabulary teaching practices that secondary preservice teachers prefer:

Hedrick, W. B., Harmon, J. M., & Wood, K. (2008). Prominent content vocabulary strategies and what secondary preservice teachers think about them. *Reading Psychology, 29*, 443–470.

The following presents an innovative teaching practice that connects vocabulary learning with real world observing and participating

Blachowicz, C. L. Z., & Obrochta, C. (2005). Vocabulary visits: Virtual field trips for content vocabulary development. *The Reading Teacher, 59*, 262–268.

Good sources of words to present when teaching morphemes and other word features are in the following:

Bear, D., Invernizzi, M., Templeton, S., & Johnston, F. (2007). *Words their way: Word study for phonics, vocabulary, and spelling instruction* (4th ed.). Upper Saddle River, NJ: Prentice-Hall.

Johnston, F., Invernizzi, M., Bear, D., & Templeton, S. (2008). *Words their way: Word sorts for syllables and affixes spellers* (2nd ed.). Upper Saddle River, NJ: Prentice-Hall.

Templeton, S., Johnston, F., Bear, D. R., & Invernizzi, M. (2008). *Words their way: Word sorts for derivational relations spellers* (2nd ed.). Upper Saddle River, NJ: Prentice-Hall.

Another good source of words to present when teaching morphemes and other word features are in the following:

Ganske, K. (2000). *Word journeys: Assessment-guided phonics, spelling, and vocabulary instruction*. New York, NY: The Guilford Press.

Ganske, K. (2006). *Word sorts and more: Sound, pattern, and meaning explorations K–3*. New York, NY: Guilford.

Ganske, K. (2008). *Mindful of words: Spelling and vocabulary explorations 4–8*. New York, NY: Guilford.

This book also presents words to present when teaching word features. It has an especially extensive list of homophones.

Fry, E. B. (2004). *The vocabulary teacher's book of lists*. San Francisco, CA: Jossey-Bass.

Books like the following that present the origins of English words and phrases help develop your and your students' word consciousness:

Barnhart, R. K. (1995). *The Barnhart concise dictionary of etymology*. New York, NY: Collins Reference.

Funk. W. (1992). *Word origins: A classic exploration of words and language*. New York, NY: Gramercy.

Lederer, R. (1991). *The play of words*. New York, NY: Pocket Books. (Lederer has produced many joyful books on English; all are recommended.)

Safire, W. (2004). *The right word in the right place at the right time*. New York, NY: Simon & Schuster.

Online Resources

These two online etymologies are valuable sources of word origins and morphological links.

Online Etymological Dictionary
http://www.etymonline.com

Word Information
www.wordinfo.info/

Selected online dictionaries and collections of dictionaries are available here.

American Heritage Dictionary
http://www.bartleby.com/am/

Dictionary.com
http://dictionary.reference.com

Merriam-Webster OnLine
http://www.m-w.com/

My Word
http://myword.info/

Onelook
www.onelook.com

Among other things, this multipurpose site allows you to cluster words by spelling patterns.

All Words
www.allwords.com

Two portals to online references for word study and word games are as follows.

Megalist of Word Links
http://home.earthlink.net/~ruthpett/safari/megalist.htm

Word Play
http://www.wolinskyweb.net/word.htm

References

Beck, I. L., Mckeown, M. G., & Kucan, L. (2002). *Bringing words to life: Robust vocabulary instruction.* New York, NY: The Guilford Press.

Blachowicz, C. L. Z., & Fisher, P. (2004). Keep the "fun" in fundamental: Encourage word awareness and incidental word learning in the classroom through word play. In J. F. Baumann & E. J. Kame'enui (Eds.), *Vocabulary instruction: Research to practice* (pp. 218–237). New York, NY: The Guilford Press.

Blachowicz, C. L. Z., Fisher, P. J. L., Ogle, D., & Watts-Taffe, S. (2006). Vocabulary: Questions from the classroom. *Reading Research Quarterly, 41,* 524–539.

Brozo, W. G., Valerio, P. C., & Salazar, M. M. (1996). A walk through Gracie's garden: Literacy and cultural expectations in a Mexican American junior high school. *Journal of Adolescent and Adult Literacy, 40*(3), 164–170.

Carlo, M. S., August, D., Snow, C. E., Dressler, C., Lippman, D. N., Lively, T. J., & White, C. E. (2004). Closing the gap: Addressing the vocabulary needs of English-language learners in bilingual and mainstream classrooms. *Reading Research Quarterly, 39,* 188–215.

Cunningham, A. E., & Stanovich, K. (1998). What reading does to the mind. *American Educator, 22*(1), 8–15.

Duke, N. K., & Pearson, P. D. (2002). Effective practices for developing reading comprehension. In A. E. Farstrup & S. J. Samuels (Eds.), *What research has to say about reading instruction* (pp. 205–242). Newark, DE: International Reading Association.

Edwards, E. C., Font, G., Baumann, J. F., & Boland, E. (2004). Unlocking word meanings: Strategies and guidelines for teaching morphemic and contextual analysis. In J. F. Baumann & E. J. Kame'enui (Eds.), *Vocabulary instruction: Research to practice* (pp. 159–176). New York, NY: The Guilford Press.

Graves, M. F. (2000). A vocabulary program to complement and bolster a middle-grade comprehension program. In B. M. Taylor, M. F. Graves, & P. van den Broek (Eds.), *Reading for meaning: Fostering comprehension in the middle grades* (pp. 116–135). New York, NY: Teachers College Press.

Graves, M. F. (2006). *The vocabulary book: Learning and instruction.* New York, NY: Teachers College Press.

Graves, M. F., & Watts-Taffe, S. (2008). For the love of words: Fostering word consciousness in young readers. *The Reading Teacher, 62,* 185–193.

Harmon, J. M. (2002). Teaching independent word learning strategies to struggling readers. *Journal of Adolescent and Adult Literacy, 45,* 606–615.

Harmon, J. S., Wood, K. D., & Medina, A. L. (2009). Vocabulary learning in the content areas: Research-based practices for middle and secondary school classrooms. In K. D. Wood & W. E. Blanton (Eds.), *Literacy instruction for adolescents: Research-based practice* (pp. 344–367). New York, NY: Guilford.

Hyland, K., & Tse, P. (2007). Is there an academic vocabulary? *TESOL Quarterly, 41,* 235–253.

Kieffer, M. J., & Lesaux, N. K. (2007). Breaking down words to build meaning: Morphology, vocabulary, and reading comprehension in the urban classroom. *The Reading Teacher, 61,* 134–144.

Krashen, S. (2004). *The power of reading* (2nd ed.). Englewood, CO: Libraries Unlimited.

Nagy, W. E., Berninger, V. W., & Abbott, R. D. (2006). Contribution of morphology beyond phonology to literacy outcomes of upper elementary and middle-school students. *Journal of Educational Psychology, 98,* 134–147.

Nagy, W., & Anderson, R. C. (1984). How many words are there in printed school English? *Reading Research Quarterly, 19,* 304–330.

National Reading Panel. (2000). *Teaching children to read: An evidence-based assessment of the scientific research literature on reading and its implications for reading instruction: Reports of the subgroups.* Bethesda, MD: National Institute of Child Health and Human Development, National Institutes of Health.

Ruddell, M., & Shearer, B. (2002). "Extraordinary," "tremendous," "exhilarating," "magnificent": Middle-school at risk students become avid word learners with the Vocabulary Self-Collection Strategy (VSS). *Journal of Adolescent and Adult Literacy, 45,* 352–363.

Scott, J. A., & Nagy, W. E. (2004). Developing word consciousness. In J. F. Baumann & E. J. Kame'enui (Eds.), *Vocabulary instruction: Research to practice* (pp. 201–217). New York, NY: The Guilford Press.

Templeton, S. (2004). The vocabulary-spelling connection: Orthographic development and morphological knowledge at the intermediate grades and beyond. In J. F. Baumann & E. J. Kame'enui (Eds.), *Vocabulary instruction: Research to practice* (pp. 118–138). New York, NY: The Guilford Press.

Venezky, R. L. (1999). *The American way of spelling: The structure and origins of American English orthography.* New York, NY: The Guilford Press.

CHAPTER 7

Writing

If you come upon someone who is sitting with a pen or pencil in hand or fingertips poised over the keyboard and staring at the blank page or screen, you might ask, "What are you doing?" The person will often respond, "I'm thinking."

Continuing to observe, you will see the person eventually move into the drafting phase, but the writing is not nonstop. If you are rude enough to interrupt during a stop and ask, "What are you doing?" the writer will probably again respond, "I'm thinking." Eventually, the writer will finish the first draft. The writer may put the piece away for a while or ask someone to "take a look at this and tell me what you think." Later the writer will return to the piece to revise and edit. Words will be changed and paragraphs added, moved, or deleted. Again, the writer will pause from time to time during this after-writing phase; if you ask the writer what he or she is doing, you will likely get the familiar response, "I'm thinking!"

This scenario shows that writing is, at its essence, thinking made external, thinking you record with a pen, pencil, or computer. Students who write as they are learning tend to think more and thus learn more (Bangert-Downs, Hurley, & Wilkinson, 2004; Newell, 2008). The following three keys head the contents of this chapter:

1. Vary informal writing.
2. Provide scaffolds for challenging tasks.
3. Teach writing strategies.

VARY INFORMAL WRITING

Informal writing can take just a few minutes but can help students focus on what they know, what they don't know, and what they are learning (Graham & Perin, 2007). In some classrooms, students regularly record short bursts of thoughts about a topic, recording their ideas, questions, and feelings throughout a unit. In this section, we describe informal writing that can occur on a daily basis as a tool for learning content.

Capture Ideas

Capture Ideas (Collins Writing Program, n.d.) is a timed practice where writers brainstorm a minimum number of items or lines in response to a topic. Students' work is assessed with a plus or minus. A more developed type of informal writing is Respond Correctly, which shows what writers know about a topic. It is a response to a specific question that is graded as a quiz.

Quick Writes

1. We are about to begin learning about machines. Take thirty seconds and write down all you can tell about machines. The clock starts now!
2. Before we begin our exploration of matter, write down everything you know about matter. You have one minute.
3. We have been talking about communities today. Write one sentence that expresses your own definition for community. Try to include the big ideas we have talked about.
4. We have been learning about habitats. List as many habitats as you can in thirty seconds.
5. Today's math lesson had some difficult concepts. List at least one thing you don't fully understand. We will work on it tomorrow.
6. I didn't hear from many of you today and I am wondering what you are thinking. Tell me in a sentence or two what you thought of today's activity.
7. The topics of race and prejudice are emotional ones. Tell me in a few sentences how you are feeling about the difficult issues we have talked about today.

These are all examples of quick writes used in content area classrooms. Quick writes are the least formal kind of writing and in some ways the easiest ones to fit into a crowded content curriculum. Quick writes are used for a variety of purposes.

- Examples 1 and 2 are previewing quick writes, intended to help both students and teacher assess entry-level knowledge about a new topic.
- Examples 3 and 4 are quick writes that help students synthesize the day's learning and let teachers assess how well the concepts were understood.
- Examples 5, 6, and 7 are self-assessment quick writes. Students assess their understanding, their involvement, their attitudes, and their emotions.

By reading these quick writes, you could determine common confusions, evaluate the success of the lesson, and determine if an emotional topic under consideration was at or beyond students' comfort levels.

What you do with quick writes depends on why you did them and how much time you have. If the quick writes are like examples 1 and 2 and intended to get students accessing prior knowledge and thinking about a topic, use them for a unit's introductory grabber as Chapter 3 suggested. You may want to have students tell what they have written down as you list this on the board and point out that this is the starting point, the "what we know" from Chapter 5. You may also ask volunteers to share what they have written in response to examples 3 and 4 in order to let students see how others defined *community* or how many habitats they have listed. This helps students cement their learning and monitor their level of understanding.

If you collect the quick writes, you may tell students not to put their names on them to make sure students know you are evaluating the lesson, class learning, mood, and so forth, and not individuals. Many teachers hand students small index cards for these assessment quick writes. Index cards are unintimidating and help students to view this writing as different from some of the more formal class assignments. Collecting the cards as an informal exit slip is a good way to manage this practice and bring closure to the day's lesson.

CUBING   *Cubing* is a quick-write practice that emphasizes different purposes for writing about the same topic. The name, *cubing*, comes from the practice of designating a purpose for each side of a cube (totaling six), then rolling it to see which one emerges. Cubing is a good way to practice writing; many teachers use it to prepare students for state-level writing assessments. Cubing differs from process-writing approaches that emphasize continual shuttling among planning, drafting, and revising to produce finished products. Cubing has become a fast-paced approach that emphasizes short bursts of output. Students have relatively brief amounts of time to produce final products.

You might designate writing purposes that correspond with your state tests along with ones considered important in their own right. For instance, given any topic, students might set out to perform the following:

- *Analyze*: Identify its parts and explain how they relate.
- *Narrate*: Tell a story connected with it.
- *Persuade*: Convince someone of an assertion related to it.
- *Respond*: React to it and support your reaction.
- *Specify*: Provide exact directions or details related to it.

First, teach students how to perform each of the tasks with simple topics. Then randomly select one for students to accomplish in a brief amount of time. If the Grand Canyon were the lesson topic, students might have the following purposes:

- Analyze the natural forces that carved the canyon.
- Narrate a story with the Grand Canyon as the physical setting.
- Persuade potential tourists that the canyon is a natural wonder.
- Respond to the word *grand* in the Grand Canyon's name.
- Specify how to enjoy the Grand Canyon best.

Like most teaching practices, cubing can be modified multiple ways. As with this example, you might leave one side of the cube blank and have someone in your class select the writing purpose when the blank side turns up. You might gradually decrease the amount of time students have to complete the tasks, generating excitement while inducing concentration on writing. You might include one purpose (e.g., persuade) more than once and delete another (e.g., narrate) according to your curricular emphases. Cubing can be performed readily with topics as diverse as the Grand Canyon, cell division, fractions, and personal identity.

TIMED WRITING   Timed Writing reflects the on-demand time-sensitive writing people frequently do for reports, proposals, and correspondence such as e-mail (Gere, Christenbury, & Sassi, 2005). It is designed to promote written fluency, to accelerate the flow of written words. Timed Writing is meant to promote a habit of focusing and producing text quickly. In content area classrooms, it directs students to concentrate on aspects of the current topic of study.

The inclusion of Timed Writing in many state tests, as well as in the SAT and ACT college entrance exams, has encouraged its practice in many classrooms. During Timed Writing, students compose in response to a prompt or choice of prompts for a specified amount of time, from thirty seconds to an entire class period. Note that the first two quick writes listed earlier contain a time deadline:

- We are about to begin learning about machines. Take **thirty seconds**, and write down all you can tell about machines. The clock starts now!
- Before we begin our exploration of matter, write down everything you know about matter. You have **one minute**.

These quick write/timed writes allow very brief amounts of time because they are meant only to help students call up prior knowledge. Others might allow more time for composing better-developed thoughts, although a deadline still is vigorously enforced.

When students produce timed writings, you might select the papers from particular groups of students for editing and assessing. Your students might edit first at home, then at school, before submitting the preliminary and final drafts to you for assessment. This practice helps you manage the paper load by dealing only with selected groups, and it focuses students' attention on their timed writing when they realize you could randomly select them to develop their writing.

Content Journals

A content journal is a place for your students to record their personal insights, questions, confusions, disagreements, and frustrations about what is being learned. (Some teachers call these journals *learning logs*.) Journal writing is primarily writing students do for themselves; it helps them sort through their thinking about what they are learning.

Content journals may have a great deal of structure or very little. When there is little structure, students choose what to write about. One student might write a diary-style account of what was learned, while another might write you a letter, complete with visuals, explaining his or her reaction to what is being studied. When students have control over the specific content they are writing about, the journals are said to have *low structure*.

With *high-structure* content journals, you require students to react to specific ideas they are exploring in class. Students may be asked to explore some controversial issue associated with the content. For instance, if westward expansion were the unit of study in American history, students might be asked to record their impressions of the similarities between nineteenth-century movement by U.S. citizens into Texas and twentieth-century movement by Mexican citizens into Texas. Students could be asked to call up impressions they had before beginning the class and compare them with their current impressions. They might be asked to summarize chapters or articles they are reading. The structure is high because the teacher assigns the writing task; students have little to say about what they are to write.

Typically, students are expected to write in their journals from five to ten minutes each day. Some teachers begin class each day with a five-minute journal-writing time. During the five minutes while students are completing their journal entries, you do the routine chores of attendance, talking to a student who was absent, and so on. On some days, a high-structure entry is required and prompted by a sentence or two written on the board. On other days, your students write whatever they want related to the topic being studied. Teachers who establish this five-minute beginning-of-class journal-writing routine report that journal writing does not take away from their teaching time because they must spend a few minutes at the beginning of each class with routine chores, and they see students settle in and get back into the content of the class much more readily.

Journals are collected several times a term in order to make sure students have been writing regularly, and to determine whether students are learning course content and reacting thoughtfully to the ideas they are encountering. While reading the journals, some teachers write comments to the students, creating a written dialogue, about how well students are learning the course material and how clearly they express what they have learned. Students' attitudes and efforts regarding journal writing seem to be directly related to the frequency and quality of a teacher's comments in the journals. Weekly reactions are ideal, although biweekly or monthly input is generally more feasible. Most teachers don't grade each journal entry, but they do give students points for keeping their journal up to date and for demonstrating good thinking.

TRY IT OUT

Plan three informal writing practices you might implement during a particular unit of instruction. Describe the practices in sufficient detail so a substitute teacher could perform them. Then share your descriptions with a few classmates to personalize and apply your knowledge of the types of informal writing presented here.

Students clarify their understandings of classroom experiences by writing.

PROVIDE SCAFFOLDS FOR CHALLENGING TASKS

Imagine that you have a frame for a particular instructional unit as described in Chapter 3, and you are satisfied with your objectives, essential question, culminating activities, and so forth. If you have decided that students will do more than write informally during this unit of study—perhaps they will produce an exhibit that features writing—then planning how to provide scaffolds for this task is your next step (Langer, 2002; Pressley, Mohan, Raphael, & Fingeret, 2007).

Planning Writing Scaffolds

With regard to planning, as we said about comprehension in Chapter 5, you decide on clear learning purposes, then decide how to engage students and build their background knowledge so they can achieve these purposes. When planning writing scaffolds, you follow similar steps.

DETERMINING WHAT STUDENTS ARE TO WRITE ABOUT Planning scaffolds for students' writing during subject matter study begins with determining what everyone is to write about. First, examine your unit's objectives for the one that (a) seems most promising for students to maximize their learning by writing about and (b) warrants the time and energy to have students write and make their thinking external about. Every unit's objectives present a host of possibilities for writing. For instance, the unit on immigration talked about in Chapter 3, "Instructional Units," presents the following four content objectives:

1. Students will be able to describe noteworthy immigrations.
2. Students will be able to portray personal experiences of immigrating.
3. Students will be able to explain conditions that produce immigrations.
4. Students will be able to evaluate the consequences of immigrations.

Note that the key verbs in each of these objectives, *describe, portray, explain,* and *evaluate,* are promising occasions for writing. Students potentially could write in response to all four objectives. Indeed, you will see that the verbs in any set of objectives lend themselves to writing. Even actions like *calculate, compute,* and *solve* that often are found outside the humanities are candidates for written responses (e.g., "Explain how to calculate . . ."; "Describe how to compute . . ."; "List the steps in your solution . . ."). If the unit plan on immigration did not establish a literacy objective that called for writing, then you would select the content objective that seemed most appropriate for a writing concentration, and you would be on your way to determining what everyone is to write about.

However, recall that the immigration unit plan in Chapter 3 included the following literacy objective:

In this case, you already linked a content and literacy objective. You already devised a writing objective that corresponded with one of your content objectives:

Now you would determine what everyone is to write by explicitly linking the two objectives:

Students will write an explanatory multiparagraph essay about the conditions that produce immigrations.

At this point you are ready to plan scaffolds for the task.

DESIGNING AN AUTHENTIC WRITING TASK   In Chapter 5, we noted that once you decide what you want students to read, you design a task that will focus their attention. When writing, once you know what you want students to write about, you design a task that focuses their attention, too. Additionally, ensure that the task is authentic, that it is not just academic. Authentic literacy tasks are "those that replicate or reflect reading and writing activities that occur in the lives of people outside of a learning-to-read-and-write context and purpose" (Duke, Purcell-Gates, Hall, & Tower, 2006, p. 346). Students engaged in authentic literacy tasks have genuine, personal desires to communicate. They read and write for bona fide reasons. To design authentic writing tasks, consider their topic, form, audience, and role.

Topic   The topic is both the "what?" and the "what for?" of writing: the content and the purpose. The topic includes what your students will write about and the purpose they will attempt to accomplish during writing. As presented in the informal writing section on Cubing, some common purposes for writing, which frequently turn up on state and national tests, include the following:

Analyze: Identify parts of the topic and explaining how they relate

Narrate: Tell a story connected with the topic

Persuade: Convince someone of an assertion related to the topic

Respond: React to an aspect of the topic and supporting your reaction

Specify: Provide exact directions or details related to the topic.

Form   Form is the medium of writing. How are students going to write about the topic? Are they going to write a poem, a story, an essay, or a newspaper article? Writers use a variety of forms, and their choice of form is related to their purpose. If you intend to persuade people, then you might write an ad, editorial, essay, campaign speech, or position paper. If your purpose is to specify exact information, you might write a brochure, lab report, contract, set of directions, observational notes, or recipe.

Specifying the form of a passage usually includes specifying its length. Knowing the expected length of their writing helps students understand how much information to include. Imagine that you are assigning a paper describing the metric system. Do you expect the paper to be one page or five pages long? A one-page paper would leave space for few examples, but a five-page paper would need many examples. Assigning approximate lengths for writing helps clarify the depth of discussion you expect to find in the writing. Often, you will have more success by setting a maximum length than a minimum one. For students to meet the demands of the topic within a certain length, they will have to plan carefully before writing.

Much school writing is limited to a few forms—paragraphs, stories, letters, poems, and reports. Actual writing, however, contains countless forms. People write lists, journal entries, and directions. The following gives just a sampling to get you thinking about the possibilities for writing forms:

A Sampling of Writing Forms

ads	allegories	announcements
autobiographies	biographies	book jackets
book reviews	brochures	campaign speeches

email

character sketches	children's books	debates
commercials	contracts	directions
dialogues	diaries	epitaphs
editorials	encyclopedia entries	interviews
essays	fables	letters
journals	lab reports	mathematical solutions
lists	magazine articles	and proofs
memoirs	memos	mysteries
myths	newspaper articles	newspaper columns
obituaries	observational notes	plays
poems	position papers	posters
powerPoint	questionnaires	recipes
presentations	reviews	scenarios
reports	song lyrics	stories
scripts	comic strips	thumbnail sketches
summaries		

Audience   Imagine this vignette:

It was a dark and foggy night, and you were driving home from class. You did not stop at a STOP *sign that had only recently been installed at a familiar intersection. Fortunately, there were no other cars in the intersection, so you got through safely. Unfortunately, a police officer was parked along the curb ahead. You were given a ticket for running the* STOP *sign.*

Now imagine that you are going to write a letter about this incident to a seven-year-old cousin, your best friend, or the judge who will decide your fine. The topic and form will be the same for all the letters, but the audience for each is quite different. Think about how the three letters would be different.

Audience refers to the person or persons who might read your writing. When scaffolding your students' writing, an authentic audience is preferable. For example, students write pieces to be read by their classmates, students in other classes, younger children, pen pals, parents, school personnel, newspaper readers, and public officials. Sometimes the audience cannot really read the piece, but the writer writes as if the audience could. For example, letters are written to George Washington, and descriptions of life as it is today are put into time capsules for some possible readers years or even decades into the future.

Often writers write for themselves. People keep diaries and journals; make lists, schedules, and notes; and write to clarify their thinking rather than to communicate that thinking to others.

In schools, a common audience is the teacher-as-examiner, probably the hardest audience for whom to write. Students who know that you will be the only reader often leave important information unstated because they know you already know it. They also come to see writing only as a way to earn a grade rather than to promote and crystallize their learning. Writing to you as an interested aunt or uncle, newspaper editor, public official, community member, and so on enriches your students' writing.

Having an authentic audience other than the teacher-as-examiner has been shown to improve the quality of student writing (Purcell-Gates, Duke, & Martineau, 2007). Students write more clearly and use more examples when they know that someone who really needs the information is going to read it. Whenever possible, students should write for a variety of audiences, including themselves, their classmates, and people outside of school. Before students begin to write, they should be clear about who will be the audience for that piece of writing.

Role Role is the identity, or the perspective, you take. Often you write from your own perspective, so you do not think about your role; sometimes you write from different perspectives. Assuming different roles helps produce clear, interesting writing.

Students could write to Abraham Lincoln, so Lincoln would be the audience; or they could write what they think Abraham Lincoln would say in a speech today, so they would assume the role of Lincoln. For actors, getting into the part, believing they are who they are portraying, is crucial for believable acting. For writers, assuming different roles helps produce more writing.

A writing task thus has four components: RAFT (Holston & Santa, 1985) is a mnemonic device for remembering the four components:

Role—Who is doing the writing?

Audience—For whom are you writing?

Form—In what format will you write about the topic? How long will your writing be?

Topic—What are you writing about and for what purpose?

RAFTing writing tasks encourages students to shift their perspectives on a topic. It helps clarify expectations and engages students. Consider the writing task determined earlier for a unit on immigration:

Students will write an explanatory multi-paragraph essay about the conditions that produce immigrations.

In its current fashion, this task presents a conventional, academic assignment. RAFTing helps convert it to an authentic assignment. To begin RAFTing writing tasks, maintain the topic (explain the conditions that produce immigration) and form (explanatory multiparagraph essay), then enrich the assignment by generating possibilities as follows:

Topic	Role	Audience	Form
explain the conditions that produce immigration	• immigrant child • newspaper reporter	• friendly young citizen of the host country • annoyed adult citizens of the host country	• formal letter • newspaper article

Given the possibilities generated above, you might decide on the following tasks:

As an immigrant child, write a letter to a friendly young citizen of the host country that explains the conditions causing you to immigrate.

Acting as a newspaper reporter, write an article that explains the conditions that produce immigration to annoyed adult citizens of your country.

When you design a writing task, think about the topic first and then the forms, audiences, and roles that would help students think deeply about the topic. Writing tasks have these four components, but you do not have to specify all four. Sometimes you may want to decide on the topic and form but let students choose their audience and role; other times you may want to specify the topic and let students decide the rest.

TRY IT OUT

Design an authentic writing task that fits one of your units of study. First determine what your students are to write about. Next, follow the guidelines just presented and start with your topic, then generate possible roles, audiences, and forms. Blend these components into a clear, authentic task or set of tasks. Finally, share what you produced with a few classmates to personalize and apply your knowledge of designing authentic writing tasks.

DESIGNING A SCORING GUIDE Although teachers frequently look over informal writing just to determine whether or not it represents students' reasonable efforts, more formal writing typically is assessed. As Chapter 3, "Instructional Units," indicated, students as well as teachers have legitimate rights and needs for assessments. Assessments help you and your learners focus attention on what is important; they are sources of feedback regarding ongoing efforts. Assessments indicate expectations for your students' writing. Scoring guides, or rubrics, as presented in Chapter 3 are useful when you deem writing assessment to be appropriate.

The 6+1 Trait Writing Scoring Guide, produced by the Northwest Regional Educational Laboratory (www.nwrel.org/assessment), is found in practically every state, and several educational governing boards have adopted this scoring guide for their state- and district-level assessments. This instrument contains the following seven traits:

1. Ideas
2. Organization
3. Voice
4. Word choice
5. Sentence fluency
6. Conventions
7. Presentation

Note that the term *trait* is a synonym for the term *criterion* as used in Chapter 3 of this text. The following is a skeleton version of this popular scoring guide, showing maximum and minimum performance indicators for each of the traits:

Ideas

5	1
This paper is clear and focused. It holds the readers' attention. Relevant anecdotes and details enrich the central theme.	As yet, the paper has no clear sense of purpose or central theme. To extract meaning from the text, the reader must make inferences based on sketchy or missing details.

Organization

5	1
The organization enhances and showcases the central idea or theme. The order, structure, or presentation of information is compelling and moves the reader through the text.	The writing lacks a clear sense of direction. Ideas, details, or events seem strung together in a loose or random fashion; there is no identifiable internal structure.

Voice

5	1
The writer speaks directly to the reader in a way that is individual, compelling, and engaging. The writer crafts the writing with an awareness and respect for the audience and the purpose for writing.	The writer seems indifferent, uninvolved, or distanced from the topic and/or the audience.

Word Choice

5	1
Words convey the intended message in a precise, interesting, and natural way. The words are powerful and engaging.	The writer demonstrates limited vocabulary or has not searched for words to convey specific meaning.

Sentence Fluency

5	1
The writing has an easy flow, rhythm, and cadence. Sentences are well built, with strong and varied structure that invites expressive oral reading.	The reader needs to practice quite a bit in order to give this paper a fair interpretive reading.

Conventions

5	1
The writer demonstrates a good grasp of standard conventions (e.g., spelling, punctuation, capitalization, grammar, usage, paragraphing) and uses conventions effectively to enhance readability. Errors tend to be so few that just minor touch-ups would get this piece ready to publish.	Errors in spelling, punctuation, capitalization, usage, and grammar and/or paragraphing repeatedly distract the reader and make the text difficult to read.

Presentation

5	1
The form and presentation of the text enhances the ability of the reader to understand and connect with the message. It is pleasing to the eye.	The reader receives a garbled message due to problems relating to the presentation of the text.

Appropriate criteria, or traits, for your writing tasks balance issues pertaining to your prior instruction, students' competencies, school or school district curriculum guides, state standards, and the task at hand. Create a set of about five criteria that are feasible and build incrementally from the past; including more or less than five depends on the sophistication of your students.

Appropriate criteria also connect directly with the task's subject matter. For instance, if your students are writing an essay that explains the conditions that produce immigration, you might include only three criteria from the list: organization, word choice, and conventions. Then you might create two criteria that are specific to this task, such as the following:

Accuracy

5	1
Explanation of the conditions that produce immigration is accurate.	Explanation of the conditions that produce immigration is not accurate.

Push-Pull Balance

5	1
Forces that push people out of a country are balanced with forces that pull people to a country.	Forces that push people out of a country are not balanced with forces that pull people to a country.

PREPARING TO BUILD BACKGROUND KNOWLEDGE Once you know what you want students to write about and how to assess the writing task they will perform, you can decide what knowledge you need to build to enable them to carry out the task. Building knowledge for writing is no different from building background knowledge for reading. Ask yourself what students need to know to complete the task; then think about how most efficiently to build that knowledge.

Background knowledge for writing usually includes content related to the topic but may also include how to write the form. Students cannot successfully write a letter, an essay, or a TV commercial if they do not know how to write the particular form. If you are having students write as an immigrant child and compose a letter explaining their reasons for immigrating, then you are obliged to equip students with the knowledge of why people immigrate as well as how to write such a letter.

PREPARING TO HELP STUDENTS PLAN Your student's writing will be better if they plan what they are going to say. This is the point at which students prepare outlines or webs, jot down what they may include, discuss with others what they want to say, develop a working title, or compose a final sentence.

Decide how you will help students plan. You might decide to have them engage in some class activity that will involve them in the planning. If research is involved, you might decide to help them organize their findings into a writing plan before they begin

Developing a plan for writing enhances writing.

their paper. One caution: Because writing is a discovery process, do not set out to insist that students follow their plan too closely, even though there will be some relationship between the plan and the paper.

Implementing Writing Scaffolds

In a manner similar to comprehension scaffolds, implementation of writing scaffolds occurs in phases. Discernible beginnings, middles, and endings are apparent in writing scaffolding just as in comprehension. The following is an example of writing scaffolds based on the following central question and task:

> *Central question*: Does heredity mold personality?
>
> *Task*: As a genealogist, produce a poster for classmates that explains your major personality traits that seem molded by your heredity.

BEFORE WRITING   Assume that this writing task occurs during a middle-grades unit on human nature. Since you have determined what students are to write about and designed an authentic writing task, you present this to your students, showing how it fits the unit as well as their lives. You would present a scoring guide for their posters, too, clarifying its criteria and performance indicators and possibly having students generate additional criteria. Then you would turn to building background knowledge and helping students plan their compositions. All these actions and products are scaffolds; they support students' production of their compositions.

Tell how research with identical twins who were separated at birth is providing insights into the heredity versus environment issue. Tell how scientists at the University of Minnesota Center for Twin and Family Research have found amazing similarities between identical twins who were separated at birth. Present students with data from the Minnesota Twin Family Study, which indicate that leadership, cheerfulness, and optimism are strongly influenced by heredity. Other traits, such as ability to establish emotional intimacy and the propensity to be sensible and rational, appear to be less influenced by heredity.

Write these traits on the board in two columns under these headings: *Personality Traits More Influenced by Heredity* and *Personality Traits Less Influenced by Heredity*. Next, have the class brainstorm other personality traits such as these: hot-tempered, impatient, cooperative, laid back, high-strung, nervous, and cautious. Write these traits on the board but not under either heading, then explain that some personality traits seem to be more influenced by heredity than others. Students then compare their personality traits with those of their family members and try to conclude, based on their own family experiences, which traits they seem to share with other family members.

After building content knowledge, move to building knowledge of the writing form. Display excellent and poor examples of posters and point out their features like overall appearance, balance between text and graphics, organization and flow of main points, presentation of sources, and summary of findings. Post and talk through the steps in producing such posters.

Next, arrange for your students to plan their posters as they finish gathering information. You might have them produce an initial, small-scale, rough depiction and obtain feedback from a partner, group, or yourself before moving to the actual product. Again, these scaffolds assist students in accomplishing the writing task.

DURING WRITING   Once your students have a good basis for their posters and are creating them, you scaffold their ongoing efforts. Confer with groups and individuals, offering feedback as needed. You might schedule conferences and meet at a certain location, or you might circulate about the class and improvise comments. Have the scoring guide for the posters on hand so you can compare students' ongoing work with the stated criteria. As you advise students in this phase of writing, you move in and out of their worlds opportunistically. Make sure that students have enough time to produce their posters but not so much time that they move off task.

AFTER WRITING   When your students have finished the final drafts of their posters, conduct a culminating activity. You might have students exhibit their work in order to share and celebrate what they have accomplished. Display the posters and have your class, other classes, or family, school and community members take a gallery walk among them. You might have students apply the scoring guide to the final draft of their posters, then compare your assessment with each student's. Such a comparison can promote reflection about the process of creating the poster and its relative strengths and limitations. You might have students discuss as a class or with a classroom guest the personality characteristics that seem molded by heredity. Determine what agreements and disagreements exist among the class.

LISTEN, LOOK, AND LEARN

Visit a classroom to observe writing instruction or watch a videotape. Summarize what you saw during each phase of writing, then assess it according to the information presented in this section. Were appropriate scaffolds presented in the before, during, and after phases of writing? What scaffolds were most effective? If scaffolds that might have strengthened the students' writing were missing, what are they?

TEACH WRITING STRATEGIES

Teaching students strategies for writing and learning fosters their independence for the present as well as for the future; it promotes lifelong learning. Some writing strategies that have been shown to promote content and literacy learning include ones that occur in the before, during, and after stages of writing (Graham, 2008). Strategies enable students to write independently.

As a general rule, determine the writing you intend students to perform regularly throughout your course. To illustrate, many English/language arts teachers have students write in reading response journals, mathematics teachers have students record class notes, science teachers utilize laboratory reports, and social studies teachers employ time lines and summaries. Teachers across the curriculum have students maintain word books.

At the beginning of the school year, as you are teaching the routines expected in your classroom, teach students how to do the regular writing that you require. Teach students the writing strategies for producing what you expect. Following the direct explicit model for teaching strategies presented in Chapters 5 and 6, describe the strategy, model it, then collaboratively use it. As your students become competent, guide their application of it. Eventually fade your scaffolding even more and support their independent application of it.

Additionally, many teachers team with English/language arts teachers during certain units to help students accomplish certain writing expectations. For instance, interdisciplinary teaming happens when history teachers link up with English/language arts teachers as students report their inquiries into the events and leaders of a particular era. History teachers scaffold students' history learning in cooperation with English/language arts teachers who scaffold the students' abilities to report what they are learning. The teachers from both subjects mutually, yet differentially, support their students' literacy and content learning.

You also might teach somewhat general writing strategies needed in particular units. These strategies can be divided among the before, during, and after phases of writing.

Before Writing

The before-writing phase is sometimes called *prewriting* or *planning*. Some people call it *fixing to write*, and others call it *getting it together*. There are various strategies that help students get ready to write. They all center about devising a plan for writing.

One part of devising a plan for writing involves establishing a focus. In line with RAFTing, presented earlier in this chapter, writers independently clarify their role, audience, form, and topic. If they are responding to a prompt, they unpack its requirements by underlining what they are to write about (e.g., "explain the conditions that produce immigration") and circling how they should develop their writing (e.g., "write an article").

Another part of devising a plan for writing involves generating and organizing ideas. Writers generate ideas by brainstorming what they know already, talking with others, and consulting print and digital texts. They list key words, frequently arranging them in graphic organizers such as charts, story maps, outlines, and webs. They also number ideas in their planned order of use, and many establish a central, or controlling, idea as a goal for their writing.

Finally, some writers determine how they will allot their time to the task. They establish a rough work flow plan and timetable so they complete the writing efficiently and on time.

During Writing

If the before-writing prewriting phase is *getting it together*, the during-writing phase is *getting it down*. During-writing strategies center about the production of text. These strategies influence the ways writers go about recording their thoughts. Depending on the situation, such as when writing creatively or poetically, students might plunge into a first draft without a formal plan. However, when writing informatively, students do well to create a draft that strategically sticks to an initial focus and makes use of preliminary ideas and organization.

Once writers begin drafting, they can benefit from strategies to form effective communications. Three during-writing strategies include communal efforts, technology, and conventions.

COMMUNAL EFFORTS Writing is usually conceived of as an individual activity, but many excellent pieces of writing (this textbook, for example) are group-written. Students often achieve much and enjoy learning when it is arranged in some kind of cooperative learning format. This is especially true of writing.

Students benefit from learning to work in a group of three or four. This communal writing seems to work best if everyone contributes ideas, individuals produce their own drafts, then all group members respond to what one another has written. This communal strategy of *plan collaboratively—draft individually—revise collaboratively* blends group effort with individual accountability. Individuals have access to group support, but they submit their writing individually and no classroom grades are awarded to the group. This promotes group interaction while eliminating the free-rider problem of students being rewarded for efforts they didn't exert.

For a lengthy piece, students might learn how to divide up the sections (as we did with the first draft of this book). They would first plan which part each would write and set some guidelines about the writing focus, ideas, and organization. Each person writes his or her part, to which everyone in the group responds. The group works together producing sections that make up one product to which all contributed.

TECHNOLOGY   In classrooms today, students write using computers. Those who have regular access to computers for word processing are more willing to write, write more, revise more, and feel more confident in their writing. In addition to basic word-processing programs that allow students to write, edit, check spelling, and so forth, other software supports writing in much more sophisticated ways (Bruce & Levin, 2003). Programs like *Inspiration* (www.Inspiration.com) and *Expression* (www.Sunburst.com) are available that provide computer-assisted brainstorming, idea mapping, and outlining. Other software, like *Author's Toolkit* (www.Sunburst.com), extends prewriting planning to drafting and editing. And still others, like *Kidspiration* (www.Inspiration.com), take it one step further by enabling young writers to hear their work read aloud by the computer or by their own recorded voices. *Webspiration* (www.Inspiration.com) is a free online visual thinking tool.

Students record their thoughts in the writing phase.

Desktop publishing software such as *Print Shop 23 Deluxe* (www.Broderbund.com) allows writers to customize their own professional-looking books, reports, announcements, and so on, by formatting text with student-made illustrations, clip art, and other visuals. Popular presentation software, like *PowerPoint* (www.Microsoft.com), enhances written notes students might display during multimedia presentations. And Web sites such as *Homestead* (www.Homestead.com) readily enable older students to embed writing with music, video, pictures, and other media on their own Web sites. Your role is to provide students the strategies for using this information and communication technology efficiently and wisely.

CONVENTIONS Fixing spelling, and many more conventions such as grammar and punctuation, is what you can teach while students produce their first drafts. In some classrooms, teachers work with individuals or small groups who are revising an already completed first draft while the rest of the students are writing their first drafts. These writing conferences are usually conducted quietly in a corner of the room so that the writers are not disturbed.

Spelling, of course, is a concern, but it seems best to underemphasize it during first-draft writing. Students should be taught to brainstorm lists of words, use a dictionary (if they know how and want to), and write words as best they can. Some teachers encourage students to leave blanks for letters about which they are uncertain or put an asterisk in the margin where they think their spelling is probably wrong.

The procedure just described sounds easier than it is. Because students generally are concerned about misspelling words, you feel a natural tendency to want to help. But your students will write longer drafts and use more sophisticated words if they are freed from real or perceived perfect spelling demands on their first-draft writing. Students should learn that perfect spelling is not required for them to share their work with a small group and that they fix spelling when their writing is to be publicly displayed or graded.

After Writing

During the culminating, after-writing phase, possibilities range from doing nothing, to sharing the writing by reading it aloud, to revising, editing, and publishing it. Consider the doing-nothing option. If your goal for having students write is to promote their learning of content, you may have accomplished this goal with the thinking engaged in by the students before and during writing. In this case, you would simply check to see that the writing was done and that a sufficient effort was made.

The problem with the doing-nothing response is that students do not learn after-writing strategies for revising ideas and editing conventions. If you have used the terms *getting it together* and *getting it down* to help students conceptualize the before- and during-writing phases, you might want to tell them that now they are engaged in *getting it right*.

Here again, students could work with a partner, a small group, or you to learn revising and editing processes. The goal is for writers to determine what is needed for the piece to be as understandable and suitable as possible for a real audience. The message should be dealt with first, then attention can focus on conventions.

PQS (praise, question, suggest) is a nifty mnemonic for a strategy to help students remember how to help one another revise. Each writer shares his or her paper with a willing partner or partners (teacher, buddy, or small group). The writer elicits **praise** by

A writer getting editing help from a friend.

asking something like this: "What did you like about it?" The partner or partners then offer positive comments:

"You really learned a lot by interviewing your grandparents."

"Your reasons for your adventurous and competitive nature really made sense to me."

Next, the writer elicits **questions** by asking, "Do you have any questions?" or "Was there anything you didn't understand?" These are sample responses:

"I didn't understand if your characteristics are all equal or not."

"You lost me on the right-hand side of your poster."

Finally, the writer asks the partners to **suggest** how to improve the paper. The writer might ask, "Can you think of ways to make the writing more informative?" Using the comments, the writer has some concrete things to do in order to revise the piece.

The next step is editing for conventions, with which students and teachers can help. The goal of editing for conventions is to produce a final draft that presents the message effectively. How good that needs to be depends on the age and ability of the students and the expectations of the audience who will read the final copy.

Once the writer has had help revising the message and editing for conventions, the piece should be recopied, retyped, or reprinted. This finished product can then be displayed or published because the reason for revising and editing first drafts is to make them more readable for a new reader.

To be sure, individuals also can develop strategies for independently revising and editing their written work (Sandman, 2006). To produce independent lifelong writers, you encourage responsibility and reflection and help students develop self-assessment strategies. Some teachers provide students with a reflection sheet they can use to evaluate any piece of writing they do. The reflection sheet might include questions such as these:

- What do I like best about what I wrote?
- What is not clear? How can I make it clearer?
- Will the reader be interested in reading it?

Many teachers use scoring guides to help students learn the strategy of assessing their own writing. Scoring guides fit specific writing projects or tasks and may take the form of checklists in which questions are answered with a "yes" or a "no."

- Does the paper give clear and accurate definitions?
- Does the paper provide appropriate examples in the right places?
- Does the paper use a variety of sentence structures?

Scoring guides need to be explained to students before they write to clarify expectations. After writing, students work with a peer to evaluate their paper according to the criteria set up in the guide. Some teachers send the guides home and ask parents to help the writer read the piece to determine if the criteria are being met. The essential factor with guides is that students are taught how to use them to improve their own writing.

While scoring guides help students learn what is expected in their writing and how to assess their own writing, there is a danger that students will become too dependent on these devices and write to the formula. The most successful teachers use these devices but gradually help students determine what the writing criteria should be and eventually help students reflect upon and assess their writing based on their own criteria.

Writers get editing help from a teacher.

TRY IT OUT

Plan a specific writing strategy you might teach. Describe the strategy, then explain how you would teach it so students have it for life. Share your description and explanation with a few classmates to personalize and apply your knowledge of the writing strategies presented here.

DISCIPLINARY LITERACIES

Writing in English/Language Arts Classrooms

Countless opportunities exist for writing in English/language arts classes. Indeed, if you review the English/language arts classroom suggestions for comprehension and vocabulary in the preceding chapters, you will see writing activities already incorporated (e.g., maintain a response journal, compose a resolution to the central question, record passage sections containing words worth remembering). The following suggestions go beyond the ones already presented, building on ideas introduced in this chapter specifically related to quick writes, journals, and authentic tasks. The following would be appropriate for students engaged with the novel *Shabanu, Daughter of the Wind*.

QUICK WRITES   Quick writes help when calling up prior knowledge on a topic. Students might produce quick writes in response to the following:

- What three things should nomadic people do when desert sandstorms occur?
- What wedding customs have you seen or heard of?

To have students predict what comes next in *Shabanu*, you might offer these prompts:

- What will happen to Shabanu's betrothal to Rahim-Sahib?
- What will happen in the next chapter?

Synthesizing ideas about the novel can be elicited by having students write in response to these items:

- What Islamic customs differ from the ones you are used to?
- List the similarities and differences between Shabanu and her sister, Phulan.

To help students reflect on their processing of *Shabanu*, they might write briefly on the following:

- What part of *Shabanu* has been confusing?
- Why is *Shabanu* maintaining—or losing—my interest?

JOURNALS   Journals contain writings that take numerous forms. Indeed, students might maintain reactions to these quick-write prompts listed above in their journals. To facilitate writing, students might have available a menu of generic prompts from which to react. Here are some generic prompts we have found to be productive that would fit *Shabanu*:

- What have I learned from reading this passage?
- What images did I experience while reading this passage?
- What do I not really understand so far?
- What did this passage remind me of?
- What would I like to see changed?
- How did I feel when reading this passage?

DESIGNING AUTHENTIC WRITING TASKS Thinking of RAFTs (roles, audiences, forms, and topics) when designing tasks for writing helps produce meaningful and connected learning opportunities. Students tend to find writing tasks explicitly based on RAFTs more engaging than traditional ones. If the topic you are addressing is the wedding of Shabanu's sister, Phulan, here are some ways RAFTing could be done to transform academic writing tasks to authentic ones.

Modifying Forms Students benefit from modifying forms of expression while maintaining essentially the same role and audience. We call this practice *translation writing*. After students read the passage describing Phulan's wedding, they might rewrite the description of it in a form selected from the following:

play	song lyrics
interview script	newspaper article
illustrated strip	diary
poem	contract
personal letter	

Modifying Roles Considering different roles that writers might assume also contributes to the design of writing tasks. For instance, if students decide to produce a poem or a set of diary entries centering on Phulan's wedding, they might consider the multiple perspectives that are available. They might write a wedding poem while acting in the role of Phulan, Shabanu, the girls' mother, or the girls' father. They might write poems from the points of view of all four story characters.

Modifying Audiences When thinking about possible wedding poem audiences, students again have several options. They might write for those in attendance, for Phulan's husband, for other members of the family, for younger children, or for readers of a literary journal. Associating different roles and forms with different audiences as we have done here produces writing task possibilities with space for most students' interests and abilities.

Supporting Writing The tasks listed provide good momentum for students writing about *Shabanu* in English classrooms, but there certainly is more to writing instruction than this. Students require support, or scaffolding, to accomplish goals along with opportunities to reflect on and assess their writing performance. This section concentrated on tasks for writing because teaching and learning are greatly facilitated when there are clearly stated engaging tasks guiding the attention and action of teachers and students.

Writing in English Language Development Classrooms

Writing in English language development classrooms is much the same as writing in English/language arts classrooms. Students plan what they will write, produce written drafts, and sometimes revise what they have written. The main difference between writing in one's first language and a new language involves the support that is required.

CONNECTIONS   Writers who easily sustain a line of thinking are able to concentrate on overcoming the word choice, grammar, spelling, and other such challenges a new language presents. One way effective teachers support writers and help sustain their lines of thought is by offering them access to life experience topics that have personal connections.

Topics from life experiences enable writers to focus on expressing themselves. Life experience topics include students' favorites with regard to the following:

foods	books/comics/magazines
clothes	weekend activities
sports	adventures
games	pets/animals
hobbies/collections	television shows/movies
friends	songs/musical groups

Teachers often suggest topics such as one's preferences for food, entertainment, and clothing, and students go into depth on particular ones. Of course, when describing one's preferences, students should realize they are free to decide how much they will reveal about themselves.

Oral history projects with family or community members are good ways for English learners to capitalize on life experiences and personal connections. When students interview parents and grandparents, aunts and uncles, and neighbors and business people in their communities, they are connecting the stories of others' lives with their lives. They can see how past actions might have affected their lives and how conflicts and circumstances from the past might be similar to those of the present. Writing comes into play during oral history projects when students research the times in which people lived, prepare questions, record interviewees' responses, and write up reports.

Finally, writers who address topics associated with their cultures also have ready access to personal connections. Practically everyone has personal experiences and understandings of distinctive holidays, foods, ways of dress, and pastimes. Addressing such topics allows writers to concentrate on expressing themselves, and it provides opportunities to honor and celebrate differences in culturally diverse classrooms. Teachers who share their interest and respect for others' cultures model ways that students can do the same.

COLLABORATION   Promoting collaboration is another good way to support students who are writing in a new language. Collaborative writing projects call for students to work together in whole-class, small-group, or paired situations. Students with high proficiency and those with low proficiency in English might collaborate sometimes, and those with similar levels of proficiency might collaborate other times.

One key to the success of collaborative writing is the instruction students receive about how to act. Teachers typically demonstrate positive face-to-face interactions (e.g., praising others, encouraging participation, finding common ground) so students will do the same when they interact. Teachers often specify particular interactions; then they and the students reflect on their interaction during and after collaborative work.

Collaboration during the planning, before-writing phase occurs many ways. If students are writing in their new language about particular life experiences, they first might jointly brainstorm possibilities. They could list key words that are related to what each plans to write. They could help each other decide on terms that would most appropriately articulate what they want to say. They could talk about the order in which they would use the words, stating orally what they plan to express in print. They could talk with each other about what they want to write.

When students are getting their writing down, they still can benefit from collaboration. They might request a partner's help with a particular term or a grammatical form, or they might consult about the spelling of a word. Writers who cannot produce a particular word or phrase in their new language might insert a few words from their first language to get past the difficulty, later getting help to replace the first-language terms.

Collaboration also is appropriate in the after-writing phase. Students can read their writing orally to a single partner or to a small group, and all concerned individuals can listen for points to praise and to question. Rather than listening, partners and small-group members can read what one has written, looking for points to praise and to question. Teachers typically model before a whole class the dynamics of small-group revisions. They demonstrate how to attend to specific features of writing as well as how to comment appropriately when they spot difficulties.

Writing in Mathematics Classrooms

For many, writing was not a part of mathematics class. Recently, however, all content areas have become concerned with students' ability to learn and communicate, and writing is one of the major ways of promoting both of these. Here are some specific ways that math teachers use quick writes, journals, and word problems to help students learn and communicate mathematically.

QUICK WRITES   As previewing activities, math teachers ask students to

- List as many kinds of different triangles as you can in thirty seconds.
- Draw and label three shapes that have different names.
- List ways you use decimals in real-life activities.

To synthesize what was learned at the end of a class, ask students to

- Define in your own words what parallel lines are.
- Write in words what this formula means. (Present a formula.)
- Use the symbols =, <, and > to write three true sentences.

To help students self-assess understanding, attitudes, and so on, you could use these prompts:

- What did you not understand about today's lesson?
- List one or more terms you cannot clearly define.

- I have the feeling many of you are not "with me" on this topic. Write what you are feeling about what we are doing and if there is anything I could change to help you feel more involved and successful.

JOURNALS Journals call for more extended entries than quick writes and are most successful if used on a daily basis. Both high-structure and low-structure journals can be used in math class. Here are some examples of high-structure journal prompts math teachers use:

- Draw and label pictures that will help you remember each of the shapes we have studied so far.
- Write a paragraph using as many of the following words as possible. (List math terms you are studying.)
- Analyze the mistakes made on your homework (or in-class work). What have you learned that will help you avoid making these same mistakes again?
- Write an explanation of why we need to study _____, which would make sense to a younger friend who hasn't yet taken this course.

WORD PROBLEMS Solving word problems is an essential math skill but one that presents problems for many students. To understand word problems from the inside out, students are often helped by learning to write some. Most teachers find that because this is a difficult task, it is one at which students are more successful and are willing to tackle if they write cooperatively as a team of two or three members. Team members are asked to write word problems similar to the ones they have been solving, and then two teams are paired to try to solve each other's problems. The solving team points out any missing information or unclear language and the writing team rewrites. Finally, the combined team picks its best problem for the whole class to solve.

Guidelines for changing word problems into easier ones include the following:

- Using fewer words
- Using shorter sentences
- Using smaller numbers
- Using simpler figures
- Having fewer steps or operations
- Putting the information in the order it will be used
- Including a chart or diagram
- Suggesting the use of manipulatives

Writing in Science Classrooms

Scientists are inveterate writers. They write down hunches and sketch possible arrangements of whatever they are studying. They observe carefully and write down their observations. They conduct experiments and write down what they think will happen as well as what they actually observe. They write interpretations of what they have observed. Writing and sketching are important tools scientists use to help themselves think. Here are some specific ways that science teachers use quick writes, journals, and lab reports to help students learn and communicate like scientists.

QUICK WRITES   As previewing activities, science teachers ask students to

- List as many different animals with backbones as you can in thirty seconds.
- Draw and label the parts of a tomato plant.
- List ways that chemistry is important to us in real-life activities.

To synthesize what was learned at the end of a class, you might offer students these prompts:

- Define in your own words what an ecosystem is.
- Your book says, _____. Write what that means in your own words.
- Use the words _____ and _____ and _____ to write a true sentence.

To help students self-assess understanding, attitudes, and so forth, you could offer these prompts:

- What did you not understand about today's lesson?
- List one or more terms you cannot clearly define.
- I have the feeling many of you are not "with me" on this topic. Write what you are feeling about what we are doing and if there is anything I could change to help you feel more involved and successful.

JOURNALS   Journals call for more extended entries than quick writes and are most successful if used on a daily basis. Both high-structure and low-structure journals can be used in a science class. Here are some examples of high-structure journal prompts science teachers use:

- Draw and label the parts of the digestive system.
- Arrange the following words into a web that shows their relationships.
- Analyze how you did with today's experiment. Were you able to follow the directions? Did the experiment turn out as you had predicted?
- Explain to a younger person (brother, sister, cousin) why it is important for everyone to understand about toxins in our environment.

LAB REPORTS   Many students feel about lab reports the same way they feel about book reports. They don't mind the lab (book) and even enjoy it sometimes, but they detest writing it up.

Successful science teachers find ways to make the writing of the lab report less tedious and more successful. They usually begin by modeling the writing of lab reports. This is not the same as giving the students an already completed model because as the teacher writes, he or she thinks aloud, allowing students to see how the teacher decided what to include and how to word it. Most teachers do the modeling and thinking aloud themselves several times and then continue modeling but asking students to give them ideas of what to write next and how to write it. Once students are participating in the writing being modeled by the teacher, they move to a small-group writing team.

Many teachers display a frame for a lab report in the room that will serve as a reminder of the essential elements. A generic frame is given here but should only be considered as an example and not as *the* frame for lab reports. Frames more specific to the particular area of science being studied, the age, and scientific sophistication of your students will support student writing of lab reports.

Laboratory Report

Problem

Why does . . .?

Hypotheses

I think that . . .

Materials

(List materials used)

Procedures

(List in order what you did)

Data

(List what you observed, including numbers, pictures, etc., as appropriate)

Conclusions

My problem was . . .

The results showed that . . .

These results supported (did not support) my hypotheses because . . .

Writing in Social Studies Classrooms

Writing in social studies is quite common. Because you are studying people and events, there are endless opportunities for students to think things through while writing.

QUICK WRITES   As previewing activities, social studies teachers ask students to

- List as many names of people important in the Civil War as you can in thirty seconds.
- Write down one question you have about our federal budget.
- List three major inventions of the twentieth century.

To synthesize what was learned at the end of a class, ask students to

- Define in your own words what a democracy is.
- List two things that changed after the *Brown v. The Board of Education* ruling.
- Use the words *interest rates, inflation*, and *stock market* to write a true sentence.

To help students self-assess understanding, attitudes, and so forth, offer these prompts:

- What did you not understand about today's lesson?
- List one or more terms you cannot clearly define.
- I have the feeling many of you are not "with me" on this topic. Write what you are feeling about what we are doing and if there is anything I could change to help you feel more involved and successful.

JOURNALS   Journals call for more extended entries than quick writes and are most successful if used on a daily basis. Both high-structure and low-structure journals can be used in a social studies class. Here are some examples of high-structure journal prompts social studies teachers use:

- We have been studying the controversial topic of our tax system and the law that limits tax deductions. Are you for or against this law? On balance, is it going to make us a better or worse society? If you could have voted on this issue, how would you have voted? List three reasons to justify your vote.
- Arrange the following words into a web that shows their relationships.
- Explain to a younger person (brother, sister, cousin) why it is important for everyone to understand the concept of global interdependence.

In addition to content-oriented journal entries such as these, many social studies teachers use historical figure diaries to help students relate to events often far away in time and space. While studying the Vietnam War, students may become major players such as John F. Kennedy, Lyndon Johnson, Henry Kissinger, Ho Chi Mihn, Ngo Dinh Diem, or common people such as a marine sent to Vietnam, a college student with a draft deferment, a soldier in the Viet Cong, a civilian living in North Vietnam, and the child of an American soldier left in Vietnam. Teachers may let students choose their character or have them pick a character from a hat so that all points of view are represented. As the unit continues, characters write each day diary style what they are doing and thinking. If two people have the same character, they can write separately or can collaborate on a joint entry. To make this more effective, have the common people characters name themselves and decide on their personal characteristics (age, occupation, family status, etc.) before beginning. From time to time, let characters share their diary entries with the whole class or in small groups.

Getting students involved in events that occurred long before their birth is not easy. Having students assume the role of a person in a historical setting promotes their use of the imaging and evaluating thinking processes. Keeping a diary is an authentic writing task. Anne Frank kept one, as did Richard Nixon!

ORAL HISTORY PROJECTS Oral history projects use interviews with real people who have experienced an event as the primary source of information. They can be used any time the event or phenomenon being studied is one that friends and relatives of your students have experienced. Many teachers use oral history projects when studying immigration or societal changes. Often the oral history project begins in the middle of the unit when the students have enough background information to construct good questions. The first time this project is used, it is probably best to lead the class as a whole to construct the questions. As this format is incorporated into other units, students can work in small groups to construct questions and finally construct their own questions. Students may conduct the interviews individually or with a partner. After conducting the interview, students can report to the class what they learned. In many classes, students write a book in which each interview is summarized and printed, perhaps with a picture of the person being interviewed.

Oral history projects make history come alive for students. Learning about the flood of immigrants that arrived after a particular war and the personal and societal upheaval that accompanies immigration takes on a whole different dimension when someone you actually know was one of these immigrants. Students develop new respect (and sometimes even awe!) for neighbors and relatives often previously ignored. Teachers of

English learners and newcomers to the U.S. find that incorporating oral history projects into their social studies classrooms involves and validates the experience of students struggling with English and with a new culture. Of course, personal involvement increases motivation and engagement, and writing becomes a tool for thinking as students write down the questions, write down the answers, and construct the written summary of what was learned. The name *oral history* refers to how the student gathers the information but, for the student, oral history projects involve a lot of purposeful, focused writing.

Writing in Activity Classrooms

Teachers seeking ways to get students to think more deeply about their subjects find writing is one way to focus and organize thinking. Here are some specific ways that teachers of activity courses use writing to help students learn and think.

QUICK WRITES As previewing activities, ask students to

- List as many different materials sculptors might use as you can in thirty seconds.
- Sketch what you think a miter box looks like.
- List ways that knowing first aid is important to us in real-life activities.

To synthesize what was learned at the end of a class, ask students to

- Define in your own words what syncopated rhythm is.
- Draw a stick figure to show what the backhand position looks like.
- Use the words _____ and _____ and _____ to write a true sentence.

To help students self-assess understanding, attitudes, and so forth, you could offer these prompts:

- What did you not understand about today's lesson?
- List one or more terms you cannot clearly define.
- I have the feeling many of you are not "with me" on this topic. Write what you are feeling about what we are doing and if there is anything I could change to help you feel more involved and successful.

JOURNALS Journals call for more extended entries than quick writes and are most successful if used on a daily basis. Both high-structure and low-structure journals can be used in activity classes. Here are some examples of high-structure journal prompts:

- Draw and label a _____.
- Arrange the following words into a web that shows their relationships.
- Analyze how you did with today's activity? Were you able to follow the directions? What problems did you experience? What did you do to help yourself understand?
- Explain to a younger person (brother, sister, cousin) why it is important for everyone to know how to do CPR.

INTERVIEWING PEOPLE ABOUT ON-THE-JOB WRITING Mechanics, technicians, computer specialists, and store managers expend a huge amount of time and effort writing everything from letters to orders to e-mail messages to reports. Every student needs to see writing as an important part of any job to which he or she aspires. Of course, preaching this to them is rarely effective. Some teachers of activity-oriented courses send the students out to find out for themselves. Students select some people in a variety of nonacademic jobs and then interview them to find out specifically what they write. When all the information obtained from these interviews is compiled and shared with the whole class, students can see authentic reasons for learning to write clearly and well.

REWRITING DIRECTIONS   Directions can be hard to read. Students who experience frustration reading directions benefit when teachers demonstrate an "It's not your fault; they should write them more clearly" attitude. Students are more willing to work through a set of directions and try to make sense of them when they realize that not being able to follow the directions easily says more about the writer of the directions than it does about their own reading ability. One effective writing activity to use when you and your students are faced with complex written directions is to rewrite them. When you come across poorly written directions, have the students work together in small groups to first try to follow the directions. Once they have assembled the object or carried out the procedure, have them rewrite the directions so that they are easier to follow. Here are some guidelines for making directions easier to follow:

1. Use shorter sentences.
2. Use "plain" English words instead of technical terms.
3. Include only one thing in each step.
4. Make sure the steps are in logical order.
5. Include a drawing for each step when possible.
6. Include a list of materials/parts with each one clearly labeled.
7. List important "don'ts" at the beginning. (Sometimes, knowing what not to do is more important than knowing what to do!)

LOOKING BACK

Writing can be a tool for learning. Learners who record thoughts in print crystallize and refine them and cement them in memory. In this chapter, you encountered ways to promote the power of writing. The ideas are divided among three headings: (1) Vary informal writing, (2) provide scaffolds for challenging tasks, and (3) teach writing strategies.

ADD TO YOUR JOURNAL

Reflect upon the three key ideas presented in this chapter and decide what you think. Do you see ways that writing can help your students think and learn? Do certain informal writing practices appeal to you more than others? Can you imagine yourself providing scaffolds that promote students' success with challenging writing tasks? What strategies for independent writing do you see yourself teaching? Describe your reactions to the three key ideas and generalize about the role of writing in your classroom.

Additional Readings

A persuasive case for attention to writing is provided by the following:

National Commission on Writing. (2003). *The neglected R: The need for a writing revolution.* Retrieved August 14, 2005, from the National Commission on Writing website: www.writingcommission.org.

These books are devoted solely to content area writing:

Daniels, H., Zemelman, S., & Steineke, N. (2007). *Content-area writing: Every teacher's guide.* Portsmouth, NH: Heinemann.

Strong, W. (2006). *Write for insight: Empowering content area learning, grades 6–12.* Boston, MA: Pearson/Allyn & Bacon.

Comprehensive views of best practices in general writing instruction are found in the following:

Bromley, K. (2006). Best practices in teaching writing. In L. B. Gambrell, L. M. Morrow, & M. Pressley (Eds.), *Best practices in literacy instruction* (3rd ed., pp. 243–263). New York, NY: The Guilford Press.

Graham, S., Macarthur, C. A., & Fitzgerald, J. (Eds.). (2007). *Best practices in writing instruction.* New York, NY: Guildford.

These two resources are comprehensive research reviews of writing instruction:

Graham, S., & Perin, D. (2007). *Writing next: Effective strategies to improve writing of adolescents in middle and high school.* Washington, DC: Alliance for Excellent Education. Retrieved December 13, 2007, from all4ed.org

Macarthur, C., Graham, S. & Fitzgerald, J. (Eds.). (2008), *Handbook of writing research.* New York, NY: Guilford Press.

The following is a good account of how to scaffold the content writing of English learners interactively:

Carter, M. J., Hernandez, A. C., & Richison, J. D. (2009). *Interactive notebooks and English Language Learners: How to scaffold content for academic success.* Portsmouth, NH: Heinemann.

This article provides a compelling sketch of a young person's writing and writing instruction from elementary to high school:

Casey, M., & Hemenway, S. I. (2001). Structure and freedom: Achieving a balanced writing curriculum. *English Journal, 91,* 68–75.

This survey describes the classroom writing experiences of high school students:

Scherff, L., & Piazza, C. (2005). The more things change, the more they remain the same: A survey of high school students' writing experiences. *Research in the Teaching of English, 39,* 271–296.

Online Resources

This professional development network is dedicated to improving the teaching of writing in U.S schools.

National Writing Project

http://www.nwp.org

This site posts writing resources that were created and shared during professional development events.

Writing Fix: Home of Interactive Writing Prompts

http://writingfix.com/index.htm

This site offers many resources for self-help in advanced writing.

Purdue On-line Writing Lab (OWL)

http://owl.english.purdue.edu

This is the site for the 6+1 Traits of Writing.

Northwest Regional Educational Laboratory

http://www.thetraits.org/index.php

References

Bangert-Drowns, R. L., Hurley, M. M., & Wilkinson, B. (2004). The effects of school-based writing-to-learn interventions on academic achievement: A meta-analysis. *Review of Educational Research, 74,* 29–58.

Collins Writing Program. (n.d.). *Collins Writing Program.* West Newbury, MA: Author. Retrieved April 5, 2009, from www.collinseducationassociates.com

Duke, N. K., Purcell-Gates, V., Hall, L. A., & Tower, C. (2006). Authentic literacy activities for developing comprehension and writing. *The Reading Teacher, 60,* 344–355.

Gere, A. R., Christenbury, L., & Sassi, K. (2005). *Writing on demand.* Portsmouth, NH: Heinemann.

Graham, S. (2008). Strategy instruction and the teaching of writing: A meta-analysis. In C. MacArthur, S. Graham, & J. Fitzgerald (Eds.), *Handbook of writing research* (pp. 187–207). New York, NY: Guilford Press.

Graham, S., & Perin, D. (2007). *Writing next: Effective strategies to improve writing of adolescents in middle and high school.* Washington, DC: Alliance for Excellent Education. Retrieved December 13, 2007, from all4ed.org

Langer, J. A. (2002). *Effective literacy instruction: Building successful reading and writing programs.* Urbana, IL: National Council of Teachers of English.

Newell, G. E. (2008). Writing to learn: How alternative theories of school writing account for student performance. In C. A. MacArthur, S. Graham, & J. Fitzgerald (Eds.), *Handbook of writing research.* New York, NY: The Guilford Press.

Pressley, M., Mohan, L., Raphael, L. M., & Fingeret, L. (2007). How does Bennett Woods Elementary School produce such high reading and writing achievement? *Journal of Educational Psychology, 99,* 221–240.

Purcell-Gates, V., Duke, N. K., & Martineau, J. A. (2007). Learning to read and write genre-specific text: Roles of authentic experience and explicit teaching. *Reading Research Quarterly, 42,* 8–45.

CHAPTER 8

Studying

LOOKING AHEAD

Have you ever heard a joke, laughed out loud at the punch line, then found yourself unable to retell it to friends a few days later? If so, you experienced the difference between comprehending and studying. You understood the joke well, but you did not learn it well.

Studying is understanding and remembering. It involves specific strategies and general approaches that enhance long-term learning. Students in K–12 schooling seldom develop effective and efficient study abilities from merely being required to do so. Explicit instruction in how to study is necessary if most students are going to acquire those abilities. Study strategy instruction involves, among other things, teaching students how to take notes, question themselves, and organize what they read.

Thinking processes are the building blocks of studying; they are its fundamental elements. The essential thinking processes described in Chapter 1—connect, preview and predict, organize, generalize, image, monitor and fix up, evaluate, and apply—are also the processes of studying. Students learn more and remember it longer when they actively think about a subject. Setting the thinking processes in motion is the antidote to the passive rote learning achieved by reading something over and over until it is memorized. That which is memorized by rote is usually forgotten soon after a test. This chapter presents five key ideas:

1. Studying is complex.
2. Studying includes learning strategies.
3. Studying includes taking tests.
4. Studying includes managing resources.
5. Important principles of instruction apply to studying.

STUDYING IS COMPLEX

The term *study* denotes any conscious effort to learn independently. Students study when they deliberate over subject matter, working to understand and, especially, to remember it (Devine & Kania, 2003). Studying is something students do for themselves, orchestrating and monitoring their own learning. Because reading and writing are major tools for learning, most studying involves reading, writing, or both.

Studying is particular to the content area being learned. As we discussed in Chapter 1, content teachers can teach content area reading and writing best because different subjects' perspectives on the world require different literacies, because students are most receptive to receiving help in literacy when they need it to accomplish specific assignments, and because content teachers best know how to read and write in their subjects. For these same reasons, it is difficult to teach students how to study in a generic way. When students try to transfer generic approaches to a particular content area, they often find that they are unable to get them to work, given the demands of that subject. For example, being taught how to take notes outside of math class often fails to help students take notes in math because it ignores the sequential, step-by-step nature of mathematics.

Self-regulated studying calls for proficient learners to do what it takes to learn. This involves control and motivation (Baumeister & Vohs, 2007).

Control

Self-regulated learners control their learning actions. If deep understanding of a passage is needed, these students may preview it, take notes, and question themselves about it. If mastery of specific facts is the learning goal, these learners may decide to create mnemonic devices. Furthermore, they know whether an abbreviation, acronym, or acrostic is the best type of mnemonic device for the particular set of facts they intend to learn.

When self-regulated learners control what they read, they sometimes move forward at a medium rate, they sometimes skim, and they sometimes slow down considerably. They change their reading rate according to the demands of the material and their purpose for reading. If the passage is easy and learners want an overview of it, they read rapidly. If the passage is difficult and learners want to master the contents, they read more slowly, maintaining their focus.

Proficient learners control themselves as they move through print, centering on ideas that they know to be important. At times, they regress to an earlier point in the passage and reread it to fix it in their minds or to compare it with a later one. These learners also focus on confusing ideas. If they are unclear about something, they return and attempt to clarify it or seek a third source to resolve an apparent conflict. This control of strategies and reading rate is essential for learning.

Think of a person skilled in a craft such as plumbing. Good plumbers have many tools and control them selectively to accomplish specific purposes. Plumbers might size up a situation, then begin working with a socket wrench. If that tool is not getting the job done, they might employ a crescent wrench. When plumbers are at a delicate part of a job, they will slow down to be sure to get it right. Students with control use learning strategies like skilled craftspeople use tools. They plan to use strategies appropriate to specific learning tasks, check on how well they are progressing, and make adjustments as needed. They have well-developed, flexible repertoires.

Motivation

Along with having control, self-regulated learners are motivated. Students might be full of study strategy knowledge, but it will help only if they are motivated to apply it. Habit and will are as important as content and skill. Self-regulated learners have the predisposition to accomplish academic goals and persist with tasks even when they become difficult. They engage learning tasks with their full attention, blocking out distractions.

Students with little control of their efforts often attempt to escape learning. They may try to distract teachers or make excuses for their performance. They often create highly charged emotional scenes, acting out verbally and physically or withdrawing sullenly. Feelings of frustration and embarrassment rather than confidence and pride influence their actions.

A productive way to directly address the motivational aspects of self-regulation is to focus on students' academic identities as noted in Chapter 1. Acknowledging the influence of students' identities as readers, writers, and learners leads to many actions. Teachers recognize learners' difficulties but emphasize what students do well and begin instruction with these capabilities in mind. Such teachers maintain high standards and positive expectations for success. They promote learners' awareness of how academic success fits with personal fulfillment and career goals. They invite to the classroom role models from the community who attest to the value of reading, writing, and studying. Taking academic identity seriously means showing children and youth that studying in school counts for something, and individuals have the power to control it.

The motivational aspects of self-regulation deserve as much instructional attention as controlled strategic aspects. The roles of identity, curiosity, persistence, and confidence in learning should not be shortchanged.

LISTEN, LOOK, AND LEARN

Interview a few high-achieving and a few low-achieving public school students of the same grade level. You may use the study questionnaire presented in Figure 8.1. Describe the similarities and differences between the students' reported approaches to studying. Explain how your beliefs about studying instruction were affected by interviewing the students.

Interviewer _____ Date _____

Student _____ Grade _____

School Subject _____

Note: If students are confused by a question, explain it until they understand. In addition, probe students' responses until they have no more to say about each item.

1. What do you do when you want to learn the information being presented in your (school subject) class? How do you go about understanding and remembering the information you need for this class?

2. How do you prepare for tests in (school subject)?

3. What do you do to understand and remember what you read?

4. How did you learn how to study?

5. When and where do you study?

6. How much reading do you do each week in (school subject)?

FIGURE 8.1 Study Questionnaire.

STUDYING INCLUDES LEARNING STRATEGIES

Philosophers have commented on studying throughout recorded history, and U.S. educators have published voluminous research-based and professional reports about it starting in the 1920s (Moore, Readence, & Rickelman, 1983). A major component of study involves learning strategies. Strategies are plans for accomplishing specific actions. They are how-to forms of knowledge (Kiewra, 2002). Practically all meaningful learning with print elicits some evidence of strategies.

Defining Learning Expectations

Proficient learners define expectations by clarifying what they intend to learn. One way of defining learning expectations is *previewing*, when proficient learners look over what they are to learn before examining it closely. They preview printed materials by surveying many sources of information: titles, headings, italic and boldface print, and other typographical aids; illustrations, maps, graphs, and other pictorial aids; introductions, first sentences of paragraphs, summaries, and conclusions; guiding questions, stated objectives, end-of-chapter exercises, and other adjunct aids. Previewing helps learners define learning expectations by establishing a general idea of what a passage has to offer.

Another aspect of defining learning expectations involves *setting a purpose*. Learners set purposes when they discern what they should acquire. Learners incorporate what they gathered from a preview with their understanding of the learning task to decide what deserves special attention. They attend to their instructors' stated and unstated cues about what they should learn. The age-old tradition of "psyching out" vague instructors to anticipate what should be in a paper or might be on a test exemplifies part of this strategy. When learners set a purpose, they decide what they want to learn, then they go after it.

Questioning

Students who read and then answer questions tend to learn more than students who only read.

ANSWERING PREPARED QUESTIONS Answering prepared questions often seems like busywork to students, but it can be a potent strategy. Help students see that answering prepared questions can be a strategy rather than just a conventional comprehension exercise. Show them how answering comprehension questions is a legitimate check of their understanding that can lead to them repairing any misunderstandings.

SELF-QUESTIONING An independent form of questioning involves self-questioning. To learn how to self-question, students might be encouraged to pattern their questions after yours, using certain stems like the ones on page 105–106 in Chapter 5, *Comprehension*. More open-ended self-questions that promote learning include the following:

- What might be other examples of _____?
- What conclusion can I draw about _____?
- Why is it important that _____?
- What would happen if _____?
- What do I have to say about _____?

Organizing Information Graphically

Graphic representations arrange key terms in order to depict their relationships. *Outlines, time lines, Venn diagrams*, and *webs* (which are discussed in Chapter 5, pages 101 to 102) are different formats for graphically organizing concepts. They all show how selected concepts are organized. A graphic representation of the desert, for example, could consist of terms arranged about such topics as climate, location, plant life, and animal life; it would not be an illustrated scene of coyotes and cactuses. Graphic organizers have been shown to affect immediate comprehension as well as long-term learning (Nesbit & Adesope, 2006). Having learners examine preconstructed organizers as well as construct their own tends to help them retain knowledge.

Writing

Writing strategies that promote learning progress from simply recording facts to assimilating and reflecting on bodies of knowledge. These strategies activate thinking when learners compose the message; they also provide a record for review.

STUDY CARDS   Study cards are one kind of writing strategy. Each study card usually contains a question or vocabulary term on one side with a corresponding answer or definition on the other. These cards are especially useful for factual learning. Many students would not have been successful in fact-filled courses without resorting to study cards. Teaching students how to produce study cards through direct, explicit instruction is presented later in this chapter.

NOTE TAKING   Another writing strategy that promotes learning involves notes. Note taking assumes many forms. Learners sometimes copy definitions and key ideas verbatim from a passage, comment in the margins of texts, paraphrase information, or add personal examples. Learners benefit from rewriting their notes, clarifying and consolidating information from class presentations and readings. They might use sticky notes to insert symbols that represent various aspects of thinking. Common symbols are as follows:

✓   "I knew this already." This is used when encountering ideas and information already known.

—   "I thought differently." This is used when encountering contradictory ideas and information.

?   "I don't understand this." This is used when encountering confusing ideas and information.

+   "I didn't know this." This is used when encountering new ideas and information.

SUMMARIZING   Selecting and condensing important information into summaries is a powerful learning strategy. When summarizing, students abstract important contents. In at least one paragraph, they state what the text mostly is telling about its topic. General steps for summarizing are as follows:

1. Identify the key words that indicate what the author thinks is important.
  • Delete trivial and repeated ideas; collapse lists.
2. State the main idea of the selection as your first (topic) sentence.
3. Put the key terms together to sum up what the author wants you to know.
  • Follow the order of the selection.
  • State the ideas and information in your own words.

LEARNING LOGS/JOURNALS Learning logs/journals are a record of information from class presentations, readings, or outside experiences. Students sometimes develop their logs into more lengthy compositions. In addition, they sometimes use learning logs or journals to pose questions or state confusions about what they are learning. Many mathematics teachers have students write—rather than orally ask—questions about their homework in order to clarify the questions. This practice often leads students to reach independent solutions.

ESSAYS Analyzing subject matter by writing essays about it promotes content learning. Analytic writing often is in response to essential questions like "Why did the Civil War happen?" and "How do you factor quadratic equations?" Learners produce a set of responses to these prompts, providing evidence and examples to confirm their responses. The goal is to produce trustworthy claims about the topic.

Creating Mnemonic Devices

Mnemonic devices—memory aids named after the Greek goddess of memory, Mnemosyne—include several disparate techniques (Glynn, Koballa, & Coleman, 2003).

ANALOGIES Similarities between phenomena can be expressed well through analogies. For instance, the cell structure of a plant might be compared with the factory structure of an industry. Effective speakers, writers, and teachers frequently use analogies to help students use what they already know to help them understand and remember new knowledge.

IMAGES Images become mnemonic devices when they are used to represent abstract concepts. For example, a visual image of mist coming from a block of dry ice might be used to represent the physical process of sublimation, the change of a solid directly into a gas. Most of us associate personal or public events of the past with certain images that make those events come alive for us even now.

SPECIAL VERBAL FORMS Mnemonic devices also take special verbal forms that aid in the retrieval of information. Only certain types of information fits these special verbal mnemonic devices. Examples of these devices are as follows:

- *abbreviations* (FBI, NAACP, NCAA),
- *acronyms* (HOMES for the first letters of the Great Lakes),
- *acrostics* ("Every good boy does fine" for the notes of the treble clef),
- *phrases* that help with meaning ("Hang on tight" for remembering that stalactites are on cave ceilings rather than floors) as well as pronunciation ("It's hot again" indicates the accent to Betatakin, a cliff dwelling in Arizona's Navajo National Monument), and
- *rhymes* ("In 1492 Columbus sailed the ocean blue").

MEANINGFUL WORD PARTS Meaningful word parts, or morphemes, are found in derived words with their prefixes, roots, and suffixes. Contractions and compound words also contain these parts. Students often benefit from attending to the meaningful parts of such words as *underground, triangular,* and *immortalize.* Identifying the meaningful parts of words provides control of them and a tool for identifying new words.

IDIOSYNCRATIC ASSOCIATIONS Idiosyncratic associations are similar to meaningful word parts, although the word parts are not from our linguistic heritage. Knowing that the princi**pal** should be your **pal** and that latitude lines resemble a ladder represent idiosyncratic associations.

The *mnemonic keyword method* requires first an acoustic link, then a visual one. For instance, to remember that a credenza is a piece of furniture like a buffet or sideboard, the students might recode the word to an acoustic link, such as dents. A visual image of someone bumping into and denting the furniture could then be constructed.

Mental Learning

This somewhat amorphous category of study strategies produces no written or visual products. It stresses learning activities to be done either with others as part of a study/discussion group or inside one's own head.

SELF-EXPLANATION A good way to initiate mental learning is through self-explanation. After reading, students individually or in groups recount what has been learned. They put new ideas in plain words, explicitly clarifying relationships among concepts within the text, connecting them with previous knowledge. Sometimes they focus on specific information, repeatedly paraphrasing it. When uncertainties occur, proficient learners return to the source to clarify it or make a note to ask the instructor for an explanation.

DISCUSSING Discussing is an open-ended arrangement for students to come together and refine their learning. They might retell particular portions of subject matter, teach it to one another, or ask and answer questions about it.

Reciprocal Teaching

Reciprocal teaching (RT) (Palincsar & Brown, 2009) is a highly acclaimed set of strategies. In reciprocal teaching, students in small groups take turns leading discussions about sections of a piece of reading material they have all read and have open in front of them. RT consists of the following four strategies:

Summarize—Identify and integrate the most important information in the passage.

Question—Pose information in question form to test self and ascertain understanding.

Clarify—Identify specific impediments to understanding (e.g., unfamiliar terms, unclear ideas) and take necessary measures to restore meaning.

Predict—Preview upcoming text and hypothesize what it contains.

The student leader begins the group's discussion of the section by having the designated *questioner* ask questions of the other students about the section's content. After the question–answer period, the student discussion leader as the designated *summarizer* summarizes the section aloud for the others. The rest of the students in the group respond to this summary and, if there are disagreements, everyone returns to the text until a consensus is reached. After consensus on an oral summary is achieved, attention turns to clarifying. A *clarifier* specifies troublesome aspects of the text, such as unclear referents, unfamiliar vocabulary, disorganized structure, incomplete information, and unusual expressions. Older readers often respond best to this strategy by pointing out what younger readers might need to have clarified. Next, the student discussion leader has the *predictor* elicit predictions from the others about the content of following sections. The leader may also add predictions of his or her own. This ends the group's discussion of the section. If another section is to be discussed reciprocally that day, another student in the group may become the discussion leader for the new text section, and group members change discussion roles.

After introducing reciprocal teaching, you move around, scaffolding questions, summaries, clarifications, or predictions for students. You also provide suggestions and feedback. As your students improve in their ability to discuss text segments reciprocally, you fade your guidance until each group is functioning independently.

Collaborative Strategic Reading

Collaborative strategic reading (CSR) (Klingner, Vaughn, Arguelles, Hughes, & Leftwich, 2004) consists of a set of four strategies patterned after Reciprocal Teaching. The strategies provide a clear sequence that occurs before, during, and after reading. They are as follows:

Preview—Activate background knowledge, stimulate interest and questions about the text, and generate informed predictions about the text to be read.

Click and Clunk—Monitor and fix up comprehension while reading. Students *click* when they recognize familiar material and extend what is provided in the text. They *clunk* when they identify confusing material they need to know, then work to figure it out. Students might reread the unclear part of the text slowly to themselves, specify the problem, and search the surrounding words for clues to meaning. They continually explain the text to themselves as a way to check their understanding, moving on when their understanding becomes sufficient or when continued attempts to clarify become counterproductive.

Get the Gist—Identify the most critical information while reading. State in a few words what the author evidently wants readers to know.

Wrap Up—After reading, consolidate understandings of the selection's most significant ideas. Ask and answer questions about critical information, and state in a few words what the author evidently wants readers to take away from the entire selection.

Sets of study strategies like RT and CSR share an important characteristic with your unit and lesson plans: They have a beginning, a middle, and an end. Learners' sets of study strategies and your instructional frameworks call for learners to think deliberately about a passage before, during, and after reading. Preparation is done in the prereading, beginning stage; actual reading is done in the middle stage; and follow-up occurs in the postreading stage. Proficient learners realize this progression when studying with a set of strategies.

STUDYING INCLUDES TAKING TESTS

Test-taking Strategies

As standards-based accountability systems increasingly control education, students take more and more tests. And test performance substantially influences the futures of students and their schools. Consequently, preparing students for tests is a study strategy that now is an educational priority.

Test preparation is not the same as test practice (Kraemer, 2005). As one student who felt authentically ready for testing put it, "You prepare us for the test without teaching to the test." You prepare students for tests authentically by connecting test demands with coursework, integrating what is tested into the ongoing curriculum rather than only allocating separate time to isolated activities. You do not focus on raising schools' test scores; you focus on improving youths' reading proficiencies. You first teach students how to improve their reading, then you teach how to succeed with tests.

When the focus is on succeeding with tests, approach the task like any other genre. Explain the special forms and functions of tests, calling attention to how tests are similar to and different from other types of reading. Engage students in the genre, talking through the process of understanding it. Have students read test items carefully, deliberate with others over appropriate answers, and generate guidelines for succeeding with this genre. Figure 8.2 contains a list of test-taking strategies that are appropriate for middle-grade and older students. Note the three types: (1) general, (2) objective (i.e., response select), and (3) essay (i.e., response construct).

General Strategies

1. Survey the test. Estimate its difficulty and plan your time for each section.
2. Read each direction or question carefully. Underline the important words in each direction or question. Be especially alert for closed terms
   such as *always, never,* and *most.*
3. Answer every required question (unless there is a penalty for guessing).
4. Do not spend too much time on any one question.
5. Drink water and eat a nutritious snack as needed.
6. Take a deep breath if you are becoming anxious.
7. Think like a test maker.

Strategies for Objective Tests

1. Answer the easy questions first. Mark the ones you skip and go back to them when you are ready. Remember that information contained in later items can help you answer previous items.
2. Look for the most correct answer when two items seem to be similar.
3. Narrow multiple-choice items to two, then make your choice when you are not sure of an answer.
4. Rephrase questions and answer questions in your head before inspecting the choices.
5. Change your answers only if you misunderstood the question the first time or if you are absolutely sure that your first response was wrong.
6. Shuttle among the passage, the question, and the choices.

Strategies for Essay Tests

1. Briefly outline all answers before writing. Jot down key terms and then add to those terms while working on your answers.
2. Include only information that you believe is correct.
3. Plan your time for each question and stick to that schedule.
4. Include topic sentences and supporting details in each paragraph.
5. Proofread your writing.

FIGURE 8.2   Test-taking Strategies.

Question-answer Relationships

Question–answer Relationships (QAR) (Raphael & Au, 2005) is a useful, strategic approach to taking multiple-choice tests. QAR enhances students' control of tests by providing a way to think through test items, by leading students to determine where to find answers to comprehension questions. QAR classifies comprehension test items according to the following locations of their answers:

In the Book: The answer is in the text.

> *Right There*: You can find the answer in one place in a sentence. You can point directly to the answer.

> *Think and Search*: The answer is in different parts of text. You link ideas across sentences, paragraphs, or even chapters and books to find the answer the question.

In My Head: The answer is not in the text.

> *Author and Me*: You link ideas in the text with what you already know to figure out the answer the question.

> *On My Own*: You use your own ideas and experiences to figure out the answer the question.

Test Talks

Benchmark tests frequently are administered at the end of each grading period to assess how well your students are learning your state's performance objectives. After scores are obtained, you can conduct test talks to help students analyze their performances, obtaining insights into their scores and the choices they made on the multiple-choice tests. Begin by providing all students in your class a copy of their scores as well as class, grade-level, and district scores. Provide a copy of the test for your students to reference during the test talk.

Show your students a graph, by test item, of the percent of students in your class who got each item correct. Direct your students to the items that all or most of the class answered correctly, and have your students figure out why the items were so easy. Briefly discuss what made the items easy.

Then direct attention to the graph showing items that few if any students in your class answered correctly. Again, direct your students to these items, then have your students figure out why each was so difficult. Briefly discuss what made the items difficult and generate strategies for solving them.

Make notes about why your students thought the easy questions were easy and why the difficult ones were difficult. Analyze the responses to identify areas not taught well (or not taught as tested) and plan follow-up instruction accordingly.

STUDYING INCLUDES MANAGING RESOURCES

One of the authors wanted to attend a time management seminar offered during the writing of this book but couldn't find the time. Resource management is easier to talk about than to control. You probably will find this to be the case with your students. You can teach students to apply strategies through direct, explicit instruction, but you can only encourage students to manage their resources. Managing personal resources like time and effort involves beliefs and habits, and these are human characteristics that you do best cheering for and urging your students to take up. Recommendations for managing resources that enhance learning include the following:

1. *Maintain a routine.* Establish a consistent time and place to study.
2. *Create a productive environment.* Establish appropriate levels of noise, light, and temperature. Make sure school supplies are nearby. Have access to food and beverage. Take short breaks.
3. *Complete tasks in an efficient order.* Sequence tasks in an order such as easy to difficult, short to long, interesting to boring, or most favorite to least favorite (or vice versa). Then complete them in the way that is most efficient for you.
4. *Complete tasks on schedule.* Keep up with readings and assignments; do not procrastinate.
5. *Review information at regular intervals.* Conduct frequent short reviews rather than infrequent long ones.
6. *Seek help when needed.* Contact friends, classmates, or teachers to clarify information. Use tutors or study centers. Initiate study groups or pairs.
7. *Set goals.* Chart a course to the future that includes career pathways and personal fulfillment.
8. *Get along with others.* Collaborate as a team member more than a lone wolf. Develop teamwork skills, societal and workplace etiquette, and assertive communication. Channel emotions; manage stress and anger.

You can help students improve their resource management by informing them and providing occasional opportunities during class for students to share how they manage resources. Schools can support students' development of good resource management by sending home descriptions of resource management, focusing on the eight principles, and explaining how important home support is in helping students do well with them.

IMPORTANT PRINCIPLES OF INSTRUCTION APPLY TO STUDYING

At this point you probably realize the complexity of studying. Studying has many aspects, and many of these aspects rely on mental habits. For instance, such strategies as note taking, self-questioning, and graphically organizing information cannot be broken down into a fixed sequence of steps that always produce the same results. Long division can be reduced to such a series, but study strategies usually cannot. Because self-regulation is a major component of studying, the application of study strategies requires countless decisions about the relative importance of information and the relationships among ideas. The individuality of knowing what some ways of studying are, understanding which ones to employ in particular situations, and being motivated to do so add to the intricacies of studying.

You can and should be explicit when you teach students how to study, but you cannot expect an answer key to help you check students' notes, questions, or visual representations. Their approaches to studying should produce some common outcomes, but students' individual interpretations, preferences, and dispositions will also cause these outcomes to vary.

TRY IT OUT

Compare the complexity of long division with that of study strategies. With a fellow student or teacher, compute an answer to an identical long-division problem; then both of you take notes on an identical passage. Compare both sets.

Given the complexity of studying, you do well to explicitly present general guidelines for strategies, tests, and resources, then structure regularly occurring situations so students construct what works for them. This section describes three aspects of effective study instruction.

Isolated and Integrated Instruction

An effective way to combine study strategy instruction with content teaching is by mixing isolated and integrated instruction (Langer, 2002). To illustrate, a school might focus on note taking as a study strategy all students will learn well. You initially might demonstrate and have students practice note taking in isolation, with materials unrelated to unit topics. You would set aside brief portions of class time devoted only to this strategy. You might use short, skill-building, commercial reading materials that are unrelated to the particular unit's topic. You would demonstrate and explain how to go about taking notes. Such an introduction is a way of separating a particular strategy such as note taking from the ongoing flow of class life and highlighting it for your students' undivided attention. It marks note taking for future use and signals its importance.

As your students become proficient with note taking, you would ensure that it soon is integrated into instructional units with the actual tasks at hand. For instance, in science class, your students initially might summarize materials unrelated to cell division, but, as their proficiencies increase, they would take notes when reading about the cardiovascular system and the nervous system. Your students might record notes in journals or notebooks, then use them during inquiry projects or when preparing for a test.

Many upper-grade teachers introduce particular study strategies during the first few weeks of school to help students study better throughout the semester or year. Teachers identify a few preferred ways to study or take ones from a school's curriculum guide, then present them to students immediately. For example, if you expect students to keep learning logs throughout a semester, you demonstrate how to do so at the beginning. Or, if mnemonic devices make especially good sense and are applicable to a subject you are teaching, you introduce the creation and use of mnemonic devices to students as early in the semester or year as possible.

Ways to study can also be presented after a semester or school year has gotten under way. Different ways to represent information visually might be presented throughout the year as opportunities and students' needs arise. In social studies, time lines might be appropriate during each unit of study, but outlining might be introduced only when your students create the table of contents for a report. If your students are having special difficulty with a portion of subject matter, then self-questioning might be introduced at that point to help them overcome that special challenge.

Direct, Explicit Instruction

Direct, explicit instruction is an effective approach for teaching students study strategies (Schunk & Zimmerman, 2007). As explained in earlier chapters, it occurs when you show students how to perform a reading or writing strategy, then gradually move back so your students do it on their own. You fade out, and your students fade in as you gradually release responsibility.

Direct, explicit instruction requires planning on your part to make sure it happens. Teachers often lead students through particular learning procedures, never fading out to relinquish control to students. But think about it: If you always ask the questions, when do your students learn to question themselves? If you always present an outline of course topics, when do your students learn to outline independently?

There is no question that teachers should fade out during instruction in how to study, but sometimes teachers can fade too quickly. Sometimes teachers simply tell students to "take notes on the upcoming material" or "get ready for a quiz on Friday," with little or no instruction on how to take notes or prepare for a quiz. Teachers sometimes assume students are proficient with these strategies when they are not. Guard against not fading out and fading out too soon. Plan studying instruction that balances the five steps of the direct, explicit model of instruction.

DESCRIBE THE STRATEGY   During the description step, you begin as the dominant figure in the class. You label and define the strategy by naming it, presenting a general description of it, and making analogies to it whenever possible. Explain the relevance of the strategy by indicating when and why it is useful. When describing word study cards, you might tell your students something like this:

> Today I will present word study cards to you. These cards are ways to focus on the technical vocabulary of this class. They are like snapshots of individuals rather than a total class picture. Word study cards contain a vocabulary term on one side and ways to understand the word on the other. Making these cards will help you understand the terms, and reviewing the cards will help you remember them.

To explain the relevance of the strategy, you might say something like this:

> Using these cards is one way to cope with the terrific amount of new terms you'll be encountering here. Knowing this strategy will help you in other situations, like getting a new job or being on a sports team, when you suddenly have to learn a lot of specific new ideas.

MODEL THE STRATEGY   As you model the strategy, say something like this:

> Watch how I produce word study cards. First, I acquire a stack of index cards. Then I decide which terms to transfer to the cards. I select words in boldface print, ones listed at the end of the passage, and ones that seem important to me. As you can see, I chose *monarch* as one of the words, so I print it on the front of the card. Then I turn the card over and produce learning aids that will help me understand and remember this word. I decide to write a definition, "Ruler. A king or queen"; a sentence containing the term, "Queen Elizabeth is the monarch of England"; and a note on word parts "mon = one (monorail)." I could have drawn a picture or produced other examples of monarch, but what I have here seems to be enough. Now I put this word card into my pile to review later. I might simply quiz myself on the meanings, separate known from unknown words, get with someone else and take turns quizzing each other, or group the words into different categories.

List prompts that specify as well as possible the strategy you followed. Prompts are general guidelines; they are not rules that always lead to the same outcome. You might tell your students something like this:

> As you saw, I followed the three steps that I posted on the bulletin board:
>
> **1.** Identify important terms.
> **2.** Record one term on one side of a card and learning aids on the other.
> **3.** Review the cards regularly.

COLLABORATIVELY USE THE STRATEGY   After describing and modeling the strategy, begin handing it over to your students. As a whole class, select a few key terms, record each term on one side of a card, then mutually decide what learning aids to enter on the other side. Comment on your students' suggestions for learning aids, focusing on their suitability for the task at hand.

GUIDE APPLICATION OF THE STRATEGY   Next, provide guided practice in the strategy. Direct students to use it and provide feedback while they do. You might say, *Now it's your turn to produce your own study cards. Work with a partner or on your own. We'll get together as a whole class in fifteen minutes to check on progress.* As you move around to work with students, you can probe their understanding of the strategy, praise and encourage their efforts, remind them of missing steps, and suggest improvements.

SUPPORT INDEPENDENT APPLICATION OF THE STRATEGY   Showing your students a strategy, then having them practice it several times as you provide cues and feedback is a good beginning, but learners need to apply the strategy independently and regularly to make it their own. During the independent application stage, plan situations for your students to use and refine the strategy; determine your students' grasp of it and reteach what is needed.

TRY IT OUT

Select a study strategy and plan an introductory lesson that contains the first four steps of direct, explicit instruction. Conduct the lesson with a group of peers or students. Evaluate the lesson: Describe what you would keep and what you would change if you were to do it again. Also describe your next steps to follow up this introductory lesson with opportunities for independent application.

Scaffolded Instruction

As noted earlier, construction workers use scaffolding to prop up structures and gain access to them as they are being erected; scaffolds are used in various ways until the building can stand on its own. In education, scaffolds are the supports you and your students use to construct new knowledge. Dialogue among students and teachers is a central feature of scaffolded instruction (Stone, 2001). Students benefit from a nonevaluative setting to verbalize their understandings and beliefs about study strategies so you and other students can suggest the right actions at the right times.

When you plan and present studying lessons, decide what scaffolding is needed. Working closely with your students will help you determine the supports to include, gradually decrease, and eventually remove. Thinking about the following types of scaffolding helps you plan instruction: instructional routines, self-assessment, prompts, analogies, classroom grouping patterns, reading materials, strategy complexity, and process checks.

INSTRUCTIONAL ROUTINES   Plan your teaching so your instructional routines incorporate study strategies, and so your students succeed in class when they apply them. Open-notebook quizzes exemplify this type of planning. Regularly provide class time for students individually or in groups to take notes from their readings. Then allow students to use these notes, but not the readings themselves, during quizzes. Many teachers also collect students' learning logs or journals, comment on them, and record a plus or minus grade depending on the amount of writing students produced. Graphically organizing information becomes an instructional routine when every Monday you randomly select a student to share what he or she produced for an assigned reading. You ensure that self-questioning leads to success when student-produced questions appear on quizzes.

SELF-ASSESSMENT   The necessary complement to your fading is for students to self-assess during studying instruction. For instance, as with any writing, you could have your class complete score guides for their notes, learning logs, graphic organizers, or self-questions before you check them.

You could have your class complete open-ended questions such as the following:

- What did I find difficult to understand? What can I do to improve my understanding of _____?
- Does _____ make sense with what was presented before? If not, what can I do to make sense of _____?
- What did the author/teacher present to help me understand _____?

PROMPTS   Prompts stimulate thinking. They are questions or directions that cue learners to the critical features of the strategy. They induce learners to think a certain way.

Like the outcomes of a traditional task analysis, prompts indicate the actions to perform in multistep procedures. The three guidelines for producing study cards, presented earlier, exemplify prompts (identify important terms; record one term on one side of a card and learning aids on the other; review the cards regularly). Mathematics teachers usually present a multistep strategy for solving word problems with prompts such as the following:

1. Survey the problem.
2. Determine what is given and what is asked for.
3. Determine what operations to use and when to use them.
4. Estimate the answer.
5. Solve the problem.
6. Determine if the solution is reasonable.

Record the prompts for students' reference. The prompts might be placed on a bulletin board, distributed on cue cards, or copied into students' class notes. You should refer to the prompts frequently at first, then begin to fade out.

Prompts do not specify invariant rules; they signal general actions. The *clarify* part of reciprocal teaching, for instance, involves examining many parts of a passage in no particular order. Despite their generality, prompts are valuable supports that guide learners.

ANALOGIES   Another form of scaffolding to include in studying instruction is analogies that compare a study strategy to something vivid. Analogies can motivate students and make strategies concrete and sensible. They are good vehicles for discussions.

Many types of analogies are available. You can compare word study cards to snapshots, note taking to gold mining or eating digestible bites of food, and graphically organizing information to sketching a picture or framing a building. Teachers sometimes compare readers to detectives: Both search for clues, form hunches, and support their generalizations.

If you cannot think of an analogy for the strategy or system you are presenting, ask students for one. Their analogies frequently are more vivid and apt than the ones adults produce.

CLASSROOM GROUPING PATTERNS   Adjusting classroom grouping patterns is a good way to scaffold instruction. Students can develop strategies when participating in whole-class, small-group, learning-pair, and individual configurations. You can change classroom grouping patterns to keep your instruction fresh, accommodate the type of lesson you are presenting, and promote dialogue.

Teachers often demonstrate ways of studying to a whole class, then begin fading by jointly performing the procedure with students still grouped as a class. After collaborating with students in a whole-class setting, have them perform the strategy or system in small groups or learning teams. Students who take turns sharing a strategy with one another go far in refining their knowledge of it. Small-group or learning-pair production of questions, visual representations, or mnemonic devices are clear tasks that fit group work nicely. Individuals can perform strategies on their own and then join a group or a partner to share what they produced and receive feedback. Finally, group support can be removed as students work to internalize the strategy on their own.

READING MATERIALS   Ensuring that your instruction offers an appropriate challenge is an important feature of scaffolded instruction. The materials you use when introducing ways to study should present minimal difficulties to your students so they can concentrate on the strategy. Many studying lessons have been torpedoed by lengthy, difficult reading materials; the students became confused about the material and, consequently, the strategy.

When you introduce a strategy, one way to ensure appropriate materials is to use ones already studied in class. Return to a passage that your class already read and show how the strategy applies to it. Another way is to locate very easy topic-related materials. Secondary-school English teachers often introduce such literary elements as plot, setting, theme, and symbolism with children's literature. After introducing a strategy with short, easy materials, you can begin increasing the length and difficulty of the materials to meet your students' abilities. Once students have a strategy for identifying the plot of *The Three Little Pigs*, they can begin transferring it to *Charlotte's Web* and eventually *War and Peace*.

COMPLEXITY   Another way to control the difficulty of studying instruction involves the strategy being taught. Be sure that the prompts are appropriate for your students. If a step in summarizing is "Determine the main idea of the passage," you would need to ask yourself if your students can accomplish this step. Perhaps this main idea prompt should be modified to "Determine the topic of the passage."

You can regulate the difficulty of a multistep procedure by presenting each prompt gradually, teaching manageable yet meaningful portions a step at a time. Ensure that your students can perform the first step before beginning the second. If your students are to ask themselves or one another generic questions, be sure that they understand each question and know how to go about answering it.

Students can learn study strategies while working in groups.

STRATEGY CHECKS. A final way to scaffold instruction involves strategy checks. These checks are good ways to keep students in pursuit of learning how to study, directing them to maintain what they are learning. Have students take stock of their use of study strategies or systems at various intervals. When they are preparing to read, ask them, "What are some things you might do to learn this information?" At other times simply remind students of strategies they have learned: "Remember what you know about imaging when you read this passage."

Questions such as the following check on students' strategy:

Before Reading
How will you remember this?
What can you do to learn this?

After Reading
How did you figure this selection out?
How did you approach this selection?

Strategy checks focus students on how they studied rather than on what they learned. If a student claimed that the Spanish conquistadors were criminals rather than heroes, a product-oriented check would be: "What did they do that was criminal? Were the French settlers any more criminal or heroic?" Conversely, the following would be a strategy check: "Why do you say that? What led you to that conclusion?"

DISCIPLINARY LITERACIES

Studying in English/Language Arts Classrooms

English/language arts curriculums include a broad array of outcomes. Among other things, students in English/language arts are expected to learn how to write essays, letters, memos, and poems; understand advertisements, plays, short stories, and novels; present themselves during interviews, public presentations, and work groups; and value, appreciate, and personally respond to literary accomplishments. Concentrating on study techniques that provide students initial access to these outcomes is one way English/language arts teachers manage such crowded curriculums.

Reciprocal Teaching (RT) as an approach to studying English/language arts deserves consideration. RT denotes an instructional approach for teachers as well as a set of study strategies for students. It offers a set of specific learning conditions as well as a set of specific mental operations.

The RT instructional approach emphasizes teacher–student and student–student conversations, or dialogues, about understanding texts. It calls for cooperative effort and sharing. While reading short sections of a passage, for example, you and your students think aloud, describing the mental processes you are using to make sense of what you are reading.

Fade your instruction during RT. Initially take the lead in describing particular strategies you are applying, then gradually relinquish this role as your students describe their use of the strategies with other segments of text. When participating in small groups, have your students record their responses for whole-class sharing. Scaffold instruction during RT by commenting on your students' efforts ("That's a good start. What do others of you think might be important to say?"), offering additional modeling ("I think the reason for selling the camel needs to be included here."), and hinting at next steps ("Now what should you do to make sense of this passage?"). Praising valid actions, providing passages at different levels of difficulty, and posting written prompts about RT strategies are additional possible scaffolds. Explain why and when particular strategies are appropriate.

The RT, repertoire of mental operations consists of four cognitive strategies: summarize, question, clarify, and predict. Teachers and students talk about how they are employing these mental actions relative to specific sections of reading materials. If your class or a small group was reading *Shabanu, Daughter of the Wind*, individuals would take turns describing their summaries, questions, clarifications, and predictions. For the episode when Shabanu's father sells Guluband, the family's prize camel, one student might briefly summarize what happened, produce a question such as "Why was Guluband sold?", clarify the way Shabanu's father went about selling the animal, and predict what will happen next. As the student talks about these things, others chime in with their thoughts. They might add to the summary, suggest additional questions, offer other items for clarification, and produce their own predictions.

The RT learning target is independence. After multiple focused conversations about passages conducted in groups, individuals are expected to conduct their own dialogues internally. Individuals are expected to become independent and think through their own summaries, questions and answers, clarifications, and predictions. When emphasizing this individual action phase of RT, you might call it "talking to yourself" or "having an internal dialogue." This aspect obliges individuals to utilize inner speech—the voices within their minds—to determine text meanings. Students are expected to address possible interpretations and evaluations internally before settling on certain ones.

When using RT in English/language arts class with narrative passages, you might retain its approach to instruction but modify its cognitive strategies. Consider modifications such as reducing the number of strategies from four, having students select only the one or two they believe most appropriate for a particular section, or substituting strategies. You might replace the original RT strategies (summarize, clarify, question, predict) with some of the essential thinking processes described in Chapter 1, such as connect, generalize, or image, if these seem more appropriate for your students and the materials they are reading. For instance, students internally might orchestrate connections among text ideas and previous experiences, think through possibilities for a passage's overall message, and construct and reconstruct images of key scenes until they are satisfied. Indeed, RT's value seems to come from its collaborative, explicit, sense-making approach to instruction more than from its specific strategies being taught. Students benefit when they exert concentrated efforts to learn and make public what they are doing.

Studying in English Language Development Classrooms

Helping students become independent lifelong learners is a central goal of education. This means developing students' desires and abilities to continue their language learning after graduation. Promoting effective instructional settings and word-learning strategies are two ways to approach this goal in English language development classes.

INSTRUCTIONAL SETTINGS As noted in Chapter 2, the overall setting of a classroom substantially affects learning. English learning is no exception. You play an especially crucial role in promoting settings that begin a lifetime of English learning.

English learners typically benefit from classes that engage them in learning by being interactive, challenging, and enjoyable, that actively involve them in learning. Debates as well as back-and-forth conversations that encourage them to think on their feet and put their ideas quickly into English are beneficial. The best classes engage them in games or hands-on activities as opposed to taking notes and listening to lectures. These classes employ plays and literature circles.

Effective instruction also uses students' primary languages as scaffolds for learning English. When English learners are confused, clarify the issue in their primary language generally before continuing in English. Comparing English language structures with students' primary language structures also is effective.

WORD-LEARNING STRATEGIES   Teachers who present only the meanings of words encountered during class shortchange students when they leave class. English learners with few word-learning strategies are limited when they encounter unfamiliar terms and their teacher is not available to explain them. To avoid this situation, emphasize word-learning strategies.

A frequently underestimated word-learning strategy is determining the depth of knowledge needed for particular terms. Knowing only that *truffles* are edible and that *taupe* is a color might be sufficient for some situations but not for others. Learners need to become adept at determining the words that warrant their attention and the degree of knowledge that they require. English language teachers promote this adeptness by involving students in selecting words for study and determining their meanings. Regularly have students identify the important words in reading materials, presentations, and audiovisuals, and have students talk about the meanings they produce for the words. To stimulate these practices, regularly hold discussions in response to questions such as these two:

"Which terms should be learned?"

"What needs to be known about each term?"

Emphasize word-learning strategies by helping students become "word detectives," sleuths who take advantage of word-meaning clues. Stress context as a powerful clue to word meanings. After deciding on a passage's terms that should be emphasized, help students figure out their meanings by examining the ways they are presented. Regularly talk about students' reactions to a question such as this one:

"What does the passage reveal about the meaning of this term?"

Searching for cognate relationships (e.g., discerning the connections between the Spanish *naturalmente* and the English *naturally* as described in Chapter 6) is another good way to utilize word meaning clues. Accustom students to search habitually for shared meanings among words that look and sound alike by regularly asking students:

"Do you know any words that look and sound like this word?"

"Are any of these look-alike/sound-alike words related to each other?"

To see how contextual and morphemic clues combine, consider this sentence: *All rocks formed from fiery hot magma are called igneous rocks.* The context clearly implies that *igneous* means *formed from fiery hot magma.* And since the beginning of *igneous* looks and sounds something like the beginnings of *ignite* and *ignition*, a morphemic connection based on *ign* becomes apparent. Students can generalize the meaning of *igneous* to something like, "rocks formed by fire or volcanic action." To help students combine contextual and morphemic clues, you might ask something like:

"What are the connections between what the passage reveals about the word and its relation to look-alike words?"

If contextual and morphemic clues are insufficient, then independent learners consult references such as dictionaries, glossaries, encyclopedias, and other people. References are consulted only after determining that a term is important to understand and that the available clues do not fully reveal its meaning. Indeed, learners consult references to confirm and refine word meanings as much as to gain completely new understandings. In the preceding example, learners might seek confirmation to the meaning of *igneous*, and they might look up *magma* for initial ideas if they don't have any clue to its meaning. To help students consult references at appropriate times, you could ask:

> "When understanding a word is crucial and the clues to its meaning are insufficient, what do you do?"

Finally, making and reviewing word study cards is a time-honored word-learning strategy. Recording new terms on the front of study cards and supplying clarifying information on the back is a powerful tool for continually upgrading English learning. Writing the clarifying information in one's native language enlarges the possibilities of what can be included. Learners might record definitions, explanations, sentence contexts, mnemonic devices, related words, and illustrations to clarify the unfamiliar word meanings. Reviewing the study cards, separating the words that are understood immediately from the ones that are not, and resolving difficulties are additional steps that promote word learning over time.

Studying in Mathematics Classrooms

When students are doing math homework or preparing for a math test, their lack of effective study procedures can lead to frustration and poor performance. Here are some ways math teachers help students become more successful and independent in their learning of mathematics.

STUDY CARDS   Having students make a set of study cards during a math unit and then teaching them how to use that set of cards to study for a test helps students develop an important study strategy that only a few high-achieving students probably do on their own.

After each type of problem covered in the unit has been taught and practiced, have students pick one problem of that type from their math book. Choosing one of moderate rather than low or high difficulty is generally best. Have each student write that problem on one side of a four-by-six index card. (See Figure 8.3 for an example of a math study card from a middle-school math class.)

$$
\begin{array}{r}
23.2 \\
\underline{\times 14.1}
\end{array}
$$

23.2 × 14.1

23.2 14.1

(23.2) (14.1)

FIGURE 8.3   Math Study Card Front.

pages 187-189

1. Copy the problem in vertical form.
2. Check to see if the decimals line up.
3. Check to see if the numerals line up.
4. Multiply the top number by the first numeral on the right of the lower number.
5. Put a zero on the right, then multiply by the second numeral of the lower number.
6. Put two zeros on the right, then multiply the third numeral of the lower number.
7. Add the part answers together, starting on the right and keeping numerals straight.
8. The answer has the number of decimal places that the two numbers have together.

$$\begin{array}{r} 23.2 \\ \underline{\times 14.1} \\ 232 \\ 9280 \\ \underline{23200} \\ 327.12 \end{array}$$

FIGURE 8.4   Math Study Card Back.

On the other side of that same four-by-six index card, have each student write the page number(s) in the book where the explanation of how to work that kind of problem is to be found, followed by the steps recommended for solving that kind of problem, followed by the problem worked correctly. (See Figure 8.4.)

After each student has completed this study card, it can be handed in or checked by a partner. Once it has been checked, it is added to the student's growing deck of math study cards.

Before a test, demonstrate how to use the deck of math study cards for study. Shuffle your deck and then pick the top card. Work the problem on the front without looking at the back of the card. Then turn the card over to check both your answer and how you worked it. It is helpful to students if you get one or two problems right and then "miss" one. On the one you miss, show them how to use the card to check, step by step, what you did. Show them how to use the pages from the book that explain how to do that kind of problem when you can't remember exactly what one of your steps means or what your teacher said about it.

Provide time during class for students to study for the next test using their deck of math study cards. Encourage them to use their study cards outside of class as they prepare for the test. Students who use their deck of cards for study and feel that it helps them are more likely to begin developing their own decks of math study cards.

SELF-REGULATION   No component of studying is more important for mathematics than self-regulation. Consider the kinds of students who usually do well in math. They know when they "have it" and expend little effort and exhibit little anxiety afterward on that concept. On the other hand, they also know when they are having difficulty and seem able to formulate the right questions to ask to elicit the help they need. Moreover, they seem to know when a parent, a fellow student, or a teacher is the most likely person to know the answer to a particular question. At times, they are able to keep working at one or more problems until they figure out what they need to know without help. The successful student of mathematics is almost always a self-regulated student.

Successful teachers of mathematics help students become self-regulated by having them predict and self-monitor during math lessons. Instead of starting out by working a problem for the class, present a problem to the class and ask them to predict individually whether they can solve it correctly or not. If a number of students are certain that they can or uncertain about whether they can or not, take a minute and have students try to solve the problem at their seats. The correct answer is shared and students discuss any difficulties. Then, help them determine how they could have anticipated where they would have trouble. If most of the students seem certain that they cannot solve the problem, have different students explain what there is about the problem that has them stymied. In either case, teach everything you would have otherwise taught, but only when students are aware that they really need to know what is being taught.

Studying in Science Classrooms

Science is an extremely important subject that many students have difficulty learning. Here are some ways science teachers help students become more successful and independent in their learning of science.

GRAPHIC ORGANIZERS   Graphic organizers are an extremely important tool for giving students the big picture and showing them relationships between that big picture and science facts, terms, and concepts. Just as importantly, your students can learn to create their own graphic organizers independently so that they can assist in their own mastery of both the parts and wholes of science.

For example, some chemistry teachers make the Periodic Table of the Elements on the wall of their classrooms an integral part of their course. In the beginning, explain what a chemical element is and contrast it with a compound. As students are taught the concept of *atomic number*, refer to the Periodic Table to show them how the elements are arranged in increasing order of atomic number from left to right and top to bottom. As your students learn that the elements can be subdivided into groups that act somewhat alike when forming compounds, and share other properties as well, refer to the Periodic Table to show them how sections of it cluster together into identifiable groups such as alkali metals or noble gases. Later, as your students learn the chemistry of these different groups of elements, they learn about the K, L, M, N, O, P, and Q electron shells. The teacher then regularly refers to the Periodic Table to show the students how the number of electron shells that an element has determines which of the seven rows or "periods" that element is in. As you teach the students that the number of electrons in the outer shell of an element determines how it forms compounds with other elements, you also show students that the number of electrons in the outer shell determines which column of the table that element is in. Once they understand how it works, students are encouraged to refer to the Periodic Table in their chemistry textbook as they study. Throughout, students are not allowed to forget that all the specific facts, terms, and concepts about chemical elements they are learning fit together into a grand scheme.

A *data chart* (labeled rows and columns with information in the cells) like the Periodic Table is only one kind of graphic organizer that you can use to show the relationships between the whole of a course, unit, or topic and its parts. With respect to studying, however, it is important to follow the effective use of graphic organizers with activities that have students work in small groups to represent graphically the relationships they understand among a set of facts, terms, or concepts. For example, at the end of a unit on electricity in a middle-school physical science course, your students could be put in mixed groups of four or five and given a list of key terms from the unit: *current, conductor, induction, insulator, resistance, semiconductor,* and *voltage.* The task would be for them to web "electricity" using those terms and others they find helpful. The groups can record these webs on sheets of chart paper and some can be shared with the whole class. Of course, this task assumes that you have previously taught webs as graphic organizers while teaching the course.

As your students improve in their ability to represent graphically the key terms, facts, or concepts of a science topic or unit, they can be shown how such an activity helps them prepare to answer test questions about the relationships among those terms, facts, or concepts. This motivates the construction of graphic organizers as a study strategy.

MNEMONIC DEVICES   What are the colors of the rainbow in order? You probably know the answer to this question because you remember the memorable nonsense word, *roygbiv,* or strange name, Roy G. Biv (red, orange, yellow, green, blue, indigo, violet). One of us still remembers eras in the order he learned decades ago in historical geology by constructing the sentence, "Come over soon; don't miss pepperoni pizza" (Cambrian, Ordovician, Silurian, Devonian, Mississippian, Pennsylvanian, Permian).

No other subject is so vocabulary intensive as science. The number of terms that must be learned in any science course is often daunting for students. Teaching them a few mnemonic devices that you have found helpful will increase their ability to remember sets of terms. With respect to them learning how to study science better, it is important to have the class construct a mnemonic occasionally to help them remember a particular set of important terms. The students who find these mnemonics helpful are more likely to produce ones on their own when studying science outside of class.

Studying in Social Studies Classrooms

Social studies courses are often marked by their breadth of content coverage and thoughtfulness of conceptual issues. If students are to take advantage of this breadth and thoughtfulness, they must learn how to study both social studies content and its conceptual implications. Here are some ways social studies teachers help students become more successful and independent in their learning.

GRAPHIC ORGANIZERS   To learn social studies, a student has to acquire a large number of facts, terms, and concepts. Unfortunately, teaching this basic level of social studies knowledge causes many students to become unable "to see the forest for the trees" and to conceive of social studies as "just one darn thing after another!" Graphic organizers help portray the big picture and relationships among facts, terms, and concepts.

For example, use data charts to help your students see the significance of the people, events, and dates they are learning. A *data chart* is a graphic organizer consisting of labeled rows and columns with information in the cells. Figure 8.5 is an example of a data chart that helps students see relationships among the specifics they are learning about the years leading up to the Civil War.

After having students fill the cells of this data chart with information from their textbook, class notes, and other sources, you can lead them to consider expansion, slavery, and the economy across the five administrations instead of only within each. Moreover,

	Expansion	Slavery	The Economy
James K. Polk (1845–1849)			
Zachary Taylor (1849–1850)			
Millard Fillmore (1850–1853)			
Franklin Pierce (1853–1857)			
James Buchanan (1857–1861)			

FIGURE 8.5   The Five Presidential Administrations Leading Up to the Civil War.

the chart facilitates your students in seeing relationships among expansion, slavery, and the economy during these years. The data chart increases the likelihood that students will think about the possible relationships across administrations and factors without you having to tell them directly what those relationships are.

A data chart is only one kind of graphic organizer that an American history or other social studies teacher can use to show the relationships between the whole of a course, unit, or topic and its parts. With respect to studying, however, it is important to follow the effective use of graphic organizers with activities that have students work in small groups to represent graphically the relationships they understand among a set of facts, terms, or concepts. For example, at the end of a unit on types of government in a middle-school social studies course, your students could be put in mixed groups of four or five students each and given a list of key terms from the unit: *anarchy, aristocracy, authoritarianism, autocracy, capitalism, communism, democracy, fascism, monarchy, oligarchy, republic, socialism, totalitarianism.* The task would be for them to web "government" using those terms and others they find helpful. The groups can record these webs on sheets of chart paper and some can be shared with the whole class. Of course, this task assumes that you have previously used webs as graphic organizers while teaching the course.

As students improve in their ability to represent graphically the key terms, facts, or concepts of a social studies topic or unit, they can be shown how such an activity helps them prepare to answer test questions about the relationships among those terms, facts, or concepts. This motivates the construction of graphic organizers as a study strategy.

DISCUSSING   In social studies, critical thinking is crucial. That is why successful social studies teachers use as many essay questions on tests and have students write as many short papers as they have time to handle. Perhaps the best way to prepare students to do the kind of thinking that essay questions and short papers require is to have class discussions from time to time on responding to the kinds of questions you ask and paper topics you assign. Clarify your expectations for critical thinking, perhaps explaining what it takes to understand specific events. Draw attention to (a) sourcing, noting authors' particular backgrounds and purposes; (b) contextualization, situating an event in its particular social, political, and economic time and place; and (c) corroboration, comparing documents that pertain to the same event.

TWO-COLUMN NOTES   Two column notes help students organize information under specific topics and give them a study strategy that they can use alone or with a partner. Students take notes on one side only of loose-leaf notebook paper. Before taking notes, they draw a line vertically down the paper, leaving a three-inch column on the left. They leave this left column blank, making their notes based on the lecture, video, or reading only in the wider right-hand column. When they finish taking their notes, they go back through them and label each with a word or phrase that tells the topic of each section of notes. To study from these notes, they work by themselves or with a partner, folding their paper so that they can only see the left column with the topics. Trying to anticipate questions that might be asked, they answer the questions, using information they remember from the folded-away right column of details. To check their recall of important facts, they fold back the paper and see if they have included all pertinent ideas. While studying, they deal with all notes that have a particular topic entry, even if these are separated by other topic entries. If students who have taken notes on the same lecture, video, or text section study together, they can compare notes and add details from each other's that they omitted to enter into their own notes and then test each other by constructing possible questions for each topic and trying to recall the pertinent details.

Studying in Activity Classrooms

Think of the studying you have done as you have learned the field you teach. While reading and writing play a significantly smaller role in your field than they do in social studies, science, or English, they have helped you at times to learn what you now know and can do. Your students may not be aware that reading and writing have *any* part to play in your course. Here are some ways teachers of activity courses use literacy to help students become more successful and independent in their learning.

STUDY CARDS   Having students make a set of study cards while they are learning a procedure in your class and then teaching them how to use that set of cards to study for a test helps students develop an important study strategy that only a few high-achieving students would probably figure out on their own.

As you are teaching the procedure, select an important term, step, or rule that your students in the past had trouble remembering. Have each student write that term, step, or rule on one side of a four-by-six index card. On the same side of that card, have each student write the page number(s) in the book, if there is one, where the explanation of that term, step, or rule is to be found.

On the other side of that same index card, have each student write the question that the term, step, or rule on the other side is the answer to. If the term, step, or rule on the other side is the answer to more than one question, then more than one question should be written.

After each student has completed this study card, it can be handed in or checked by a partner. Once it has been checked, it is added to the student's growing deck of study cards for this procedure or the procedures being taught during this unit.

Before a test, demonstrate how to use the deck of study cards to study from. Shuffle your deck and then pick the top card. Ask the question(s) on the front aloud and then try to answer it (them) aloud without looking at the back of the card. Then turn the card over to check whether you answered with the right term, step, or rule. It is helpful to students if you get one or two terms, steps, or rules right and then miss one. On the one you miss, show them how to use the card to study that term, step, or rule (put it in a "missed" pile that you review after going through the deck one time). Show them how to use the pages from the book that explain that term, step, or rule when you can't remember exactly what your answer means or what was said about it. Provide time during class for students to study for the next test, using their deck of study cards. Encourage them to use their study cards outside of class as they prepare for the test. Students who use their deck of cards to study with and feel that it helps them are more likely to begin developing their own decks of study cards for difficult terms, steps, or rules.

WRITING SUMMARIES OF PROCEDURES   After you explain or demonstrate how to do a particular procedure, have students write a quick summary of the steps and rules you have taught them. Then, pair the students and have them swap their summaries. Each student reads her partner's written summary to see if she understands and agrees with it. This process is faster and less threatening than if you watch each one of the students try to do the procedure, and yet it usually reveals many of the misunderstandings and gaps in what the students understand about how to do the procedure. Respond to the questions that arise.

IMAGES AND RHYMES   Mnemonic devices help learners remember difficult or tricky procedures. Many people still remember how to use a screwdriver or wrench properly by reciting the ditty: "Righty tighty, lefty loosey." Great basketball players often practice

Literacy in an activity class.

hitting crucial, last-second free throws over and over again in their minds so that, if the situation arises, they will have an image to help them remember how it feels to make those shots when the pressure to panic is intense.

Share with your students any images or rhymes you have used to help you remember procedures at difficult or stress-filled times. Encourage and give them time to construct their own images or rhymes to help them remember the procedures you are teaching them or to prepare for tests or performance situations when they might forget under pressure.

LOOKING BACK

You can instruct and encourage students in how to study. More and better studying would help all students be better prepared to learn from their current courses, future schooling, and lifelong learning opportunities. You encountered five key ideas in this chapter: (1) Studying is complex; (2) studying includes learning strategies; (3) studying includes test-taking strategies; (4) studying includes managing resources; and (5) important principles of instruction apply to studying.

ADD TO YOUR JOURNAL

Record in your class journal your reactions to this chapter. What lessons or units in how to study have you experienced? What were their strengths and limitations? What were their similarities and differences? Which study strategies will you emphasize with your students? How do you plan on implementing studying instruction in your teaching?

Additional Readings

A good source for teaching students how to study is found in the following:

Flippo, R. F. (2004). *Texts and tests: Teaching study skills across content areas*. Portsmouth, NH: Heinemann.

These three classics present scholarly descriptions of study strategies:

Novak, J. D., & Gowin, D. B. (1984). *Learning how to learn*. New York, NY: Cambridge Press.

Pressley, M., Johnson, C. J., Symons, S., McGoldrick, J. A., & Kurita, J. (1989). Strategies that improve memory and comprehension of text. *Elementary School Journal, 90,* 3–32.

Weinstein, C. E., & Mayer, R. E. (1986). The teaching of learning strategies. In M. C. Wittrock (Ed.),

Handbook of research on teaching (3rd ed., pp. 315–327). New York, NY: Macmillan.

Self-regulated learning is explained well in the following scholarly collection:

Baumeister, R. F., & Vohs, K. D. (Eds.). (2007). *Handbook of self-regulation: Research, theory, and applications*. New York, NY: Guilford.

Many how-to-study handbooks written for students are available. These are written for intermediate-grade students:

Rozakis, L. (2002). *Super study skills*. New York, NY: Scholastic.

Woodcock, S. K. (2006). *SOAR study skills*. New York, NY: Grand Lighthouse Publishers.

This how-to-study handbook is written for middle-school students:

Ernst, J. (2004). *Middle school study skills*. Westminster, CA: Teacher Created Resources.

These how-to-study handbooks are written for secondary students:

Fry, R. (2004). *How to study* (6th ed.). Florence, KY: Delmar Cengage Learning.

Moss, S., & Schwartz, L. (2007). *Where's my stuff?: The ultimate teen organizing guide*. San Francisco, CA: Orange Avenue Publishing.

These how-to-study handbooks are written for students entering college:

Carter, C., Bishop, J., Kravits, S. L. (2007). *Keys to college studying: Becoming an active thinker*. Upper Saddle River, NJ: Pearson/Prentice Hall.

Turner, J. (2002). *How to study: A short introduction*. Thousand Oaks, CA: Sage.

Online Resources

These sites present strategies and tips intended to help older students study successfully.

HowtoStudy.com
http://www.how-to-study.com/

Skills4Study
http://www.palgrave.com/skills4study/index.asp

Study Guides and Strategies
http://www.studygs.net/

Successful Math and Science Study Skills
http://wc.pima.edu/~carem/studyskills.html

References

Baumeister, R. F., & Vohs, K. D. (Eds.). (2007). *Handbook of self-regulation: Research, theory, and applications*. New York, NY: Guilford.

Devine, T. G., & Kania, J. S. (2003). Studying: Skills, strategies, and systems. In J. Flood, D. Lapp, J. R. Squire, & J. M. Jensen (Eds.), *Handbook of research on teaching the English language arts* (2nd ed., pp. 942–954). New York, NY: Macmillan.

Glynn, S., Koballa, & Coleman, D. (2003). Mnemonic methods. *The Science Teacher, 20*, 52–55.

Kiewra, K. A. (2002). How classroom teachers can help students learn and teach them how to learn. *Theory into Practice, 41*, 71–80.

Klingner, J. K., Vaughn, S., Arguelles, M. E., Hughes, M. T., & Leftwich, S. A. (2004). Collaborative Strategic Reading: "Real-world" lessons from classroom teachers. *Remedial and Special Education, 25*, 291–302.

Kraemer, D. J. (2005). Fighting forward: Why studying standardized tests with our students is important. *English Journal, 94*, 88–92.

Langer, J. A. (2002). *Effective literacy instruction: Building successful reading and writing programs*. Urbana, IL: National Council of Teachers of English.

Moore, D. W., Readence, J. E., & Rickelman, R. R. (1983). An historical exploration of content area reading instruction. *Reading Research Quarterly, 18*, 419–438.

Nesbit, J. C., & Adesope, O. O. (2006). Learning with concept and knowledge maps: A meta-analysis. *Review of Educational Research, 76*, 413–448.

Palincsar, A. S., & Brown, A. L. (2009). Interactive teaching to promote independent learning from text. In D. Lapp & D. Fisher (Eds.), *Essential readings on comprehension* (pp. 101–106). Newark, DE: International Reading Association.

Raphael, T. E., & Au, K. H. (2005). QAR: Enhancing comprehension and test taking across grades and content areas. *The Reading Teacher, 59*, 206–221.

Schunk, D. H., & Zimmerman, B. J. (2007). Influencing children's self-efficacy and self-regulation of reading and writing through modeling. *Reading & Writing Quarterly, 23*(1), 7–25.

Stone, C. A. (2001). Promises and pitfalls of scaffolding instruction for students with language learning disabilities. In K. G. Butler & E. R. Silliman (Eds.), *Speaking, reading, and writing in children with language learning disabilities: New paradigms in research and practice* (pp. 175–198). Mahwah, NJ: Erlbaum.

CHAPTER 9

Inquiry through Digital Literacies

LOOKING AHEAD

A group of primary-grade children inspects the charts they are producing with a wizard software function. One claims, "We need to show the difference between those who eat sugar cereal for breakfast and those who don't." Group members talk about how this might portray classmates' eating habits, and they decide to make the comparison. A class of middle-school youth call out ways to reduce, reuse, and recycle as their teacher at the interactive whiteboard records ideas under a heading entitled "Conservation." In a high school media center, young adults are searching online for possible solutions to selected U.S. foreign policy issues. These glimpses of school life show learners engaged in inquiry through digital literacies, investigating meaningful issues and informing others about what was learned through technological resources. This chapter describes how to facilitate such inquiries.

Recognizing the need for information, locating good sources, synthesizing what is found, and communicating ideas digitally are critical competencies. Well-formed decisions about personal, social, and occupational issues depend on well-developed inquiry processes.

Many consider inquiry and research to be mysterious and specialized endeavors. However, these terms can be demystified by thinking of them as states of mind. *Inquiry* and *research* refer to the process of producing convincing answers to interesting questions. People become curious about something, so they set out to learn more about it, increasingly through 21st-century digital means.

This chapter describes inquiries that engage students with a range of materials and methods for independently learning about and interacting in the world. These are its keys:

1. Inquiry is a special feature of instruction.
2. Ask engaging researchable questions.
3. Locate sources and information within sources.
4. Synthesize information.
5. Represent what is being learned.
6. Teach independent inquiry.

INQUIRY IS A SPECIAL FEATURE OF INSTRUCTION

Many models of teaching involve student inquiry. General educators (Lambros, 2004; Ronis, 2008) have long promoted learner-centered investigations. Many secondary schools now have graduation requirements that call for students to exhibit the products of inquiries conducted over several months. Inquiry advocates believe that the most permanent and transferable learning occurs through personal involvement and self-controlled analyses. Inquiry-based educators believe that students who receive just teacher-directed instruction are at risk of learning to perform only on command.

The professional literature typically groups *inquiry* with educational concepts such as problem solving, project-based learning, research projects, and experiential learning. Unlike direct didactic teaching, inquiry-based approaches take a somewhat indirect, facilitative role in students' learning. You provide support in whole-class, small-group, and individual settings as your students assume primary responsibility for planning, conducting, and evaluating their investigations. During inquiry activities, you act as a guide on the side more than as a sage on the stage.

Digital literacies refers to the knowledge and skills associated with the information and communication technologies of the 21st century. Today's literacy tools such as video screens, Web sites, and podcasts are merging with and sometimes replacing conventional ones like paper, printed books, and pencils. The professional literature tends to group digital literacies with educational concepts like information literacy, new literacies, and 21st-century skills. It centers about the ways of processing ideas and information in computerized, online environments such as wikis, blogs, and videogames. Digital literacies focus on nonlinear critical thinking, problem solving, and decision making; they feature participation, innovation, and distributed expertise. Instruction in digital literacies occurs nicely amid your students' inquiries.

Student inquiry readily occurs during instructional units. If a unit focuses on heroes, alienation, inventions, weather, space, or careers, then students take the lead in exploring aspects of these topics in depth. They might concentrate solely on the central question of a unit (e.g., "What does it take to become a hero?") or they might address a particular favorite sport hero (e.g., "What can I learn about this hero?").

Once students begin conducting inquiries, they take the lead—or at least share it. But even as a partner in the inquiry process, you play a significant role in developing learners' proficiencies. Students require support posing engaging and researchable questions, finding information, synthesizing ideas among multiple sources, and representing what is being learned (Rouet, 2006). You support, or scaffold, students' efforts when they conduct inquiries through digital literacies. The next four sections present ways to help students ask questions, locate information, synthesize information, and represent what is being learned.

DO IT TOGETHER

As a group or pair, think back to the inquiry projects you completed in elementary and secondary school. Which projects were your favorites? Why? Which were your least favorite? Why? Have each group or pair briefly summarize its discussion for the rest of the class.

ASK ENGAGING RESEARCHABLE QUESTIONS

Asking engaging and researchable questions leads to effective inquiries. Engaging questions elicit a sense of connectedness. They involve students by linking academic contents with personal concerns. Students address issues and ideas that they choose and that they perceive to be useful and interesting in the present rather than in some unforeseen future.

Inquiring into what it takes to be considered a hero tends to be engaging and researchable for middle-grade students. Neither naming one hero from Greek mythology nor describing every recognized hero in the world would be engaging or researchable. Indeed, problem *finding* might be an inquiry activity that is as important as problem *solving*.

Introduce inquiry by engaging students' attention and arousing their curiosity. Kick off units with concrete objects that stimulate thinking and questioning. When launching upper-grade inquiries into advertising practices, you might spend time showing video clips and talking about selected advertisements, reading aloud some newspaper and magazine ads, and having students recall memorable ones. You might read aloud a brief article on how advertisers position their products. Since taking your classes on a field trip to advertising agencies probably is not going to happen, you might bring advertising agencies into your classes digitally. Present portions of DVDs and Web sites that briefly portray how ads are produced. Some call this stage of inquiry *presearch,* the time when learners acquire sufficient knowledge and interest for a productive inquiry. Immersing learners in a topic before inquiring into it goes far in setting the stage for rich research (Guthrie, Wigfield, & Perencevich, 2004).

Research entails multiple aspects of literacy.

Students learn to use a variety of information and communication technologies to investigate an issue and generate possible solutions. For instance, they might examine their community's economic and lifestyle attractions. They learn to use digital tools to test hypotheses and build models of systems. They conduct simulations in which they vary certain quantities to test if–then scenarios (Limson, Witzlib, & Desharnais, 2007).

Brainstorming is appropriate for helping students form engaging researchable questions. KWL, as presented in Chapter 3 of this text, is a popular way to generate questions. Other powerful practices include WH Poster Questions and Self-assessing Questions, which can be performed with the whole class, small groups, or individuals.

WH Poster Questions

For WH Poster Questions, a topic is presented on a sheet of chart paper or the whiteboard, or projected with a computer presentation program, so students can brainstorm questions with you. The *wh* words, who, what, when, where, why, and how, are the entry points for inquiries. Initiate the topic to be studied—*danger*, for example—then help students frame inquiries by attaching *wh* words to the organizing center. A central question for the whole class, one for each small group, or one for each individual could be produced this way. Students could ask questions such as, "*Who* are the most dangerous people we meet?" "*What* dangers occur inside and outside school?" "*When* do we encounter danger?" "*Where* are the most dangers encountered?" "*Why* do dangers exist?" and "*How* can we overcome dangerous situations?" Many more questions could be posed for each *wh* word.

The questions can be displayed digitally for inspection. Those that are too narrow for engaging inquiry (e.g., "*Who* set the Chicago fire?") might be moved aside. Those that are too broad (e.g., "*What* dangers occur outside school?") might be reduced (e.g., "*What* common dangers exist in a kitchen?"). Commenting on questions at this point enables you to make public the question generation process. You and your class might think through the production of good questions, explaining the decisions you make. Refining questions this way so they are engaging and researchable has been called the "funneling process" (Kellett, 2005, p. 39), with classmates responding to ideas and you supporting the efforts.

Question stems add several words to the WH ones, guiding students somewhat directly. Question stems take WH Poster Questions a step further by pointing students in particular directions. The following illustrate some possible stems that might be displayed in class to guide inquiries:

- What problems . . .
- What happens/happened when . . .
- What causes/caused . . .
- What are/were the effects/results of . . .
- What are the connections among . . .
- What is/was the role of . . . in . . .
- What is/was the difference between . . . and . . .
- What is the value of . . .

When exploring danger, question stems might be expanded to "*What problems* face those wishing to end stranger danger?" "*What causes* danger while cooking?" and "*What is the role of* police in dangerous situations?"

Students brainstorm researchable questions during inquiry units.

Self-assessing Questions

Posting a set of criteria such as the following helps you and your upper-grade students self-assess their questions:

- Neither too broad nor too narrow
- Interesting to the researcher
- Connected with the unit
- Resources available

Criteria such as these guide the self-assessments of possible questions to guide inquiries. Sometimes you might configure students into small groups and have them act as critical friends, commenting on each other's questions.

LOCATE SOURCES AND INFORMATION WITHIN SOURCES

Along with engaging researchable questions, students need access to information. Efficiently locating sources and their appropriate information is essential to inquiry. A productive way to help students in this endeavor is to emphasize key words, online resources, critical thinking, and interviews.

Key Words

Key words open storehouses of printed information such as libraries and the Web (Callison & Preddy, 2006). Key words encompass many concepts. "If you are going to the store for milk, orange juice, root beer, and diet cola," you might say to your class, "what word could you use to refer to all those items?" Discuss students' responses, such as *beverages* and *drinks*, in order to demonstrate that a few key words lead to many, many specifics. Point out how a few different key words can be combined with *and* and *or* to uncover the items. Adding *soft* to *drinks* specifies the list for the store.

New ideas and information are being added to the Web constantly, and users are contributing to the work of others, commenting on their creations, and creatively tagging the work to annotate and classify it (Alexander, 2008). Rather than nest traditional subordinate topics (*root beer, diet cola*) hierarchically within a main topic (*soft drink*), social tagging, or collaborative bookmarking, applies more personal associations. A user might apply the tag *refreshing* to the site, leaving space for others to apply their own tags. This system reflects the user community's opinions rather than traditional cataloguers' rules. As this emerging digital practice becomes more common, you might alert students to it as an alternate way of locating Web contents.

Key Word Scavenger Hunt is a teaching strategy that allows students to practice locating information. It addresses information location strategies for multiple topics rather than for a student's particular inquiry. Students first are led as a whole class through introductory exercises to see how to locate information that answers various questions. They learn how to generate and combine key words. Then they work in pairs or as individuals to locate information for a Key Word Scavenger Hunt list. The following are some practice items used with intermediate-grade students using search engines and the library.

1. A word used in New England for factory is mill. What kinds of mills are there?
2. What are some synonyms for *mill*?
3. Compare a mill with a sweatshop.

Online Resources

The Web increasingly offers more and more opportunities for students to access, synthesize, and communicate subject matter while conducting inquiries (Boss, Krauss, & Conery, 2008; Eagleton & Dobler, 2007). When preparing to guide your students to these resources, consider the use of search engines, WebQuests, and critical thinking.

SEARCH ENGINES When opening the Web to students' searches, many schools focus on approved outlets. They provide access to youth-appropriate search engines such as Ask Jeeves for Kids (www.askkids.Com.com/) and KidsClick (www.Kidsclick.org). They link with services such as Thinkfinity (www.thinkfinity.org) that provide panel-reviewed links to Web sites, a search engine limited to those sites, and professional development resources. They visit portals that recommend subject directories arranged hierarchically with general topics divided into subtopics. For instance, Kids Web from Syracuse University (www.npac.syr.edu/textbook/kidsweb/) allows youth to progress from *science* to *biology and life sciences* to the *human body* to the *human heart*. The online exploration of the heart offers amazing print and visual information presented through static as well as streaming sources. They install filtering software to screen out objectionable material.

WEBQUESTS WebQuest (www.Webquest.org) names a particularly sensible type of inquiry activity conducted online. Short-term WebQuests last one to three class periods; long-term ones last between one week and one month. In a WebQuest, teachers or media specialists bookmark some or all of the information from online sites for students to access.

Student researchers are not left to wander through cyberspace, hoping their search engines point them toward pay dirt. WebQuest designers include direct links to documents, searchable databases, experts' e-mail addresses, and nonprint media. This practice is especially sensible with younger students because the Web is so unwieldy at present.

To illustrate, you might search a matrix of WebQuests and find a topic you teach. If you use a WebQuest for young students on the Cinco de Mayo celebration of Mexican independence, you introduce this topic and then present a task such as creating a book that describes this event's history and portrays its traditional dances, music, costumes, and food. You have students click on a launch page's links to access preselected Web pages that provide age-appropriate information. And you present a rubric to guide students' inquiries.

Critical Thinking

Digital illiteracy can exist, so your students can benefit from instruction in critically navigating, assessing, and gathering the wealth of information available through digital technology (Katz, 2005). Instruction is needed so your students can go beyond Wikipedia. Once a search engine displays links related to particular key words, your students face the challenge of determining which links to follow (Coiro, 2005). They can benefit from your help in evaluating the links, noting whether or not their key words directed the search engine appropriately and which links are most promising. Once they open a Web site, they face the challenge of accessing its contents efficiently. They can benefit from your help in evaluating the menu choices and determining how to move among the general mix of images, music, graphic arts, video, and print.

When your students locate pertinent content, they need to determine its credibility (Bråten, Strømsø, & Britt, 2009). Checklists for evaluating the credibility of Web sites are available for K–12 students (http://school.discoveryeducation.com/schrockguide/eval.html) as well as more advanced students (http://www.library.cornell.edu/olinuris/ref/webcrit.html); guidelines for producing credible Web sites (http://credibility.stanford.edu/guidelines/index.html) also are helpful (Baildon & Damico, 2009). To assess credibility, these instruments focus on features like the reputation of the Web site's author or sponsoring institution, currency of the information, and objectivity of the presentation. Teaching your students how to critically examine Web sites with instruments like these enables them to identify trustworthy contents when engaged in future digital inquiries.

Interviews

Conducting oral interviews seamlessly blends reading, writing, listening, and speaking as student researchers gain access to information (Kellett, 2005). Interviews can range from highly structured question–answer sessions between an expert and a novice or conversations among several people with varying degrees of expertise on a topic to informal questions posed during guest presentations. Interviews are outstanding features of inquiry projects.

When involved in somewhat structured question–answer interviews, young students should begin with familiar, friendly sources. Family members, school personnel, and peers are appropriate candidates for interviews in the early grades. Secondary students can begin interviewing unfamiliar people who are expert in students' inquiry topics. Once a person has agreed to be interviewed, send the person a brief letter outlining the nature of the students' projects and a description of how the information will be used. Such a letter is especially helpful if the interview is to be tape-recorded.

Question–answer interviews work most efficiently when the researcher has specific inquiries written in a set order. If students investigate schools of the past, asking the interviewee to "Tell me about your school days" may not be very productive. Instead, the students should be prepared to ask questions about teachers, other students, lessons, tests, discipline, and so on. These key words should be jotted down at first and then developed into complete questions before interviewing a subject. Interview questions, like the ones guiding an overall inquiry, should be specific, but not so narrow that they can be answered with a "yes" or "no." Asking source people follow-up questions such as, "Can you tell me more about that?" or "What else do you remember?" is a useful way of getting more complete information.

Tape-recording the interview is a good way to maintain a record of what was said; taking notes during the interview is also recommended. After leaving the interviewee, students should write down what they learned. This summary might be shared with the interviewee in order to check for accuracy and elicit additional pertinent information.

Before sending students out to conduct interviews, teachers frequently demonstrate the procedure by interviewing a guest in the classroom. Students also may want to practice interviewing one another before going outside the classroom.

TRY IT OUT

Form groups of about three. Conduct interviews with each other. Then talk about how you think these sessions would play out in a K–12 classroom. What would you need to do to ensure their success?

SYNTHESIZE INFORMATION

Synthesizing information is an ongoing task facing student researchers (Burke, 2002). Young researchers who are seeking answers to "What do bears eat?" soon discover that information is available about the eating habits of different types of bears, at different times of the year, and at different ages and locations. Older students looking into how people measure time soon discover the great complexity with which scientists have addressed this issue. Students frequently report all the information they find because they consider everything to be of equal importance ("If it's not important, then why was it there?").

Computer software such as *Inspiration* and *Kidspiration* (www.Inspiration.com) helps students synthesize their data by providing basic report structures or writing frames. Such software enhances students' abilities to produce notes, categorize information, and, in some instances, cite information. It helps students visualize patterns and relationships among ideas.

Producing Notes

A good way to introduce note taking is to produce them on an interactive whiteboard during a unit. Think aloud your decision-making process while recording the notes you think most appropriate. Doing this in the midst of the video clips, blogs, and print found online is challenging. To show students how to move beyond simply copying and pasting Web site contents, provide Word templates for your students to complete with space for a site's address and relevant contents. To trigger students' thinking about the site's contents, provide prompts such as the following:

- The key points of this site are:
- This site helps answer my question by:
- This site connects most closely with other ones such as:

After demonstrating and explaining your process several times, have your students volunteer their notes. Offer feedback, remembering that there are many avenues to good study strategies. Have your students meet in small groups to produce notes jointly or to react to what each member produced individually. Again, display the notes so everyone can see the products.

Categorizing Information

As notes accumulate during an inquiry, your students need to categorize what they find. It is not efficient to write bits of information on separate file cards or computer documents, then organize them at the end of a project. It is far better to establish categories and group facts into categories as the research progresses. In this way, your students can see which categories are lacking information and whether new information corroborates or contradicts earlier findings. When categorizing information, your students might see the need for establishing new categories or revising old ones.

Data charts are productive tools that help students categorize information. Make a grid with the research questions listed across the top and the resources to be used listed along the side. Each box of the grid then contains the source's information related to the question. Sparsely worded notes are used in order to conserve space and encourage your students to use their own words when writing the report. If a particular source provides no information about one of the questions, an X is placed in that square. Figure 9.1 shows a data chart for investigating the career of Ernest Hemingway. Show your students

Sources	What was his life like?	What themes did he pursue?	What was his influence?
Smith & Jones			
lostgeneration.com			
Linn			

FIGURE 9.1 Data Chart for Ernest Hemingway Report.

Animals	What does the animal eat?	Where does the animal live?	What dangers does the animal face?
Tiger			
Leopard			
Lion			

FIGURE 9.2   Data Chart for Wild Animals Report.

how to record information in the proper location of the chart. Students should also locate other sources to add to the left column.

Another type of data chart lists questions across the top and aspects of the questions down the side. For example, if the topic is wild animals, the questions across the top might be "What does the animal eat?" "Where does the animal live?" and "What dangers does the animal face?" Down the side, rather than listing sources, several different wild animals such as tiger, leopard, and lion are listed. Figure 9.2 is an example of this type of data chart. Data charts are useful for arranging information, and they help your students evaluate what they have gathered. For example, your students might be directed to the wild animals chart and asked to decide which animal ate the widest variety of food, lived in the most unusual habitat, or faced the greatest dangers.

Citing Information

An important point to convey to your students is the need to record their sources accurately. Accurate records are necessary both for others to check the information and for your students, themselves, to return to if necessary. These records help students follow fair use practices and protect others' intellectual property. The simplest way to record sources is to make a numbered list of all sources by title and date, including all online, oral, and print sources. When students find something they want to use, they can jot down the information, placing the appropriate identification number after the information, and including a page number if using a print source.

Maintaining and Clarifying the Focus of Research

A word of caution: Students who are seeking information frequently lose their focus. They often become so involved with tangential information that they are led far astray of their original question. One way to help students remain focused is to have them confer during the week and talk about how their projects are progressing (Rogovin, 2001). These conversations help students crystallize their learning and their next steps. When students meet with peers to talk about the status of their inquiries, they put into words what otherwise might be unclear. They stimulate each other to articulate what is being learned, what gaps exist in their knowledge, and how everything is fitting together. They think through what they intend to say in their final reports.

Teacher–student conferences also help young researchers maintain and clarify the focus of their inquiries. As you circulate among the class, you might serve the same function as peers by stimulating students to think deeply about their topics and articulate their research status and plans. You might support their research efforts by answering questions and suggesting specific actions. You might prompt students to consult particular references or think about their questions in new ways. Praise good efforts and encourage ongoing ones.

Scheduling process checks is a good way to promote students' progress with specific aspects of inquiry. Scheduled checks add a certain formality to your role and signal inquiry as serious business, even though you can readily maintain a facilitative collaborative demeanor. Many teachers produce sheets specifying the date for checking each stage of inquiry and the possible points for that stage. Students attach these sheets to their research folders. Stages of inquiry such as the following might be designated:

1. Research topic and essential question   10
2. Resource log   10
3. Information gathered   30
4. Synthesis scheme   15
5. Representation plan   15

Scheduled checks allow you to intervene with students requiring additional support. When used to promote growth, these process checks take on a positive role.

TRY IT OUT

This section has described a number of ways to help students synthesize information. Select one of the strategies you have used in the past. Think about any problems you had applying the strategy and what you might have to do to make it easier for students to use.

REPRESENT WHAT IS BEING LEARNED

Student researchers at all levels benefit from representing and sharing with others what they are learning. This step deepens the understanding both of those who did and did not conduct the inquiry.

Student researchers generally feel compelled to display all the material that they garnered during their searches. They want credit for all the information that they worked so hard to obtain and frequently have difficulty paring down the information to that which directly answers specific questions. Such reporting results in undesirably long and convoluted pieces. Inform your students that expert researchers generally know more than they include in their reports and that students should likewise not try to include every bit of information they gather.

Representing and sharing what is being learned sometimes is done in an informal, casual manner. After consulting the Classroom 2.0 site (http://wiki.classroom20.com/), you might have students share their findings digitally through collaborative computer technologies such as blogging, collaborative documents and idea maps, online meetings, video conferencing, video sharing, and wikis, to name a few. Students sometimes are assembled after spending time conducting their inquiries in order to tell what they have learned in impromptu fashion. If the class spent time in the library investigating customs of dress, then a discussion about those customs might ensue; if students were sent home with the task of asking available adults how they came to their current occupations, then the findings can be informally shared the next day.

Your students benefit from several options for how to represent ideas. Findings can be written up, or they might be shared through multimedia formats. Students might dramatize scenes. No matter what form is used, scoring guides for self-assessment and external assessment are appropriate. The following presents four ways to represent and share information.

Multimedia Representations

Your students can create illustrations, storyboards, time lines, murals, maps, collages, and models. They can collect objects and arrange them for others. They also can use computer technology to produce multimedia representations (Kist, 2005). The term *multimedia* combines *multi*, more than one, with *media*, a means of mass communication; students combine several methods of exchange into one communication. Popular forms of media include **images** such as graphs, maps, photographs, and drawings; **texts** that range from captions to multiple paragraphs; **sounds**, such as voice recordings, music, and sound effects; and **motion**, like animation, video, and moving transitions among slides (Christel & Sullivan, 2007). Students select the media that fit their purpose for reporting their inquiry's findings. For instance, students present the products of their inquiries in a podcast when they want to tell a story or demonstrate something, in a PowerPoint slide show when they want to control the user's path through their presentation, and in a Web site when they want users to control their own paths. Multimedia representations could be incorporated as part of an oral or a written sharing.

To help these projects meet the communication expectations teachers have for inquiry reports, you could follow some of the guidelines given for science fair projects. Science fair projects need to be highly visual, self-descriptive, focused, and succinct. Communicating this to students means explaining that the display ought to be appealing, eye-catching, neat, and interesting. The question being investigated and shared ought to be clear to anyone looking at the display. The research topic being shared should be an interesting one to investigate and of a scope that is neither too large nor too picayune for the students' research capabilities.

Multigenre Representations

Multigenre representations are like collages; they consist of self-contained pieces that merge into a valid whole (Allen & Swistak, 2004; Putz, 2006). They are snapshots of a single topic taken from different vantage points. More than one genre, such as poetry, exposition, drama, music, painting, photography, recorded conversation, diary entries, and so on, join with each other to provide different entry points into one topic. Representing and sharing the products of inquiry in multigenre form blur categories.

When investigating westward expansion in U.S. history, students readily could represent what they learn through multigenre means. For instance, they might design a cardboard box as a covered wagon storage bin and fill it with possible items from the trip. They might include the following:

- A handbill or newspaper column enticing settlers to head west
- Diary entries of different family members recounting the same or different events (e.g., starting out, establishing order among the travelers, family life, encountering obstacles, arriving)
- Scenic illustrations (e.g., towns, wagon trains, river crossings, hunting)
- Maps annotated with significant sites
- Time line of events
- Poems or song lyrics expressing feelings about the journey
- Letters sent home
- Tools
- Videotaped reenactment of significant events

Multigenre means could represent diverse perspectives on westward expansion. Students might produce plausible artifacts from Native Americans, Chinese and Irish immigrants, congressional leaders from the eastern and western United States, and land speculators.

Digital technology is leading to rich possibilities for representing and sharing the products of inquiry through multigenre representations. Presentation software, video sharing, and multimedia creativity and authoring tools enable students at every grade level to represent ideas imaginatively. Even a cursory review of selected catalogs from vendors such as Broderbund (www.broderbund.com), Software Express (www.swexpress.com), and Tom Snyder Productions (www.tomsnyder.com/) reveals numerous computer tools that enable students to do the following:

- Produce or transfer artwork and graphics to adorn what they write
- Stream video and audio images into original productions
- Add sound effects, animation, music, and narration to a visual display
- Present professional-quality tables, graphs, and charts
- Construct Web sites

Writing

Students typically require support transferring information from their inquiries into written form. Reporting the information gathered onto a data chart, however, can be quite straightforward. For example, the data chart in Figure 9.1 can be the basis for a traditional essay. The first paragraph is the introduction, which prepares people for the upcoming questions (e.g., "Three aspects of Hemingway's life seem to have been very important"). It may also tell why the topic is important (e.g., "Ernest Hemingway was one of the most influential and well-known American authors of the twentieth century"). The middle paragraphs address the three questions, turned into topic sentences, along the top of the data chart (e.g., "Hemingway had a vigorous lifestyle," "Hemingway focused on five primary themes in his writing," and "Hemingway influenced a generation of writers").

The final paragraph is a summary of important findings. A data chart works especially well for short reports.

Once information has been organized, students draft and revise their written reports. Reports can be improved by having students go through the revising step of the writing process. Peer response groups work especially well; because each student has been trying to write a similar type of paper, he or she brings to the group the same knowledge of the paper's form.

At the beginning of the year in elementary school, where teachers have inexperienced students, a structured approach to sharing reports is frequently useful. For a unit on domestic animals, for example, the class would generate a series of basic questions. Questions might include these: "How does this animal help us?" "Where does it live?" "What does it eat?" and "What does it look like?" Each child selects a different domestic animal from a group students have previously called up and completes a graphic organizer about the animal.

When it is time to produce the written report, the children decide how many paragraphs each report should have, as well as the order of the paragraphs. They might also talk about what the introductory and concluding paragraphs should include. Each student then goes off to write a short report on his or her domestic animal, using illustrations if possible. These individual reports are revised through writing conferences with the teacher and peer editing groups, and the revised reports are bound into a classroom book on domestic animals.

Speaking

Transferring information for spoken reports is slightly different from the procedures for written reports. Students giving oral reports rely on note cards, PowerPoint frames, or some other type of reminder to help keep the order of presentation straight. Key words and apt phrases should be recorded so that students can glance at them to maintain their flow of speech.

A good aid for students presenting oral reports is to support their talks with digital aids. Technological tools allow speakers to maintain focus by discussing the aspects illustrated by each display. Oral reports allow immediate questioning, prompting researchers to give additional information about what they have learned. Thus, allow time for questions after an oral report.

One possibility to save class time during oral reports is putting students into teams to prepare a panel presentation. Each panel member is responsible for researching an aspect of the topic. Additionally, some teachers station students with reports to give at separate locations throughout the classroom and then have various groups of listeners rotate among the presenters. This strategy requires presenters to repeat themselves, but repetition can be beneficial and the class routine has been varied a bit.

LISTEN, LOOK, AND LEARN

Briefly describe to a teacher each of the four ways to represent and share information presented here. Ask the teacher which ones he or she has used and why. Ask the teacher to describe strengths and limitations of each of the sharing formats used. Would the teacher try any of the others you have described? Which one(s) and why?

TEACH INDEPENDENT INQUIRY

Students become independent when they receive support accomplishing meaningful tasks, and then the support fades away as students become proficient. This process applies to digital literacy inquiries, also. When students are engaged in inquiry, help them identify questions, locate information, synthesize information, and represent information. Students as a whole class can observe how to accomplish certain strategies; then they can perform the strategies in small groups and individually as teachers gradually release their guidance. Such fading occurs throughout the school year.

In the elementary grades, you might walk the whole class through an inquiry unit. Show students how to investigate and report a subject, with you and your students jointly producing a finished product. When a different unit is studied, remind your students of the processes they used before. For the second unit to be researched, your students might work in small groups rather than with the whole class. As your students develop research skills, they are able to carry out the research task more and more independently.

At the secondary level, refine students' research skills. If your students are already adept at locating information through search engines, show them how to use sophisticated features like advanced searching. Practically all upper-grade students benefit from attention to their note making skills. Remind students of the skills they learned in earlier grades.

Avoiding Plagiarism

Students who copy from another source often do so out of ignorance and desperation. They are unaware of any other system for generating a report. Several techniques can help prevent copying in your classroom (Galus, 2002; Howard & Davies, 2009).

Academic integrity begins with values. Student who respect the work of others tend to be unwilling to copy it verbatim. Explain this attitude to your students and bring it to life with examples from their lives when they were cheated or had their property stolen. Furthermore, students with a desire to learn tend to make new knowledge their own. Students who are invested in learning and sharing the results of authentic inquiries tend to put ideas and information in their own words according to their own styles.

Instruction is a key to preventing plagiarism. Teach your students how to apply the citation guide governing their inquiries so they credit their sources appropriately. As noted in earlier chapters, teaching students how to apply a strategy like citing sources means first explaining and demonstrating it, then collaboratively performing it, and finally guiding students' applications of it. Along with teaching your students how to cite sources, teach them how to write from the sources. Teach your students how to identify key terms and generate main idea statements and summaries. This teaching occurs best when your students have deep knowledge of source contents, when they have materials that make sense.

Taking students through the steps described in this chapter will model the research process for them. You might want to require checkpoints to monitor progress. These checks should not be presented as punitive; rather, make it clear that all students need feedback about how successfully they are dealing with the various stages of a project. Thus, if a student is organizing information on a data chart, check whether key words are being used, whether a variety of sources has been located, and whether sources are being identified with page numbers. Such checking, by the way, helps prevent student procrastination.

Making all initial reports oral or visual, with students not permitted to read reports but permitted only to use PowerPoint slide notes, stresses original work. Most students are unable to memorize a long selection from Wikipedia, so they use their own words. When you enhance their ability to speak from notes, you raise their confidence in their ability to write their own reports and present themselves to others.

Assessment

Assessing student reports is an essential aspect of instruction (Stiggins, 2007). Giving students a score guide allows them to see how you weigh the different criteria, and it offers explicit guidelines for self-assessment and self-reflection. Learners can assess their own work when they know the criteria for assessment. Allow room on the list for comments for each evaluation area. Be specific with your comments. If you write nothing or only innocuous comments, such as "good job," evaluations are largely ignored, whereas more specific comments receive attention.

Journal Writing

In many classrooms, students record in a journal thoughts and reactions about their inquiries in order to clarify and self-monitor their proficiencies. You might set aside ten to fifteen minutes for students to conduct an inner dialogue—a metacognitive conversation—with themselves. Make opportunities available for students to share their thoughts and reactions with partners, small groups, or the whole class. Upper-grade students might respond to prompts such as the following:

- What about inquiry is becoming clear to you?
- What inquiry skills are you developing?
- Who or what helped you the most with your current inquiry?
- What aspects of inquiry are easiest for you?
- What aspects of inquiry are most difficult for you?
- How might you overcome inquiry difficulties?
- What advice about inquiry might you give young children?
- What might you do differently with a future inquiry?

LOOKING BACK

Learning the inquiry process is more important than producing a polished report; otherwise, teachers could be satisfied with students who submitted reports purchased from commercial services. Therefore, help your students develop the excitement and eagerness to answer questions that will carry them through this process; in this way, research becomes something they look forward to rather than dread. We have described six keys in this chapter to help you better teach the inquiry process: (1) Inquiry is a special feature of instruction; (2) ask engaging researchable questions; (3) locate sources and information within sources; (4) synthesize information; (5) represent what is being learned; and (6) teach independent inquiry.

ADD TO YOUR JOURNAL

When involved in inquiry projects, were you introduced to strategies similar to the ones presented here? Compare the way you generated research questions in elementary and secondary school with the procedures described here. Do you consider yourself an independent researcher? Why? What can you apply from your own background to your future classroom? What kinds of inquiry experiences will you give your students? Why? How often will your students be engaged in these activities? Why?

Additional Readings

Four accessible and informative guides for conducting inquiry-based projects in today's digital environments are as follows.

Boss, S., Krauss, J., & Conery, L. (2008). *Reinventing project-based learning: Your field guide to real-world projects in the digital age.* Washington, DC: International Society for Technology in Education.

Callison, D., & Preddy, L. B. (2006). *The blue book on information age inquiry, instruction and literacy.* Englewood, CO: Libraries Unlimited.

Eagleton, M. B., & Dobler, E. (2007). *Reading the web: Strategies for Internet inquiry.* New York, NY: Guilford Press.

Forcier, R. C., & Descy, D. E. (2007) *The computer as an educational tool: Productivity and problem solving* (5th ed.). Upper Saddle River, NJ: Pearson/Merrill-Prentice Hall.

Multiple perspectives on the role of the new, digital literacies in schooling are found in these resources.

Knobel, M., & Lankshear, C. (2007). *A new literacies sampler.* New York, NY: Peter Lang.

Leu, D. J. (2006). New literacies, reading research, and the challenges of change: A deictic perspective. In J. V. Hoffman, D. L. Schallert, C. M. Fairbanks, J. Worthy, & B. Maloch (Eds.), *55th Yearbook of the National Reading Conference* (pp. 1–20). Oak Creek, WI: National Reading Conference.

Partnership for 21st Century Skills (n.d.). *Beyond the 3Rs: Voter attitudes toward 21st century skills.* Tucson, AZ: Author. Retrieved February 12, 2008, from the Partnership for 21st Century Skills site: http://www.21stcenturyskills.org/

These two books address school applications of social networking and information sharing. They emphasize online users' capacities to control what they take in from the Read/Write Web.

Herndon, J. G. (2008). *RSS for educators: Blogs, newsfeeds, podcasts, and wikis in the classroom.* Washington, DC: International Society for Technology in Education.

Schrum, L., & Solomon, G. (2007). *Web 2.0: New tools, new schools.* Washington, DC: International Society for Technology in Education.

A presentation of writing instruction in digital environments is presented in this text.

Herrington, A., Hodgson, K., & Moran, C. (Eds.). (2009). *Teaching the new writing: Technology, change, and assessment in the 21st-century classroom.* New York, NY: Teachers College Press.

This chapter reports research on Reciprocal Teaching practices applied to online reading comprehension.

Leu, D. J., Jr., Coiro, J., Castek, J., Hartman, D. K., Henry, L. A., & Reinking, D. (2008). Research on instruction and assessment of the new literacies of online reading comprehension. In C. C. Block & S. Parris (Eds.), *Comprehension instruction: Research-based best practices* (pp. 321–346). New York, NY: Guilford Press.

These handbooks of research address multiple topics related to digital and multimedia literacies.

Coiro, J., Knobel, M., Lankshear, C., & Leu, D. J. (Eds.). (2008). *Handbook of research in new literacies.* Mahwah, NJ: Erlbaum.

Flood, J., Heath, S. B., & Lapp, D. (2007). *Handbook of research on teaching literacy through the communicative and visual arts* (vol. 2). Mahwah, NJ: Erlbaum.

This scholarly book details successful uses of technology that enhance general literacy learning.

Warschauer, M. (2006). *Laptops and literacy: Learning in the wireless classroom.* New York, NY: Teachers College Press.

Looking back more than seventy-five years to published recommendations for inquiry-based instruction provides perspective on current recommendations. Three substantial writings from the early 1900s on this topic are as follows:

Good, C. V. (1927). *The supplementary reading assignment.* Baltimore, MD: Warwick & York.

Kilpatrick, W. H. (1919). *The project method.* New York, NY: Teachers College Press.

Whipple, G. M. (Ed.). (1920). *New materials of instruction* (Nineteenth Yearbook of the National Society for the Study of Education, Part I). Bloomington, IL: Public School Publishing Company.

Online Resources

This is the original source for WebQuests.

WebQuest

http://webquest.org/index.php

This is a good introduction to the Web 2.0 resources becoming available to schools.

Classroom 2.0 Wiki

http://wiki.classroom20.com/

Here is a portal leading to many free Internet resources.

Internet4Classrooms

http://www.internet4classrooms.com/

This professional organization is dedicated to advancing the effective use of technology in PK–12 and teacher education.

International Society for Technology in Education

www.iste.org

This advocacy organization focuses on infusing 21st-century skills into education.

The Partnership for 21st Century Skills

www.21stcenturyskills.org

This single document is an established guide for producing and assessing inquiry projects.

How to analyze a curriculum unit or project and provide the scaffolding students need to succeed. *Horace, 15*(2). Retrieved July 19, 2009, from the Coalition of Essential Schools site: http://www.essentialschools.org/cs/resources/view/ces_res/85

References

Alexander, B. (2008). Web 2.0 and emergent multiliteracies. *Theory Into Practice, 47*, 150–160.

Allen, C. A., & Swistak, L. (2004). Multigenre research: The power of choice and interpretation. *Language Arts, 81*, 223–232.

Baildon, M., & Damico, J. S. (2009). How do we know?: Students examine issues of credibility with a complicated multimodal web-based text. *Curriculum Inquiry, 39*(2), 265–285.

Boss, S., Krauss, J., & Conery, L. (2008). *Reinventing project-based learning: Your field guide to real-world projects in the digital age.* Washington, DC: International Society for Technology in Education.

BråTen, I., Strømsø, H. I., & Britt, M. (2009). Trust matters: Examining the role of source evaluation in students' construction of meaning within and across multiple texts. *Reading Research Quarterly, 44*(1), 6–28.

Burke, J. (2002). *Tools for thought: Graphic organizers for your classroom.* Portsmouth, NH: Heinemann.

Callison, D., & Preddy, L. B. (2006). *The blue book on information age inquiry, instruction and literacy.* Englewood, CO: Libraries Unlimited.

Christel, M. T., & Sullivan, S. (Eds.). (2007). *Lesson plans for creating media-rich classrooms.* Urbana, IL: National Council of Teachers of English.

Coiro, J. (2005). Making sense of online text. *Educational Leadership, 63*(2), 30–35.

Eagleton, M. B., & Dobler, E. (2007). *Reading the web: Strategies for Internet inquiry.* New York, NY: Guilford Press.

Galus, P. (2002). Detecting and preventing plagiarism. *Science Teacher, 69,* 35–37.

Guthrie, J. T., Wigfield, A., & Perencevich, K. C. (Eds.). (2004). *Motivating reading comprehension: Concept-oriented reading instruction.* Mahwah, NJ: Erlbaum.

Howard, R. M., & Davies, L. J. (2009). Plagiarism in the Internet age. *Educational Leadership, 66*(6), 64–67.

Katz, I. R. (2005). *Beyond technical competence: Literacy in information and communication technology.* Princeton, NJ: Educational Testing Service. Retrieved January 24, 2008, from the Educational Testing Service site: http://www.ets.org

Kellett, M. (2005). *How to develop children as researchers.* Thousand Oaks, CA: Sage.

Kist, W. (2005). *New literacies in action: Teaching and learning in multiple media.* New York, NY: Teachers College Press.

Lambros, A. (2004). *Problem-based learning in middle and high school classrooms: A teacher's guide to implementation.* Thousand Oaks, CA: Corwin.

Limson, M., Witzlib, C., & Desharnais, R. A. (2007). Using Web-based simulations to promote inquiry. *Science Scope, 30,* 36–42.

Putz, M. (2006). *A teacher's guide to the multigenre research project: Everything you need to get started.* Portsmouth, NH: Heinemann.

Rogovin, P. (2001). *The research workshop: Bringing the world into your classroom.* Portsmouth, NH: Heinemann.

Ronis, E. L. (2008). *Problem-based learning for math and science: Integrating inquiry and the Internet.* Thousand Oaks, CA: Corwin.

Rouet, J. F. (2006). *The skills of document use: From text comprehension to web-based learning.* Mahwah, NJ: Erlbaum.

Stiggins, R. J. (2007). *Student-involved assessment for learning* (5th ed.). Upper Saddle River, NJ: Pearson/Merrill-Prentice Hall.

CHAPTER 10

Responsive Instruction

LOOKING AHEAD

In a primary-grade classroom, students are working in pairs to illustrate the life cycle of a particular animal they selected. In an intermediate classroom, students form groups to become expert on the characteristics of a certain vertebrate (mammal, fish, reptile, or amphibian); now they are sharing their expertise with their original teams. Before discussing the basic principles of heredity, middle-grade students choose to either read silently to themselves, take turns reading aloud with a partner, or follow along with an audiotaped reading of the passage. High school students learning to describe the roles of organic and inorganic chemicals in living things select from a list of possibilities how they will present their descriptions.

The content area reading, writing, and subject matter instruction in these classrooms diverges from classrooms where everyone is doing the same thing. The instruction in these classrooms is responsive; it responds to the immediate situation. It is adapted to fit particular students in particular classrooms.

Responsive instruction addresses the needs and strengths of diverse learners. It contrasts with unresponsive instruction that follows a one-size-fits-all approach, making no adjustments for individual and group differences. It involves personalization, arranging classroom conditions to accommodate disparate human beings. You respond to students' differences by providing fair access to learning and fair opportunities to demonstrate what has been learned. The keys presented in this chapter are:

1. Learners deserve fair opportunities for success.
2. Begin with a climate of respect.
3. Use students' backgrounds as academic scaffolds.
4. Make the most of your instructional goals.
5. Utilize supportive people.
6. Provide structured freedom.

LEARNERS DESERVE FAIR OPPORTUNITIES FOR SUCCESS

Numerous factors influence student learning, so educators have developed numerous approaches to address these factors. Bilingual education and sheltered English programs are available for students who are learning English along with subject matter (Peregoy & Boyle, 2008). Special education programs are available for students who demonstrate extraordinary cognitive differences as well as emotional problems, physical impairments, and specific learning disabilities (Hallahan & Kauffman, 2008). Special reading programs are available for students who struggle with literacy (Bixler, 2009). Teachers in regular classrooms adjust their instruction because they know that not everyone learns the same way, that individuals have preferred ways to process information and ideas (Denig, 2004), as well as different racial and ethnic backgrounds, career aspirations, and identities (Ladson-Billings, 2009).

Effective teachers assume that learners follow different paths to learning. These teachers realize that some students who are learning English might benefit from working alongside others who speak the same first language yet are slightly more proficient in English. These teachers realize that students who are distracted by classroom activity benefit from seats in relatively quiet areas away from distractions. They know that some students do well in discussions where individuals interrupt each other to jointly produce ideas, whereas others do well silently writing down ideas in a personal reflective journal.

Given today's unprecedented high-stakes educational accountability measures, responsive instruction can be seen as a prerequisite for fair, just, and equitable treatment of students (McTighe & Brown, 2005). The U.S. commitment to excellence, to all students being proficient with high levels of literacy, means that all learners are expected to reach rigorous standards for literacy. The challenge is providing students fair opportunities to accomplish these standards. Students who start out with different levels of academic preparedness, different approaches to learning, and different interests deserve multiple instructional pathways to accomplishing uniform standards of achievement.

DO IT TOGETHER

Form groups of about three, and brainstorm ways you and your peers experienced responsive instruction as students in your K–12 classrooms. Discuss your personal reactions to these experiences: Did they promote your literacy and subject matter learning effectively or ineffectively? What did you like or not like about them?

BEGIN WITH A CLIMATE OF RESPECT

Establishing a climate of respect is an important first step in responsive instruction (Moore & Hinchman, 2006). You start out establishing a climate of respect during the very first day of class, acknowledging learners' diversities and expressing plans to honor them. Affirm the values of diversity by describing everyone's inherent dignity and explaining how people with multiple perspectives and strengths benefit society. Inform your classes that everyone will be treated like members of a club.

Forming personal connections with students demonstrates respect. Meet and greet students at the classroom door when they enter class. Sometimes shake hands and inquire about students' days. Having students complete *getting to know you* cards the first day of school provides insights into their lives outside of school. When time is available after class, talk with students about the subject at hand as well as about everyday events and personal issues. These actions demonstrate respect for students as individuals with human needs and desires as well as learners with academic requirements.

Demonstrate respect by holding high expectations for all. Do not patronize students with watered-down curriculums. State your expectations explicitly, and regularly encourage students to put forth what it takes to achieve the expectations. Be sure to praise and reprimand students fairly; do not treat any individual or group preferentially, thereby disrespecting others.

Responsiveness also depends upon respect from students. As Tomlinson (2001) says, "Mutual respect is nonnegotiable" (p. 22). Students must act courteously and acknowledge the advantages of working with others. To accomplish this, assert everyone's right to be heard. Regularly provide each student opportunities to express himself or herself during whole-class, group, paired, and individual situations. Do not tolerate rudeness or insults.

When assigning membership for projects and other group activities, show respect by using flexible groupings. Find ways and times for students to work with various groups of classmates. You might divide your classes into groups of four or five students at different levels of academic proficiency and have them remain together for several weeks. Have group members put their desks together and create a group name to promote their group identity. Have members work on projects and other tasks together; have them take tests and other assessments individually. Such flexible grouping encourages students to see themselves as being at liberty to interact with others, not to see themselves as restricted by the opinions and expectations of others.

Flexible grouping promotes responsive instruction.

Finally, establish a climate of respect by helping students see themselves succeeding with academic expectations as others similar to them have done. Adorn your classroom walls with positive, inclusive images of your past and present students of different ethnicities. Regularly invite role models from various sectors of the community to speak about their successes.

In essence, establishing a climate of respect makes your students feel welcome and accepted in your classroom. It makes your students feel that they belong to a community, a safe neighborhood, a caring family. They do not fear ridicule when they ask for help, express their confusion, or work with alternative materials. Students who see themselves as respected despite their learning differences are best able to benefit from different opportunities to learn.

DO IT TOGETHER

Form groups of about three and call up teachers from your pasts who effectively established climates of respect in their classrooms. Share your memories: How did those teachers establish those climates of respect? How did those teachers' classrooms compare with others not characterized by climates of respect?

USE STUDENTS' BACKGROUNDS AS ACADEMIC SCAFFOLDS

Culturally diverse learners benefit when their everyday funds of knowledge and ways with words are linked with new academic knowledge (Lee, 2007). They do well when they connect what they know and can do outside of school with the curriculum inside school. Consequently, link what your students already have learned through their families, communities, peer groups, and popular media with your academic content and literacy instruction. To illustrate, students typically have encountered most literary elements (e.g., plot, setting, characterization) in the media outside of school, so linking those experiences with their literary texts inside of school is a productive teaching practice (Smith & Wilhelm, 2006). Show students how tracking the plot of a television show or movie compares with tracking a plot in literature. In biology, students might link their knowledge of sickle cell anemia, Crohn's disease, tongue rolling, and dimples with genetics (Schmidt, 2005). In physics, students might sing and play inexpensive musical instruments, listen to popular music, then connect this background with a unit on sound terminology such as *resonance, amplitude,* and *frequency.* Responsive instruction uses students' backgrounds as academic scaffolds.

Another way to use your students' backgrounds to scaffold their academic learning involves comparing informal and formal expectations (Hall, 2009). Working collaboratively with your students, detail the ways they use literacy differently among their family and friends. Then explain how literacies in school vary along the same lines. Show how your expectations for reading and writing differ from outside-of-school expectations as well as from those of your colleagues. For instance, you might expect wide-ranging discussions of texts while your colleague next door expects meticulous attention to details. Explaining these different expectations early in the school year promotes your students' understandings of what is needed to succeed in your class.

Another way to use students' backgrounds as academic scaffolds involves linking English learners' linguistic knowledge with your new academic knowledge (Goldenberg, 2008). Linguistically diverse students benefit when their primary languages are connected to the new academic language. When possible, introduce new ideas and information in your students' primary languages, guide students through the contents in English, then culminate the activity in the students' primary languages. Regularly clarify confusing ideas and information in students' primary languages. During units of instruction, compare related words (pharmacy/farmacia) and phrases (cold water/agua fria) across languages. Show how comprehension strategies such as "preview and predict" and "monitor and fix up" that are used with a primary language apply to English as well.

Realize that English learners require academic English vocabulary to be taught far beyond what native speakers typically require. A middle-grade science description of *valley glacier* as a *river of ice* might be appropriate for native English speakers, but it might confuse ELs with underdeveloped meanings for *river, of,* and *ice.* So take such explanations to the next level by linking the new terms with ones in your students' home languages, showing visuals, and having students act out the process.

LISTEN, LOOK AND LEARN

Observe a class with culturally and linguistically diverse students. Note how students' backgrounds are used as academic scaffolds. Compare the practices described in this section with what you observe.

MAKE THE MOST OF YOUR INSTRUCTIONAL GOALS

Making the most of your instructional goals is another way to respond to culturally and linguistically diverse students in your class. Today's standards-based curriculums emphasize clear instructional goals, so build on this by explaining them fully to yourself and your students. Spell out in detail what is needed to accomplish each content and literacy objective, state the objectives in student-friendly language, and post them for ongoing display. Such presenting and posting can help you focus your instruction and scaffold your students' learning. The more you realize the complexities of your instructional goals, the better you can respond to your students' differing efforts to achieve them.

A second way to make the most of your instructional goals is to provide opportunities for students to go beyond the basics. As noted in earlier chapters, engaging your students with open-ended projects that have no single simple answers extends their learning. Providing learning space through open-ended objective-based tasks responds to the differences students always will exhibit in your classroom. As noted in Chapter 3, one of your objectives might be "Students will be able to explain conditions that produce immigration." You can make the corresponding learning task open ended by asking, "Why do people immigrate?" and having students report their answers through panel discussions, editorials, multimedia productions, or other designs of their choice. Going beyond the basics involves providing problems to solve, issues to think through, and response formats that match your students' distinctive backgrounds, interests, and talents.

LISTEN, LOOK AND LEARN

Observe a class with culturally and linguistically diverse students. Note how the most is made of the class's instructional goals. Compare the practices described in this section with what you observe.

UTILIZE SUPPORTIVE PEOPLE

An effective and common method for responsive instruction involves supportive people. Make yourself and others available during class to support your students' literacy and learning, and connect students with support that is available outside class.

Instructional aides, sometimes called paraprofessionals or teaching assistants, are one category of supportive people to help your learners with their content area reading, writing, and subject matter. Many schools and school districts provide aides to work with students who have language differences or special learning needs, and these people often assist other members of the class when their clients are working independently. Aides might come to your classroom every day or only a few days per week. They can assist with every dimension of content area literacy and learning. To illustrate, they might support students' literacy efforts, synthesizing information and ideas in response to a unit's essential question. They might help plan ways to produce a unit's culminating exhibit. They might assist with the graphic organizers learners use as a postreading, prewriting, or study strategy. And they might review meaning vocabulary.

Instructional aides respond to learners' differences.

Groups of peers are another category of people who can support content literacy and learning. Many teachers encourage students to work with learning partners, or study buddies. Individuals are paired; then they sit beside each other in class, working together on literacy and learning tasks. Although they perform academic work collaboratively, their achievement is assessed individually.

Along with learning partners, flexible groups of four or five go far to support each other's literacy and learning (Gillies, 2007). Teachers sometimes place students in groups, and students sometimes place themselves in groups. Sometimes, class assignments are given to the groups, and sometimes the groups select their assignments.

Consider the ways small groups might address content area literacy and learning. During writing assignments, students in groups might discuss ideas and help one another plan what they will write, allow each member to write individually, then respond to what has been written and help revise the draft. When studying for a unit test, groups might collaboratively generate mnemonic devices for new vocabulary, and they might generate and answer questions they expect to encounter.

When reading novels, group collaboration is common in the form of book clubs or literature circles. For instance, all members of a group might read the same book, perhaps *The Watson's Go to Birmingham* in the intermediate grades or *Roll of Thunder, Hear My Cry* in the middle grades, and perform certain roles. The following are some of the more familiar roles enacted during literature circles (Daniels, 2001):

content connector:	relates the novel to others group members have read or to personal experiences
discussion director:	serves as the group manager; ensures all participants fulfill their roles
summary spokesperson:	summarizes each chapter
vocabulary virtuoso:	selects and explains the meanings of unfamiliar words

The set of roles listed next are time-honored, generic ones that contribute to the management of any cooperative learning situation (Kagan, 1997). You might combine these roles with the ones above—or create your own—to best serve your content literacy and learning purposes:

active participant:	contributes to group proceedings in a lively and involved manner
encourager:	promotes efforts at accomplishing the task; cheers on participants
mayor:	leads the group's efforts
record keeper:	notes the group's decisions; serves as the scribe
time keeper:	monitors the timetable for accomplishing the group's task

After reading one or a few chapters, group members gather to discuss what they read according to their designated roles. When needed, group members help individuals refine what they produced in response to their particular role.

A concern about assigning roles is that students might become overly dependent on them. Consequently, if you assign roles to help your students with discussions, eventually fade out this practice. Once your students learn discussion roles, lead them to taking up the roles independently. Eventually, if someone is monopolizing the discussion, students can act on their own as time keepers and move the discussion to others. Students can independently monitor who has not participated and draw them into the conversation. Fading to independence with group roles leads to rich discussions and to a life skill students can use outside of school.

DO IT TOGETHER

Form groups of six to seven classmates. Assign individuals to roles such as active participant, encourager, mayor, and time keeper. Using the assigned roles, for 10 minutes talk about what is becoming clear and what is unclear relative to the section *Learners Deserve Fair Opportunities for Success* in the beginning of this chapter. Have one person record the group interactions. After 10 minutes, end the discussion and have the observer–recorder share his or her notes. Then assess the practice of assigning roles during discussions and plan the use of discussion roles in your classroom.

Tutors are another category of supportive people who enact responsive instruction. Tutors generally work one to one with a learner outside of the classroom. Tutors can be peers, those from the same classroom, cross-age, those from the higher grades, and mentors from the community outside the school (Gordon, 2007). The best tutoring is connected with classroom objectives so that learners are able to focus on a few outcomes at a time. Tutors can address the dimensions of content area literacy outside of class in the same way as aides and groups of peers address the dimensions inside of class.

Finally, you position yourself as a supportive person when you make yourself available to help individuals. Circulating about the classroom when your students are working independently and conferring with individuals on the fly is a common supportive practice. Many teachers schedule conferences during class to converse with individuals about their progress and intervene when appropriate. Some conduct conferences about the unit-related materials individuals are reading as well as about the writing assignments and inquiry projects individuals are pursuing. Some teachers make themselves available to work with individuals before school begins, during lunch, and after school ends. They offer their services through email and Web site postings, and they utilize homework hotlines and networked communication systems like Blackboard.

LISTEN, LOOK, AND LEARN

Think back to your K–12 school days as well as your classroom observations during your current teacher-preparation program. Call up the uses of supportive people you have experienced and connect them with the categories presented here:

- aides
- pairs and groups of peers
- tutors
- teachers making themselves available inside and outside class time

Do the uses of supportive people you have observed fit the categories presented here? What other categories might you include? Compare the positive features of each category.

PROVIDE STRUCTURED FREEDOM

Structured freedom refers to a balance between classroom control and order on the one hand and student liberty and decision making on the other. Structured freedom blends your plans and directions with your learners' voices and choices. Classroom freedom is offered, but it is within limits. Effective classrooms combine structure and freedom, sometimes referring to it as *managed options* or *controlled choices* (Alington & Johnston, 2002; Daniels & Bizar, 2005).

Structured freedom moves according to a rhythm as whole-class, small group, paired, and individual grouping patterns appear, disappear, and reappear. For instance, teachers and the whole class typically are together when a unit is launched, and they remain together to begin the first standards-based outcome. Once learners are prepared to work on their own, teachers begin fading out and learners fade in. Freedom is most evident during this guiding, or fading, phase of instruction as students apply, explore, and extend content area literacy and learning on their own. Teachers and the whole class frequently reconvene for brief amounts of time at regular intervals to monitor progress, share understandings, and gear up for further study. Whole-class meetings also typically occur when culminating instruction.

Structured freedom helps you respond to your students as individuals. Having your students select from a menu of choices allows each person to pursue what he or she finds most meaningful. It shares responsibility for learning, allowing individuals to engage academic content on their own terms.

The table below on planning structured freedom outlines possible types of choices. Two factors border the table, Material and Task. *Material* refers to what students read; *Task* refers to the assignment(s), or academic work, students do. When structuring students' freedom, think about offering same and different materials as well as same and different tasks.

Planning Structured Freedom

		Material	
		Same	*Different*
Task	*Same*	1 same material, same task	2 different materials, same task
	Different	3 same material, different tasks	4 different materials, different tasks

Same Material/Same Task

Even though the first cell in the table contains the word *same* for both material and task, several options still are available. The ways students address the same material and task can be differentiated. For instance, during an upper-grade unit on survival, you might give students the identical material to read (e.g., the novel *Into Thin Air*) and the identical task (e.g., produce a response-to-reading journal, then discuss responses); however, you could have students proceed through the novel in several ways. You could have them go to different learning stations, or locations, designated in the classroom to either

a. read silently to themselves,
b. form a group that includes you and take turns reading aloud,
c. form a pair with their learning partner and take turns reading aloud and talking about what they have read, or
d. read along with an audiotaped version of the novel.

Along with these choices, you could make available a listening guide, a brief outline of the text, and allow students to decide whether or not to use it. You also could establish limits, such as specifying how many words, sentences, paragraphs, or pages are the minimum and maximum for students' journal entries, and have them decide what to produce within those limits. Finally, you might have all your students complete the same three tasks (e.g., summarize a section, produce a storyboard depicting it, and enter personal reactions in a journal), but allow them to perform these tasks in any order they choose.

DO IT TOGETHER

Form groups of about three and discuss how you could use the same material and task yet vary the ways students proceed with them. Apply this approach to units you have planned or observed.

Different Materials/Same Task

The second cell in the Planning Structured Freedom table highlights different materials with the same task. Here students all work toward the identical end product, but they use different reading materials to produce it. For instance, you could take the upper-grade unit on *survival* mentioned in the first cell and have students read different topic-related novels individually or as members of a group. The task might still be to produce a response-to-reading journal and then participate regularly in whole-class discussions, but the reading materials could be varied. Your students might have access to *Into Thin Air* as before, but they also could have access to *survival* novels written at different levels of complexity such as *Between a Rock and a Hard Place, Endurance: Shackleton's Incredible Voyage, Hatchet,* and *The Cay.* In bilingual classrooms, students might read books written in their native languages along with simplified English-language texts.

Using different materials and the same task is common during student inquiry projects. If you present a unit on *survival* as an inquiry project, all students might work on the same culminating task (e.g., write a narrative with a theme of survival), but they could have available several different reading materials. Going beyond novels, the school media specialist could provide a text set, a collection for the class of picture books and other books of varying complexities and genres that center about the unit's topic. Students could access a launch page with links to Web sites such as *Five Basic Survival Skills in the Wilderness* (www.adventuresportsonline.com/5basic.htm). They could interact with commercial multimedia programs. A screenplay or a readers theater passage could be used. Again, all students would be producing a narrative, but they would be using multiple materials to gather ideas and information for the task.

DO IT TOGETHER

Form groups of about three and discuss ways you could use different materials and the same task. Apply this approach to units you have planned or observed. Determine how it could respond to students who are learning English or who have special learning needs.

Same Material/Different Tasks

The third cell of the Planning Structured Freedom table uses the same material yet different tasks. This method involves supporting all the students in a class through the same reading material while providing substantive choices when responding to the passage. During the upper-grade unit on *survival*, you might have students read *Into Thin Air* while using a framework to generate different tasks. For instance, following a multiple intelligence framework (Noble, 2004), you could make available choices such as the following:

Verbal/Linguistic:	write a speech arguing either for or against limiting access to Mount Everest
Logical/Mathematical:	prepare a chart relating climbing casualties with mountains' locations
Visual/Spatial:	produce a storyboard of key events on the mountain
Bodily/Kinesthetic:	role play a scene as climbers who want to continue their summit attempt and those who want to turn back argue with each other
Interpersonal:	conduct a panel discussion of whether or not the team leaders acted appropriately
Intrapersonal:	produce a reflective journal recounting the personal thoughts of one of the climbers
Musical:	perform a song inspired by the tragic events on Mount Everest

Taking the RAFT framework (Role, Audience, Form, and Topic) from Chapter 7, you and your students could generate tasks in response to *Into Thin Air* such as these:

- You are Rob Hall, an expert guide who dies on Mount Everest. Recount what you were saying on your radio as you suffered from the cold and lack of oxygen.
- You are an outdoor activist speaking to the Nepalese authorities about limiting permits to climb Mount Everest. You know that some individuals pay as much as $65,000 to be led to the summit, even though many are unprepared for the rigors of the climb. What would you say?
- You are Beck Weathers, a physician who survives a freezing night exposed on Mount Everest. Explain to a friend your thoughts as you made your way to shelter.

Following a more focused, restricted framework like Reciprocal Teaching, you could have students respond to each chapter of *Into Thin Air* by choosing among four strategies:

Summarize   Clarify
Question   Predict

When employing different tasks, many teachers require learners to complete one or more assigned ones (e.g., everyone produces a journal) along with one or more self-selected ones (e.g., everyone completes one task from the multiple intelligence list). This clearly balances structure with freedom.

DO IT TOGETHER

Form groups of about three and discuss ways you could use the same material and different tasks. Apply this approach to units you have planned or observed. Determine how it could respond to students who are learning English or who have special learning needs.

Different Materials/Different Tasks

The final way to plan structured freedom calls for different materials and different tasks. This is the most ambitious method, one that you typically would fade into over time. Starting out this way in the first unit of the school year might overwhelm students who are unaccustomed to choices.

This method combines the different materials and tasks presented earlier, although with some minor adjustments. When presenting the *survival* unit, you would provide different reading materials (e.g., *Into Thin Air, Between a Rock and a Hard Place, Endurance: Shackleton's Incredible Voyage, Hatchet,* and *The Cay*). You also would provide different assignments (e.g., produce a reflective journal, write a speech, role play a conflict). However, note that only generic stems of the multiple intelligence framework could be used, as listed here:

Verbal/Linguistic:	write a speech
Logical/Mathematical:	prepare a chart
Visual/Spatial:	produce a storyboard of key events
Bodily/Kinesthetic:	role play a conflict
Interpersonal:	conduct a panel discussion
Intrapersonal:	produce a reflective journal
Musical:	perform a song

You would use only generic stems so each one could apply to all the novels (e.g., Write a speech praising . . . Aron Ralston; Write a speech praising . . . Ernest Shackleton). Your students would choose a task's stem, then fit it to the novel they had selected.

To remain on track while guiding students through a unit on survival, you might have one third of the class produce an interpersonal response, one third a visual/spatial response, and one third a verbal/linguistic response. Then you might offer choices within the categories. For the interpersonal task, some students might choose a panel discussion to present to the class while others might produce a mock TV news report. Those working on visual/spatial tasks might produce a series of pictures showing key events from a novel, and others could make a poster representing the book. Students producing a verbal/linguistic product could choose to prepare a traditional essay while others might write a speech. You maintain the integrity of your instruction by specifying the content and literacy standards your students are to demonstrate and how their products will be assessed.

DO IT TOGETHER

Form groups of about three and discuss ways you could use different materials and different tasks. Apply this approach to units you have planned or observed. Determine how it could respond to students who are learning English or who have special learning needs.

LOOKING BACK

The strengths and needs of diverse learners require responsive instruction. You make your teaching responsive when you arrange conditions to fit individuals and groups. This is especially important during an era of high-stakes expectations to accomplish uniform standards of achievement. The keys presented in this chapter are (a) learners deserve fair opportunities for success, (b) begin with a climate of respect, (c) use students' backgrounds as academic scaffolds, (d) make the most of your instructional goals, (e) utilize supportive people, and (f) provide structured freedom.

ADD TO YOUR JOURNAL

Reflect on your K–12 classroom experiences. Can you think of ways to teach responsively that were not mentioned in this chapter? Reflect on classrooms you have experienced, with and without climates of respect. Did the teachers go beyond the ideas presented here to establish that climate? Does one particular method seem most appropriate to you? Why?

Additional Readings

This is a comprehensive and scholarly treatment of responsive literacy instruction.

Morrow, L. M., Rueda, R., & Lapp, D. (Eds.). (2009). *Handbook of research on literacy and diversity.* New York, NY: Guilford.

These two chapters examine the effects of culturally responsive literacy instruction with older students.

Moje, E. B. (2007). Developing socially just subject-matter instruction—A review of the literature on disciplinary literacy teaching. *Review of Research in Education, 31*(1), 1–44.

Moje, E. B., & Hinchman, K. A. (2004). Developing culturally responsive pedagogy for adolescents.

In J. Dole & T. Jetton (Eds.), *Adolescent literacy research and practice* (pp. 331–350). New York, NY: Guilford.

These two introductions to multicultural education present authoritative background on responsive literacy instruction.

Banks, J. A. (2008). *An introduction to multicultural education*. Boston, MA: Pearson/Allyn & Bacon.

Grant, C. A., & Sleeter, C. (2007). *Doing multicultural education for achievement and equity*. New York, NY: Routledge.

This is a good introduction to literacy instruction for English Learners.

Peregoy, S. F., & Boyle, O. F. (2008). *Reading, writing and learning in ESL: A resource book for teaching K–12 English learners* (5th ed.). Boston, MA: Pearson/Allyn & Bacon.

Reviews of research on teaching English Learners are provided here.

August, D., & Shanahan, T. (Eds.). (2006). *Developing literacy in second language learners: Report of the National Literacy Panel on Language Minority Children and Youth*. Mahwah, NJ: Erlbaum.

Genesee, F., Lindholm-Leary, K., Saunders, W. M., & Christian, D. (2006). *Educating English language learners: A synthesis of research evidence*. New York, NY: Cambridge University Press.

Goldenberg, C. (2008, Summer). Teaching English language learners: What the research does—and does not—say. *American Educator*. Retrieved August 13, 2008, from http://www.aft.org/pubs-reports/american_educator/issues/summer08/index.htm

Short, D. J., & Fitzsimmons, S. (2007). *Double the work: Challenges and solutions to acquiring language and academic literacy for adolescent English language learners—A report to Carnegie Corporation of New York*. Washington, DC: Alliance for Excellent Education. Retrieved August 13, 2008, from http://www.all4ed.org/publication_material/reports/double_work

Here is a good source for responding to diverse learners through a multiple intelligences framework:

Kornhaber, M. L., Fierros, E., & Vennema, S. (2004). *Multiple intelligences: Best ideas from theory and practice*. Boston, MA: Allyn & Bacon.

The following are useful resources for differentiating instruction:

Gregory, G. H., & Kuzmich, L. (2005). *Differentiated literacy strategies for student growth and achievement in grades 7–12*. Thousand Oaks, CA: Corwin Press.

Strickland, C. A., & Tomlinson, C. A. (2005). *Differentiation in practice: A resource guide for differentiating curriculum, grades 9–12*. Alexandria, VA: Association for Supervision and Curriculum Development.

Online Resources

These centers emphasize culturally responsive education.

Center for Research on Education, Diversity & Excellence

http://www-gse.berkeley.edu/research/crede/index.html

The National Center for Culturally Responsive Educational Systems

http://www.nccrest.org/

Numerous resources for teaching English, literacy skills, and academic content to English learners are presented here.

Colorín Colorado

http://www.colorincolorado.org/educators/content

National Association for Bilingual Education

http://www.nabe.org/

National Clearinghouse for English Language Acquisition and Language Instruction Educational Programs

http://www.ncela.gwu.edu

Teachers of English to Speakers of Other Languages

http://www.tesol.org

TEFL.net – Because You Teach English

http://www.tefl.net/

References

Allington, R. L., & Johnston, P. H. (2002). *Reading to learn: Lessons from exemplary fourth-grade classrooms*. New York, NY: Guilford Press.

Bixler, J. K. (Ed.). (2009). *Negotiating literacy learning: Exploring the challenges and achievements of struggling readers*. Boston, MA: Pearson/Allyn & Bacon.

Daniels, H. (2001). *Literature circles: Voice and choice in the student-centered classroom* (2nd ed.). York, ME: Stenhouse.

Daniels, H., & Bizar, M. (2005). *Teaching the best practice way: Methods that matter, K–12*. Portland, ME: Stenhouse.

Denig, S. J. (2004). Multiple intelligences and learning styles: Two complementary dimensions. *Teachers College Record, 106*, 96–111.

Gillies, R. M. (2007). *Cooperative learning: Integrating theory and practice*. Los Angeles, CA: Sage.

Goldenberg, C. (2008, Summer). Teaching English language learners: What the research does—and does not—say. *American Educator*. Retrieved August 13, 2008 from http://www.aft.org/pubs-reports/american_educator/issues/summer08/index.htm

Gordon, E. E. (2007). *The tutoring revolution: Applying research for best practices, policy implications, and student achievement*. Lanham, MD: Rowman & Littlefield Education.

Hall, L. A. (2009). Struggling reader, struggling teacher: An examination of student–teacher transactions with reading instruction and text in social studies. *Research in the Teaching of English, 43*, 286–309.

Hallahan, D. P., & Kauffman, J. M. (2008). *Exceptional learners: Introduction to special education* (11th ed.). Boston, MA: Pearson/Allyn & Bacon.

Kagan, S. (1997). *Cooperative learning*. San Clemente, CA: Kagan Publishing.

Ladson-Billings, G. (2009). *The dreamkeepers: Successful teachers of African American children* (2nd ed.). San Francisco, CA: Jossey-Bass.

Lee, C. (2007). *Culture, literacy, and learning: Taking bloom in the midst of the whirlwind*. New York, NY: Teachers College Press.

McTighe, J., & Brown, J. L. (2005). Differentiated instruction and educational standards: Is détente possible? *Theory into Practice, 44*, 234–244.

Moore, D. W., & Hinchman, K. (2006). *Teaching adolescents who struggle with reading: Practical strategies* (2nd ed.). Boston, MA: Pearson/Allyn & Bacon.

Noble, T. (2004). Integrating the revised Bloom's taxonomy with multiple intelligences: A planning tool for curriculum differentiation. *Teachers College Record, 106*, 193–211.

Peregoy, S. F., & Boyle, O. F. (2008). *Reading, writing and learning in ESL: A resource book for teaching K–12 English learners* (5th ed.). Boston, MA: Pearson/Allyn & Bacon.

Schmidt, P. R. (2005). *Culturally responsive instruction: Promoting literacy in secondary content areas*. Naperville, IL: Learning Point Associates. Retrieved September 7, 2008, from www.learningpt.org/literacy/adolescent/cri.pdf

Smith, M., & Wilhelm, J. (2006). *Going with the flow: How to engage boys (and girls) in their literacy learning*. Portsmouth, NH: Heinemann.

Tomlinson, C. A. (2001). *How to differentiate instruction in mixed-ability classrooms* (2nd ed.). Alexandria, VA: Association for Supervision and Curriculum Development.

CHAPTER 11

Reading Proficiency

LOOKING AHEAD

The National Assessment of Educational Progress (NAEP) consists of a series of tests and explanatory materials that offer a national perspective on the academic reading achievement of children and youth. NAEP states what young people are expected to do with print in school and then compares their expected performance with their actual performance. Due to its national scope, authoritative presentation, and sensible approach to assessment, NAEP is an excellent starting point for understanding official expectations for proficient reading.

In a manner similar to our statements about high-stakes testing in Chapter 12, we want you to know that we have mixed opinions about NAEP. We believe the NAEP literacy assessment has many positive features, but no single assessment is able to reveal the complexities of proficient reading. This chapter on reading proficiency explains the shortcomings of single assessments. It contains three key ideas:

1. NAEP expectations are starting points for describing reading proficiency.
2. NAEP expectations present readers many challenges.
3. Students deserve instruction that goes beyond NAEP expectations.

NAEP EXPECTATIONS ARE STARTING POINTS FOR DESCRIBING READING PROFICIENCY

The National Assessment of Educational Progress, often called the nation's report card, is a "nationally representative and continuing assessment of what America's students know and can do in various subject areas" (National Assessment of Educational Progress, n.d.). It periodically has assessed the reading of a representative sample of fourth-, eighth-, and twelfth-grade students across the U.S. since 1969. The National Center for Education Statistics, which is part of the U.S. Department of Education, is responsible for conducting and reporting NAEP.

NAEP has distinguished itself over the years as a legitimate and trustworthy large-scale academic reading assessment, so it is a good starting point for understanding and evaluating current reading expectations. We present it in this chapter because educational policy makers use it nationally to gauge academic performance, and many state assessments are patterned after it. But to be sure, the NAEP offers only a starting point for describing state-level reading expectations because practically every state has produced its own set of standards and tests. (To learn what officially counts as reading proficiency in your state, go to your state department of education's Web site). To repeat, the following expectations are from NAEP as it fulfills its charge of "providing information about the knowledge and skills of students in the nation as a whole, in each participating state, and in different demographic groupings (National Assessment of Educational Progress, n.d.). NAEP is not an exit exam used for determining who does and does not graduate, nor is it a state-level measure of accountability of federal provisions.

This section describes NAEP reading expectations of youth at the fourth-, eighth-, and twelfth-grade levels. The following section then analyzes these expectations, providing perspective on the challenges they present. The final section goes beyond NAEP expectations to explain other legitimate reading goals.

NAEP Expectations

In order to assess reading performance across the United States, NAEP establishes desired academic achievement levels for all students. NAEP then compares students' desired achievement with their actual achievement. Determining what achievement levels are desired of students is a policy decision made by the National Assessment Governing Board (NAGB). The NAGB is a bipartisan committee whose members include governors, state legislators, local and state school officials, educators, business representatives, and members of the general public. The U.S. Secretary of Education appoints NAGB members, but they are independent of the Department of Education.

The NAGB has stipulated three achievement levels, Basic, Proficient, and Advanced, for grades four, eight, and twelve. *Proficient* is what constitutes solid academic performance at the particular grade levels in particular subjects. It designates a higher level of performance than what might be considered a middle, or average, level for a grade level. Here is the policy definition of the Proficient level:

> *Proficient.* **Solid academic performance** for each grade assessed. Students reaching this level have demonstrated competency over challenging subject matter, including subject-matter knowledge, application of such knowledge to real-world situations, and analytical skills appropriate to the subject matter. (National Assessment of Educational Progress, n.d.)

This description of the Proficient level provides a general guideline; however, it only hints at what actually is needed relative to academic reading. Table 11.1, which comes from NAEP's 2009 Framework, contains a more detailed description of the Proficient reading achievement level for grades four, eight, and twelve. Note that even though the Table 11.1 descriptions are somewhat detailed, they still do not fully illustrate what makes up expectations of solid academic reading performance. The descriptions found in Table 11.1 still leave too much to the imagination.

TABLE 11.1 Descriptions of NAEP Proficient Reading Achievement Levels for Grades 4, 8, and 12

Grade Level	Description
4	Fourth-grade students performing at the *Proficient* level should be able to integrate and interpret texts and apply their understanding of the text to draw conclusions and make evaluations.
8	Eighth-grade students performing at the *Proficient* level should be able to provide relevant information and summarize main ideas and themes. They should be able to make and support inferences about a text, connect parts of a text, and analyze text features. Students performing at this level should also be able to fully substantiate judgments about content and presentation of content.
12	Twelfth-grade students performing at the *Proficient* level should be able to locate and integrate information using sophisticated analyses of the meaning and form of the text. These students should be able to provide specific text support for inferences, interpretative statements, and comparisons within and across texts.

To fully understand NAEP's take on what it means to be at the Proficient level, you need to examine (a) the passages that youth are expected to read, (b) the prompts that direct youth how to react to the passages, and (c) the written performances that are considered acceptable reactions. NAEP changes the contents of its main tests about once a decade to correspond to educational movements, so you will need to stay up to date with this instrument.

Sections from the NAEP that illustrate reading at the Proficient level are reproduced below to more fully portray NAEP's current expectations. These examples are from the 1992–2007 Framework because, to date, NAEP has not posted examples from the 2009 Framework. Due to page space constraints, we have reproduced from the extended passages only those particular excerpts that relate directly to the test prompts; test takers must identify these excerpts on their own.

GRADE 4: READING TO INFORM

Passage Excerpt:
Blue Crabs, by George W. Frame

The female blue crab mates only once but receives enough sperm to fertilize all the eggs that she will lay in her lifetime. Usually she lays eggs two or three times during the summer, and then she dies. When the eggs are fertilized and laid, they become glued to long hairs on the underside of the female's abdomen. The egg mass sometimes looks like an orange-brown sponge and contains up to two million eggs until they hatch—about nine to fourteen days later. Only one of the blue crabs that we caught last summer was carrying eggs, and we returned her to the water so her eggs could hatch.

Prompt:
Describe the appearance of a female blue crab that is carrying eggs.

Proficient Performance:
Acceptable responses mention that she carries an orange-brown sponge or she has eggs on her abdomen or underside (e.g., "Long hairs with glue holding 2 million eggs.").

GRADE 4: LITERARY READING

Passage Excerpt:

Sybil Sounds the Alarm, by Drollene P. Brown

Covered with mud, tired beyond belief, Sybil could barely stay on (her horse) Star's back when they rode into their yard. She had ridden more than thirty miles that night. In a daze, she saw the red sky in the east. It was the dawn. Several hundred men were milling about. She had roused them in time, and Ludington's regiment marched out to join the Connecticut militia in routing the British at Ridgefield, driving them back to their ships on Long Island Sound. Afterward, General George Washington made a personal visit to Ludington's Mills to thank Sybil for her courageous deed. Statesman Alexander Hamilton wrote her a letter of praise.

Prompt:

Sybil's ride was important mainly because

A she rode 30 miles
B she was exhausted when it was over
C the British lost at Ridgefield
D her mother allowed her to ride after all
Proficient Performance:
C the British lost at Ridgefield

DO IT TOGETHER

Gather in pairs or a group and compare the NAEP Grade 4 reading test with your state or school district's reading test designed for the intermediate grades. How are the NAEP and your local test the same? How are the NAEP and your local test different?

GRADE 8: READING TO INFORM

Passage Excerpt:

Dorothea Dix: Quiet Crusader, by Lucie Gerner

On her first day, she (Dorothea Dix) discovered that among the inmates were several mentally ill women. They were anxious to hear what she had to say, but she found it impossible to teach them because the room was unheated. Dix, angry at this neglect on the part of the authorities, asked noted humanitarian Samuel Howe for his help in taking the case to court. . . . Encouraged by Howe and education reformer Horace Mann, she spent two years visiting every asylum, almshouse, and jail in Massachusetts, quietly taking notes on the conditions.

Prompt:

Based on the passage, what is the most probable reason Howe and Mann encouraged Dorothea Dix to push for reforms?

Proficient Performance:

Appropriate answers indicate the following:

- They believed in what Dorothea was doing.
- They truly thought Dorothea could make a difference.
- They understood the plight of people with mental illness.

GRADE 8: LITERARY READING

Passage Excerpt:

Finding a Lucky Number, by Gary Soto

One laughed with hands in his hair
And turned to ask my age.
"Twelve," I said, and he knocked
My head softly with a knuckle:
"Lucky number, Sonny." He bared
His teeth, yellow and crooked
As dominoes, and tapped the front one
With a finger. "I got twelve—see."
He opened wide until his eyes were lost
In the pouches of fat cheeks,
And I, not knowing what to do, looked in.

Prompt:

Do you think the title of the poem "Finding a Lucky Number" is a good title for the poem? Explain why or why not using evidence from the poem.

Proficient Performance:

Evidence of Full Comprehension: These responses support an opinion with a clear explanation of the relationship between the title and the poem. They summarize or articulate information from the poem and tell whether or not it relates to the title. Or, they indicate that the title is a bad one and offer an explanation which is consistent with a plausible interpretation of the poem.

DO IT TOGETHER

Gather in pairs or a group and compare the NAEP Grade 8 reading test with your state or school district's reading test designed for the middle grades. How are the NAEP and your local test the same? How are the NAEP and your local test different?

GRADE 12 READING TO INFORM

Passage Excerpt:

The Civil War in the United States: The Battle of Shiloh

Here are two perspectives on the battle of Shiloh which was part of the American Civil War. Each of the two passages was taken from a different source; the first is from a soldier's journal and the second is from an encyclopedia. Read them and see how each passage makes a contribution to your understanding of the battle of Shiloh and the Civil War. Think about what each source tells you that is missing from the other source, as well as what each one leaves out.

Prompt:

Each account of the battle of Shiloh gives us information that the other does not. Describe what each account includes that is omitted by the other. Does this mean that both accounts provide a distorted perspective of what happened in the battle?

Proficient Performance:

Extensive: These responses provide at least two ideas about what is included or excluded in the journal and at least two ideas about what is included or excluded in the encyclopedia article, in addition to an opinion about the perspectives. (These opinions may or may not answer "yes" or "no," but they go beyond a "yes" or "no" response by focusing on the different viewpoints or perspectives that are offered by both passages, or they identify different potential uses for the two passages.)

Essential: These responses provide one idea about what is included or excluded in the journal and one idea about what is included or excluded in the encyclopedia article, in addition to an opinion about the perspectives. (These opinions may simply be "yes" or "no" responses to the question.)

GRADE 12 LITERARY READING

Passage Excerpt:

The Flying Machine, by Ray Bradbury

The emperor looked into the sky.

And in the sky, laughing so high that you could hardly hear him laugh, was a man; and the man was clothed in bright papers and reeds to make wings and a beautiful yellow tail, and he was soaring all about like the largest bird in a universe of birds, like a new dragon in a land of ancient dragons.

. . . "What have you done?" demanded the Emperor.

"I have flown in the sky, Your Excellency," replied the man.

"What have you done?" said the Emperor again.

"I have just told you!" cried the flier.

"You have told me nothing at all … I do not fear you, yourself, but I fear another man."

"What man?"

"Some other man who, seeing you, will build a thing of bright papers and bamboo like this. But the other man will have an evil face and evil heart, and the beauty will be gone. It is this man I fear."

"Why? Why?"

"Who is to say that someday just such a man, in just such an apparatus of paper and reed, might not fly in the sky and drop huge stones upon the Great Wall of China?" said the Emperor.

No one moved or said a word.

"Off with his head," said the Emperor.

Prompt:

Who does the Emperor believe should be responsible for an invention? Why does he think this?

Proficient Performance:

Acceptable responses must answer both parts of the question and may include the following:

The Emperor, because he is the ruler.

The Emperor, so he can control its use.

He (the Emperor) thinks this way because he believes that progress will destroy their peaceful existence.

If the inventor realizes that his/her invention may destroy or alter their peaceful existence, then it should not be invented.

Note: The answer to the first part of the question may be implicit in the explanation.

GRADE 12 READING TO PERFORM A TASK

Passage Excerpt:

Instructions for Form 1040EZ

Use this form if:

- Your filing status is single.
- You do not claim any dependents.
- You were under 65 and not blind.
- Your taxable income (line 5) is less than $50,000.
- You had **only** wages, salaries, tips and taxable scholarships or fellowships and your taxable interest income was $400 or less. **Caution**: If you earned tips (including allocated tips) that are not included in Box 14 of your W-2, you may not be able to use Form 1040EZ. See page 23 in the booklet.

Prompt:

Name two factors that would make you ineligible to file a 1040EZ tax return.

Proficient Performance:

Acceptable responses state any two of the following:

- you are married;
- you have dependents;
- you are over 65 and blind;
- your taxable income is over $50,000;
- your taxable interest income is over $400
- you have income other than wages, salaries, tips, taxable scholarships or fellowships.

DO IT TOGETHER

Gather in pairs or a group and compare the NAEP Grade 12 reading test with your state or school district's reading test designed for high school. How are the NAEP and your local test the same? How are the NAEP and your local test different?

NAEP EXPECTATIONS PRESENT READERS MANY CHALLENGES

If you are like many college-educated adults with whom we have worked, you might consider the NAEP expectations for fourth, eighth, and twelfth grade reading at the Proficient level to be rather light. You might be surprised by what seem to be rather easy reading and responding tasks, and you might believe that more should be asked of upper-grade students. However, many who have studied U.S. adolescents' NAEP performance have concluded just the opposite. Robert Linn, past president of the American Educational Research Association and the American Evaluation Association, put it this way: "The NAEP achievement levels are quite ambitious performance standards . . . the target of 100% proficient or above according to the NAEP standards appears more like wishful thinking than a realistic possibility" (2003, p. 5).

After examining the percentage of U.S. students actually reading at NAEP's Proficient level or higher, Linn (2003) concluded that expecting the NAEP level of Proficient for all U.S. youth in the near future is unrealistic. He found that in 1998 only 33 percent of eighth-grade students and only 40 percent of twelfth-grade students scored at the Proficient level or above. Stated conversely, in 1998 the majority of U.S. youth (66 percent of eighth graders and 59 percent of twelfth graders) did not read at the Proficient level or higher.

NAEP long-term testing from 1971 to 2008 shows diminishing increases in U.S. students' reading scores when viewed across the grades. Fourth-grade students' scale scores rose 12 points, eighth-grade students' scores rose 5 points, and 12th-grade students' scores rose just 1 point (National Center for Education Statistics, n.d.). This trend might be viewed positively with the realization that U.S. demographics have shifted toward a greater representation of students who traditionally have been academically underprepared and underserved. On the other hand, this trend can be viewed negatively given the ever increasing academic, economic, social, and workforce demands that require advanced literacies of high-school graduates.

Many contend that U.S. educational policymakers might aspire to—or at least hope for—all youth attaining a Proficient level of reading on the NAEP; however, they rightfully might expect all youth to attain the Basic level of reading in the next few years (McCombs, Kirby, Barney, Darilek, & Magee, 2004; Rothstein, Jacobsen, & Wilder, 2006). Reading at NAEP's Proficient level ought not be confused with state- and district-level expectations for reading proficiency. The reading demands exemplified by the NAEP test samples at the Proficient level are unrealistically demanding for large numbers of youth who still are striving to develop their academic reading competence.

To understand the challenge that NAEP expectations present, you need to understand what makes up reading comprehension. A workable breakdown is provided in the influential document *Reading for Understanding: Toward a Research and Development Program in Reading Comprehension* (RAND Reading Study Group, 2002), often called the *Rand Report on Reading Comprehension* or just the *Rand Report* in honor of its sponsor, the Rand Corporation. The Rand Report divides reading comprehension into three elements—text, activity, and reader—and places these elements within a sociocultural setting. Understanding the elements and their setting offers good insight into expectations for academic reading.

Text

Understanding the demands of a passage that students are expected to read is a starting point for understanding the expectations of readers. What is the reading load that youth are expected to manage?

The **vocabulary** of a text consistently influences readers' performance (Blachowicz, Fisher, Ogle, & Watts-Taffe, 2006). For instance, words from the fourth-grade NAEP passages that can be expected to challenge some fourth-grade readers include the following:

mates	fertilize	regiment
sperm	abdomen	militia

Words from the eighth-grade NAEP passages that can be expected to challenge some eighth-grade readers are these:

inmate	dominoes	humanitarian
almshouse	asylum	bared

And here are words from the twelfth-grade NAEP passages that can be expected to challenge some twelfth-grade readers:

expediency	miniature	annihilated
apparatus	executioner	deduction

Readers must employ complicated mental operations to know these terms. For instance, knowing that *almshouse* refers to a publicly funded institution that once sheltered poor people calls for intricate intellectual efforts and resources. If the word *almshouse* were unfamiliar to readers, they might pronounce it, hoping they recognized its sound as a known word, then attaching meaning to it. They might try to figure it out by the way it is used in the context of the passage, looking for clues to its meaning in the surrounding words. They might look up *almshouses,* in a dictionary, hoping to find a meaning that makes sense with the way the word is used in the passage. And they might look at its meaningful parts, separating *alms* from *house* and examining the fit. Of course, these readers need to realize that the common *sh* spelling pattern in *almshouse* does not represent the initial sound of *shake* and *ship* and that a meaningful break in the word surprisingly occurs between the *s* and *h*. Finally, after gaining an initial sense of this unfamiliar word's meaning, proficient readers would try to develop their understanding of it by connecting it with experiences and related words they know already.

Sentence structure, or syntax, is another aspect of text that readers are expected to control. The ways authors sequence words in sentences can place a tremendous load on readers' working memories and thinking processes. The following question on a U.S. Census questionnaire illustrates the challenge of syntax: "Approximately how many miles was it one way to the place you hunted small game most often in this state?" (RAND Reading Study Group, 2002, p. 98). You probably could figure out what this sentence was asking, but we suspect you needed to reread it, deliberately segment parts of it, and determine relationships among the parts. This is the challenge syntax often presents.

With the NAEP examples just presented, the somewhat convoluted syntax of the first sentence of the *Dorothea Dix* excerpt might challenge eighth-grade readers. The sixty-word sentence beginning with *And* in Ray Bradbury's *The Flying Machine* might challenge twelfth graders. Sentence structures like these can be especially challenging if reader's first language is not English. Because the positions of nouns, verbs, and adjectives in sentences often vary across languages, those who are learning English require substantial syntactic knowledge to get them straight.

Genre is a third aspect of text that might challenge readers. Genre classifies passages according to how writers formalize ideas and arrange texts to portray the formalizations. Literary scholars from Plato in ancient times to Bakhtin in current times have presented countless—and often overlapping—genres such as the following:

autobiography	folklore	online chat	teen magazine
blog	fantasy	podcast	text message
diary	farce	science textbook	Web site
drama	graphic novel	slave narrative	western adventure
exposition	narration	technical manual	wiki

Readers encountering these different genres need to understand the different purposes authors have, the different ways authors organize their writing to accomplish their purposes, and the different principles authors apply when choosing words. Knowing that drama portrays gripping human events, whereas technical manuals present mundane procedures, helps readers access these written forms.

The twelfth-grade NAEP readers face a personal journal and an encyclopedia entry in one section (*The Civil War in the United States: The Battle of Shiloh*), a folk tale in another section (*The Flying Machine*), and a procedural text in a third (*Instructions for Form 1040EZ*). Realizing how passages such as these are constructed (e.g., a chronological account), then using this knowledge to understand and remember the passage (e.g., mentally listing events chronologically) are crucial yet complicated ways to meet reading expectations.

Accessing a text's vocabulary, syntax, and genre in order to understand that text's message can be challenging. Moreover, texts challenge students at every grade level because vocabulary, syntax, and genre become more complicated at every level. Students certainly can be expected to rise to these challenges, but appropriate instructional conditions are needed.

Activity

The activity of reading is something else to examine when considering reading expectations. The activity of reading involves purpose; it is the answer to the question, "What is the reader to do with the text?" For example, youth might step into a text world for the purpose of experiencing it vicariously. Adolescents who immerse themselves in the sights, sounds, and feelings of a novel such as *The Outsiders* often do so mainly to live through it virtually, inferring the feelings and sensations of the characters. Other times youth might read for the purpose of informing themselves, grasping new ideas and information and storing them for later. Readers who spend time with informational texts like *Animals on the Trail with Lewis and Clark* often intend to understand and remember for a long time what the material has to offer.

Youth also might read somewhat brief texts for short-term use such as cooking a meal, assembling an engine, completing a work application, or running a software program. They read these materials for the purpose of performing certain actions. And youth might scrutinize what they find in print, critically examining the unstated beliefs and assumptions in a school newspaper's editorial or the implied promises of an advertisement in a magazine like *Spin*.

The NAEP reading expectations presented above involve only one particular type of activity, answering questions, and the NAEP questions are limited to a few types. Although answering certain types of test questions is a time-honored academic pursuit, it is only one of many possibilities that occur inside and outside academic circles. Other types of questions vary according to the following:

PEOPLE WHO ASK THE QUESTIONS In school, teachers often assign ready-made questions or generate their own, and these questions often are used to test students' comprehension. Outside of school, youth typically respond to questions from family members or friends who actually are interested in what the individual is reading and don't already know the answers to the questions. The NAEP questions are established by outsiders, people whom the youth will never meet, to test their understanding.

HOW READERS ANSWER THE QUESTIONS Some activities require youth to compose answers in their own words, and others require youth to select from the multiple choices that are provided. The NAEP reading tests generally have youth write out—rather than select—answers. Composing answers in print certainly is a worthwhile practice, although it occurs rarely outside of school and tends to complicate the assessment by connecting writing to reading.

HOW ANSWERS RELATE TO THE TEXT Some activities call for youth to recover facts that are directly stated, and others call for complex reasoning and problem solving that go beyond the text. The NAEP reading activities typically go beyond the text. To illustrate, eighth-grade youth are asked about the "most probable reason" for two historical figures encouraging Dorothea Dix to push for reform. Since the reasons for encouragement are not stated explicitly in the passage, readers need to think through what the text said, connect it with what they know already, and put together a plausible response. Again, expecting readers to infer ideas and information not stated directly in the passage certainly should be encouraged, but it adds to the challenge readers face.

THE NUMBER OF TEXTS INVOLVED Some reading activities involve multiple texts, while others involve a single one. For instance, the twelfth-grade section of NAEP on the Battle of Shiloh juxtaposes a personal journal with an encyclopedia account. All other passages are treated individually. Having readers synthesize what they gather from more than one text reflects real-world activity, but it also increases test complexity.

Although the NAEP has many positive features, it still requires a particular approach to print. Educators sometimes refer to this approach as *assessment literacy*, a way of reading and writing when taking tests. Many educators are concerned that overemphasizing assessment literacy shortchanges youth, focusing on a narrow aspect of reading and writing and limiting students' capacities for worthwhile inside- and outside-of-school activities. These educators advocate a set of activities that go beyond writing out short answers to test questions that address brief texts. They expect readers to do sophisticated things with texts, like discussing one another's interpretations, thinking critically, solving problems, and making decisions. Educational policy makers more and more are calling on schools to prepare students fully for college (ACT, 2006), to ensure that students match up well against international counterparts (Provasnik, Gonzales, & Miller, 2009), and to develop students' 21st-century skills in information and communication technologies (Partnership for 21st Century Skills, n.d.).

Reader

Suppose two students take the reading portion of NAEP. One student performs at the Proficient level, and the other does not. What have these readers brought to the NAEP—and to other reading situations—that explains their different performances?

As presented earlier, readers bring to the page different amounts of linguistic knowledge, different understandings of vocabulary, syntax, and genre. Indeed, twelfth graders who already know the distinctions between personal journals and encyclopedia entries would not even have to read the NAEP text on the Civil War to complete its corresponding activity, "Describe what each account (*personal journals and encyclopedia entries*) includes that is omitted by the other." Readers who already know that journals typically include personal experiences and encyclopedias include vast amounts of condensed information would not be challenged by this activity.

As Chapter 1 of this text pointed out, readers employ thinking processes such as connecting, organizing, and evaluating to make sense of text. The psychological literature on these processes (see, for example, Huey, 1908/1998; McNamara, 2007) is clear that readers differ substantially in their use. Some readers organize ideas efficiently and some do not. Substantial differences are found relative to these processes even within individuals; some readers are adept at forming images but limited at applying ideas to new situations. Children and youth bring different mixes of thinking processes to what they read.

Literate identity is another quality adolescents bring to texts that affects their performance. As Chapter 1 explained, literate identity is the constellation of motivations, purposes, and perspectives individuals hold for themselves as readers and writers. Productive literate identities mean that individuals think of themselves as members of a literate community, as part of an invisible reading and writing club. They believe that they are responsible for and in control of improving their literacy performance. They expect to succeed with print, bringing a can-do attitude to texts. They seek opportunities to read and write, building literate foundations that lead to improved reading and writing. Youth who identify themselves as academic readers and writers increase their chances for proficient performance on the NAEP.

Finally, readers bring to the page different amounts of topic knowledge, different degrees of familiarity with a text's subject matter. Eighth-grade youth who already are acquainted with the topic of the mentally ill and who are already familiar with the historical figures Dorothea Dix, Samuel Howe, and Horace Mann would be expected to do better with *Dorothea Dix: Quiet Crusader* than youth who do not have this background. Twelfth-grade youth who have toured Shiloh National Military Park in Tennessee and who already know about the 24,000 killed or wounded there would be expected to read *The Civil War in the United States: The Battle of Shiloh* and do better with it than those who have not visited this site. Already knowing the ideas and information that a text presents substantially enhances readers' performances with that text.

In brief, the intellectual and motivational qualities that readers bring to a passage go far in explaining differences in their performance with that passage. Youth with well-developed linguistic knowledge, thinking processes, literate identities, and topic knowledge can be expected to read more proficiently than those impoverished in these qualities.

Sociocultural Setting

Youth take up reading and writing in part according to the beliefs, values, and norms derived from their sociocultural setting, which is defined by markers such as gender, ethnicity, income, nationality, religion, and neighborhood. For instance, many boys disregard academic reading according to stereotypic masculine customs constructed about what it means to be male rather than through biological determinations (Guzzetti, Young, Gritsavage, Fyfe, & Hardenbook, 2002). The boys' beliefs, values, and norms associated with their gender are influencing them to act a certain way toward reading. Members of sociocultural groups (e.g, African American, Asian, Latino, limited-English proficient, low income, Native American, White) vary in academic reading performance due to their social and cultural settings rather than their biology.

A key feature of sociocultural settings involves opportunity to learn. Stated simply, *opportunity to learn* is the chances individuals have to gain new knowledge. It calls attention to whether youth from different sociocultural settings have equitable chances to achieve in school. Distinguishing metaphors from similes and interpreting charts and graphs are fair expectations only when youth from all sociocultural settings have had adequate chances to learn to do so. Some major aspects of opportunity to learn that account for differences in reading performance among sociocultural groups are presented in Table 11.2.

TABLE 11.2 Opportunity to Learn

Aspect	Features
Class size	Appropriate number of students (often less than 25) according to student characteristics, subject matter, and teacher ability
Curricular rigor	Academics aligned with challenging standards and higher-order thinking; nondiscrimination policies that minimize tracking; coursework requirements for graduation that involve high levels of literacy
Language compatibility	Bridges between language spoken at home and at school; home–school connections among such things as vocabulary and social customs of speaking; translation services
Parent participation	Communication between teachers and parents; sense of welcome by the school; attendance at school functions and meetings; membership in school organizations and committees; expectations for academic success
Print accessibility	Abundant time in and out of school for reading and writing; abundant materials that students can and want to read; access to rich software and Internet sites
School community	Respectful, caring relationships among students and teachers; collegial interactions; civil discourse; safe and secure facilities; orderly environment in good repair
Student attendance	Continued enrollment in a school; regular daily presence; stable classroom membership
Teacher quality	Experienced; certified; teaching within college major or minor; effectively supported with staff development; ethic of professional responsibility for student learning
Teaching practice	Gradual release of responsibility; discussion-based approaches amid high academic demands; responsiveness to formal and informal assessments

As Table 11.2 suggests, affluence is a key feature of opportunity to learn. Affluent settings increase youths' opportunities to read well. Access to plentiful print in and out of school, orderly classes with reasonable numbers of students, and regular daily attendance in school afford youth the opportunities to attain reading proficiency. Highly qualified teachers who team with parents in expecting academic excellence and who guide students through challenging experiences, thinking through texts, also go far in enhancing learning opportunities. Students of poverty, those who typically are denied such settings, predictably will struggle to meet NAEP-type reading expectations (Ancess, 2003; Berliner, 2006). These students benefit from instruction that accelerates the development of their academic literacies.

LISTEN, LOOK, AND LEARN

Visit a class and observe at least three lessons. Describe how the lessons do or do not address NAEP Proficient reading achievement level. What might be done to address the Proficient reading achievement level? What might be done to go beyond the NAEP proficiencies?

STUDENTS DESERVE INSTRUCTION THAT GOES BEYOND NAEP EXPECTATIONS

This chapter so far has presented what NAEP expects and the challenges it presents readers. This final section examines what NAEP ignores. It addresses what policymakers' tests ignore but that deserve to be honored as legitimate aspects of reading.

Youth engage in many genuine, rightful literacy activities inside and outside of school (Mahiri, 2004; Street & Lefstein, 2007). What does the NAEP ignore that deserves notice? The NAEP does not have students inquire deeply into important personal issues (e.g., What career choices do I realistically have?) or social problems (e.g., Should the U.S. allow capital punishment?). It does not include entire novels, sets of work-related documents, or personally selected magazines. And it does not combine printed messages with spoken ones.

The NAEP format reflects only a small portion of the reading many youth actually do inside and outside of school. Every day, countless adolescents log on to digital texts with specialized vocabulary and presentation patterns, and they use these texts for media-based inquiries, video gaming, and instant messaging. Every day, countless adolescents digitally combine pictures and sounds with print. And every day countless adolescents read highly technical texts related to their particular passions such as animal science, automotives, cosmetology, and robotics—to name a few. Many youth who are highly proficient with these particular types of texts that fit their personal interests tend to struggle with academic texts outside those interests (O'Brien, 2006).

Describing proficient reading is a complex undertaking that raises many questions. As Rothstein (2004) puts it, "Proficiency . . . is not an objective fact but a subjective judgment" (p. 88). What counts as proficient reading? What exactly does it take to be considered a proficient reader, especially by the end of high school? Is reading proficiency the same for everyone, or should it vary? Should those who plan to enter the workforce immediately after high school be expected to read like those who plan on postsecondary education? Should those who aspire to careers in the sciences be expected to acquire literary analysis skills equal to those who are entering the humanities? Should those who entered the country recently with a language other than English or those with learning handicaps be expected to read like those whose first language is English and have no handicaps?

Further, is reading proficiency the same in every situation, or should it depend on where it takes place? Should reading practices that occur online at home receive the same attention as what occurs with print in school? Should occupational reading tasks that call for immediate on-the-job problem solving receive the same attention as school-related reading tasks that involve long-term learning of abstract ideas?

An important qualification about readers' identities described in Chapter 1 pertains to their being socially situated. Youths might identify themselves as proficient readers in one situation and struggling readers in another. They might see themselves as part of an invisible literary novel reading club but not part of a popular science reading club. They might assume responsibility for their reading after school but abdicate responsibility for it during school. They might expect to do well with personal reading of religious or entertainment materials but expect to do poorly with the NAEP. Consequently, many youth who have difficulty with the current NAEP expectations might do better with others; conversely, many who do well with the NAEP might do worse in other reading situations.

Directing readers toward one particular type of expectation, albeit an important type, is at risk of limiting or devaluing students' proficiencies with other reading expectations. Youth certainly deserve instruction that enables them to meet educational policymakers' expectations, but they deserve instruction leading to balanced and personalized expectations, too.

LOOKING BACK

Because reading proficiency is a subjective judgment rather than an objective fact, understanding what official definitions of proficiency include—and do not include—is an important aspect of professional knowledge. Such understandings enable you to provide instruction that meets students' best interests, instruction that prepares children and youth for important tests without teaching only to the tests. This chapter contains three key ideas:

1. NAEP expectations are starting points for describing reading proficiency.
2. NAEP expectations present readers many challenges.
3. Students deserve instruction that goes beyond NAEP expectations.

ADD TO YOUR JOURNAL

Reflect upon the three key ideas in this chapter and decide what you think. Are the NAEP expectations sensible starting points for describing reading proficiency? What, if anything, might be more sensible? What do you think of the challenges NAEP expectations present readers? What other challenges do they present? Are these challenges reasonable? And how far beyond NAEP-type expectations should instruction go? Should educators address outside-of-school literacies inside of school?

Additional Readings

This publication describes NAEP clearly.

Yeager, M. (2007). *Understanding NAEP: Inside the nation's education report card*. Washington, DC: Education Sector. Retrieved February 3, 2008, from the Education Sector site: http://www.educationsector.org/research/research_show.htm?doc_id=560606

A scholarly review of NAEP is provided by this text.

Jones, L. V., & Olkin, I. (Eds.). (2004). *The nation's report card: Evolution and perspectives*. Bloomington, IN: Phi Delta Kappa Educational Foundation.

To further examine the intricacies of assessing reading proficiency, consult the following sources.

Caldwell, J. S. (2008). *Comprehension assessment: A classroom guide*. New York, NY: Guilford.

Online Resources

You can test yourself with sample items from NAEP's grades 4 and 8 reading tests at this site.

The Nation's Report Card

http://nationsreportcard.gov/reading_2007/r0017.asp

These are the official sites for the nation's report card.

National Assessment of Educational Progress

http://nces.ed.gov/nationsreportcard/

National Assessment Governing Board

http://www.nagb.org/

References

ACT. (2006). *Reading between the lines: What the ACT reveals about college readiness in reading*. Iowa City, IA: Author. Retrieved September 8, 2006, from the ACT site: www.act.org/path/policy/reports/reading.html

Ancess, J. (2003). *Beating the odds: High schools as communities of commitment*. New York, NY: Teachers College Press.

Berliner, D. C. (2006). Our impoverished view of educational reform. *Teachers College Record, 108*, 949–995.

Blachowicz, C. L. Z., Fisher, P. J. L., Ogle, D., & Watts-Taffe, S. (2006). Vocabulary: Questions from the classroom. *Reading Research Quarterly, 41*, 524–539.

Guzzetti, B. J., Young, J. P., Gritsavage, M. M., Laurie M. Fyfe, L. M., & Hardenbrook, M. (2002). *Reading, writing, and talking gender in literacy learning*. Newark, DE: International Reading Association.

Huey, E. B. (1998). *The psychology and pedagogy of reading*. Bristol, UK: Thoemmes Press. (Original work published 1908).

Linn, R. L. (2003). 2003 Presidential Address—Accountability: Responsibility and reasonable expectations. *Educational Researcher, 32*(7), 3–13.

Mahiri, J. (Ed.). (2004). *What they don't learn in school: Literacy in the lives of urban youth*. New York, NY: Peter Lang.

McCombs, J. S., Kirby, S. N., Barney, H., Darilek, H., & Magee, S. J. (2004). *Achieving state and national literacy goals: A long uphill road: A report to Carnegie Corporation of New York*. Retrieved December 18, 2004 from the Rand Corporation Web site: www.rand.org/publications/TR/TR180/

McNamara, D. S. (Ed.) (2007). *Reading comprehension strategies: Theories, interventions, and technologies*. Mahwah, NJ: Erlbaum.

National Assessment of Educational Progress. (n.d.). *Reading*. Retrieved April 15, 2010, from the National Assessment of Educational Progress Web site: http://nces.ed.gov/nationsreportcard/reading/achieve.asp

National Center for Education Statistics. (n.d.). *The nation's report card: Long-term trend*. Retrieved August 7, 2009, from the National Center for Education Statistics site: http://nces.ed.gov/nationsreportcard/pubs/main2008/2009479.asp#section1

O'Brien, D. (2006). "Struggling" adolescents' engagement in multimediating: Countering the institutional construction of incompetence. In D. E. Alvermann, K. A. Hinchman, D. W. Moore, S. F. Phelps, & D. R. Waff (Eds.), *Reconceptualizing the literacies in adolescents' lives* (2nd ed.; pp. 29–46). Mahwah, NJ: Erlbaum.

Partnership for 21st Century Skills. (n.d.). *Beyond the 3Rs: Voter attitudes toward 21st century skills*. Tucson, AZ: Author. Retrieved February 12, 2008, from the Partnership for 21st Century Skills site: http://www.21stcenturyskills.org/

Provasnik, S., Gonzales, P., & Miller, D. (2009). U.*S. performance across international assessments of student achievement: Special supplement to The Condition of Education 2009* (NCES 2009-083). Washington, DC: National Center for Education Statistics, Institute of Education Sciences, U.S. Department of Education. Retrieved September 1, 2009, from the National Center for Education Statistics site: http://nces.ed.gov/pubsearch/pubsinfo.asp?pubid=2009083

RAND Reading Study Group. (2002). *Reading for understanding: Toward a research and development program in reading comprehension*. Retrieved August 11, 2003, from the RAND Corporation Web site: www.rand.org/publications/MR/MR1465/.

Rothstein, R. (2004). *Class and schools: Using social, economic, and educational reform to close the Black–White achievement gap*. New York, NY: Economic Policy Institute/Teachers College Press.

Rothstein, R., Jacobsen, R., & Wilde, T. (2006). *"Proficiency for all"—An oxymoron*. Washington, DC: Economic Policy Institute. Retrieved April 2007 from the Economic Policy Institute site: http://www.epi.org/webfeatures/viewpoints/rothstein_20061114.pdf

Street, B., & Lefstein, A. (2007). *Literacy: An advanced resource book for students*. New York, NY: Routledge.

Paris, S.G., & Stahl, S.A. (Eds.) (2005). *Children's reading comprehension and assessment*. Mahwah, NJ: Lawrence Erlbaum Associates.

CHAPTER 12

Reading Policy

LOOKING AHEAD

Since the early 1990s, educational and political policy makers have been deciding what students are to know and be able to do. Understanding these expectations relative to reading is a crucial part of your professional knowledge. Recognizing the strengths and limitations of reading policies informs your professional decisions.

Knowing what readers are expected to accomplish enables you to direct instruction effectively. You, your colleagues, and your students can concentrate on what counts according to formal expectations. By the same token, deep understandings of reading expectations allow you to teach in a principled manner. Understanding the intended—and unintended—consequences of formal policies enables you, your colleagues, and your students to go beyond mandated expectations and fully access the wonder and power of reading.

This chapter focuses on high-stakes testing, the reliance on assessments for making significant decisions about people and institutions. High-stakes tests lead to serious consequences for failing individuals and schools; they affect your teaching and your students' learning.

In the spirit of full disclosure, we want you to know that we have mostly negative opinions about high-stakes testing. On the one hand, we applaud measures that galvanize attention toward the literacy of all children and youth. On the other hand, we disapprove of overly narrow and stringent requirements for reading. As our following comments show, we believe that policies calling for high-stakes testing should be modified to serve students best.

This chapter on reading policy contains two key ideas:

1. High-stakes testing presents reading expectations as never before.
2. The opportunity—and the challenge—of high-stakes testing is to ensure that it serves students well.

HIGH-STAKES TESTING PRESENTS READING EXPECTATIONS AS NEVER BEFORE

High-stakes testing is part of the educational accountability movement that swept the U.S. in the 1990s when political leaders set out to hold educators responsible for student achievement (Hamilton, 2003). Each state now determines academic standards across the grades in literacy, mathematics, and other subjects, then implements tests that assess students' standing relative to the standards. In general, standards-based educational accountability is meant to provide a picture of student, school, and school system performance so appropriate improvements can be made.

High-stakes testing takes standards-based educational accountability to an extraordinary level. High-stakes testing sets academic goals, then applies consequences that reward those who meet the goals and sanction those who do not. The consequences (i.e., the stakes) most often linked to high-stakes testing are whether students are promoted from one grade to the next, whether students graduate, and whether schools are reconstituted or possibly closed. High-stakes testing is risky business because of the consequences. Much can be gained or lost; it places individuals' and schools' futures on the line. This section describes high-stakes reading testing at the state and national levels.

State Policies

High-stakes testing at the state level mostly involves exit exams, assessments that determine whether students graduate from high school. While the high-stakes exit exams that states require for graduation typically measure competence in several subjects, reading makes up a sizeable portion of all of them. Reading usually is one of the subject areas, and it underlies most other subjects because performance in them is assessed textually. For instance, science and mathematics items often are presented in print, so students must read and respond accordingly.

By 2012, 26 states will require high school students to pass an exit exam to graduate (Zabala, Minnici, McMurrer, & Briggs, 2008). Given the populations of these states, about 75 percent of all U.S. high school students will have to pass a test to graduate. Given the demographics of the states, which include California and Texas, about 85 percent of all U.S. minority high school students will have to pass a test to graduate. A good source for learning the high school exit exam status of your particular state or another one is the High School Exit Examinations link on the Center on Educational Policy site (http://www.cep-dc.org/).

All of the states to date that require exit exams for high school graduation offer alternative measures for students with special needs. However, only three states offer alternatives for English learners. Consequently, these youth need to demonstrate their academic competence in English while they still are learning the language.

Most states have begun providing alternative pathways to passing the exit exams. For instance, students are being allowed multiple attempts with the tests, the number of sections on the tests needed to pass is being reduced, and performance with different tests such as college entrance or locally produced ones is being accepted. States also are beginning to weigh into students' test scores their grade point averages from core courses and their performance with projects and other work samples.

A noteworthy trend involves end-of-course exams. End-of-course exams usually assess performance relative to specific, standards-based course contents. They generally are formalized instruments produced and scored by external agencies. End-of-course assessments are said to promote alignment between state standards and school coursework. Reading is implicated extensively throughout them. By 2015, 11 states will employ end-of-course exams, and three more states will utilize dual testing systems, which include end-of-course and comprehensive exams (Zabala, Minnici, McMurrer, & Briggs, 2008).

National Policy

The No Child Left Behind Act (NCLB), which President George W. Bush enacted with bipartisan congressional support on January 8, 2002, greatly expanded the federal government's role in education by placing stipulations on all fifty states that participate in its well-funded Title I program for low-income children. It is the first time the federal government held states, school districts, and schools accountable through a high-stakes testing policy. Current and future federal administrations no doubt will change the name of this legislation and its regulations, so you will need to stay abreast of national-level high-stakes testing policies as they occur. Timely and informative updates of federal educational policy are found at the following Web sites:

Achieve	www.achieve.org
Center on Education Policy	www.cep-dc.org/
Council of Chief State School Officers	www.ccsso.org
Education Commission of the States	www.ecs.org
The Education Trust	http://www2.edtrust.org
National Education Association	www.nea.org/esea/
United States Department of Education	www.ed.gov

Beginning in the 2005–2006 academic year, federal law required states to test all students annually in grades 3 through 8 in reading/language arts and mathematics. This law also required states to test grade 10 through 12 students at least once annually in reading/language arts and mathematics. By the 2007–2008 school year, it required states to implement science tests at least once during grades 3 through 5, 6 through 9, and 10 through 12.

These annual assessments need to align with state standards and include the participation of all students, including students with special needs and limited English proficiency. Test results must be reported according to the following eight student subgroups:

- African American
- Asian
- Latino
- Limited-English proficient
- Low income
- Native American
- Special education
- White

Test scores are broken out for these subgroups because their academic progress is concealed when everyone's scores are combined and reported collectively. This subgroup monitoring is an explicit attempt to identify and close achievement gaps, the performance disparities among students grouped according to language proficiency, race/ethnicity, socioeconomic status, and special-needs conditions.

Federal law to date calls for specific percentages of students to demonstrate Adequate Yearly Progress (AYP) year by year in reading (as well as math and science). To establish definitions of what constitutes AYP, federal and state officials negotiate often complex formulas based on percentages of students demonstrating certain growth or reaching certain scores on particular reading tests. In addition, AYP formulas typically include rates of graduation or school attendance. AYP formulas vary from state to state with education officials from each state meeting with federal officials to determine their particular definition.

The high-stakes dimension of federal policy involves the consequences for schools that consistently do not demonstrate AYP. The consequences involve conventional measures such as school improvement plans and tutoring services, along with bold options such as transferring students to other schools and possibly privatizing public school management. As can be seen in what follows, the consequences to date for failing to improve reading scores are incremental, moving from mild to severe across seven years.

Year one. A school goes about its business as usual.

Year two. If a school did not make AYP the previous year, then it should identify shortcomings and adjust accordingly.

Year three. If a school does not make AYP two years in a row, then it must give parents the option to use federal funds to transfer their children to higher-performing schools in the district. It also must identify shortcomings and work to remedy them with parents, teachers, and consultants.

Year four. If a school does not make AYP three years in a row, then it must provide private tutoring and other educational supplements to its low-income students.

Year five. If a school does not make AYP four years in a row, then *corrective action* is taken. Along with continuing to offer the services already instituted, a school must implement at least one of the following corrective actions: (a) replace personnel who are not contributing to AYP, (b) institute a new curriculum along with staff development, (c) decrease the school's management authority, (d) bring in an outside expert, (e) extend the school year or school day, or (f) restructure the school organizational arrangement.

Year six. If a school does not make AYP five years in a row, then *alternative governance* is begun. Along with continuing to offer the services and corrective actions already instituted, a school must implement at least one of the following alternative governance actions: (a) reopen as a public charter school, (b) replace all or most of the personnel who are not contributing to AYP, (c) contract with a private company to operate the school, (d) turn over operations to the state, or (e) implement other state-approved fundamental reforms.

Year seven. If a school does not make AYP six years in a row, then the alternative governance plan developed previously must be implemented.

DO IT TOGETHER

High-stakes testing fundamentally affects U.S. education. To determine how well informed the general public is about this policy, interview about five noneducators. Ask them to describe the key features of the following policies.

1. exit exams
2. adequate yearly progress
3. subgroup monitoring
4. consequences for not making adequate yearly progress

Compare your findings with others in class, and—based on your limited samples—tentatively characterize public knowledge of high-stakes testing.

THE OPPORTUNITY—AND THE CHALLENGE—OF HIGH-STAKES TESTING IS TO ENSURE THAT IT SERVES STUDENTS WELL

High-stakes testing policies at the state and national levels are controversial. Advocates of state-level high school exit exams believe that such testing restores meaning to diplomas, certifying that graduates are prepared for work and higher education. They see the exams specifying what is expected for high school graduation so teachers can teach strategically. They see the exams encouraging students by clarifying what is needed to graduate. On the other hand, opponents of high school exit exams view the tests as virtually meaningless because they assess a few minimum competencies rather than a range of advanced proficiencies. They see the exams demoralizing teachers as they are led to focus on rudimentary skills and take the blame for ill-prepared students' failures. They see the exams discouraging students who become preoccupied with passing tests rather than developing personal knowledge and competence.

Most educators agree with the goal of strong academic achievement for all children and closing the achievement gap. Most embrace the use of an accountability system to monitor educational effectiveness. Such goals and systems are said to extend a commitment to social justice, to reading as the *new civil right*. Nevertheless, many oppose the specifics of high-stakes testing policies. For instance, in October 2004, more than twenty education, civil rights, children's, disability, and citizens' organizations submitted to Congress a joint organizational statement of corrections calling for a shift in the federal emphasis on penalizing schools to an emphasis on holding states and localities accountable for improving the conditions that affect student achievement (Joint Organizational Statement on *No Child Left Behind Act,* 2004). This statement directs attention to an overreliance on sanctions at the expense of assistance for schools that do not achieve AYP.

A key objection to national policy centered about high-stakes testing is that the accountability requirements can be too stringent. Those who oppose such a policy claim that it places unrealistic expectations on public schools in attempts to undermine them and turn them over to private enterprise. Many political liberals are dismayed by a perceived overemphasis on test preparation and narrowing of the curriculum. They view this law as a pathway to sterile, unproductive instruction. Many political conservatives are appalled by the federal government's intrusion into educational responsibilities traditionally assumed by local and state agencies. They note that the federal government funds less than 9 percent of the nation's education program, but federal policy affects nearly all classroom activity. The following provides perspective on some of the major issues relative to high-stakes testing. Here we address four of the more challenging questions asked of this policy.

Will High-Stakes Testing Narrow the Curriculum?

A major point of contention about high-stakes testing involves whether it will focus schools' curriculums inappropriately, narrowing instruction to only what is tested (Madaus, Russell, & Higgins, 2009; Meier & Wood, 2004; Nichols & Berliner, 2007). The concern is that schools might resemble test preparation factories more than meaningful learning communities. Educators concerned about this danger contend that preparing youth for tests differs from preparing youth for life. They reject the brain cramming that occurs in many schools, advocating instead for debate, discussion, problem solving, critical evaluation, and creative expression. They expect youth to engage in literacy practices that involve thinking through topics, handling different points of view, inventing new ideas, and expressing themselves in lengthy responses. Along with academic growth, they value youths' personal development, relationships with teachers and peers, and happiness and enthusiasm. They fear that high-stakes testing will limit classrooms to timed reading and writing drills.

Extensive research on motivation suggests that simply teaching to a test harms more than helps instruction (Alderman, 2003; Schunk, Pintrich, & Meece, 2008; Wigfield & Eccles, 2002). The best teaching and learning occur when youths' goals are to master the topic, when they believe they will succeed after expending reasonable effort, and when they choose some of their own materials and activities. Working mainly to demonstrate superiority over others or to earn extrinsic rewards such as test scores results in inferior learning. Further, the classroom and school settings in which youth work affect their mind-sets (Roeser, Eccles, & Sameroff, 2000). An instructional environment that focuses primarily on external mandates undercuts youths' motivation to read better.

If schools overemphasize reading, math, and science, then other worthwhile subjects are at risk of being deemphasized. Educators might focus on tested subjects at the expense of foreign languages, the arts, and physical education. This tendency might deny "our most vulnerable students the full liberal arts curriculum our most privileged youth receive almost as matter of course" (von Zastrow, 2004, p. 9). Students are denied the opportunities to find and follow their school-related passions such as journalism, sports, or theater due to misplaced attention on reading and writing proficiencies. The challenge clearly is to enable students to score well on tests while developing relevant lifelong competencies and attitudes.

LISTEN, LOOK, AND LEARN

Observe about three meetings of a class. What evidence of *teaching to the test* was apparent? If you noted evidence of *teaching to the test*, how did students react to it? What might be done to remedy any negative situations?

Is High-Stakes Testing Sufficient to Close Achievement Gaps?

Advocates of high-stakes assessments at the state and national levels believe this policy will help close achievement gaps. Holding high school students responsible for passing exit exams and holding schools responsible for achieving Adequate Yearly Progress is seen as a way to direct educational resources and efforts to needy areas. This policy is seen as the lever for inducing schools to boost instruction for students with special needs, limited English proficiency, poverty, and marginalized cultural heritages.

On the other hand, many educational commentators consider the reading achievement gap to be the result of conditions that schools have little ability to affect. They do not see the reading achievement gap being reduced just by school practices (National Study Group for the Affirmative Development of Academic Ability, 2004).

Perhaps the most fundamental gap that frequently is highlighted involves the comparative wealth of White, Black, and Hispanic families in the United States. In 2002, the net worth of White families on average was an incredible fourteen times more than Blacks' and eleven times more than Hispanics' (Kochhar, 2004).

Disparities in wealth affect educational achievement through home, community, and school influences (Barton, 2004; Berliner, 2005; Evans, 2005; Rothstein, 2004). Young children of affluence predictably

- are born with robust birth weights, then receive nutrition suitable for proper development,
- experience a great deal of reading in their homes, frequently being read to aloud in order to have fun and start conversations about the outside world,
- are included in conversations about the adult world, developing a belief that they are entitled to solve problems collaboratively with adults and express themselves fully to adults,
- interact with role models who demonstrate expectations to excel academically, graduate from college, and enter the professions,
- have good health, missing few school days and remaining alert during class,
- live in stable neighborhoods, experiencing relatively nonviolent and orderly surroundings,
- remain in the same school, progressing through systematic programs with frequent home–school contacts, and
- enjoy experienced teachers with expertise in their subjects who are present to teach every day.

Given the discrepancies among children of affluence and of poverty, reducing differences in reading achievement involves reducing differences in social and economic conditions. Social and economic improvements include assistance for struggling mothers; affordable and high-quality day care for young children; after-school and summer programs in community centers that support academics as well as cultural, athletic, and organizational experiences; and living wages and stable housing. Social improvements connected directly with schools involve high-quality early childhood education as well as fully staffed health clinics on school grounds.

Gaps in wealth also affect youths' educational achievement through the funding their schools receive (Biddle & Berliner, 2003). Funding gaps exist in places where local property taxes are used to support schools and where the local properties are poor, as in many inner cities and some rural areas, while others are prosperous. Impoverished property tax bases as well as discriminatory allocations within districts result in school circumstances such as the following:

- insufficient and outdated textbooks
- substandard or no libraries
- underprepared teachers
- no substitutes for absent teachers
- crowded and dilapidated classrooms
- inadequate heating, cooling, and lighting

Students of poverty—along with those of limited oral English and special learning needs—require extraordinary interventions to function academically like students of affluence with full oral English and regular learning needs. To illustrate, Pogrow (2004) offers the data-based claim that educationally disadvantaged eighth graders require thirty-five to forty minutes a day of sophisticated conversation for eighteen months to two years to develop "a sense of understanding" (p. 2), a mindset for articulating and justifying complex academic thoughts. The instructional conversations need to occur in groups of ten to twelve students engaged with topics that intrigue them and stimulate academic thinking. Such intensive instruction comes with a cost.

A major point of contention about testing is the extent to which it averts resources to close the achievement gap. Many educators focus on the need for resources such as reading materials, computer technology, innovative programs, professional development, additional time, adequate classrooms, and competitive salaries. They assert that money spent on testing can be spent better on instruction. Indeed, a mobilization of resources similar to landing a person on the moon has been said to be needed to close the achievement gap. As Joftus (2003) put it, "Accountability without resources is no better than resources without accountability" (p. 13).

Another perspective on closing the racial achievement gap focuses on racism (Ogbu, 2003). While Whites frequently consider the achievement gap to be due to social class differences, many Blacks assert that racism is the root cause. Even though racial accord generally seems prevalent as of this writing, institutional forces such as low expectations, lack of encouragement, placements in academically weak tracks, and inexperienced teachers are said to contribute to low academic performance (Ferguson, 2002). Minority students often come to identify with their marginal position in U.S. schools and society. Overcoming racist beliefs and practices rather than implementing high-stakes tests is said to be the first step toward closing the achievement gap.

What Aspects of High-stakes Testing Clearly Are Deplorable?

Holding students and schools accountable for high standards and applying severe consequences is like administering powerful medicine. While it can remedy certain conditions, it also can have undesirable and potentially dangerous side effects. This section presents aspects of high-stakes testing that clearly are deplorable.

BASING DECISIONS ON INSUFFICIENT INFORMATION Basing high-stakes decisions on only one measure of reading is unacceptable. Convincing research (Amrein & Berliner, 2003; Raudenbausch, 2004) and professional association position statements (American

Educational Research Association, 2000; International Reading Association, 1999) conclude that tests can be used to screen students, teachers, and schools as possibly needing extra help, but test scores alone should not be used to decide educational issues. Multiple measures are needed to obtain the information required for consequential decisions about individuals and schools. Multiple opportunities to succeed with a test, along with multiple situations involving class work and homework, are indispensable for fair assessments, especially when traditionally underserved groups are involved (Joint Organizational Statement on *No Child Left Behind* Act, 2004).

No single test adequately reflects all the ways readers interact with print. And no single measure administered during a single test session adequately reflects growth and development over time. Restricting reading to answering questions about brief passages during one point in time exaggerates that measure and shortchanges readers. Like medical examiners assessing the health of clients, reading examiners should consult multiple measures over multiple points in time. For instance, to judge a school's performance fully, authorities should supplement single-test information with course exit exams, Advanced Placement and International Baccalaureate tests, SAT and ACT performance, school graduation rates, percentages of graduates who enroll in as well as graduate from college or trade school, and the percentages who require remediation beyond high school.

Along the same line, basing school-level decisions only on whether students perform at a certain level misses the amount of progress students make from one school year to the next. A student might enter high school speaking little English, reading English at only a primary-grade level, and acting antagonistic or apathetic toward school. If this student progresses to an intermediate-grade level in one year, then the teacher and school would deserve enormous credit, although the judgment might be *underperforming* because the student was not reading at the level specified for proficiency. Comparing reading performance before and after instruction is known as a *growth* or *value-added* measure because it tracks what schools contribute to individual students' learning over time.

Growth, or value-added, assessments are an antidote to an accountability model that focuses on getting youth to a certain level regardless of where they start (Sunderman & Kim, 2004). Before-and-after assessments work to specify the effects of teachers and schools on learning, showing the rates of growth that instruction brings about rather than the absolute levels of achievement regardless of background characteristics like poverty. Growth, or value-added, assessments that depict school effectiveness accurately and fairly permit good teachers to remain in challenging classrooms.

LIMITING HIGH-SCHOOL READING   As noted earlier, high-stakes testing tends to narrow the curriculum. This policy tends to lead high school educators, especially, to present subject matter in fragmented, test-related pieces and increase teacher-centered instruction (Au, 2007; Hillocks, 2002; Zabala & Minnici, 2007). A form of multiple-choice teaching occurs that links learning to a test rather than to students' subject matter knowledge, world knowledge, or personal experience.

Narrow instruction leads to narrow outcomes. Convincing research shows that high-stakes testing policies have produced no effects, and sometimes negative effects, on youth's reading achievement (Amrein & Berliner, 2003; Grigg, Donahue, & Dion, 2007; Grodsky, Warren, & Kalogrides, 2009; Langer, 2002; Reardon, Atteberry, Arshan, & Kurlaender, 2009). Twelfth-grade students' overall reading test scores have flatlined or declined during the high-stakes testing era. Additionally, youth who earned diplomas in states with high school exit exams later earned no higher incomes than those who earned their diplomas elsewhere, were no more likely to be employed, and were no more likely to complete college (Warren, Grodsky, & Lee, 2008). In brief, high-stakes testing policies have not been shown to be effective vehicles for increasing high school youth's reading instruction, reading performance, or later success in work or higher education.

ABANDONING LEARNERS Another deplorable aspect of high-stakes accountability systems involves abandoning learners (Booher-Jennings, 2005; Settlage & Meadows, 2002). School administrators, counselors, and teachers often analyze test data to identify those students who probably (a) will pass future tests with no interventions, (b) will pass future tests if interventions are applied, and (c) will not pass future tests regardless of interventions. Using a triage mentality of saving the most promising cases, educators are at risk of focusing efforts on the middle group, those students scoring just above or below cut-off points, called *cusp* or *bubble* students, and allowing the other students to coast.

Although positive expectations and resources for all struggling readers can emerge, they are not automatic. Some educators distance themselves from students who fall short in their classrooms, believing that these individuals lack the necessary moral character, work ethic, and commitment to mainstream values and norms to succeed academically (Anagnostopoulos & Rutledge, 2007). These educators then direct their attention and effort to the students they consider more deserving. The challenge here, plainly, is for educators to work on teaching beliefs and practices that respond appropriately to struggling students' capacities, cultures, and social and economic conditions; the challenge is to overcome deficit perspectives of struggling readers.

A perverse consequence of high-stakes testing is that the worst- and best-scoring readers tend to be disregarded (Duffett, Farkas, & Loveless, 2008; Neal & Schanzenbach, 2008). Teachers operating under this policy typically believe all students deserve equal shares of attention, but they tend to put a higher priority on students in the middle and direct more instructional attention to them than to the lowest and highest achievers. Resulting test scores show gains for middle performers and relative stagnation for low and high performers. The challenge here clearly is for schooling to be equal and excellent at the same time (Gardner, 1995).

CORRUPTION High-stakes testing can result in corruption (Nichols & Berliner, 2007). In efforts to inflate test scores, educators have been known to photocopy secure tests for use in class, read off answers during a test, provide exact items or answers during test preparation sessions, disregard test administration directions (e.g., allow extra time, ignore student copying), and change students' answers or send students back to correct wrong answers (Hamilton, 2003). In efforts to increase test scores, some schools have been known to place students in special education programs they do not need, encourage low-achieving readers to drop out and enter a General Educational Development (GED) program or alternative school (International Reading Association, 1999), or actually expel students from school.

Other forms of corruption involve wrongly excluding students from tests. Sometimes low-achieving students are assigned to a few days in a special protected class that excludes them from the state test, then are reassigned to their regular classes when the test is finished. Sometimes students who already have demonstrated proficiency are repeatedly included in later test administrations in order to produce higher overall test scores for the school, even though the particular students receive no academic benefit. And sometimes school administrators give faulty identification numbers to low-achieving students so their scores do not lower a school's scores. Dishonest practices like these can stem from inordinate pressure to perform well on a high-stakes test.

What Aspects of High-stakes Testing Are Most Promising?

As indicated earlier in this chapter, we believe that many aspects of high-stakes literacy testing are quite troublesome. Serious tensions arise from this policy. Despite these strains, we think the following aspects show some promise.

One promising aspect of high-stakes testing is that educators more and more are using assessment data to make decisions (Hamilton, 2003). Educators as never before are examining the results of instruction, determining what is and is not working, and doing something about it. Programs are being aligned and directed toward concrete results. Teaching is becoming more responsive to students' demonstrated achievement.

Another positive aspect is the change evident in many schools toward expectations for struggling readers. Rather than abandoning learners, many educators are focusing on struggling readers' and writers' achievement more than in the past. In many cases, these youth now are receiving multiple opportunities to learn; if one lesson is unproductive, another is tried. In addition, test results are being used to attract resources to students who are especially needy.

Third, schools, now more than ever, are articulating curricular purposes and goals that can be shared among school administrators and faculty, students, parents, and community members. Schools are focusing their efforts on clear outcomes, moving toward instructional consistency and direction. With these outcomes in mind, educators are better able to persuade one another to work collectively, engage students with what matters, and elicit support from parents and the community.

A fourth promising aspect of high-stakes testing involves the tests themselves. Teaching to a test can be devastating if the test is flawed, if it encourages superficial unproductive learning. However, teaching to a test can be promising if the test is appropriate, if it encourages deep productive learning (Au, 2007). High-stakes tests that certify important accomplishments have the potential to enrich education. Such assessments involve solving problems adaptively, managing multiple tasks, controlling one's actions, and performing different roles in different situations (Baker, 2007). These assessments tap 21st-century skills and are calibrated with international benchmarks. For instance, document-based questions can require students to tackle compelling problems, synthesize ideas and information across multiple texts, compose innovative responses, and exhibit compositions to external audiences. Other assessments might be in the form of certifications and licenses similar to what individuals earn in the automotive industry, health care, and legal affairs. These assessments work somewhat like merit badges in scouting, with individuals completing projects according to specified criteria and a panel of judges assessing the performance.

In general, effective educators are finding ways to work with high-stakes testing despite its limitations. To illustrate, Langer (2002, 2004) shows how excellent schools use assessments as opportunities to enrich curriculums rather than narrow them. Educators with this frame of mind do not focus on raising school test scores; they focus on improving youths' reading proficiencies. They consider reading test scores to be a means to the end of competent reading. When test results come in, students, teachers, and administrators interpret them in light of the goals and practices of the current curriculum. They connect test demands with course work, integrating test preparation into the ongoing curriculum rather than allocating separate time to isolated activities. They invest in schoolwide professional development devoted to literacy rather than only purchasing add-on reading-improvement programs. In brief, they embed in schools' cultures the determination to achieve high standards of literacy through high-quality teaching.

Bringing students into the conversation is wise. Authorizing students' perspectives on how mandated tests and course work connect with their personal, social, and cultural practices can make instruction more responsive (Noguera, 2007; Schultz, Jones-Walker, & Chikkatur, 2008). It permits you to take into account youth's experiences and perspectives relative to reading and writing. Acknowledging how young people identify themselves as readers and writers amid high-stakes standards-based expectations holds great potential for literacy development.

Conclusion

Meeting the goal of advanced literacy for all requires new ways of thinking because such a goal never has been met in the past (Berliner & Biddle, 1995; Bracey, 2004; Kantor & Lowe, 2004; Rothstein, 1998). The United States never had a golden age where all students from all walks of life obtained a high-quality intellectual education. Reports of extraordinary school and school district achievements relative to academic rigor certainly exist, but they typically were exceptions. High-achieving groups of students typically emerged in schools, but many other groups remained at limited levels. Students of poverty and of color, along with those of limited oral English and special learning needs, had especially limited expectations and opportunities to achieve academic excellence. Due to the high-stakes testing policy described here, attention to high levels of reading for everyone currently is at unprecedented levels. The opportunity—and the challenge—of this policy is to ensure that it serves all students well.

LOOKING BACK

This chapter is meant to provide deep understandings of a dominant educational policy that affects not only reading, teaching, and learning but students' lives. It is meant to inform your professional decision making in light of official expectations. It contains two key ideas: (1) High-stakes testing presents reading expectations as never before and (2) the opportunity— and the challenge—of high-stakes testing is to ensure that it serves students well.

ADD TO YOUR JOURNAL

Record in your class journal your reactions to this chapter. What do you think of high-stakes testing? How might this policy affect your teaching? How will you respond to it?

Additional Readings

These books provide guidance for teaching well amid high-stakes testing policies.

Boudett, K. P., City, E. A., & Murnane, R. J. (Eds.). (2005). *Data wise: A step-by-step guide to using assessment results to improve teaching and learning*. Cambridge, MA: Harvard University Press.

Langer, J. A. (2002). *Effective literacy instruction: Building successful reading and writing programs*. Urbana, IL: National Council of Teachers of English.

The following two resources present sensible everyday advice for coping with high-stakes tests.

Cizek, G. J., & Burg, S. S. (2006). *Addressing test anxiety in a high-stakes environment: Strategies for classrooms and schools*. Thousand Oaks, CA: Corwin.

Tileston, D. W. (2006). *What every parent should know about schools, standards, and high-stakes tests*. Thousand Oaks, CA: Corwin.

This collection accentuates the positive features of standardized testing.

Phelps, R. P. (Ed.). (2005). *Defending standardized testing*. Mahwah, NJ: Erlbaum.

The four books listed here caution educators about the negative features of high-stakes testing.

Au, W. (2008). *Unequal by design: High-stakes testing and the standardization of inequality*. New York, NY: Routledge.

Madaus, G., Russell, M., & Higgins, J. (2009). *The paradoxes of high-stakes testing: How they affect students, their parents, teachers, principals, schools, and society*. Charlotte, NC: Information Age Publishing.

Nichols, S. N., & Berliner, D. (2007). *Collateral damage: How high-stakes testing corrupts America's schools*. Cambridge, MA: Harvard Education Press.

Valli, L., Croninger, R. G., Chambliss, M. H., Graeber, A. O., Buese, D. (2008). *Test driven: High-stakes accountability in elementary schools*. New York, NY: Teachers College Press.

These two related documents by reputable professional associations draw attention to the appropriate uses of educational testing.

American Psychological Association. (2007). *Appropriate use of high-stakes testing in our nation's schools*. Washington, DC: Author. Retrieved June 24, 2008, from the American Psychological Association site: http://www.apa.org/pubinfo/testing.html

American Educational Research Association, American Psychological Association, and National Council on Measurement in Education. (1999). *Standards for educational and psychological testing*. Washington, DC: American Educational Research Association.

An accessible justification for basing important educational decisions on multiple measures is provided here.

Fuller, D., Fitzgerald, K., & Lee, J. S. (2008). *Infobrief: The case for multiple measures*. Retrieved June 9, 2009, from the Association for Supervision and Curriculum Development site: http://www.ascd.org/publications/newsletters/infobrief/winter08/num52/toc.aspx

An alternative to federal high-stakes testing policy is presented here.

Darling-Hammond, L., & Wood, G. (2008). *Democracy at risk: The need for a new federal policy in education*. Washington, DC: The Forum for Education and Democracy. Retrieved April 27, 2009, from the Forum for Education and Democracy site: http://www.forumforeducation.org/

Online Resources

This site is dedicated to preventing the misuse of standardized tests.

The National Center for Fair & Open Testing
www.fairtest.org

This center investigates the role of testing in education.

Center on Education Policy
http://www.cep-dc.org/

Among other things, these leaders in college entrance examinations publish regular reports about student achievement.

ACT
http://www.act.org/

ETS: Educational Testing Service
http://www.ets.org/

References

Alderman, M. K. (2003). *Motivation for achievement.* Mahwah, NJ: Erlbaum.

American Educational Research Association. (2000). *AERA position statement concerning high-stakes testing in preK–12 education.* Retrieved October 25, 2004, from the American Educational Research Association Web site: www.aera.net/about/policy/stakes.htm.

Amrein, A. L., & Berliner, D. C. (2003). The effects of high-stakes tests on student motivation and achievement. *Educational Leadership, 60*(5), 32–38.

Anagnostopoulos, D., & Rutledge, S. A. (2007). Making sense of school sanctioning policies in urban high schools. *Teachers College Record, 109,* 1261–1302.

Au, W. (2007). High-stakes testing and curricular control: A qualitative metasynthesis. *Educational Researcher, 36,* 258–267.

Baker, E. L. (2007). The end(s) of testing. *Educational Researcher, 36,* 309–317.

Barton, P. E. (2004). Why does the gap persist? *Educational Leadership, 62*(3), 8–13.

Berliner, D. C. (2005). *Our impoverished view of educational reform.* Retrieved August 22, 2005, from the Teachers College Record Web site: www.tcrecord.org

Berliner, D. C., & Biddle, B. J. (1995). *The manufactured crisis: Myth, fraud, and the attack on America's public schools.* Reading, MA: Addison Wesley.

Biddle, B. J., & Berliner, D. C. (2003). *What research says about unequal funding for schools in America.* Retrieved October 13, 2004, from the WestEd site: www.wested.org/online_pubs/pp-03-01.pdf

Booher-Jennings, J. (2005). Below the bubble: "Educational triage" and the Texas Accountability System. *American Educational Research Journal, 42,* 231–268.

Bracey, G. (2004). *Setting the record straight* (2nd ed.). Portsmouth, NH: Heinemann.

Duffett, A., Farkas, S., & Loveless, T. (2008). *High-achieving students in the era of No Child Left Behind.* Washington, DC: The Thomas B. Fordham Institute. Retrieved May 13, 2009, from the Thomas B. Fordham Institute site: http://www.edexcellence.net

Evans, R. (2005). Reframing the achievement gap. *Phi Delta Kappan, 86,* 582–589.

Ferguson, R. F. (2002). *What doesn't meet the eye: Understanding and addressing racial disparities in high-achieving suburban schools.* Retrieved December 3, 2004, from the North Central Regional Educational Laboratory Web site: www.ncrel.org/gap/ferg/

Gardner, J. (1995). *Excellence: Can we be equal and excellent, too?* (rev. ed.). New York, NY: W. W. Norton.

Grigg, W., Donahue, P., & Dion, G. (2007). *The nation's report card: 12th-grade reading and mathematics, 2005* (NCES 2007-468). U.S. Department of Education, National Center for Education Statistics. Washington, DC: U.S. Government Printing Office. Retrieved July 5, 2009, from the National Center for Education Statistics site: http://nces.ed. gov/pubsearch/pubsinfo.asp?pubid=2007468

Grodsky, E., Warren, J. R., & Kalogrides, D. (2009). State high school exit examinations and NAEP long-term trends in reading and mathematics, 1971–2004. *Educational Policy, 23,* 589–614.

Hamilton, L. (2003). Assessment as a policy tool. In R. E. Floden (Ed.), *Review of Research in Education* (vol. 27, pp. 25–68). Washington, DC: American Educational Research Association.

Hillocks, G. (2002). *The testing trap: How state writing assessments control writing.* New York, NY: Teachers College Press.

International Reading Association (1999). *High stakes testing.* Retrieved October 25, 2004, from the International Reading Association Web site: www.reading.org/positions/high_stakes.html

Joftus, S. (2002, September). *Every child a graduate: A framework for an excellent education for all middle and high school students.* Retrieved June 5, 2003, from the Alliance for Excellent Education Web site: www.all4ed.org/publications/Every ChildAGraduate/index.html

Joint Organizational Statement on *No Child Left Behind* Act (2004, October). Retrieved January 5, 2005, from the National Education Association Web site: www.nea.org/presscenter/nclbjointstatement.html

Joint Organizational Statement on No Child Left Behind Act (2004, October). Retrieved April 8, 2005, from FairTest: The National Center for Fair and Open Testing Web site: www.fairtest.org/

Kantor, H., & Lowe, R. (2004). Reflections on history and quality education. *Educational Researcher, 33*(5), 6–10.

Kochhar, R. (2004). *The wealth of Hispanic households: 1996 to 2002.* Retrieved October 19, 2004, from the Pew Hispanic Center Web site: www.pewhispanic.org/page.jsp?page=Reports-Reports%20Section

Langer, J. A. (2002). *Effective literacy instruction: Building successful reading and writing programs*. Urbana, IL: National Council of Teachers of English.

Langer, J. A. (2004). *Getting to excellent: How to create better schools*. New York, NY: Teachers College Press.

Madaus, G., Russell, M, & Higgins, J. (2009). *The paradoxes of high stakes testing: How they affect students, their parents, teachers, principals, schools, and society*. Charlotte, NC: Information Age Publishing.

Meier, D., & Wood, G. (2004). *Many children left behind: How the No Child Left Behind Act is damaging our children and our schools*. Boston, MA: Beacon Press.

National Study Group for the Affirmative Development of Academic Ability. (2004). *All students reaching the top: Strategies for closing academic achievement gaps*. Retrieved January 13, 2005, from the North Central Regional Educational Laboratory Web site: www.ncrel.org/gap/studies/thetop.htm

Neal, D., & Schanzenbach, D. W. (2008). *Left behind by design: Proficiency counts and test-based accountability* (NBER Working Paper No. W13293). Cambridge, MA: National Bureau of Economic Research. Retrieved August 4, 2009, from the Social Science Research Network site: http://ssrn.com/abstract=1005606

Nichols, S. N., & Berliner, D. (2007). *Collateral damage: How high-stakes testing corrupts America's schools*. Cambridge, MA: Harvard Education Press.

Noguera, P. A. (2007) How listening to students can help schools to improve. *Theory Into Practice, 46*(3), 205–211.

Ogbu, J. U. (2003). *Black American students in an affluent suburb: A study of academic disengagement*. Mahwah, NJ: Erlbaum.

Pogrow, S. (2004). *The missing element in reducing the learning gap: Eliminating the "blank stare."* Retrieved October 13, 2004, from Teachers College Record Web site: www.tcrecord.org/Content.asp?ContentID=11381

Raudenbausch, S. (2004). *Schooling, statistics, and poverty: Can we measure school improvement?* Retrieved December 16, 2004, from the Educational Testing Service Web site: www.ets.org/research/pic/

Reardon, S. F., Atteberry, A., Arshan, N., & Kurlaender, M. (2009). *Effects of the California High School Exit Exam on student persistence, achievement, and graduation*. Stanford, CA: Institute for Research on Education Policy and Practice. Retrieved July 25, 2009, from the IREPP site: http://www.stanford.edu/group/irepp/cgi-bin/joomla/index.php2002

Roeser, R. W., Eccles, & Sameroff, A. J. (2000). School as a context of early adolescents' academic and social-emotional development: A summary of research. *Elementary School Journal, 100*, 443–462.

Rothstein, R. (1998). *The way we were? The myths and realities of America's student achievement*. New York, NY: Century Foundation Press.

Rothstein, R. (2004). *Class and schools: Using social, economic, and educational reform to close the black-white achievement gap*. New York, NY: Economic Policy Institute/Teachers College Press.

Schultz, K., Jones-Walker, C. E., & Chikkatur, A. P. (2008). Listening to students, negotiating beliefs: Preparing teachers for urban classrooms. *Curriculum Inquiry, 38*(2), 155–187.

Schunk, D. H., Pintrich, P. R., & Meece, J. L. (2008). *Motivation in education: Theory, research, and applications* (3rd ed.). Upper Saddle River, NJ: Pearson/Merrill Prentice Hall.

Settlage, J., & Meadows, L. (2002). Standards-based reform and its unintended consequences: Implications for science education within America's schools. *Journal of Research in Science Teaching, 39*, 114–127.

Sunderman, G. L., & Kim, J. (2004). *Inspiring vision, disappointing results: Four studies on implementing the No Child Left Behind Act*. Retrieved November 15, 2004, from The Harvard University Civil Rights Project Web site: www.civilrightsproject.harvard.edu/research/esea/nclb.php

Von Zastrow, C. (2004). *Academic atrophy: The condition of the liberal arts in America's public schools*. Retrieved August 12, 2004, from the Council of Basic Education Web site: www.c-b-e.org/PDF/cbe_principal_Report.pdf

Warren, J. R., Grodsky, E., & Lee, J. C. (2008). State high school exit examinations and postsecondary labor market outcomes. *Sociology of Education, 81*, 77–107.

Wigfield, A., & Eccles, J. (Eds.). (2002). *Development of achievement motivation*. San Diego, CA: Academic Press.

Zabala, D., & Minnici, A. (2007). *It's different now: How exit exams are affecting teaching and learning in Jackson and Austin.* Washington, DC: Center on Education Policy. Retrieved September 21, 2007, from the Center on Education Policy site: http://www.cep-dc.org/

Zabala, D., Minnici, A., Mcmurrer, J., & Briggs, L. (2008). *State high school exit exams: Moving toward end-of-course exams.* Washington, DC: Center on Education Policy. Retrieved December 13, 2008, from the Center on Education Policy site: http://www.cep-dc.org

INDEX